FIVE THOUSAND AMERICAN FAMILIES— PATTERNS OF ECONOMIC PROGRESS

VOLUME III

Analyses of the First Six Years

of the Panel Study of Income Dynamics

Edited by Greg J. Duncan and James N. Morgan

With Contributions by Jonathan Lane, James Morgan, Greg Duncan,
Daniel Hill, Richard Coe, Robert Hampton, Everett Ehrlich,
Katherine Dickinson, C. Russell Hill, Elizabeth Roistacher,
Sandra Newman, Al Arterburn, Jacob Benus, Jan Kmenta,
Harold Shapiro, Greg Miner, and Michael Conte

Conducted Under Contracts with the Office of Economic Opportunity
(Responsibility for this project has been transferred to the Office of the
Assistant Secretary for Planning and Evaluation, Department of
Health, Education, and Welfare)

SURVEY RESEARCH CENTER
INSTITUTE FOR SOCIAL RESEARCH
THE UNIVERSITY OF MICHIGAN

ISR Code No. 4030

Five Thousand American Families—Patterns of Economic Progress, Volume III
Library of Congress Catalog Card No. 74-62002
ISBN 0-87944-175-5 paperbound
ISBN 0-87944-176-3 clothbound

Published by The Institute for Social Research
The University of Michigan, Ann Arbor, Michigan 48106

Published 1975
Manufactured in the United States of America

CONTENTS

PREFACE

This is the third of what may prove to be a series of annual reports on the most recent findings from the Panel Study of Family Income Dynamics. This volume contains analysis, both completed and in progress, by the study staff and by other researchers at Michigan and elsewhere.

We will not repeat the history of the study nor the names of those who were instrumental in its conception, support, and continuation. We are greatly indebted to many people, most of all to the thousands of respondents all over the country who by telephone, by mail, or in person continue overwhelmingly to answer our questions. Also indispensable are hundreds of interviewers, scores of editors and coders, and a variety of specialists, advisors and analysts both within and outside the Institute for Social Research.

This year we have lost three veteran staff members, Katherine and Jonathan Dickinson to the Wisconsin Poverty Institute and Jacob Benus to the Stanford Research Institute. We have been very fortunate in adding two new graduate research assistants to the staff, Dan Hill and John Holmes. Another, Saul Hoffman, will join us in January, 1975.

Greg Duncan is now Dr. Duncan. He has become a study director and assists in coordinating the study. His many contributions to its operation include editing this volume as well as writing parts of it.

Beverly Harris is now in charge of our data processing and Tecla Loup and Charles Stallman have also taken on increased responsibilities. Their experience and collective memory are invaluable.

As usual, Joan Brinser has done many things, among them some of the editing of this volume, assembling our report to the respondents and keeping the panel intact.

Although Priscilla Hildebrandt is now involved with another study, we still impose upon her good nature when we need help. Susan Finlayson has also left us

vii

but, fortunately for us, is still connected with our study in her new Field Office capacity.

Wanda Lemon oversees the endless and varied work of our office which includes the preparation of this manuscript. She has been ably assisted with the typing by Barbara Browne and, with extensive editorial advice, by Charlotte Whitney.

Our contacts at the Department of Health, Education and Welfare have been mainly with Jonathan P. Lane. He has been most generous with his help and is joint author of the first chapter in this volume. We are also indebted to Larry Orr and Oliver Moles for many useful suggestions.

In writing a preface to the preliminary findings from the sixth wave (incorporated into this volume), William A. Morrill, the Assistant Secretary for Planning and Evaluation, concludes:

> The analyses of these data which already have been performed ... represent only a small fraction of what can be pursued fruitfully. I hope that a major exploration of this unique source of information on the social and economic status of American families and individuals over time will be undertaken over the next several years.

These volumes attempt to contribute to that analysis, both in the findings they present, and as a record of who is working in what areas, enabling the coordination of these and future efforts.

James N. Morgan
Ann Arbor

INTRODUCTION

This volume reports on findings from the sixth wave of a Panel Study of Family Income Dynamics and on further analysis of the preceding waves. It can be read by itself, particularly if the reader is primarily interested in findings rather than methodology. A short history of the Study is presented in the first chapter. There are, however, substantive findings in the first two volumes that are not repeated here.[1]

Without trying to translate findings into public policy, we focus, whenever possible on policy-relevant issues. While some of the statistical methodology is complex, an attempt has been made to make the explanations and summaries of findings clear and readable. We have continued, where feasible, the practice followed in the first two volumes of searching an independent subsample of the data, leaving some untainted data for testing whether the principal findings will hold up and extrapolate to the whole population.

Most of Volume III is comprised of chapters by permanent and temporary staff members. They attempt to preserve the focus of Volume I on the main issues to which the study was directed -- the determinants of the changing economic fortunes of families. These issues are faced directly in the first two chapters. A possible policy approach to the problems of maintaining a minimum living standard for all families is investigated in Chapter Three.

---

[1] See Five Thousand American Families -- Patterns of Economic Progress, Volume I, An Analysis of the First Five Years of the Panel Study of Income Dynamics, and Volume II, Special Studies of the First Five Years of the Panel Study of Income Dynamics, Institute for Social Research, The University of Michigan, Ann Arbor, Michigan, 1973.

A set of documentation volumes for all seven years of the study is also available. See A Panel Study of Income Dynamics, Volume I: Study Design, Procedures, Available Data, Waves I-V; Volume II: Tape Codes and Indexes, Waves I-V; Wave VI Supplement: Procedures and Tape Codes, 1973 Interviewing Year; Wave VII Supplement: Procedures and Tape Codes, 1974 Interviewing Year, Institute for Social Research, The University of Michigan, Ann Arbor, Michigan.

Some of the remaining chapters cover specific problems faced by many families. Various disruptive events are looked at in Chapters Four and Five. Chapters Six and Seven examine the child care options available to working parents. The eigth and ninth chapters profit from the longitudinal nature of the study to look at several aspects of residential mobility.

The next two chapters investigate equity at various income levels of the income tax (Chapter Ten) and the recent gasoline price inflation (Chapter 11). The twelfth chapter analyzes the risk avoidance behavior of sample families as it relates to their economic fortunes.

The procedures and initial findings from three studies still in progress are incorporated in Chapter 13. They are followed by summaries of other research and reports of research published elsewhere. Some of these summaries were submitted in response to a general invitation issued each year to those using the data.

Finally, there are some appendices on the quality of the data, statistical method, and a guide to using the Sentence Completion Test on other, nonrepresentative, groups using our national averages to correct the scores.

There has been no attempt to control the direction of individual investigations nor the findings, so long as the procedures appear proper, and the conclusions connect with the statistical facts. The reader will find different styles and foci, and even an occasional implication drawn a little rashly. Scholarship and free inquiry must proceed this way, relying on competition and criticism to preserve balance and lead to truth.

Chapter 1

PATTERNS OF CHANGE IN ECONOMIC STATUS
AND FAMILY STRUCTURE
Jonathan P. Lane and James N. Morgan

INTRODUCTION

This chapter gives an overview of the Panel Study of Income Dynamics and a descriptive analysis of the fortunes of families and individuals over the time period from 1968 through 1973. We begin with a general description of the study -- its purpose, scope, and methods. Next, we look at the economic status of the families at a point in time (1973). The income of the family relative to its needs is our usual measure of economic status, although we also employ and describe its components.

Patterns of transition are examined by comparing the economic status of families in 1972 with the status of the same families in 1967. Because family composition change itself is crucial to a study of family income dynamics, we then look at changes in the structure of families and their relationships to changes in economic activity.

Poverty can be defined in terms of income below some set poverty standard or in terms of position in the distribution of income/needs. The panel data allow us to categorize families and individuals by the number of years (out of six) that they were "poor" by either definition. A descriptive analysis of families so categorized follows, using first an "absolute" and then a "relative" definition of poverty.

Finally, we repeat some of the multivariate analysis of change in economic status with the added sixth wave data, testing in several ways the stability of the five-year findings reported in Volume I.

ANALYSIS

I. History of the Study

The Panel Study of Income Dynamics was designed to investigate how and why the economic fortunes of American families change from year to year. It supplements information from surveys of the Census Bureau, which each year interviews a different sample of people and charts aggregate changes in the economic status of the population as a whole and important subgroups of the population. The panel method -- reinterviewing the same families year after year -- provides an additional dimension for analysis. Not only changes in aggregate income can be seen, but also the movement of units within the income distribution can be tracked. How much individual change exists within the rather stable overall income distribution? Which kinds of families show the most year-to-year fluctuation in income? How much change in the economic status of families results from birth, death, divorce and other changes in family composition? Why do the incomes of certain families consistently increase, while those of other families decline, even within demographically similar subgroups? These are the kinds of questions which a panel study is uniquely capable of addressing.

Questions such as these arose with special force in the mid-1960's, as the government turned its attention to problems of poverty and the relatively low economic status of blacks and other minority groups. In response, the Office of Economic Opportunity contracted with the Survey Research Center at the University of Michigan to design and conduct a large national sample survey following the same families over several years. The Survey Research Center interviewed about 5000 families in 1968 and has conducted reinterviews each year since.[1]

The panel survey thus has produced a large and unique body of data useful for answering some major questions about the dynamics of income distribution. First, the data provide a description of such items as the amount of variation in the income of families through the years, the types of families whose economic status does and does not change, and the amount of change in composition of the poverty population. In addition, panel data have several advantages for explaining the causes of change. Most existing causal analysis is based on comparing people at different income *levels* at a single point in time to determine what factors may account for past changes in their economic status. But such

---

[1]Throughout this report, the term "family" refers not only to adults with children, but also single persons and childless couples who do not live in larger households with blood relatives.

analysis cannot examine change itself because it is not based upon observations of the same individual at two different points in time. A panel study permits the *direct measurement of change* and provides information on the *time sequence of different events* so that cause and consequence of change in economic status can be distinguished with more accuracy. While these features of a panel study do not solve all the problems of analyzing the causes of change, they provide considerably better information than that available from analysis of cross-section surveys.

In order to *describe* the amount of change experienced by individual families, much information has been gathered on the amount and sources of their yearly incomes. To help in *explaining* change, a broad range of background, environmental and attitudinal information has also been gathered.

The bulk of the analysis performed to date has been directed at the latter objective; that is, at identifying conditions, events or attitudes which help to improve or weaken family economic status. Particular interest centers on factors which can be affected by individuals themselves or by government policy. While people's backgrounds -- where they grew up, their parents' occupations, their own education -- cannot be changed by either the government or by people themselves in the short run, these factors must be taken into account in order to derive unbiased estimates of the effects of other factors.

Characteristics such as race and sex are also unchanging, but their *effects* on such things as employment and earnings will change if employer policies or public attitudes change. (For example, less discrimination may affect minority earnings.) Environmental factors, such as the level of unemployment or public school expenditures, are clearly changeable. Beyond these well-studied demographic and environmental variables are a variety of attitudes and behavior patterns. A major emphasis of this study was to measure attitudes and behavior patterns and assess their effects on economic well-being over time.

THE SAMPLE OF 5,000 FAMILIES

Field work began in the spring of 1968, with a national sample of about 5000 heads of families who have been reinterviewed every spring. After five annual personal interviews, the sixth and seventh waves (the latter occurring in the spring of 1974) have been carried out mainly by telephone, with an abbreviated questionnaire.

The original sample was made up of two subsamples. Some 2930 interviews were conducted with household heads from a cross-section sample selected to be representative of the entire U. S. population. An additional 1872 interviews

were conducted with heads of low income households drawn from a sample identified and interviewed by the Census Bureau for the 1966 Survey of Economic Opportunity. The total response rate was 76 percent in 1968, the first year; 89 percent the second; and 97 percent each year since. Families who moved between
interviews were contacted at their new addresses, and members of 1968 families
who formed their own households were added to the sample as separate households.

Since 1968, the sample has increased in size because the number of newly-
formed families to join it exceeded the number that ceased to respond. After
the 1972 interviews, there were 5060 families in the sample, 1108 of them were
newly formed since the 1968 interviews. There were 5285 families interviewed
in 1973. This third volume of findings focuses on 3438 of those 5285 families,
where the head has remained unchanged since 1968. There is, however, some analysis using other subgroups or data covering less than the full six years.

Estimates based on the total sample have been adjusted by giving differential "weights" to different families for: (1) the overrepresentation of low
income families in the original sample; (2) differential nonresponse rates among
different subgroups in the population; and (3) problems caused by formation of
new families in which some members are not part of the original sample. Thus,
these estimates represent (within the limits of sampling error and any bias) the
status and experience of the population as a whole. Also, the large number of
interviews of low income families allows reliable detailed analysis of this portion of the population.

We mention the time reference of certain data to avoid confusion. The description of family composition refers, in each case, to the year of interview -- 1968 and subsequent years. Reports on income flow, consumption and
work hours refer to the calendar year prior to that of the interview -- 1967 and
subsequently. Thus tables may refer to 1972 income, for 1973 families.

II. Economic Characteristics of Families in 1972

Economic status is generally measured by the amount of earnings and other
income (such as income from capital or from public assistance) of family members
relative to the number of people which the income must support. Refinements may
include adding the value of leisure as a component of income or deducting work
expenses. The measure of economic status used most extensively in this survey
is similar to that used by the Census Bureau in its annual counts of the poverty
population: ratio of total family money income to "subsistence level" needs --
an income/needs ratio.

The need standard is based on the costs of a minimally adequate diet for the family and, hence, depends primarily on the size and age composition of the family. To this figure is added a sum for nonfood needs which is almost twice the allotment for food, with reductions for economies of scale in housing and other consumption needs of large families. The resulting need standard can be adjusted annually for changes in the Consumer Price Index to eliminate the effect of inflation on the cost of living. For a nonfarm family of four, the need standard in 1972 was $4275.[1]

The need standard is set low in order to identify those who are generally considered "poor." Most people live in families with an income/needs ratio greater than 1.00. In the Panel Study sample, about nine percent of the families score less than 1.00 on this index of economic status in 1972; the median score was 3.03.

The major components of family income and the varying importance of different components and sources for families at various levels on the income/needs measure are shown in Table 1.1. It gives a snapshot view of the families' economic status in a single year.

It is perhaps noteworthy that in over half of all families, the head's labor income was less than $7000 in 1972. (This includes those with no earned income, such as the retired.) More transfer income[2] is received by those with lower income/needs ratios than those with high ratios, but the differences in amounts going to the poor and the well-off is not as great as might be expected. On the other hand, transfer income as a percentage of total income is dramatically different for high and low income families, as Figure 1.1 indicates.

The averages in Table 1.1 include everyone in the family and involve averaging zeroes in with positive numbers. The wide disparities in earnings if we look only at those who had any earnings is indicated by Table 1.2. It shows that the

---

[1] For a detailed explanation of the needs standard used by the Bureau of the Census, see its Current Population Reports, Series P-60, No. 81. The need standard constructed for use in this Panel Study is actually 25 percent higher than that used by the Census Bureau. (It is based on the Department of Agriculture's "low" rather than "economy" food budget.) However, it is relatively easy to shift from one standard to the other in making tabulations, and, *in this chapter, the need standard employed is as close as possible to the "official" standard used by the Census Bureau.*

[2] Transfer income includes social security and private retirement funds, which account for about 40 percent and 25 percent of all transfer income, respectively. Public assistance transfers, such as Aid to Families with Dependent Children, account for only about ten percent of total transfer income; but, for those in the lowest decile, public assistance accounts for about a third of their transfer income.

TABLE 1.1

Components of Income by Deciles of Income/Needs*

Entries are the Averages for Families in Each Decile

Income/Needs Decile**	Upper Limit	Head's Labor Income	Wife's Labor Income	Head and Wife Capital Income (Rent, Interest, Dividends, Farm, Business)	Other's Taxable Income	Transfer Income Head and Wife	Transfer Income Others	Total Family Money Income
Lowest	1.11	$ 1047	$ 86	$ 33	$ 182	$1209	$ 90	$ 2650
Second	1.58	2126	257	119	262	1546	130	4440
Third	2.08	3473	410	233	431	1432	116	6096
Fourth	2.59	5236	592	336	560	1317	151	8192
Fifth	3.03	6830	969	361	738	882	132	9913
Sixth	3.56	7632	1111	562	851	930	143	11229
Seventh	4.21	8876	1343	689	969	1023	33	12932
Eighth	5.05	10187	2015	833	957	899	67	14958
Ninth	6.44	12394	2525	970	1140	630	80	17739
Highest	---	18788	3392	4371	1000	762	120	28433
Overall average		$ 7662	$1271	$ 851	$ 709	$1063	$106	$11663

*Based on the 1972 incomes of the 5285 families interviewed in 1973.

**Each decile of the distribution contains ten percent of the population. Thus, the lowest decile consists of the ten percent of the population with the lowest income/needs scores.

FIGURE 1.1

Percentage of Total Family Money Income in 1972 from Some Major Sources by Income/Needs

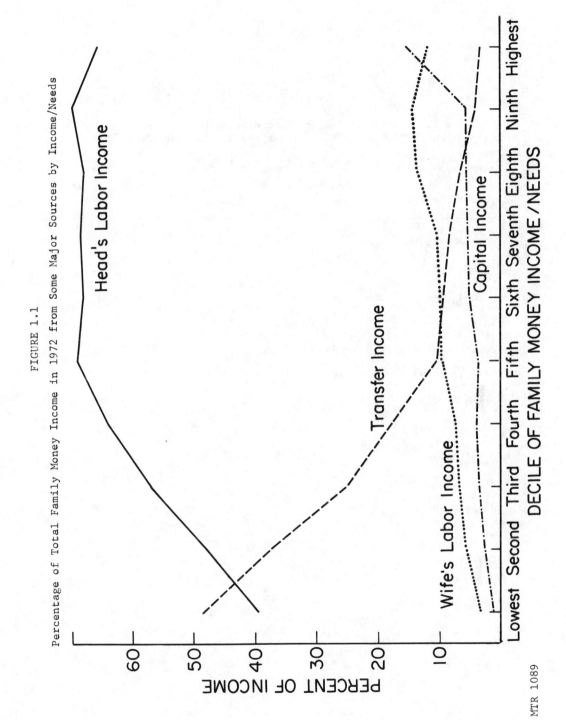

MTR 1089

TABLE 1.2

Percent in Each Income/Needs Decile
Where Head or Wife or Others Had Any Earnings in 1972

(for all 5285 families)

Income/Needs Decile	Upper Limit	Head Had Some Earnings	Wife Had Some Earnings	Others in Family Had Taxable Income
Lowest	1.11	50	9	16
Second	1.58	62	17	15
Third	2.08	75	21	20
Fourth	2.59	79	26	23
Fifth	3.03	90	35	21
Sixth	3.56	90	37	27
Seventh	4.21	90	39	26
Eighth	5.05	94	44	25
Ninth	6.44	94	49	27
Highest	--	95	49	23
TOTAL		82	33	22

MTR 1089

proportion of families where the head had earnings rises from 50 percent at the bottom decile to 95 percent at the top. The fraction of wives working rises from a tenth to a half. The proportion of families where someone *else* in the family had a taxable income (mostly earnings) rises from a sixth to more than a fourth, then declines. Any policies affecting the earnings of secondary earners will thus have different impacts from those affecting earnings of heads or of wives.

By relating total money income to needs, one ignores taxes. Table 1.3 provides estimates of the Federal income taxes paid by families in different income/needs deciles. Taxes, of course, increase with income and thus reduce the spread a little. The same table shows that the average "needs" (adjusted family size) do not vary much except at the very top where there are apparently some smaller families.

Looking only at incomes and needs (family sizes) leaves out a third important dimension of well-being, namely, the amount of free time available. Table 1.4 provides estimates of the hours spent working for money at each decile of income/needs. The averages include families where head, wife, or others do no work at all, so part of the large increase in work hours as one goes up the income/needs scale is an increase in the proportion working (with nonzero work hours). But even among workers only, heads' hours increase substantially, and wives' hours double from bottom to top. There are also more families at the lower income/needs deciles with no wife (or no husband) or with no others to earn extra income.

Some of the higher well-being in the upper deciles results from longer work hours. We do not have a comprehensive measure of leisure (per main adult) because the sixth wave did not collect data on home production, and there remains some "leisure" that is not enjoyable where people really want more work. But, in general, the average family in an upper decile has less nonwork time.

III. Change in Economic Status of Families

Turning now to a dynamic analysis of change, we must face the issue of what to do with families who changed composition. Of particular importance are the new families formed by young people leaving parental homes. Changes in society are clearly made up in part by changes in income distribution resulting from the usual and expected demographic movements through life cycle stages. The dramatic change from parental income to the initial income of a new unit --particularly when children leave home -- is offset in large measure by a reduction in the

TABLE 1.3

Claims on Income by Deciles of Income/Needs

(1972, for all 1973 families)

Income/Needs Decile	Upper Limit	Federal Income Taxes*			"Consumption" Need Standard**
		Head and Wife Taxes	Others Taxes	Total Taxes	
Lowest	1.11	$ 3	$ 6	$ 8	$3393
Second	1.58	59	6	65	3283
Third	2.08	214	20	234	3328
Fourth	2.59	465	30	495	3512
Fifth	3.03	775	56	831	3531
Sixth	3.56	973	61	1034	3420
Seventh	4.21	1258	81	1339	3354
Eighth	5.05	1645	90	1734	3279
Ninth	6.44	2269	119	2387	3136
Highest	--	5268	118	5385	3034
TOTAL		$1294	$59	$1352	$3327

N = 5285

*Estimated; see documentation referred to in footnote on page 1.

**Unadjusted for inflation. Increase by 25% for 1972 prices, by 29% for "relative equity" (change in average income per family). But to adjust only for inflation and reduce to economy standard would leave these numbers unaffected.

MTR 1089

TABLE 1.4

Components of Work by Deciles of Income/Needs

(1972, for all 1973 families)

Income/Needs Decile	Upper Limit	Head's Work Hours	Wife's Work Hours	Other's Work Hours	Total Annual Work Hours
Lowest	1.11	663	67	127	857
Second	1.58	977	163	155	1295
Third	2.08	1307	252	212	1771
Fourth	2.59	1574	300	239	2113
Fifth	3.03	1828	400	295	2523
Sixth	3.56	1910	426	315	2651
Seventh	4.21	1977	536	353	2866
Eighth	5.05	1976	635	304	2915
Ninth	6.44	2124	706	331	3161
Highest	--	2243	739	281	3263
TOTAL		1658	422	261	2341

N = 5285

MTR 1089

number of people dependent on that new unit. A family of four with an income of
$20,000 may lose a son and become a family of three with an income of $15,000,
while the son forms a new family of one with an income of $7,000.

We have calculated a set of transition tables for several measures of income
or well-being, both for the whole sample and for those units with the same head
in all six interviews (for the five-year span). We present here only a summary,
using a rank correlation coefficient (Kendall's Tau-B; see Table 1.5). It shows
the extent to which measures of status in different years are associated. The
persistence of status is clearly higher when we look only at families with the
same head and when we look only at changes from year five to year six, rather
than for the whole five years. We have deflated incomes in the later years by
25 percent for the five-year change, by five percent for the last year, and by
20 percent for ADC, AFDC where we do not have a first-year measure coded separately and must look at change from year two to year six.

The low rank correlations of transfer income in different years reflect
both the higher turnover of families with such income and the small proportion
of the population that is nonzero in these categories. For ADC-AFDC transfers,
however, the small proportions nonzero fail to reduce the correlations much,
indicating some tendency to stay on the rolls, particularly for families with
the same head during the years.

By focusing on one reasonable measure of well-being such as total family
money income/needs, we can describe families that have experienced changes and
what the total spread of experience has been. If we start with *all* families and
deflate 1972 incomes by 25 percent for price inflation since 1967, we see in
Table 1.6 a substantial spread of experience with a considerable amount of decline in status among the young (splitoffs) and those at the retirement age.
For example, about 26 percent of 1973 families with heads in the 18 to 24 year
age range have income/needs levels at least 1.0 lower than in 1967.

When we look at differences according to race, sex, and marital status (see
Table 1.7), we see a larger number of whites with substantial declines in status.
This reflects white children leaving very well off parental homes. Also start-
ing salaries (and minimum wages) are not very different for blacks and whites.

Tables 1.8 and 1.9 show changes in actual deflated income. They show an
exaggerated picture of decline by focusing on the lower incomes of splitoffs who
usually have lower needs.

Since changing family composition is crucial, we look separately at families with the same head. Also, to eliminate the effects of young people getting
into the labor force and older people retiring, we look at families with the same

TABLE 1.5

Rank Correlations of Economic Status in Different Years

(Tau-B)

Measure of Status*	All:***			Same Head Only:		
	Year 1 to Year 6	Year 5 to Year 6	Year 2 to Year 6	Year 1 to Year 6	Year 5 to Year 6	Year 2 to Year 6
Family Money Income**	.47	.70		.64	.80	
Family Money Income/Needs**	.49	.69		.59	.77	
Decile of Income/Needs	.48	.69		.57	.77	
Total Family Transfer Income**	.08			.13		
ADC, AFDC of Head and Wife		.69	.36		.76	.59

*Deflated for price increases

**These income variables are bracketed.

***Includes both original and splitoff families. For the newly-formed families, original family income is compared with splitoff family income.

MTR 1089

TABLE 1.6

Real Change in Income/Needs 1967 to 1972
by Age of Head in 1973

(deflated for 25% increase in prices; includes new families [split-offs])

Change in Income/Needs	Age of Head in 1973							All Ages
	18-24	25-34	35-44	45-54	55-64	65-74	75+	
-1.00 or less	26	17	10	12	20	25	12	17
- .50 to -.99	11	10	9	8	10	13	10	10
- .10 to -.49	14	11	18	13	10	14	19	13
- .09 to +.09	5	7	10	7	8	11	18	9
+ .10 to +.49	10	13	19	17	16	16	26	16
+ .50 to +.99	14	14	15	19	15	11	7	14
+1.00 to +1.49	8	10	8	10	8	4	5	8
+1.50 to +1.99	5	6	4	4	5	3	1	5
+2.00 to +2.99	5	8	3	6	4	2	2	5
+3.00 or more	2	4	4	4	4	1	1	3
	100	100	100	100	100	100	101	100
Number	844	1202	958	941	707	410	223	5285
Percent	12.7	20.6	17.1	17.8	13.8	11.4	6.7	100.1

MTR 1089

TABLE 1.7

Real Change in Income/Needs 1967 to 1972
by Sex, Race, Marital Status in 1973
(adjusted for 25% inflation)

Includes New Split-off Families

Change in Income/Needs	White			Nonwhite		
	Male Head		Female Head	Male Head		Female Head
	Married	Not Married		Married	Not Married	
-1.00 or less	17	25	22	8	9	8
- .50 to -.99	10	12	11	8	6	8
- .10 to -.49	13	7	15	17	13	20
- .09 to +.09	8	9	9	8	5	18
+ .10 to +.49	15	12	17	20	22	25
+ .50 to +.99	14	12	13	17	21	14
+1.00 to +1.49	8	10	8	9	13	4
+1.50 to +1.99	5	2	3	5	5	1
+2.00 to +2.99	6	7	2	5	6	1
+3.00 or more	4	5	0	3	0	1
	100	101	100	100	100	100
Number	2281	294	689	993	221	798
% of Families	58	9	19	7	2	5	100.0

MTR 1089

TABLE 1.8

Real Change in Total Family Money Income 1967 to 1972
by Age of Head in 1973

(deflated for 25% inflation of prices;
includes new families [splitoffs])

Change in Total Family Income 1967 to 1972	Age of Head in 1973							
	18-24	25-34	35-44	45-54	55-64	65-74	75+	All Ages
-5000 or less	44	15	7	11	14	11	4	15
-4999 to -2000	19	13	10	13	17	19	10	14
-1999 to - 500	9	10	10	13	18	18	21	13
- 499 to + 499	6	8	12	11	14	25	37	14
+ 500 to + 999	3	5	9	5	8	7	12	7
+1000 to +1999	4	9	13	11	10	9	7	9
+2000 to +2999	6	10	10	11	5	6	4	8
+3000 to +4999	5	13	13	10	5	2	2	8
+5000 to +7499	3	9	8	8	4	2	2	6
+7500 or more	1	8	9	7	5	1	1	5
	100	100	101	100	100	100	100	99
Number of cases	844	1202	958	941	707	410	223	5285
Percent	12.7	20.6	17.1	17.8	13.8	11.4	6.7	100.1

MTR 1089

TABLE 1.9

Real Change in Total Family Money Income 1967 to 1972
by Sex, Race, Marital Status in 1973

(deflated for 25% price inflation;
includes new families [split-offs])

Change in Total Family Income 1967 to 1972 (deflated)	White			Nonwhite			
	Male Head		Female Head	Male Head		Female Head	All
	Married	Not Married		Married	Not Married		
-5000 or less	13	29	21	7	9	10	15
-4999 to -2000	14	18	16	11	12	14	14
-1999 to - 500	12	10	16	16	15	18	13
- 499 to + 499	11	16	19	10	17	24	14
+ 500 to + 999	7	5	7	5	15	11	7
+1000 to +1999	9	9	8	10	16	11	9
+2000 to +2999	9	4	7	10	8	4	8
+3000 to +4999	10	3	3	16	4	5	8
+5000 to +7499	8	3	2	8	4	2	6
+7500 or more	7	3	1	7	0	1	5
	100	100	100	100	100	100	99
Number of cases	2290	294	689	993	221	798	5285
Percent	58	9	19	7	2	5	100

MTR 1089

head *and* little change in the head's total annual work hours. When we do this,
the spread of changes in income/needs is dramatically reduced (see Table 1.10).

We can also ignore changes in the number of other earners and their earnings
by focusing on changes in the head's annual earnings. Table 1.11 gives the distribution of changes in head's annual earnings (deflated for price changes) for
all families (in some of which a different head is compared with the present one),
for those with the same head, and for those with the same head and little change
in the head's work hours.

In order to see what differences appear by age or by race-sex-marital status,
we collapse the change into three groups, those where real annual earnings of
the head went up appreciably, went down appreciably, or changed by less than
$500. The effect of age -- and the effect of sex and marital status of head --
can be viewed differently depending on whether one looks at *all* families or only
those with the same head as five years earlier (see Tables 1.12 and 1.13).
Younger heads are much worse off when compared to their parental family than if
compared to their *own past* situation. Families which become female headed suffer more losses than those which were that way in the beginning.

It is evident that individual unchanged units are progressing while the
overall distribution is kept relatively stable by the appearance of new families
at the bottom and the retirements of a few at the upper ages.

To show that these effects persist when we move to the more comprehensive
measure of change in status -- change in family money income/needs (deflated for
inflation) -- Tables 1.14 and 1.15 demonstrate again that it is the units with
changed heads and/or changed work hours of the head that produce most of the
declines in economic *status*. These are concentrated among the very young, the
unmarried, and those near retirement age.

We have seen that changes in family composition profoundly affect changes
in income and welfare. Pushing further to look into what kinds of units had
experienced these changes in family composition (as of early 1973), we find that
age and sex together account for most of the differences. Table 1.16 shows that
the new heads of families are mostly young men and women, that a substantial
number of female heads are former wives, and that minor changes in family members other than head or wife occur most frequently in the "middle ages" (35-54).

Table 1.17 focuses on marital status in 1973, indicating clearly that only
the married and the widowed are unlikely to have experienced a recent change in
head or wife. Most of the single men and women are new heads (and young, of
course), and most of the divorced or separated have experienced that change recently. For the women, it is a wife becoming a head; for the men, a change in
wife. The greater longevity of women shows up in the much greater number of

TABLE 1.10

Change in Real Family Money Income/Needs 1967 to 1972

Changes in Income/Needs *	All Families	Only Those with Same Head All Six Years	Same Head and His Annual Work Hours Changed Less Than 200
-1.00 or less	17.0%	13.7%	8.8%
- .99 to -.50	9.9	8.9	8.3
- .49 to -.10	13.5	14.0	18.0
- .09 to +.09	8.6	9.9	14.8
+ .10 to +.49	16.0	18.4	23.3
+ .50 to +.99	14.1	15.3	15.5
+1.00 to +1.49	8.3	8.0	6.1
+1.50 to +1.99	4.5	4.1	1.6
+2.00 to +2.99	5.0	4.6	2.7
+3.00 or more	3.1	3.2	0.9
	100.0%	100.1%	100.0%
Number	5285	3438	871
Rank Correlation with age	-.04	-.12	-.05

* adjusted for 25% inflation

MTR 1089

TABLE 1.11

Change in Head's Real Annual Earnings (Deflated) 1967 to 1972 *

Change in Head's Real Annual Earnings*	All 1973 Families	Only Those with Same Head All Six Years	Same Head and His Annual Work Hours Changed Less Than 200
-5000 or less	15.1%	7.1%	3.7%
-4999 to -2000	14.4	12.3	6.8
-1999 to - 500	13.2	13.9	14.2
- 499 to + 499	13.6	16.2	29.7
+ 500 to + 999	6.7	8.4	13.8
+1000 to +1999	9.2	10.8	12.4
+2000 to +2999	8.0	9.1	8.6
+3000 to +4999	8.4	9.5	6.5
+5000 to +7499	6.0	6.9	2.5
+7500 or more	5.3	5.7	1.9
	99.9%	99.9%	100.1%
Number of cases	5285	3438	871
Rank correlation with age	.02	-.21	-.19

* 1972 income reduced 25% for price inflation

MTR 1089

TABLE 1.12

Change in Head's Real (Deflated) Earnings 1967 to 1972
by Age For All 1973 Heads, and Two Subgroups *

All 1973 Heads (some new heads)

| | Age of Head in 1973 | | | | | | | |
	18-24	25-34	35-44	45-54	55-64	65-74	75+	All Ages
Down $500 or more	72.4	38.6	26.5	37.2	48.3	48.1	35.2	42.7
Changed less than $500	6.3	8.3	11.6	10.9	14.2	24.6	36.6	13.6
Up $500 or more	21.3	53.1	61.9	51.9	37.5	37.3	28.2	43.7
	100.0	100.0	100.0	100.0	100.0	100.0	100.0	100.0
Number of cases	844	1202	958	941	707	410	223	5285

Same Head as in 1967

| | Age of Head in 1973 | | | | | | | |
	18-24	25-34	35-44	45-54	55-64	65-74	75+	All Ages
Down $500 or more	0	23.5	22.9	34.1	45.6	47.0	29.5	33.3
Changed less than $500	15.2	9.7	12.0	11.3	15.3	24.3	41.7	16.2
Up $500 or more	84.8	66.8	65.0	54.6	39.1	28.7	28.8	50.4
	100.0	100.0	99.9	100.0	100.0	100.0	100.0	99.9
Number of cases	17	604	793	854	625	361	184	3438

Same Head and Annual Work Hours Changed Less Than 200

| | Age of Head in 1973 | | | | | | | |
	18-24	25-34	35-44	45-54	55-64	65-74	75+	All Ages
Down $500 or more	0	17.0	19.7	30.9	28.9	24.3	25.5	24.7
Changed less than $500	0	20.7	18.5	15.0	35.0	35.8	48.3	29.7
Up $500 or more	100.0	62.3	61.8	54.1	36.1	39.9	26.2	45.6
	100.0	100.0	100.0	100.0	100.0	100.0	100.0	100.0
Number of cases	2	118	177	185	140	121	128	871

*1972 earnings reduced by 25% for price inflation.

MTR 1089

TABLE 1.13

Change in Head's Real Annual Earnings 1967 to 1972
by Race, Sex, Marital Status (in 1973)
For All 1973 Heads and Two Subgroups^

	All 1973 Heads						
	White			Nonwhite			
	Male Head		Female Head	Male Head		Female Head	All
	Married	Not Married		Married	Not Married		
Down $500 or more	38.5	56.4	53.4	34.0	36.2	42.9	42.7
Changed less than $500	11.2	15.5	18.7	10.1	17.3	23.8	13.6
Up $500 or more	50.4	28.0	28.0	55.8	46.5	33.2	43.7
	100.1	99.9	100.1	99.9	100.0	99.9	100.0
Number of cases	2290	294	689	993	221	798	5285

	Same Head in 1973 as in 1967						
Down $500 or more	33.8	38.6	32.3	29.7	29.6	25.4	33.3
Changed less than $500	12.4	21.7	27.6	12.2	22.0	32.9	16.2
Up $500 or more	53.8	39.7	40.0	58.2	48.5	41.7	50.4
	100.0	100.0	99.9	100.1	100.1	100.0	99.9
Number of cases	1624	183	378	636	114	503	3438

	Same Head and Annual Work Hours Changed Less than 200						
Down $500 or more	27.6	14.6	23.3	29.2	2.2	15.8	24.7
Changed less than $500	20.6	49.1	41.2	19.7	42.6	43.9	29.7
Up $500 or more	51.6	36.5	35.6	51.0	55.3	40.2	45.6
	99.8	100.2	100.1	99.9	100.1	99.9	100.0
Number of cases	347	49	178	112	33	152	871

*1972 income reduced 25% for price inflation   MTR 1089

TABLE 1.14

Absolute Change in Real Family Money Income/Needs 1967 to 1972
By Age For All 1973 Heads and Two Subgroups *

All 1973 Heads (some are new heads)

Change in Real Income/Needs	Age of Head in 1973							
	18-24	25-34	35-44	45-54	55-64	65-74	75 +	All Ages
Down by .10 or more	51.2	49.8	35.8	32.5	40.0	51.4	40.3	40.4
Changed less than .10	4.5	6.7	9.9	7.4	8.3	11.4	18.5	8.6
Up by .10 or more	44.3	43.5	54.3	60.1	51.7	37.2	41.2	51.0
	100.0	100.0	100.0	100.0	100.0	100.0	100.0	100.0
Number of cases	844	1202	958	941	707	410	223	5285

Same Head in 1973 as in 1967

	18-24	25-34	35-44	45-54	55-64	65-74	75 +	All Ages
Down by .10 or more	9.7	33.2	34.3	29.7	39.0	50.9	38.5	36.6
Changed less than .10	5.5	8.3	10.2	7.8	7.6	12.1	19.1	9.9
Up by .10 or more	84.9	58.5	55.5	62.6	53.3	37.0	42.3	53.6
	100.1	100.0	100.0	100.1	99.9	100.0	99.9	100.1
Number of cases	17	604	793	854	625	361	184	3438

Same Head and Annual Work Hours Changed Less than 200

	18-24	25-34	35-44	45-54	55-64	65-74	75 +	All Ages
Down by .10 or more	.0	38.7	41.0	32.2	28.2	30.7	38.2	35.1
Changed less than .10	.0	13.8	10.0	11.0	13.2	20.0	19.8	14.8
Up by .10 or more	100.0	47.5	49.0	56.8	58.6	49.3	42.0	50.1
	100.0	100.0	100.0	100.0	100.0	100.0	100.0	100.0
Number of cases	2	118	177	185	140	121	128	871

* adjusted for inflation

MTR 1089

TABLE 1.15

Absolute Change in Real Family Money Income/Needs 1967 to 1972
By Race, Sex, Marital Status in 1973
For All 1973 Heads and Two Subgroups

All 1973 Heads

	White			Nonwhite			
	Male Head		Female Head	Male Head		Female Head	All
	Married	Not Married		Married	Not Married		
Down .10 or more	39.4	43.6	47.5	32.6	28.0	35.9	40.4
Changed less than .10	7.9	9.1	9.0	7.7	5.4	18.2	8.6
Up .10 or more	52.7	47.2	43.6	59.7	66.5	45.9	51.0
	100.0	99.9	100.1	100.0	99.9	100.0	100.0
Number of cases	2290	294	689	993	221	798	5285

Same Head in 1973 as in 1967

	White			Nonwhite			
	Male Head		Female Head	Male Head		Female Head	All
	Married	Not Married		Married	Not Married		
Down .10 or more	38.3	31.4	34.5	35.4	29.7	28.0	36.6
Changed less than .10	9.0	12.3	9.9	8.6	6.3	22.5	9.9
Up .10 or more	52.8	56.2	55.6	55.9	63.9	49.5	53.6
	100.1	99.9	100.0	99.9	99.9	100.0	100.1
Number of cases	1624	183	378	636	114	503	3438

Same Head and Annual Work Hours Changed Less than 200

	White			Nonwhite			
	Male Head		Female Head	Male Head		Female Head	All
	Married	Not Married		Married	Not Married		
Down .10 or more	39.1	21.7	30.6	42.6	19.2	28.7	35.1
Changed less than .10	13.4	27.2	14.5	6.7	9.8	25.0	14.8
Up .10 or more	47.5	51.2	54.8	50.8	71.0	46.3	50.1
	100.0	100.1	99.9	100.1	100.0	100.0	100.0
Number of cases	347	49	178	112	33	152	871

MTR 1089

TABLE 1.16

Change in Family Composition 1968 to 1973
by Age and Sex of 1973 Head

| Change in Family Composition | Head in 1973 is | | | | | | All |
| | Male | | | Female | | | |
	18–34	35–54	55+	18–34	35–54	55+	
No change in family members	11	39	65	14	25	50	36
Change in members other than head or wife	22	48	27	4	37	20	30
Same head but change in wife	6	7	5	0	0	0	5
Wife from previous years became head	0	0	0	19	32	24	6
Female head got married to a non-sample member	3	3	2	2	3	1	3
Some sample member other than head or wife became head	39	2	2	53	3	4	15
Some female (not head) married a nonsample member	16	1	0	6	0	0	5
Other	2	1	0	1	1	0	1
	99	101	101	99	101	99	101
Number of Cases	1592	1374	823	454	525	517	5285
Percent of Sample	27	29	21	6	6	11	100

Cramer's V = .38

MTR 1094

TABLE 1.17

Change in Family Composition 1968 to 1973
by 1973 Marital Status of Head

| Change in Family Composition | Marital Status of 1973 Head | | | | | | |
| | | Single | | | | | |
	Married	Man	Woman	Widowed	Divorced	Separated	All
No change in family members	37	30	35	45	20	17	36
Change in members other than head or wife	37	5	8	20	23	18	30
Same head but change in wife	3	1	0	6	18	15	5
Wife from previous years became head	1	0	0	25	23	23	6
Female head got married to a non-sample member	3	0	0	1	3	2	3
Some sample member other than head or wife became head	11	63	56	4	11	19	15
Some female (not head) married a nonsample member	7	0	1	0	2	5	5
Other	1	1	0	0	1	1	1
	100	100	100	101	101	100	101
Number of Cases	3306	236	612	396	410	335	5285
Percent of Sample	66	5	13	7	3	5	99

Cramer's V = .29

recent widows (wife became head) relative to recent widowers (same head but change in wife).[1] But across all groups the amount and diversity of changes over this brief five-year period is substantial.

The kinds of changes in family composition being examined here suggest certain changes in the number of family members who may be earners on the one hand or dependents on the other. The relationships between changed family *composition* and changed family *size* are what one would expect and will not be shown. Where the head remains the same, or a female head gets married, there is usually only a small change up or down in family size, but splitoffs usually leave large families to form small ones.

One of the important economic consequences of these changes in family composition comes through changed work hours of the family members. Table 1.18 brings this discussion of changing family composition back to the issue of effects on economic status by showing how change in family composition accounts for changes in total family work hours. New families have the largest changes, but there are very substantial changes in total work hours even in families with no change in head or wife. It must be remembered, however, that without such change, working children may leave home, reducing the total family work hours. If a wife or child goes to work or a man loses or gains a wife who is working, it will change total family work hours substantially.

The emphasis here on changing family composition may seem like simple demographic description. A large amount of social analysis, however, consists of comparing distributions from independent cross sections, ignoring patterns of transition and the histories of the individual units at any point in time. Rather small changes in the pattern of these transitions can lead to what seem to be changes in distributions and are easily misinterpreted. An increase in units with low income because of a wave of undoubling (splitting off) is not the same as one brought about by less work hours (perhaps unemployment) of units with the same head as in previous years.

This section has shown how stages in the life cycle, changes in family composition, and other demographic factors affect the economic status of families. The final section of this chapter will go on to examine the relative effects of some other factors -- such as attitudes and behavior patterns of family heads -- attempting to "control" for the dominant demographic factors which have been described here. But first we turn to some additional descriptive analysis focusing on the poverty population.

---

[1] Of course there are some divorces in here too, but they involve as many men as women.

TABLE 1.18

Change in Total Annual Hours of Work for Money (1967 to 1972)
By Change in Family Composition

| | Change in Family Composition | | | | | | | |
| | Same Head: | | | Different Head: | | | | ALL (Includes Some Other Change Groups) |
Change in Work Hours	No Change In Members	No Change In Head Or Wife	No Change In Head (Change In Wife)	Wife Became Head	Female Head Married Nonsample Person	Sample Member (Not Head Or Wife) Became Head	Female Not Head Married A Nonsample Person	
+2000 or more	5	8	8	2	25	6	11	7
+1000 to +1999	9	11	14	4	18	8	15	10
+500 to +999	9	11	5	2	11	5	6	8
+200 to +499	8	9	11	2	5	5	6	7
-199 to +199	36	19	14	26	15	9	10	23
-200 to -499	9	9	6	6	4	5	7	8
-500 to -999	8	11	11	9	5	11	9	9
-1000 to -1999	9	12	17	23	13	23	18	14
-2000 or less	8	10	13	26	3	27	19	13
	101	100	99	100	99	99	101	99
Number of Cases	1536	1637	265	284	193	941	367	5285
Percent of Sample	36	30	5	6	3	15	5	

Cramer's V = .14

MTR 1094

IV. A Multi-Year Perspective on the Low Income Population

APPLYING THE "OFFICIAL" POVERTY STANDARD

Counting "the poor" is always an arbitrary business. The Census Bureau's annual counts are based on the number of people found below an income/needs ratio of 1.00 in a single year. Similar counts can be obtained from the Panel Study sample, where, for example, it is found that 11 percent of the sample was poor in 1968 and eight percent in 1972.[1] The strength of the Panel Study lies in having data on the same people spanning several years so that the number of persons continually below the poverty line, who move back and forth across it or who are in many years just above it (those "at risk"), can be counted.

For this kind of description, it is useful to shift from families to individuals as the unit of analysis. Since family composition changes, the meaning of the "same family" through time may be ambiguous, as we saw in the previous section. This kind of complication does not arise in examining the changing economic status of individuals. Note, though, that a person's economic status in any year is still determined by the income/needs ratio of the family to which he or she belongs in that year, since some sharing of income takes place.

We start by looking at amounts of change -- and stability -- for individuals at all levels on the income/needs ratio. Table 1.19 shows the patterns of transition for individuals between 1967 and 1972. Each column contains a group of people who started in a certain income/needs bracket in 1967. For example, the left-hand column contains all those who started in 1967 in families with an income/needs ratio of less than 1.00. By reading down this column, it is possible to see what happened to this group by 1972. Some 39 percent were still in the category less than 1.00; 26 percent had moved into the 1.00-1.49 category, and so on. Note that the majority had moved above 1.00, and four percent had an

_____

[1] The comparable Census Bureau estimates of the percentage of the population poor in 1967 and 1972 are 14 and 12, respectively. The Panel Study finds somewhat fewer people poor. Whether the Panel Study or the Census is more accurate is uncertain. Unearned and irregular income -- which is important to low-income people -- tends to be underreported in surveys. It is possible that reporting improved through repeated interviews. This would suggest that the Panel Study data are more accurate. On the other hand, the Census samples are much larger. Furthermore, very poor people may be among those most likely to drop out of a panel study, and this loss may not be completely compensated for by adjustments which have been made for nonresponse. These considerations would suggest that Census is more accurate. The two studies do show similar orders of magnitude and direction of change for poverty incidence. Which is the more nearly correct in measuring the absolute incidence is not crucial here, since the emphasis is on the amount of change for families from year to year and the *relative* size of low-income groups when measured on a one-year versus a multi-year basis.

TABLE 1.19

Income/Needs in 1972 According to Income/Needs in 1967
(for individuals)

Income/Needs in 1972	Income/Needs in 1967						
	Less than 1.00	1.00-1.49	1.50-1.99	2.00-2.99	3.00-3.99	4.00+	All
Less than 1.00	39	15	6	2	1	1	8
1.00 - 1.49	26	22	13	6	4	1	9
1.50 - 1.99	15	22	20	10	5	2	10
2.00 - 2.99	11	24	36	34	21	10	23
3.00 - 3.99	5	9	16	28	25	15	18
4.00 -	4	8	9	20	44	71	32
	100%	100%	100%	100%	100%	100%	100%
Number of persons in sample	4272	2605	2298	2975	1524	2132	15,806
Estimated percent of U.S. population	11	11	13	25	16	24 =	100

Income/needs ratios have been adjusted for inflation

income/needs ratio over 4.00 in 1972.

The underlined percentages represent persons who were in the same income/ needs bracket both years. In all but the "4.00+" column (which indicates that 71 percent were above 4.00 in both 1967 and 1972), the majority had changed their bracket by 1972, with more having increases in their income/needs ratios than decreases. Note that the table presents income/needs ratios for two years only (1967 and 1972). There were even greater changes in the intervening years in both directions.

The aggregate distributions of income/needs for the two years are shown in the bottom row (for 1967) and the right-hand column (for 1972). There has been some net upward shift in the distribution from 1967 to 1972. But there were more changes in both directions by individuals than are reflected by the aggregate figures. Over half of those poor (below 1.00) in 1967 were no longer poor in 1972. The aggregate proportion below 1.00 was not reduced by half, however, because others who had not started out poor became poor and because children were born into poverty.

Table 1.19 gives information for individuals for only two years. Table 1.20 includes some groups obtained from people's economic experience over all six years. Few people remain in poverty year after year: only 2.4 percent of the population were below 1.00 on the income/needs distribution *every one* of the six years, compared to 11 and 8 percent in the single years 1967 and 1972. On the other hand, quite a large proportion (21 percent of the population in 1972) fell into poverty *at least once* during this relatively short period. One implication of this high rate of turnover is that the number of people who might be eligible for income-tested public assistance programs *at some time* over the course of several years greatly exceeds the number eligible in any one year.

Some have suggested that the most meaningful categorization of "the poor" would be on the basis of a concept of "permanent income," e.g., average income over a number of years or even the lifetime of the individual. An approximation to this is provided in the third category of Table 1.20, "Six-year average below 1.00." This group contains fewer people than fell below 1.00 in any single year -- seven percent compared to eight percent in 1972 or 11 percent in 1967.[1]

Since the poverty line is set quite low, calculations using a 1.50 cutoff on the income/needs ratio have also been made. In any single year about one-

---

[1]Because the percent poor in single years in the Panel Survey is somewhat lower than similar figures from the Census annual counts (see footnote, p. 31), Table 1.20 may underestimate poverty incidence. However, the important comparison is between the relative size of the single-year and multi-year poverty groups.

TABLE 1.20

Percentages of Persons in Various Low-Income Categories,
Considering Their Experience Over Six Years

Low-Income Categories	Estimated Percent of Total Population in Each Low-Income Category*
Persons with Income/Needs Scores ...	
Below 1.00 in 1967	11
Below 1.00 in 1972	8
Six-year average below 1.00	7
Below 1.00 all six years	2
Below 1.00 for at least one year	21
Below 1.50 in 1967	22
Below 1.50 in 1972	17
Six-year average below 1.50	17
Below 1.50 all six years	8
Below 1.50 for at least one year	36

*Estimates are based on the experience of the 15,806 persons in the sample families in 1973.

fifth of the population falls below this low income level; less than ten percent are in families consistently below this ratio; however, over one-third of the population fell below this level at least once during the six-year period.

The relative sizes of the various groups below the 1.50 level differ some-what from the relative sizes of the groups below the 1.00 level. When the high-er cutoff point is used, larger fractions of those below that line in any *single* year are also below it *every* year and *average* below it. This means that if a higher income threshold were used as the poverty line, the poor would be a more stable group over time.

CHARACTERISTICS OF SOME LOW-INCOME GROUPS

Not only size, but also demographic characteristics of the low-income popu-lation depend upon the criteria used in defining poverty. Table 1.21 indicates how demographic characteristics differ depending on the time periods used to classify groups. It includes a comparison of various groups to the total sample. Each row describes the characteristics of one group. The first row shows the characteristics of those poor in a single year. This group is disproportionate-ly aged, poorly educated, black, female headed, and rural -- not an unexpected finding. The number at the far right of the row indicates that 85 percent of those in this group averaged no higher than 1.5 of the poverty line over the en-tire six years. Thus, while it has been shown that most of those found poor in any single year are not below the poverty line *every* year, most in this group usually are not very far above it either. The third row (below 1.00 all six years) shows a distinctly different and smaller group. Those poor every year are overwhelmingly uneducated and black, and half live in rural areas. Although it is not shown in the table, 85 percent of them live in the South.

On the other hand, the fourth group, including all those who fall into pov-erty at least once, contains smaller proportions of persons in families with these characteristics. This implies that many have fallen to this level tempo-rarily for reasons not associated with these demographic attributes. It does not necessarily indicate that most in this group do not have economic problems. In fact, almost 70 percent of them averaged no better than the 1.5 level over the six years.

The last low-income group, those who fell below 1.5 on the income/needs ratio in any year during the period, shows a low-income group most similar in the identified demographic characteristics to the total sample. Thus, many people fall quite low on the income/needs ratio for reasons unrelated to age, education, race, sex, or geographic location.

TABLE 1.21

Percentages of Persons in Various Low-Income
Groups Having Certain Characteristics

(Read *across* for characteristics of each low-income group)

Low-Income Groups Persons With Income/Needs Scores ...	Number of Sample Persons in Group*	Characteristics					Percent of Per- sons With Six-Year Average Income/Needs Less Than 1.5
		Percent of persons in families in which the head in 1973 ...					
		Is 65 or Over	Has 8 Years Educa- tion or Less	Is Black	Is Fe- male	Is Ru- ral**	
Below 1.00 in 1972	(2910)	19	49	46	44	37	85
Six-year average below 1.0	(2870)	21	58	54	46	42	100
Below 1.0 all six years	(1219)	29	78	66	52	50	100
Below 1.0 at least once	(6345)	16	40	34	34	34	69
Below 1.5 in 1972	(5211)	19	42	35	37	34	73
Six-year average below 1.5	(5626)	20	47	38	37	35	100
Below 1.5 all six years	(3129)	23	56	47	43	39	100
Below 1.5 at least once	(9080)	15	34	25	28	31	46
Total sample	(15,806)	11	21	13	16	22	17

*Each of the percentages in a row is based on all the persons in that group. Since many persons have more than one of the indicated characteristics, they will appear more than once, so the percentages in each row add to more than 100. The percentages are based on the weighted sample. The "number of sample persons" is the actual number of persons in the sample.

**"Rural" means lives at least 50 miles from nearest city of 50,000 or more.

APPLYING A PURELY RELATIVE STANDARD OF POVERTY

Income relative to a poverty needs standard is an absolute, rather than relative, measure of economic status. In a country as affluent as the United States,
where the poorest families have more income than a majority of people in some
other countries, poverty is clearly a matter of having income which is low *relative* to others in the country.[1] It is important, then, to look at changes in the
relative position of families and individuals, defined by the family money
income/needs *decile*. Since average incomes rose during the panel period, even
more than prices in most instances, a family could experience an increase in in-
flation-adjusted income/needs and yet stay in the same decile. Whether such a
family would feel better off depends on whether it compares itself with its
neighbors or with some fixed standards.

Given this definition of *relative* economic status, Table 1.22 sorts individuals in the panel according to their family income/needs decile position in
1967 and 1972. Table 1.22 (unlike Table 1.20) does not percentagize the persons
in *each column* but the total of *all* individuals. Even though most errors in the
reporting of income will tend to exaggerate the impression of change, the finding that only 25 percent of all individuals are in the same relative income position in the two years is striking, as is the number of shifts of more than one
decile.

The numbers of persons in various six-year poverty categories -- using the
relative definition of low income -- depends on where in the distribution one
sets the poverty cutoff. Of course, about ten percent are in the lowest decile
each year and about 20 percent in the lowest quintile. (It is not exactly 10
and 20 percent simply because the decile points are based on a ranking of families, while the counts are of persons within families.) We shall take the bottom quintile as our relative poverty line. Using this cutoff, only 7.8 percent
of all individuals are poor all six years, but more than a third (35.5 percent)
fall into poverty at least one year of six.[2] These proportions are about the

-----

[1] Actually, the "absolute" poverty standard used by the Census Bureau (and in the
previous section) recognizes this, in that it is based on the costs of food
available to low-income people in this country, and it provides for necessities
other than food based on the evidence that in America food is only one-third of
the family budget. It is not relative only in the sense that it is not adjusted for changes in the general level of real income through time. (It is
adjusted for inflation.) Thus, as general incomes move up (as they did in the
late 1960's), this poverty standard established in 1964 becomes relatively
lower.

[2] If the incidence of being in the bottom fifth were completely random, almost no
one would be in all six years and 74 percent would be in at least once.

TABLE 1.22

Individuals -- According to Family Income/Needs in 1967 and 1972

1972 Income/ Needs Decile	1967 Income/Needs Decile										Total
Lowest tenth	4.9	2.4	1.3	0.4	0.4	0.1	0.2	0.0	0.1	0.2	10.1
Second	2.2	2.1	2.0	1.1	0.9	0.6	0.5	0.1	0.1	0.1	9.8
Third	1.2	1.5	2.8	1.6	0.9	0.7	0.5	0.4	0.3	0.1	9.9
Fourth	0.6	1.2	1.7	2.1	2.1	1.2	0.8	0.8	0.3	0.1	10.8
Fifth	0.3	0.6	1.1	2.0	1.9	2.0	1.2	1.0	0.4	0.4	10.8
Sixth	0.2	0.4	1.1	1.5	1.9	1.7	1.6	1.0	0.6	0.5	10.5
Seventh	0.3	0.3	0.4	1.1	1.3	1.9	1.4	1.8	0.9	0.6	9.9
Eighth	0.1	0.3	0.2	0.7	0.7	1.4	1.8	1.9	1.6	1.1	10.0
Ninth	0.1	0.1	0.3	0.4	1.0	0.5	1.3	1.7	2.4	1.4	9.2
Highest tenth	0.1	0.1	0.1	0.1	0.2	0.5	0.8	1.1	2.3	3.7	9.0
Total	9.8	8.9	11.2	11.0	11.3	10.7	10.1	9.8	9.0	8.2	100.0

Rank correlation (Kendall's Tau-B) = .54

Association (Cramer's V) = .29

MTR 1098

same as the proportions who are below 1.5 on the absolute income/needs measure for the various periods (see Table 1.20).

In an earlier volume, some analysis was presented showing how various demographic characteristics were related to being in the "target population" (in the bottom quintile at least one year).[1] We shall now extend this analysis, not only to an additional year of data, but also to show the number of different years that persons of various sorts are and are not in poverty.

Table 1.23 shows for each individual age group the numbers of years out of the six (1967-1972) the individual was in a family where the family income/needs was in the lowest fifth in the nation. There are clearly people at both ends of the age distribution who are persistently poor. Others at those ages also are more likely to be temporarily poor. Heads of families and wives tend to be middle aged and are the least likely people in the sample to be poor, especially wives, as shown in Table 1.24. The individuals most apt to be poor are grandchildren and great-grandchildren, who are found in surprisingly large proportions in persistently poor families.

Table 1.25 looks at a number of different subgroups, showing, as expected, that families headed by females, high school dropouts or single persons are more frequently found in the bottom fifth than people in other categories. We also provide at the bottom of that table the proportion of each group whose *average* income/needs position for the six years is in the lowest fifth, and whether the individual was ever (during 1967-1972) in a family in the lowest *tenth* (decile) by family income/needs. The proportions of blacks in these lowest categories is extraordinary.

As a summary of the relationship of other factors to the number of years of poverty and the average six-year position, Table 1.26 gives rank correlations between characteristics of the individual or family on one hand, and each of three measures of the six-year experience on the other. Here we find women without husbands, people of a nonwhite race, or people lacking education more likely to be temporarily or persistently poor.

Figure 1.2 shows that even a little education sharply reduces the likelihood of being poor. However, only the very well educated seem to be entirely free from occasional poverty.

---

[1] Morgan, et al. (1974). That analysis was for families, not individuals.

TABLE 1.23

Number of Years Individual was in a Family with Family Income/Needs
in the Lowest Fifth of All Families

Number of years in lowest fifth on family income/needs	Age of Individual in 1973									
	Less than 5	5-14	15-24	25-34	35-44	45-54	55-64	65-74	75+	All ages
0 (never)	60	60	55	71	74	78	73	61	39	64.5
1	12	8	13	12	8	6	7	9	11	9.8
2	7	6	7	6	4	4	4	4	8	5.6
3	5	5	6	3	4	2	3	6	5	4.4
4	5	5	5	3	2	2	3	4	7	3.9
5	4	6	5	2	3	2	3	5	6	4.0
6 (all the time)	7	10	10	3	5	6	6	11	23	7.8
	100	100	101	100	100	100	99	100	99	100.0
Number of cases	1287	3942	3302	1793	1577	1448	1028	591	295	
Percent of all individuals	6.9	21.0	19.2	13.5	11.0	10.9	8.2	6.1	3.2	100.0

MTR 1115

TABLE 1.24

Number of Years Individual was in a Family with Family Income/Needs
in the Lowest Fifth of All Families, 1967-1972,
By Relation of Individual to Head of Family in 1973

Number of years in lowest fifth on family income/needs	Relation of Individual to Head in 1973						
	Head	Wife	Son or daughter	Brother or sister	Father or mother	Grand child or great-grandchild	Other relatives (in-laws)
0 (never)	64	72	62	49	77	16	62
1	11	10	9	18	8	8	5
2	6	5	5	0	6	7	13
3	4	4	5	12	2	2	3
4	4	3	4	2	0	13	5
5	4	3	5	4	1	11	3
6 (all the time)	7/100	4/101	10/100	15/100	6/100	43/100	9/100
Number of cases	4677	2749	7279	64	45	329	86
Percent of all individuals	35.4	22.8	39.7	0.3	0.3	0.8	0.4	99.7*

*Excludes a few unrelated people pooling resources and a few husbands of female heads.

TABLE 1.25

Number of Years Individual was in a Family with Family Income/Needs
in the Lowest Fifth of All Families, 1967-1972,
for All Individuals and for Selected (overlapping) Subgroups

Number of years in lowest fifth	All	Female Head in '73	High school drop-outs	No change in family composition	Black	Single person in '73
0 (never)	64.5	38.2	49.3	73.5	29.1	47.7
1	9.8	12.4	12.1	7.0	7.6	14.5
2	5.6	7.3	8.0	3.3	6.3	8.5
3	4.4	6.5	6.3	3.5	7.9	5.5
4	3.9	7.1	7.4	3.2	9.1	6.8
5	4.0	7.6	7.8	3.5	10.7	4.7
6 (all the time)	7.8	20.9	9.0	6.0	29.4	12.3
	100.0	100.0	99.9	100.0	100.1	100.0
Number of cases	15,203	3745	3508	4578	6314	995
Average is in lowest fifth	15.3	34.8	22.8	12.4	48.4	21.5
Ever in lowest decile	21.2	44.8	28.6	13.7	55.9	34.8

TABLE 1.26

Rank Correlation Coefficients for Individuals - 1968-1972

Explanatory Characteristic	Number of years in lowest fifth on family income/needs	Number of years in lowest tenth on family income/needs	Average position of family on family income/needs
Change in family composition*	.15	.14	-.10
Age of person in '73	-.06	-.06	.10
Age of Head in '73	-.01	-.02	.02
Age of Head in '68	.07	.07	-.02
Race (Non-white)	.31	.32	-.28
Sex of person (female)	.03	.03	-.02
Sex of Head (female)	.25	.25	-.20
Education of Head	-.31	-.26	.37
Number in family in '73	.09	.06	-.20
Relation to Head in '73**	.05	.04	-.10

*See Table 1.17 for ranking detail.

**Ranked as follows: Head, wife, son or daughter, sibling of head, parent of head, grandchild or great-grandchild, other, unrelated. (See Table 1.24.)

MTR 1115

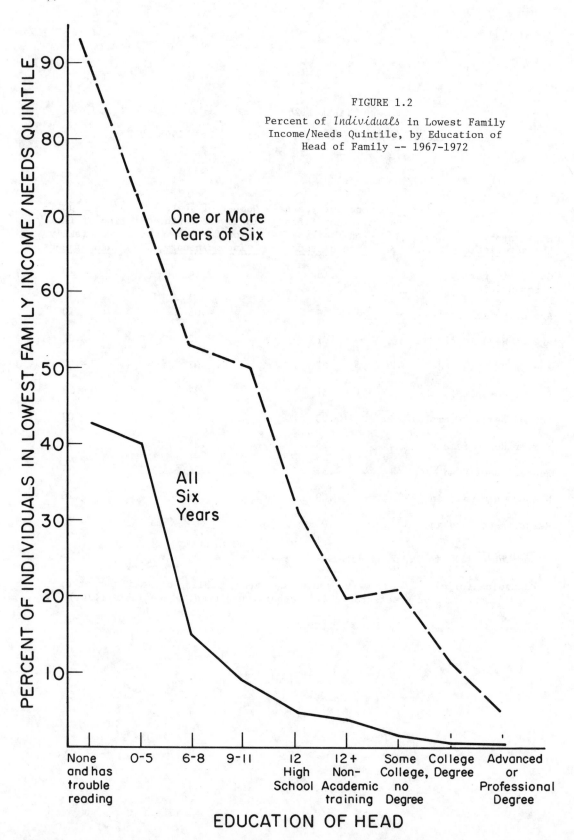

FIGURE 1.2

Percent of *Individuals* in Lowest Family
Income/Needs Quintile, by Education of
Head of Family -- 1967-1972

V. Regression Analysis of Trends in Status

In this section, we again extend and elaborate an analysis presented in an
earlier volume. We want to estimate what causes (or at least predicts) changes
in economic status when various explanatory factors are considered simultaneously. We want to see whether the important explanatory factors are different
for the population as a whole and for the target population (those who fell into
the bottom quintile of the income/needs distribution in at least one year).

Table 1.27 repeats for six years the analysis of trends in economic status
of families which was previously done for five years.[1] (It should be noted that
at this point we are switching back to the family as the unit of analysis.) It
takes a global measure -- total family money income relative to needs -- and examines the regression-estimated trend in it, relative to the six-year average.
The main findings of the earlier analysis are confirmed. Changes remain dominated by demographic forces, even when the analysis is restricted to families with
the same head all six years. The young report substantial increases in well-
being. Those near retirement age report increases insufficient to keep up with
inflation. Interestingly enough, those of advanced age report income changes
that just about keep up with inflation, though we may be averaging in some who
fall behind with others who are "ahead" only because someone left home or died.

Those with young children show lower gains until the youngest child enters
school (ages 5-7 in 1973), presumably because the mother can then reenter the
labor force.

Education has less effect than test scores, and test scores seem to matter
more for the target population, particularly for a small group in that population with very high scores (20 cases, 14 1/2 percent annual increase).

Unemployment in the county during 1968-1971, geographic mobility, race, and
sex have little effect on trends in status. Marital status is important for the
single and widowed in the target population. They have larger than average increases. The divorced (as of 1973) were the worst off.[2]

The personality measure of achievement motivation appeared to have some
effect, but only for target population members at the extreme top of the scale.
Over the rest of the range, those with the lowest scores reported greater increases in income/needs.

Neither risk avoidance nor being connected to sources of information and
help (as reported in the first two interviews) are important determinants of

---

[1]Morgan, et al. (1974), pp. 44-60.

[2]Remember these are units with unchanged heads, so divorced in 1973 means either
a woman divorced all along or a man divorced any time.

TABLE 1.27

Trend in Income/Needs Relative to Six-Year Average
For Families With Same Head All Six Years *
(All Families and Those in Target Population)

	Same Head			Target Population & Same Head		
	all 6 years		5 years	all 6 years		5 years
	eta^2	$beta^2$	$beta^2$**	eta^2	$beta^2$	$beta^2$**
Age	.049	.053	.037	.031	.031	.040
Age youngest child	.014	.020	.015	.022	.027	.035
Change in family composition	.050	.037	.019	.032	.037	.011
Education	.004	.002	.002	.013	.011	.009
Test Score	.010	.010	.008	.016	.018	.011
Achievement motivation	.002	.001	.002	.008	.013	.016
Risk avoidance years 1 & 2***	.007	.008	.004	.012	.018	.011
Planning acts	.022	.010	.006	.020	.021	.014
Connectedness	.006	.004	.006	.009	.010	.015
Marital status	.003	.004	.002	.006	.015	.010
Sex	.002	.001	.003	.001	.000	.004
Race	.003	.002	.005	.003	.002	.006
Unemployment (1, 2, 3, 4)	.001	.003	.003	.003	.006	.005
Residential mobility	.008	.002	.002	.007	.006	.003

	Adj.R^2=.11	Adj.R^2=.09	Adj.R^2=.12	Adj.R^2=.12
	N=3438	N=3568	N=1628	N=1647

---

* Unadjusted for inflation. Target population means those who were in the bottom fifth for at least one year. Trend means the slope of a regression line fit against time.

** From Table 1.17, Vol. I of <u>Five Thousand American Families</u>.

*** Effect opposite to expected effect -- risk avoiders do worse.

NOTE: Eta^2 is gross effect, $beta^2$ is net effect. See Glossary.

MTR 1056

six-year trend in well-being. Indeed, if anything, avoiding risk is associated
with less favorable trends.

Acts within the control of respondents that seem associated with trends in
well-being are the number of those acts of planning reported in the first two
interviews. Even this might be spurious, since one of the component acts was
having a better job in mind and doing something about it. Such jobs may have
just appeared, been reported in early interviews, and resulted in improvements,
but it both remains possible and makes sense that planning helps. On the other
hand, in our more detailed analysis, people's self-ratings on their time horizons
did not seem to matter. (This fits with other evidence that people's self-ratings are less reliable than their own revealing behavior in the same areas.)

These generally negative findings are all the more important because they
are contrary to many popularly held notions and because they hold up even when
we extend the period another year, to a time of somewhat less unemployment and
better times. The relative importance of the various explanatory factors
changes little.

The extreme changes experienced by those at both ends of the age scale may
well be hiding less dramatic but important changes in other groups. So may substantial changes in family composition or number of earners be hiding other factors affecting head's economic status. Hence we provide an analysis of a more
homogeneous measure for a more homogeneous group in the population -- the change
in head's annual earnings from 1967 to 1972 relative to the average of 1967 and
1972, for heads aged 25 to 54 in 1968.[1] The results are shown in Table 1.28.
We clearly are unable to explain much of the trend in head's earnings. There is
an expected relationship with age (the young are moving up). The racial minor-
ities did better, possibly reflecting some effects of the battle against prejudice.

---

[1] We have used annual rather than hourly earnings to allow differential access to
extra work or impacts of unemployment to appear.

Since some changes come intermittently from changing jobs or promotions, we did
not fit a trend using all six years but took the difference between the first
and the sixth year's earnings. Relating this change to the level at the beginning would have produced a spurious impression of "regression" toward the mean
if there were any errors of measurement or random fluctuations, and relating it
to the level at the end would have produced a spurious positive correlation between level and increase. We related change to the average of the two years.
We still found a positive relationship between level and change, indicating that
people at higher levels also had greater *percentage* increases; so we included
level of earnings as one of the explanatory variables in the analysis. It must
be kept in mind that the last year, 1972, was still a year of substantial unemployment, a possible reason why those low would stay low.

TABLE 1.28

Average Relative Increase in Head's Earnings 1967 to 1972
For 1510 Families with Same Head All 6 Years, Age 25-54 in 1968[*]
(Regression Estimates of Effects of Explanatory Factors)

	Analysis 1		Analysis 2		Analysis 3	
	eta^2	$beta^2$	eta^2	$beta^2$	eta^2	$beta^2$
Age	.023	.021	.023	.018	.023	.023
Education	.011	.011	.011	.016	.011	.016
Race	.008	.010	.008	.011	.008	.012
Sex-Marital status	.001	.001	.001	.005	.001	.003
Test score	.003	.004	.003	.003	.003	.002
Achievement motivation	.013	.013	.013	.016	.013	.016
Size largest city in area	.006	.005	.006	.010	.006	.009
Unemployment in county	.002	.002	.002	.001	.002	.001
Veteran or not	.006	.003	.006	.003	.006	.003
Occupation			.026	.020	.026	.026
Head's father's education			.004	.002		
Head's father's occupation			.002	.004		
Change in county wage			.006	.006		
Level head's labor income[**]			.013	.035	.008	.026
Change in marital status			.003	.003		
Low education, high test score			.001	.001		
How long in same job as of 1972			.027	.024	.027	.023
Connectedness					.008	.009
Real earnings acts					.005	.007
Risk avoidance					.006	.008
Planning acts					.001	.003
Money earnings acts					.006	.007
Efficacy					.002	.005
Trust-hostility index					.002	.002
Ambition-aspiration index					.004	.007

Adj.R^2=.04   Adj.R^2=.09   Adj.R^2=.09

---

[*] One-fifth of the change from 1967 to 1972, relative to average of first two years.

[**] Three categories in the second analysis, four in the third analysis.

NOTE: Eta^2 is gross effect, beta^2 is net effect. See Glossary.

MTR1091

Even with the adjustments for the effects of race, level of earnings, and age, we find again the curious effect or lack of effect of education on the relative increase in head's earnings. Those with very little education or with non-academic training posted the largest increases followed by those with advanced degrees. The explanation of this may be that education starts one out with a good income and the right occupation, and, after that, other forces take over even for those who slipped through the screening system. Those who had been on the same job a moderate length of time did best, and those with less than two years or more than 19 years seniority did least well in getting more money. Skilled blue-collar workers did worse than the unskilled, and managers and officials did better than self-employed businessmen, even after adjustments for age, level of earnings, race, and so on. There was a small systematic effect in the expected direction in which higher test scores were associated with greater increases in earnings. Our measure of achievement motivation once again had an irregular effect with those at both extremes doing worse than those in the middle.

Of considerable importance are those factors which did *not* have a systematic effect in the expected direction. None of the behavioral or attitudinal indexes made any appreciable difference in the head's earnings, nor did the average level of unemployment in the county. The general picture presented in 5000 American Families, Volume I, of changes being dominated by things largely outside of the control of the individual is reinforced.[1]

What individuals can change that matters is their family and living arrangements, the number of earners and, over the longer run, their job mobility, and the education and occupational entrance of their children. Intellectuals perhaps have extrapolated to a broader population a belief in personal efficacy which may exist only for themselves.

The use of change relative to average as the dependent variable does not completely remove the effects of level on change, so we reran the analysis using absolute change from 1967 to 1972 as the dependent variable and the average level for the four middle years 1968-1971 as one of the explanatory variables (to avoid spurious correlations). Since we were using the level in the form of six categorical (dummy) variables, no assumptions were made about the shape of the relationship between level and change. The other explanatory variables now

---

[1] At low levels of eta or beta, it is the systematic (monotonic) pattern of coefficients in the expected direction that matters. With the measure of achievement motivation, for instance, there were two reversals of direction. Irregular or reversed patterns also appeared for all the indexes.

could be seen as affecting change, adjusted for level. At the same time, we
shifted to hourly earnings, since people can take advantage of improvement in
wage rates to enjoy more leisure, and the change in annual earnings would
not show the full improvement. We again restricted the analysis to families
with the same head all six years, heads aged 25-54 in 1968, and heads who worked
at least 1500 hours (3/4 time) in each of the six years. The results are given
in Table 1.29.

Once more the attitudes and behavior patterns, averaged over the first two
years, had little effect; and, what is more, there were no systematic patterns
of effects in the expected direction for any of the attitudinal or behavioral indexes. The test score was correlated with the absolute increase in earnings,
but most of the effect disappeared when the data were adjusted for the initial
level, implying that it had already affected earnings levels, which in turn accounted for most of the change in earnings. The same crucial difference between
absolute increase in earnings and increase adjusted for initial level appears
when we look at the effects of occupation, education, and even a few of the
indexes which seemed to have some effect on the absolute changes in earnings
(economizing, risk avoidance, planning acts).[1]

SUMMARY

This has been largely a descriptive chapter, presenting data on the economic status of both families and individuals at a single point in time and over a
six-year period. It is found that families at different levels of economic status vary a great deal in the labor force participation of family members but
very little in terms of family size and hence family needs. Higher status families pay for some of that status with longer work hours.

Most changes in family economic status result from changes in family composition, which are widespread even in the relatively short period covered by
this study. Within stable families, status change is associated with changes in
work hours (including more or fewer earners), rather than by changes in the wage
rate of the head of the family. These "stable" families are likely to show more
progress in status. Decreases in status are concentrated among young splitoffs
entering the population of families, older people retiring and leaving the labor
force, and families where a female becomes head.

To examine the low-income population over the years, we switch to an exam-

---

[1]Additional detail of these results is given in Appendix 1.

TABLE 1.29

Absolute Increase in Head's Hourly Earnings, 1967 to 1972
for 1410 Families with the Same Head All Six Years,
Aged 25-54 in 1968, and Who Worked at Least 3/4 Time Each Year
(Regression Estimates of Importance of Explanatory Factors)

	Eta^2	$Beta^2$
Age	.005	.002
Occupation	.051	.013
Changed residence	.006	.005
Education	.071	.014
Race	.014	.021
Test score	.037	.014
Achievement motivation	.019	.012
Sex and marital status	.007	.000
Level of hourly earnings, 1968-1971	.151	.140
Efficacy index	.008	.006
Trust-hostility index	.003	.001
Ambition aspiration index	.004	.006
Real earning acts	.004	.001
Economizing	.015	.002
Risk avoidance	.023	.001
Planning acts	.019	.008
Connectedness	.004	.005
Money earning acts	.012	.007
Change in family needs (size)	.008	.008

R^2 adjusted = .206

N = 1410

MTR1116

ination of changes in the economic status of individuals (as distinct from families). The majority of individuals never fall below a poverty level, but others are in difficulty all six years. The latter are predominantly very young, very old, uneducated, black or those in families headed by females. Even a little education for the head of the family reduces the chance that those family members will be poor all six years, but it takes at least a high school diploma for family members to have a better-than-even chance of staying out of poverty for all six years.

When we repeat the multivariate analysis of change in family economic status using six instead of five years of data, the earlier results are generally reconfirmed. Whether we look at trends in family income/needs relative to an average level or change in head's annual earnings relative to the average of the first and last year, none of the attitudinal or behavioral indexes we constructed make much difference, and particularly not in a systematic expected direction. Much of the variance remains unexplained, though some of it was accounted for by changes in family composition which are partially under the control of the individual involved.[1] As an additional check, we introduced another analysis of changes in head's hourly earnings for 25-54 year old stable heads who worked more than three-fourths time every year. To remove the effects of level of earnings, we introduced that as one of the predictors, raising the correlation, of course, but reconfirming the general lack of effect of initial attitudes or behavior patterns. Change in residence during the period is correlated with change in hourly earnings but may well not be causal.

The six years of data now provide a relatively clear picture of the amount of persistence and change in both family composition and economic status. We still account for relatively little of the change. A longer span of time and further analysis may reveal more meaningful differences with policy implications for certain subgroups.[2]

---

[1] Even compared with the usual analysis of individuals where chance or unmeasured variables are important, the explanatory powers of the indexes is small.

[2] In fact, we can already point to some analysis which follows in Chapter 2 which indicates that for blacks there are some things that affect change in economic status and that may be subject to influence or change.

APPENDIX 1.1

ASSESSING THE IMPACT OF A PREDICTOR
ON CHANGE IN ECONOMIC STATUS

Problems of accounting for differences in initial (or average) level are
always present in studies of short-run change. An association between some explanatory variable and absolute change in earnings may be merely the product of
the positive association between the predictor and initial level of earnings and
the correlation between level and change in earnings. The final regression in
this chapter affords an interesting and relatively clear example of this, particularly because the effect of initial level is accounted for in a specific and
flexible form. Figure A1.1 shows the relationship between initial level of
head's hourly earnings and its change from 1967 to 1972. Clearly those at both
extremes have higher percentage increases than those in the middle. (A constant
percent increase means a straight diagonal line through the origin.) Adjustments
for the other variables make almost no difference.

What happens when the effects of other variables are adjusted for differences in initial level of earnings? Figure A1.2 shows the most dramatic case --
education. Education has a powerful effect on absolute increases in earnings
when initial level is not taken into account, but our adjustment for initial
level eliminates the effect except for the two highest groups -- the college
graduates and those with advanced degrees. And even they might have shown no
relative advantage in the short run if we had taken more detailed account of
their very high initial levels. Indeed, other analyses using percentage increases in earnings show no effect of education.

The effects of other factors on changes in earnings are also altered when
we take account of differences in initial level of earnings. The racial differences are reversed (Table A1.1). For three of the behavioral indexes, the simple relationships with absolute increase in earnings are mostly eliminated when
initial level is controlled. Figure A1.3 shows the patterns.

The implication of the adjustment, since it is mostly for initial level, is

54

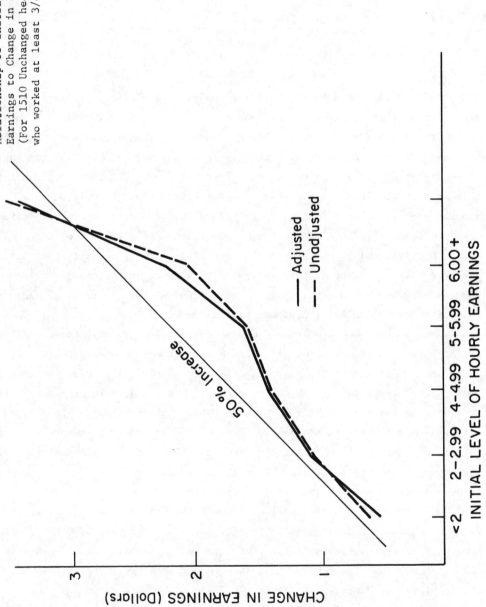

FIGURE A1.1

Relationship of Initial Level of Hourly
Earnings to Change in Earnings 1967-1972
(For 1510 Unchanged heads, 25-54 in 1968,
who worked at least 3/4 time each year)

MTR 1116

50 % increase

Adjusted
Unadjusted

<2   2-2.99 4-4.99 5-5.99 6.00+
INITIAL LEVEL OF HOURLY EARNINGS

CHANGE IN EARNINGS (Dollars)

3

2

1

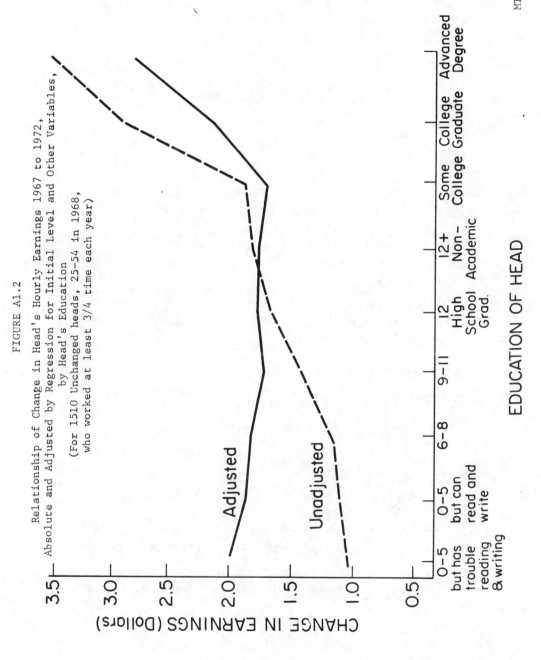

FIGURE A1.2

Relationship of Change in Head's Hourly Earnings 1967 to 1972,
Absolute and Adjusted by Regression for Initial Level and Other Variables,
by Head's Education

(For 1510 Unchanged heads, 25-54 in 1968,
who worked at least 3/4 time each year)

Adjusted

Unadjusted

CHANGE IN EARNINGS (Dollars)

3.5
3.0
2.5
2.0
1.5
1.0
0.5

0-5
but has
trouble
reading
& writing

0-5
but can
read and
write

6-8

9-11

12
High
School
Grad.

12+
Non-
Academic

Some
College

College
Graduate

Advanced
Degree

EDUCATION OF HEAD

TABLE A1.1

Change in Head's Hourly Earnings, 1967 to 1972,
by Race and Sex-Marital Status

	Unadjusted	Adjusted
White	−$1.88	+$1.80
Black	−$1.61	+$2.46
	$\eta^2 = .014$	$\beta^2 = .021$
Single man	$1.82	$1.77
Single woman	$1.15	$1.78
Married man	$1.97	$1.92
	$\eta^2 = .007$	$\beta^2 = .000$

η^2 = Gross effect = squared correlation ratio. See Glossary.

β^2 = Net effect = Normalized regression coefficient. See Glossary.

Absolute and adjusted by regression for initial level and other variables
(for 1510 unchanged heads, 25-54 in 1968, who worked at least 3/4 time
each year)

MTR 1116

FIGURE A1.3

Relationship of Change in Head's Hourly Earnings 1967 to 1972,
Absolute and Adjusted by Regression for Initial Level and Other Variables,
by Three Behavioral Indexes

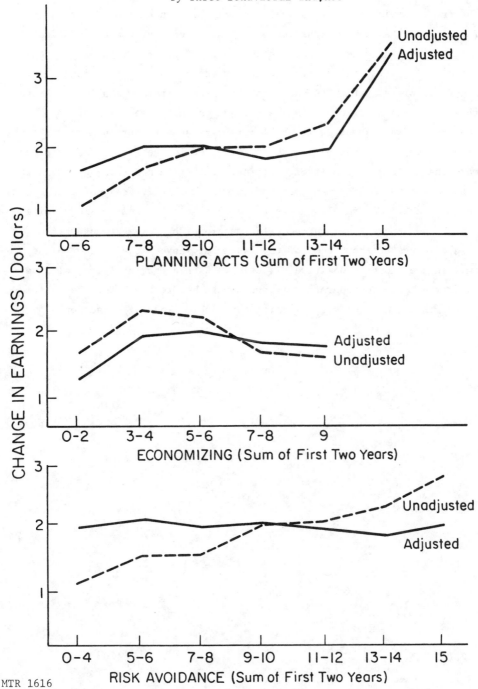

MTR 1616

that if there is a strong effect on absolute change and little or none on adjusted change, then that variable has presumably had its main influence by put-
ting the individual in a favorable situation before the panel started.

The one exception to this is when the variable can be thought of as the result rather than the cause of the economic status, so that the correlation with
the initial level indicates economic experience affecting attitudes and behavior
rather than being affected by it.   The longer the period of experience after
measuring the initial attitudes and behaviors, the better we shall be able to
sort this out.   The next chapter makes a start on the process.

The cause-effect question is still more serious with our index of achievement orientation or motivation, which was measured in the fifth year.   It has
even more chance to be a result of experience rather than a cause of it, even
though the *theory* of achievement motivation posits that it does not change much
after adolescence.   Figure A1.4 shows that adjustment for initial level wipes
out much of the apparent serpentine relationship of achievement motivation with
change in earnings at both ends of the index but leaves some effect in the middle range in the expected positive direction.   With a few more years of panel
data, we may be able to separate the wage change before and after the measurement of the index and feel more certain of probable lines of causation.

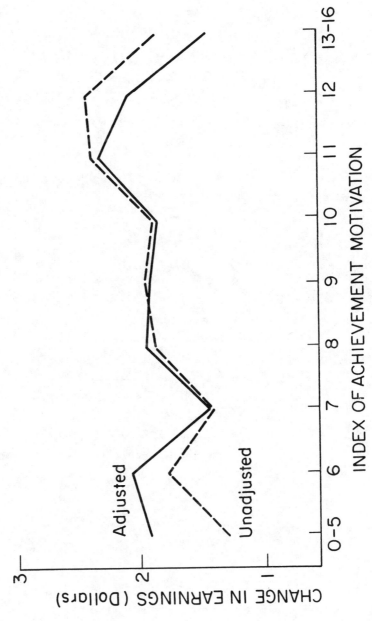

FIGURE A1.4

Relationship of Change in Head's Hourly Earnings 1967 to 1972,
Absolute and Adjusted by Regression for Initial Level and Other Variables,
by Index of Achievement Motivation

(for 1510 Unchanged Heads, 25-54 in 1968, Who Worked at least 3/5 Time each Year)

MTR 1116

Chapter 2

ATTITUDES, BEHAVIOR, AND ECONOMIC OUTCOMES:
A STRUCTURAL EQUATIONS APPROACH
Greg Duncan and Daniel Hill

INTRODUCTION

The Panel Study of Income Dynamics was designed, in part, to investigate the short run relationship among attitudes, behavior patterns, and economic status. The design model underlying the study holds that changes in attitudes lead to change in certain behavior patterns which, in turn, affect economic status. When status change itself is hypothesized to change attitudes, then the circle is closed and the system becomes a recursive model of short run income dynamics.

The notion that certain attitudes and behavior patterns both affect and are affected by economic status is not new. Numerous studies[1] have established cross-sectional associations between economic status and certain values and behavior patterns and have inferred system dynamics from those associations. For example, "culture of poverty" theorists propose that poverty leads to certain attitudes and behaviors which in turn keep people poor. A representative statement of this dynamic process was issued by the Council of Economic Advisors:

> Poverty breeds poverty. A poor individual or family
> has a high probability of staying poor. Low incomes
> carry with them high risks of illness; limitations on
> mobility, individual access to education, information
> and training.... Lack of motivation, hope and incen-
> tive is a more subtle but not less powerful barrier
> than lack of financial means.[2]

The dynamics of the relationship between attitudes, behavior and economic status might conform to explanations other than the culture of poverty theory. A complementary explanation might be termed the "culture of affluence" theory.

---

[1]Rossi and Blum (1968) review this literature.

[2]Council of Economic Advisors (1964), p. 64.

According to it, economic success would change attitudes and behavior so that chances of further success would be increased. Attitudes and behavior might also relate to income change in accordance with a theory of "coping behavior" in which actions are viewed as responses to economic adversity. Such behavior may operate to *reverse* changes in economic status rather than to exacerbate them.

The first chapter of Volume I reported the results of an extensive statistical search for attitudes and behavior patterns that were associated with changes in economic status. Status changes were measured and scaled in a variety of ways. The search methods employed assumed neither additive nor linear relationships, and both sequential and simultaneous statistical control was applied to predictor variables. The results of this search were summarized as follows:

> We have not been able to find much evidence that people's
> attitudes or behavior patterns affect the trends in their
> well being.... (F)or public policy purposes and for argu-
> ments about the extent to which we could reduce dependency
> in our society by changing the behavior and attitudes of
> dependent members, the findings certainly do not encourage
> expectations that such change would make much difference.[1]

This paper will expand the analysis of that chapter in two ways. First, our investigation of attitudes, behavior and economic status will include not only a search for attitudes and behavior which seem to affect change in family well-being, but also an exploration for evidence of effects of economic status in changing attitudes and behavior patterns. Both lines of causation need empirical testing before a recursive model of income dynamics can be accepted. Either or both may explain the static associations between economic status on the one hand and certain attitudes and behavior patterns on the other.

Second, we estimate separate models for blacks and whites. This was not done in the searches reported in Chapter I, Volume I, even though arguments and evidence have been presented which indicate that the income determination process works differently for blacks and whites.[2]

The model we fit provides estimates of the extent to which five-year changes in status (measured by the logarithm of annual earnings of the head of the household and by the family's total income relative to its needs) is associated with initial attitudes and behavior patterns, and estimates of the association between initial status and subsequent five-year change in attitudes and

---

[1]Morgan et al. (1974), p. 339.

[2]Duncan (1968), Moynihan (1965).

behavior patterns. These estimates are made after the effects of other factors which might influence attitudes and status (i.e. education, cognitive skills, and labor force experience) have been taken into account.

We will analyze the sample of families having the following character-istics: 1) male head of household between the ages of 21 and 45 in 1968 who worked at least 1000 hours for each of the six panel years, and 2) the wife, if present in 1968, remained in the household for each of the six years. This restriction of the sample to young, stable families with a male head contin-uously in the labor force leaves a reasonably homogeneous set of families with the greatest chance of translating the effect of the attitudes and behavior pat-terns into a measurable income advantage. The effects that attitudes and beha-vior might have on the incomes of the excluded families (e.g., those headed by a female, with heads older than 45 years, experiencing extensive unemployment or illness or dramatic change in family composition) may be obscured by labor mar-ket constraints or family disruptions.

Our presentation is organized as follows: Section I describes some sim-ple associations among attitudes, behavior indexes and earnings both at a point in time and across time. Section II discusses the status attainment model. Estimates of the model are presented in the third section for each of the atti-tude and behavioral indexes, separately for black and white families. The fourth section summarizes the results.

ANALYSIS

I.   Simple Associations

Responses to questions asked in the first and fifth interviewing waves can be used to construct a variety of attitudinal and behavioral indexes.[1] Self-reported attitude indexes can be developed from questions on sense of per-sonal efficacy, trust and aspiration-ambition. Behavioral indexes fall into two groups. The first is comprised of four types of behaviors which may cause improvement in economic status. We shall call them "advantageous behavior". They include the avoidance of undue risk, connectedness to sources of informa-tion and help, horizon proxies, and money earning acts. The second kind of

---

[1]The indexes are thoroughly documented in Morgan (1972) and are briefly described in the Glossary. In this section we report results on the indexes as originally coded. In later sections we use (and describe) modified indexes.

behavior -- called "coping behavior" -- is more a reaction to adversity than a
possible cause of betterment. Economizing and real earning acts are the descriptive names given to the coping behavior indexes.

The simple correlation (r) between the 1972 index scores and the total
labor income of the head in 1972 (reported in 1973) is given in Table 2.1.
Additional analysis has shown that the direction and magnitude of these intra-
year correlations do not depend upon the year in which both are measured nor do
they change much when total family income relative to needs is substituted for
earnings as the outcome measure.

Most of the attitudes and advantageous behavior indexes have a moderate,
positive association with earnings. The exceptions -- aspiration-ambition and
money earning acts -- contain components such as planning for or doing something
about a better job which would be associated with unsatisfactory employment
(and perhaps income). The two coping behavior indexes have the expected negative associations with earnings.

The extent of temporal stability of these indexes is indicated by the
correlation between the 1968 and 1972 index scores. These correlations (along
with those of earnings and income/needs) appear in Table 2.2. Most of the
cross-year correlations fall into the .3 to .5 range. The risk avoidance index
has greater temporal stability than any other attitude or behavior index: its
correlation (.59) almost equals that of the family income to needs measure.
The components of the risk avoidance -- e.g., fastening seat belts and cigarette
consumption are thus rather stable events. The lowest cross-year correlation
is that attached to the horizon proxy index. Some components of this index include explicit plans to change jobs or move. Because these events are rarer
than the events included in the other indexes, the temporal correlation for the
horizon proxy index is lower.

As our chief concern is with the association between changes in the indexes
and change in economic status, we calculate the correlations between the percentage change in each of the indexes and the percentage change in labor income
(see Table 2.3). All correlations are quite low, never exceeding .10. The
strongest association, .08, is between income change and the risk avoidance index. All others are within four-hundredths of zero. These low correlations
suggest that dramatic attitudinal or behavioral effects on income (or vice
versa) are not likely to show up when we estimate a structural model of income
determination.

TABLE 2.1

Simple Association (r) Between 1972 Attitude
and Behavior Patterns, and 1972 Labor Income of Head

Index	(r)
Attitudes	
Efficacy	.17
Trust	.19
Aspiration-ambition	-.02
Advantageous Behavior	
Risk avoidance	.32
Connectedness to sources of infor- mation and help	.05
Horizon proxies	.12
Money earning acts	-.08
Coping Behavior	
Economizing	-.22
Real earning acts	-.12

TABLE 2.2

Simple Association (r) Between 1968 and 1972
Measures of Attitudes and Behavior Indexes

Index	(r)
Attitudes	
Efficacy	.39
Trust	.41
Aspiration-ambition	.32
Advantageous Behavior	
Risk avoidance	.59
Connectedness	.43
Horizon proxies	.11
Money earning acts	.23
Coping Behavior	
Economizing	.41
Real earning acts	.36
Annual labor income	.71
Total family income/needs	.62

TABLE 2.3

Simple Association (r) between Percentage Change
in Index 1968 to 1972 and Percentage Change
in Labor Income 1968 to 1972

Index	(r)
Attitudes	
Efficacy	-.01
Trust	.03
Aspiration-ambition	.02
Advantageous Behavior	
Risk avoidance	.08
Connectedness	-.02
Horizon proxies	-.04
Money earning acts	.03
Coping Behavior	
Economizing	-.02
Real earning acts	-.03

II. The Model

The general system of relationships we will estimate is depicted in Figure
2.1 using the example of "risk avoidance" behavior.

The variables of this system can be grouped into three sets according to
the time frame in which they were determined. These sets are:

1. Predetermined or background variables;

2. 1968 measures of economic status, and attitudes or behavior
    patterns; and,

3. 1972 measures of economic status, and attitudes or behavior
    patterns.

As background variables we use years of education, years of labor force experience, and the respondent's cognitive skills as measured by the sentence completion test given in the 1972 interview. These variables are predetermined in
the sense that they are not affected by any of the other variables in the system. The double-headed curved arrows shown in Figure 2.1 indicate intercorrelation among these variables without asserting any direction of causation.

The second set of variables are the 1968 observations on economic status
and one of the nine attitudes or behavioral characteristics. Because none of
the attitudes or behavior patterns are directly measured by a single variable,
we are forced to combine several indicators of each concept into an index. We
do this by standardizing each index component and then summing them.[1]

The third group of variables are the 1972 measures of economic status and
attitudes or behavior corresponding to those measured in 1968.

Because of the sequential nature of these sets of variables, several conclusions about the direction of causation can be drawn. Since events in the
present cannot possibly affect or "cause" events in the past, any causal connec-
tion between two of our sets must be from the past to the present. Hence the
single-headed arrows in Figure 2.1 are causal paths indicating the direction of
causation between variables in the system.

---

[1] We are aware that more sophisticated statistical techniques have been developed
to scale index components in the context of the entire structural system. We
spent several weeks trying to estimate the system with Joreskog's LISREL program (See Joreskog (1973)). Because our indicators seemed to have correlated
errors, the simple Joreskog model was not appropriate for our data and we were
forced to estimate the system with ordinary least squares regression. It
should be noted that estimates for the paths of interest (i.e., those running
between 1968 index and 1972 economic status and the path between 1968 status
and 1972 index) are quite similar in the LISREL and regression estimates.

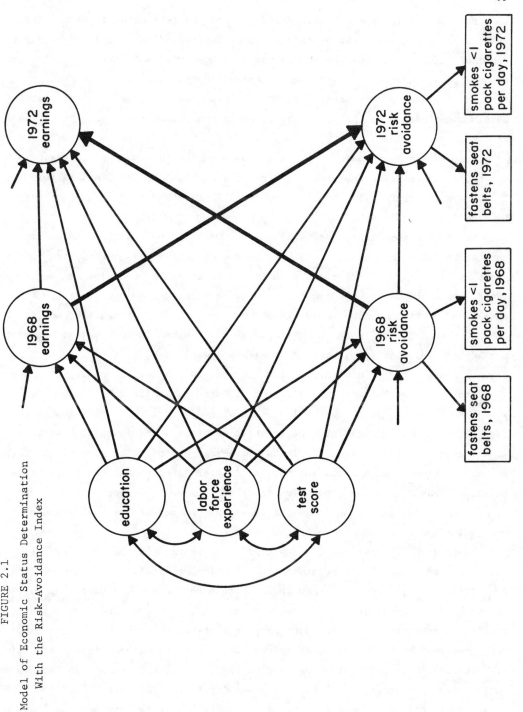

FIGURE 2.1

Model of Economic Status Determination
With the Risk-Avoidance Index

The 1968 attitude and behavior indexes and the 1968 economic well-being measure are hypothesized to be determined by background variables and by other residual factors not included in the model. These residual factors are further assumed to be uncorrelated with the background variables. The lines running from the background variables represent the hypothesized causal paths. Arrows which do not come from the other variables in the system represent the residual factors.

The 1972 economic outcome and attitudes or behavior indexes are taken to be determined by the 1968 measures, background variables, and residual factors. The arrows in Figure 2.1 which lead to the 1972 variables correspond to these hypothesized causal paths.

No simultaneous causation is allowed between economic status and an attitude or behavior in a given year. The reasoning behind this restriction is simply that time is required before a change in attitudes or behavior can be translated into a change in economic status or vice versa. A change in risk avoidance behavior indicated by the decision to stop smoking, for example, would not be expected to result in an immediate increase in economic well-being, but such a change in well-being may occur over several years time.

The most interesting causal paths are the crossed arrows running from the 1968 attitudes and behavior to 1972 economic status, and from 1968 economic status to 1972 attitudes or behavior. The size of the former indicates the extent to which the initial level of an attitude or behavior index is associated with change in economic status over the five-year period. The size of the latter shows the strength of association between initial earnings and change in attitudes or behavior. Strong, positive cross effects would support a recursive, cumulative income determination model in which economic status both influences and is influenced by an attitude or behavior pattern.

The system of relationships depicted in Figure 2.1 can be estimated with four different multiple regressions (the equations themselves are discussed in Appendix 2.1). The size of arrows running from the background variables to 1968 economic status is given by the standardized regression coefficients estimated when the 1968 status variable is regressed on the three background variables. Paths between the background factors and the 1968 index of behavior or attitude are obtained in a similar fashion from regression of the index on the background variables. The importance of the paths running to the 1972 status and index of behavior or attitude from all of the other variables in the system come from regressions of the 1972 measures on the 1968 measures and background variables.

As noted earlier, because researchers have found that the effect of education and other background factors on status depend upon race, we estimate the system separately for blacks and whites.

Two different measures of economic status are used in the analysis. The first is the logarithm of annual labor earnings of the household head. Labor earnings are the product of the wage rate and the annual number of hours worked. Each of these components could be affected by changes in attitudes or behavior. The logarithm of earnings is used both because it has been shown to be the most appropriate measure for theoretical reasons,[1] and because the transformation shifts the emphasis from changes in income at the high end of the income distribution to changes at the low end.[2]

While labor earnings reflect the outcome of labor market events, there are other factors which may influence the economic status of the family and may also be affected by the attitudes and behavior of the head. These include decisions regarding family composition and labor force participation of the family members. For this reason we perform the analysis for both the logarithm of annual labor earnings, and the total family income relative to the family's needs standard. This measure accounts for both income from other sources than the head's labor income (wife's earnings, asset earnings, etc.) and for variation in the income *needs* resulting from differences in family composition.

III. Results

We have formulated our model to use the six years of Panel data in order to answer the following two questions: 1) to what extent are initial attitudes and behavior patterns associated with short-run changes in economic status; and 2) what is the strength of relationship between initial status and subsequent change in attitudes and behavior? The estimates of the associations sought by these two questions are made after the linear effects of education, labor force experience and cognitive skills have been taken into account.

The answers to these questions, as explained earlier, are the regression coefficients obtained when the 1972 status and behavior variables are regressed on the 1968 measures and background variables. We will limit our discussion of

---

[1] Mincer (1972)

[2] A statistical advantage of the transformation is that results are not likely to be dominated by a few extreme cases.

results to the coefficients that differ from zero at the 95% probability level.[1]
It should be noted that since the number of observations for blacks is considerably smaller than the number of observations of whites (321 versus 891), this
restriction makes the minimum acceptable *size* of coefficients larger for blacks
than whites.

While complete regression estimates are listed in Appendix Tables A2.1, a
more compact summary of results is given in Table 2.4. The rows of the table
are comprised of the various attitudes and behavior indexes, the columns delin-
eate possible effects of these measures by race, measure of economic outcome and
line of causation. The first two columns are marked if the attitude or behavior
had a significant association with the change in the outcome measure for whites;
columns five and six represent this same contingency for blacks. If, on the
other hand, the initial measure of status was found to have significant relationship with five-year change in attitudes or behavior of whites, then columns
three or four will be marked, depending upon the outcome measures. For blacks,
the corresponding columns are numbers seven and eight.

Results presented in the summary table are noteworthy for a variety of
reasons. First, significant effects do show up for many of the attitude and
behavior indexes. In two cases, the pattern of effects suggests a cumulative
recursive feedback cycle. Second, the fact that the indexes have a much more
consistent association with the outcome measures for blacks than whites means
that these results do not contradict those reported in Volume I. Because blacks
constitute only about ten percent of the (weighted) sample, significant results
for them would not show up if they are combined with the rest of the population.

Another interesting racial difference in the pattern of relationships
shown in the summary table is that labor income has a significant association
with attitudes and behavior for whites, while income/needs works much better for
blacks. The difference between these measures, as mentioned before, comes from
the labor income of the wife and others in the family and the composition and
size of the family. This suggests that whites can translate attitude or behavior change more readily into labor market success while blacks must work indi-

_____

[1] The significance tests used here are based upon the assumption of simple random
sampling. The Panel data came from a clustered sample so that there are
"design effects" which increase the critical t-ratios. For a discussion of design effects, see Morgan (1974), Appendix B.

TABLE 2.4

Summary Table of Results For Effects of Attitudes and Behavior
on Outcomes and Vice Versa, by Race

Index	White				Black			
	Is index associated with change in:		Is change in index associated with initial level of:		Is index associated with change in:		Is change in index associated with initial level of:	
	Log earnings	Income/needs	Log earnings	Income/needs	Log earnings	Income/needs	Log earnings	Income/Needs
Attitude								
Efficacy	+		+			+		
Future orientation					+	+	−	
Trust						+	+	
Aspiration-ambition								−
Advantageous Behavior								
Risk avoidance	+					+	+	+
Connectedness								
Money earning acts						+		
Coping behavior								
Economizing			−	−				
Real earnings acts								

NOTE: "+" indicates coefficient is positive and significantly different from zero at 5% level; "−" indicates coefficient is negative and significantly different from zero at 5% level.

rectly through family planning or the labor force participation of family members.

A third noteworthy point is that the attitude or advantageous behavior indexes generally have the expected, positive association with economic status while the coping behavior indexes have a negative relationship with status.

A final encouraging result is that some indexes had very little or no importance for any of the status measures for either race so that the reader need not brace himself for an excessively long discussion of results. Connectedness to sources of information and help neither influenced nor was influenced by economic status. Results obtained for this index will appear only in the Appendix Tables A2.1(f) and A2.4. Similarly, results for indexes measuring aspiration-ambition and money earnings acts are of little importance and will appear only in Appendix Tables A2.1(d), A2.1(g), A2.2 and A2.3.

We will now consider each remaining index in turn, beginning with the risk avoidance behavioral index, proceeding to the attitudinal measures and finally to the two indexes of coping behavior.

RISK AVOIDANCE

The behavioral measure which relates most successfully to economic outcomes is the risk avoidance index. The type of risk measured by the index is not the potentially beneficial entrepreneurial risk but rather is undue or unnecessary risk, indicated by excessive cigarette smoking, failure to fasten seat belts, having inadequate medical insurance or savings or operating uninsured vehicles. Such behavior might be expected to affect economic status in a number of ways. Avoidance of undue risk might reduce the amount of time lost from the job because of illness or accident. The tendency to maintain certain savings levels or medical insurance should enable families to cope better with emergencies. Savings may have additional importance by allowing families to take advantage of distant labor market opportunities by facilitating mobility. Risk avoidance might also influence the effectiveness of family planning and consequently the labor force participation of the wife.

The risk avoidance index is constructed by summing the standardized responses to the questions listed in the first column of Table 2.5. The table also presents the average scores on each component in both 1968 and 1972, for both blacks and whites. With the exception of the two insurance components, the average scores for whites declined somewhat over the five year period. For blacks, on the other hand, only the average score on the "seat belts" question declined.

TABLE 2.5

Mean Scores On Risk Avoidance Questions
in 1968 and 1972, by Race

Question	Code	1968 White	1968 Black	1972 White	1972 Black
Do you have insurance on all or some of your autos?	all = 3 some = 2 none = 1	2.82	2.60	2.88	2.82
Do you fasten your seat belt?	all of the time = 3 some of the time = 2 never = 1	1.82	1.79	1.70	1.68
Is your family covered by medical insurance or do they have access to free medical care?	whole family covered = 3 some of the family covered = 2 no coverage = 1	2.79	2.68	2.83	2.76
Do you smoke less than a pack a day?	yes = 1 no = 0	0.61	0.56	0.55	0.59
Do you have savings for emergency purposes?	normally have two months pay or more saved = 3 normally have some savings, but less than two months pay = 2 don't have savings = 1	2.66	2.23	2.62	2.44

When the risk avoidance indexes are included in the estimation of the model outlined in the previous section, several significant results emerge. For whites, the 1968 risk avoidance index was a significant predictor of 1972 earnings, but not of income/needs. The 1972 risk avoidance index was not well predicted by either 1968 earnings or income/needs.

For blacks, however, the 1972 index was predicted by *both* measures of economic status. Furthermore, the 1968 index was found to affect the 1972 income/needs variable. Since the most interesting results are for blacks when income/needs is used to measure economic status, complete estimates for that model are presented in Figure 2.2.[1] Only the paths that are statistically significant are shown.

The paths of greatest interest run from the 1968 index to 1972 income/needs and from 1968 income/needs to the 1972 risk avoidance index. Both are positive and significant for this black subsample. The latter path is twice as strong as the former. That income/needs influences subsequent risk avoidance is partially explained by the fact that components of the index are income related.[2] It requires a certain level of income to accumulate savings or to acquire medical or car insurance. This, however, is only part of the reason for such a strong path. For whites, the corresponding coefficient is only one-fifth the size of that for blacks. Blacks, therefore, appear more prone to react to income gains by purchasing insurance, accumulating savings, or engaging in the other risk averse behaviors measured by the index. The strong association between 1968 economic status and subsequent risk aversion also appears when the logarithm of the head's labor market earnings is used to measure status.

The risk avoidance index is not only affected by income/needs but also affects it. Higher initial risk avoidance scores have a positive, significant association with subsequent changes in income/needs, and those in the highest income/needs categories in 1968 experience the greatest positive gains in subsequent risk avoidance. The significant, positive path that runs from 1968 risk avoidance to 1972 income/needs completes the culture of poverty (or affluence) circle of causation for blacks for the income/needs measure of economic well-being.

---

[1] The estimates of the other three models are given in Appendix Table A2.1.
[2] This is pointed out both in Dickinson (1972) and in Chapter 12 of this volume.

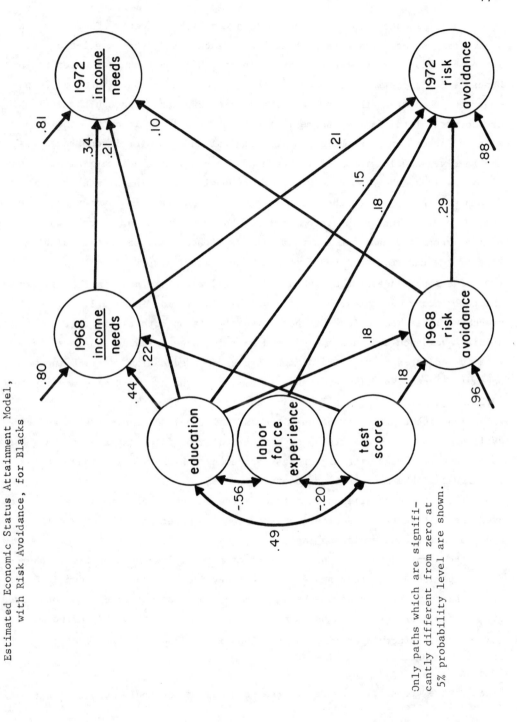

FIGURE 2.2

Estimated Economic Status Attainment Model,
with Risk Avoidance, for Blacks

Only paths which are significantly different from zero at
5% probability level are shown.

Family income relative to needs is a composite concept. That it has a significant association with past risk avoidance raises the question of which of its components is most affected by the index. Using a technique described by Duncan[1], it is possible to decompose the income/needs measure into its components and then trace the total effects of risk avoidance through the various components. Total family income is the sum of the labor income of the head, wife and other family members plus the capital and transfer income received by the family. The logarithm of income/needs is equal to the logarithm of income minus the logarithm of needs. Thus the composite income/needs measure can be decomposed in two ways. When this is done we find that risk avoidance increases income/needs by increasing income but *not* by reducing needs. Furthermore, most of the income increase comes from additions to head's labor income, although some of the change also comes from the wife's labor income.

The importance of the risk avoidance index is best seen in the context of the full income determination model, which is shown in Figure 2.2. The background variable "education" has pervasive effects on both the initial *levels* of risk avoidance and income/needs and on the change in these two measures. This is indicated by the size of the arrows from "education" to 1968 income/needs (.44) and 1968 risk avoidance (.18) and by the arrows from education to 1972 income/needs (.21) and 1972 risk avoidance (.15). The test score variable is a significant predictor of only the initial levels of income/needs and risk avoidance. When the effects of education and labor force experience are taken into account, blacks with higher test scores have higher family income/needs and higher risk avoidance index scores.

Labor force experience affects only the amount of change in risk avoidance over the five years. The older workers[2] tend to experience the greatest increases in the risk avoidance index.

The magnitude of the total effects of risk avoidance, education, labor force experience, and test score on 1972 money income/needs are shown in Table 2.6. The total effects of the background variables are divided into both direct effects (as shown by the paths running directly from them to 1972 economic/needs) and indirect effects operating through 1968 income/needs. These indirect ef-

---

[1] Duncan (1965), pp. 7-10.

[2] Recall that the sample was restricted to heads of households who were between 21 and 45 years old in 1968.

TABLE 2.6

Effects of Background Variables and 1968 Risk
Avoidance Index on 1972 Income/Needs, for Blacks

| | | Effects | | |
| | | | | |
Predictor	Direct	Indirect via 1968 Income/Needs	Indirect via 1968 Risk Avoidance	Total Effect
Education	.21	.15	.02	.38
Experience	---	---	---	.00
Test Score	---	.07	.02	.09
Risk Avoidance	.10	---	---	.10

fects are simply the product of the path between the background measures and
1968 income/needs, and the path between the 1968 and 1972 income/needs variables.
For education and test score, there are also indirect effects operating through
1968 risk avoidance. Table 2.6 shows that the total effects of risk avoidance
are comparable to those of the test score variable, larger than that of the
experience variable[1] and considerably smaller than the total effects of the
education variable.

A final set of numbers in Figure 2.2 reflect the extent of intercorrelation among the background variables. They are located next to the curved,
double-headed arrows among the three variables. Education and labor force
experience are negatively related (r = -.56) because one cannot begin working
until after the completion of school.[2] Education and test scores have a positive
correlation (+.49). Labor force experience and cognitive skills have a moderate
negative correlation (-.20).

Thus the relationship between risk avoidance and income/needs for blacks
is consistent with a short run cumulative-effects system of income dynamics.
Blacks with high initial income/needs experience the greatest increase in risk
avoidance over the five years. High initial risk avoidance scores, in turn, are
associated with significant increases in income/needs between 1968 and 1972. A
similar, although not as powerful system of effects holds for blacks when the
logarithm of earnings is used to measure economic well-being. Figure 2.3 shows
the part of the income determination model for blacks with the logarithm of
earnings and also a comparable part of the income/needs model. The effects of
earnings and income/needs on subsequent risk avoidance are quite similar (.17 vs
.20, respectively), while risk avoidance does considerably better in predicting
the income/needs measure than the logarithm of earnings.

In contrast to the important risk avoidance effects for blacks, neither
earnings nor income/needs are consistently related to risk avoidance for whites.
The size of the effects for whites are shown in Figure 2.4. The only significant
path for whites runs between the 1968 risk avoidance index and 1972 log earnings.
The *size* of this path, however, is quite small (.06). Totally insignificant results show up for the income/needs outcome measure for whites.

---

[1] While labor force experience has a positive, significant effect on head's earnings, it is not a significant predictor of total family income/needs. For this
composite variable, the importance of experience on head's earnings is cancelled out by the relationship between experience and family size.

[2] Since we have no direct measure of experience, we define it to be age minus
years of education minus five.

FIGURE 2.3

Estimated Economic Status Attainment Model,
With Risk Avoidance Index, for Blacks

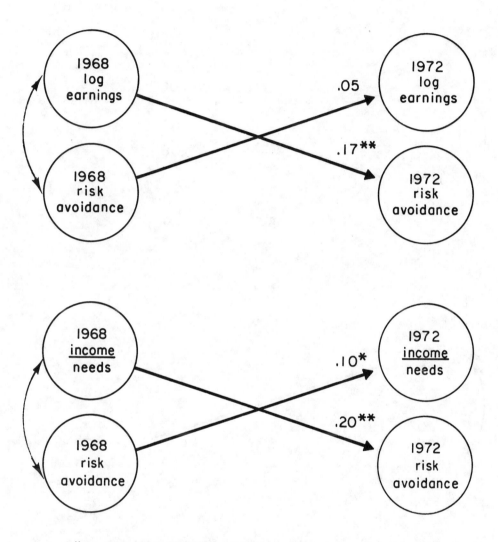

* path is significantly different from zero at 5% probability level.

** path is significantly different from zero at 1% probability level.

Note: Path coefficients come from full status attainment model. See Appendix
Table A2.1 for complete estimation of the model.

FIGURE 2.4

Estimated Economic Status Attainment Model,
With Risk Avoidance Index, for Whites

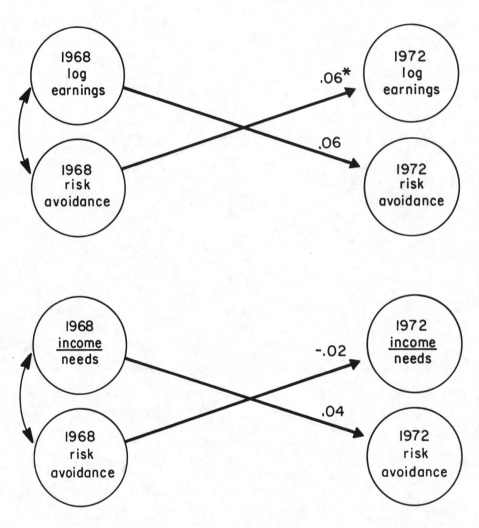

* path is significantly different from zero at 5% probability level.

NOTE: Path coefficients come from the full status attainment model. See
Appendix Table A2.1 for complete estimation of model.

EFFICACY

A factor analysis performed on the original efficacy index[1] suggests that this index in fact measures two distinct concepts -- a personal sense of effectiveness in carrying out plans and a more general future orientation. Accordingly, we have divided the original index into two measures called "efficacy" and "future orientation". The efficacy index is constructed from the response to two questions, each of which is coded on a five-point scale:

> 1) Have you usually felt pretty sure your life would work out the way you wanted it to, or have there been more times when you haven't been very sure about it?
>
> 2) When you make plans ahead, do you usually get to carry out things the way you expected or do things usually come up to make you change your plans?

The mean scores for whites and blacks on these two questions is given in Table 2.7. On the average, whites have higher efficacy scores than blacks, although blacks had a slightly larger increase (both relative and absolute) in reported efficacy between 1968 and 1972 than did whites.

TABLE 2.7

Mean Efficacy Index Score in 1968 and 1972, by Race

Race	Year	
	1968	1972
White	3.77	3.97
Black	2.99	3.30

Various researchers have established both theoretical and empirical connections between the sense of personal efficacy and achievement. Gurin and Gurin (1974) report that "personal control has been related to behavior that reflects competence and realistic achievement orientations, e.g., grades of high school and college students, ... student's aspirations for prestigious

---

[1] See Dickinson (1972).

occupations that simultaneously represent a realistic challenge." (p.5)
Furthermore, they cite longitudinal evidence for a reinforcing feedback system
that is precisely the type we seek in the Panel data:

> In one instance where we had longitudinal data, we
> were able to demonstrate the causality of the rela-
> tionship between personal control and economic
> achievement: trainees in a manpower program who
> had higher scores on personal control while still
> in the training program had higher economic earn-
> ings in the six months following the completion
> of the program. At the same time, their higher
> earnings also served to increase their feeling of·
> control as measured at that later post-program
> point, even with the initial feelings of control
> partialed out.[1]

The status determination model outlined in the previous section was estimated with the efficacy index for both the logarithm of earnings and income/
needs, and separately by race. Of the four sets of results, the earnings model
for whites was the most interesting. Complete estimates for the model are shown
in Figure 2.5. Only the paths that are statistically significant are shown. As
noted before, the paths of greatest interest are those which run from the 1968
efficacy index to 1972 earnings, and from 1968 earnings to the 1972 efficacy
index. That both of these paths are positive and significant suggests feedback effects between efficacy and earnings for whites. Those with the
highest efficacy scores in the first year experienced the greatest gains in earnings between 1968 and 1972, and those with the highest initial earnings tended
to have greater increases in scores on the efficacy index. This cycle of effects could also be phrased in a negative way: those with the lowest initial
efficacy scores gained the least in earnings and those with low earnings in
1968 had declines or only small increases in reported efficacy.

Although the coefficients that suggest these cumulative effects are statistically significant, their absolute sizes, .05 and .10, are not large. Table
2.8 compares the sizes of the estimated efficacy effects with those of the
background variables. As pointed out in the discussion of the risk avoidance
index, the *total* effect of the background variables on 1972 earnings is composed
of both direct effects (as shown in the paths running directly from them to the
1972 earnings measure) and indirect effects operating through 1968 earnings.

---

[1] Gurin and Gurin (1974), p. 15, citing from Gurin (1968).

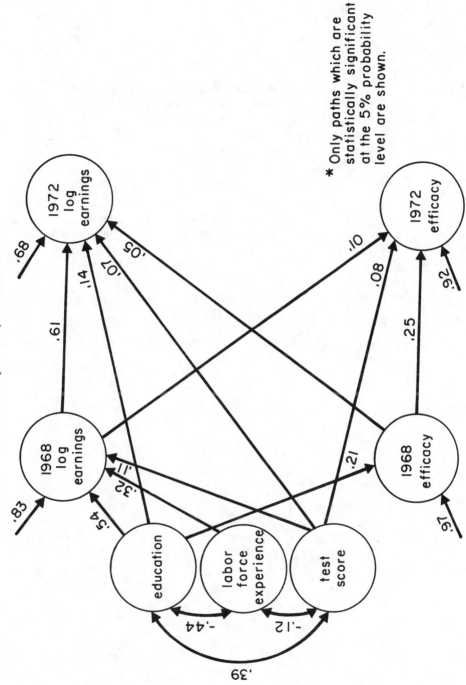

FIGURE 2.5

Estimated Economic Status Attainment Model,
with Efficacy Index, for Whites*

* Only paths which are
statistically significant
at the 5% probability
level are shown.

TABLE 2.8

Effects of Background Variables and 1968
Efficacy Index on 1972 Earnings, for Whites

| Predictor | Effects | | | |
	Direct	Indirect via 1968 earnings	Indirect via 1968 efficacy	Total effect
Education	.14	.33	.01	.48
Experience	---	.20	---	.20
Test Score	.07	.07	---	.14
Efficacy	.05	---	---	.05

For education there is also an indirect effect operating through the 1968 efficacy measure. Table 2.8 shows that the coefficient on efficacy is about one-third to one-fourth the size of the total effects of labor force experience and cognitive test score, and about one-tenth as important as the education variable. While this type of comparison is somewhat sensitive to the way in which the model is specified, the *relative* importance of the various predictors is not likely to change.

The relationship between the background variables and the efficacy variables shown in Figure 2.5 is also interesting. Neither test score nor experience are significant determinants of efficacy, while education is important. This result is consistent with other empirical research on the relationship between education and personal efficacy.[1]

Turning to the results for the other economic outcome measure and for blacks, we find that the efficacy index does *not* have a significant association with the income/needs variable for whites nor is it consistently important for blacks. The full detail of these regressions is given in Appendix Tables A2.1(a). Of greatest interest are the size and significance of the paths running between the efficacy and earnings variables. These coefficients and their standard errors are given in Table 2.9. One significant result shows up for blacks: the 1968 efficacy index has a significant, positive association with change in income/needs over the five year panel period. The estimated *size* of this effect (.11) is more than twice as large as that for whites (.05) when efficacy was related to change in earnings.

That efficacy relates to total family income relative to needs for blacks, but not to the labor income of the head, suggests that either changes in family size and composition or in some other component of income are affected by efficacy. When the income/needs are decomposed, it is found that efficacy "works" mostly through changes in the earnings of the wife and secondarily through the income of others in the family. Efficacy did *not* increase income/needs for blacks by reducing the family's needs standard.

FUTURE ORIENTATION

The second half of the original efficacy index relates to the respondent's

---

[1] Gurin and Gurin (1974).

TABLE 2.9

Coefficient (and Standard Errors) for Effects
of Efficacy on Economic Status and Vice Versa, by Race

Path from 1968 efficacy index to:				Path to 1972 efficacy index from:			
1972 log income		1972 income/needs		1968 log income		1968 income/needs	
White	Black	White	Black	White	Black	White	Black
.05*	.00	.01	.11*	.09*	.04	.04	-.05
(.02)	(.04)	(.03)	(.05)	(.04)	(.06)	(.03)	(.07)

*Significantly different from zero at 5% probability level.

orientation toward the future.   The future orientation index is constructed
from responses to the following three questions:

> 1) Are you the kind of person that plans his life ahead
> all the time, or do you live more from day to day?
>
> 2) Would you rather spend your money and enjoy life
> today, or save more for the future?
>
> 3) Do you think a lot about things that might happen in
> the future, or do you usually just take things as they come?

Responses were coded on a five point scale, standardized and summed.   Mean scores
on the index for blacks and whites in 1968 and 1972 are presented in Table 2.10.

TABLE 2.10

Mean Future Orientation Scores in 1968 and 1972, by Race

	Year	
Race	1968	1972
White	3.17	2.98
Black	3.23	2.92

It shows that there are virtually no racial differences in index score for either
year.   In contrast to the efficacy index presented earlier, both groups report
less future orientation in 1972 than in 1968.

When the economic status determination model is estimated with the future
orientation index, it is found that for whites the index neither affects nor is
affected by either earnings or family income/needs.   Significant effects *are*
found for blacks, however, and the estimates of these effects are shown in
Figure 2.6.   For both income concepts, the initial future orientation index has
a significant, positive association with change in income.   Initial economic
status, on the other hand, relates *negatively* to change in the future orientation index.

For blacks, the income dynamics of the future orientation concept are thus
not cumulative and reinforcing but rather are dampening.   Being oriented toward
the future is associated with short run earnings gains, but these gains, in turn,
appear to *reduce* the extent of future orientation.

The similarity of effects of the 1968 index on both earnings and income/

FIGURE 2.6

Estimated Economic Status Attainment Model,
With Future Orientation Index, for Blacks

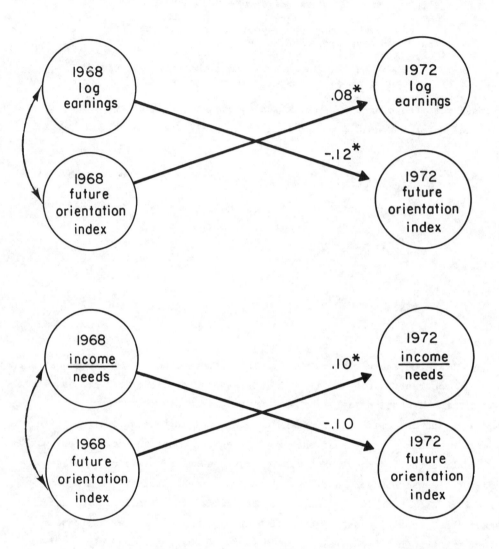

* path is significantly different from zero at 5% probability level.

Note: Path coefficients are from the full status attainment model.
See Appendix Table A2.1 for complete estimation of the model.

needs suggests that the component of income/needs that is most responsive to future orientation is head's labor income. Decomposition analysis performed on the income/needs measure confirms this notion and further suggests that changes in wife's labor income are also affected by future orientation. While it is plausible that family planning decisions might also relate to an orientation toward the future, it is found that five year increases in family needs are *greater* for those with high initial scores on the future orientation index.[1]

TRUST-HOSTILITY

The final attitudinal index that has a significant relationship with short-run income change is the trust-hostility index. It is formed from the responses to the following five questions:

1) Do you get angry fairly easily, or does it take a lot to get you angry?

2) How much does it matter what other people think about you?

3) Do you trust most people, some, or very few?

4) Do you think the life of the average person is getting better or is it getting worse?

5) Are there a lot of people who have good things they don't deserve?

Responses indicating trust are given higher scores.

Since most questions are considerably more heterogeneous than the questions which are included in the efficacy or future orientation indexes, the mean scores for blacks and whites in the first and fifth interviewing years are given for *each* question in Table 2.11. The mean index score for whites is higher than for blacks in both years. An examination of the index components, however, shows that blacks score lower than whites on some, but not all, questions.

For whites, contrary to the maxim, nice guys finish neither first nor last: the trust-hostility index neither affects nor is affected by economic status. Trust *does* have significant effects for blacks, however, and the pattern of relationships for them is shown in Figure 2.7.

The 1968 trust-hostility index has a positive association with change in

---

[1] Higher needs do not necessarily mean that children were born to the family. This may be due to the growing up of children present in 1968.

TABLE 2.11

Mean Scores in Trust-Hostility Questions
in 1968 and 1972, by Race

		1968		1972	
Question		White	Black	White	Black
i)	Don't get angry easily	3.92	4.29	4.03	4.20
ii)	Matters what others think	2.43	1.93	2.57	1.96
iii)	Trust most other people	4.10	2.95	4.07	2.66
iv)	Average man getting better	3.76	4.12	3.77	3.84
v)	People with good things deserve them	3.89	3.63	3.71	3.36
	Mean	3.62	3.38	3.63	3.20

FIGURE 2.7

Estimated Economic Status Attainment Model,
With Trust-Hostility Index, for Blacks

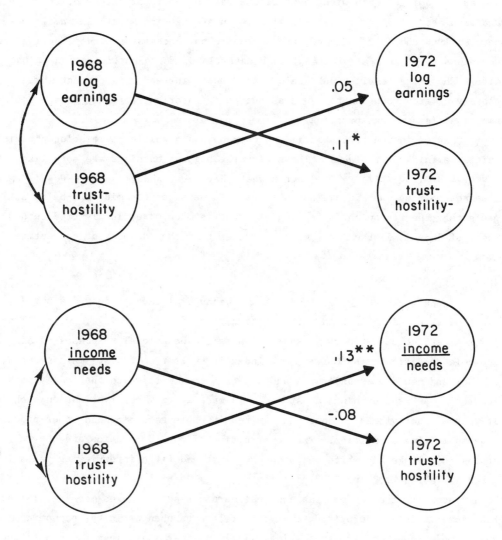

* path is significantly different from zero at 5% probability level.

** path is significantly different from zero at 1% prob-
ability level.

NOTE: Path coefficients come from the full status attainment
model. See Appendix Table 1 for complete estimation
of model.

both earnings and family income/needs, but only for the latter status measure is the relationship statistically significant. When the income/needs variable is decomposed, it is found that the index's effect operates through the labor income of the wife and through family needs. Higher scores on the initial index are associated both with positive changes in the labor income of the wife *and* with decreases (or at least smaller than average increases) in family needs between 1968 and 1972. The two phenomena are not necessarily independent since decisions to limit family size allow greater labor force participation of the wife. Why these results would relate to "trust" instead of a concept more closely related to planning (such as future orientation, efficacy or aspiration-ambition) is somewhat puzzling.

Changes in the trust-hostility index have a significant relationship with initial earnings for blacks. Those with the highest earnings are more likely to trust others, to feel people deserve what they have, and so on. That this result does not hold up when income/needs is used to measure economic well-being suggests that the respondent's feeling of trust is much more closely tied to how successful he is in the labor market, rather than the adequacy of the entire family income relative to its size.

Indexes of Coping Behavior

In contrast with the attitudinal and behavioral indexes just discussed which might be expected to influence the pattern of short-run earnings, two additional indexes were constructed as measures of possible behavioral responses to adverse economic conditions. An *economizing* index is built from reports on cigarette, alcohol and new car expenditures and the frequency with which the family eats together. A "real earnings acts" index is made up from observations on such do-it-yourself activities as home and car repair, home gardening and other productive spare time activities. The construction of the two indexes and the mean scores for blacks and whites in both the first and fifth interviewing years is given in Tables 2.12 and 2.13.

Since both the economizing and real earnings acts indexes measure similar behavior, it is not surprising that they relate to changes in the economic status measures in a similar fashion. While neither index matters much in the black models, both are important for whites. For whites, changes in these indexes over the five years are negatively related to initial level of economic well-being. These negative effects are strong and significant in three out of four cases.

Estimates for the economizing index for whites are given in Figure 2.8. For both income measures, the paths running from the 1968 economizing index to

TABLE 2.12

Mean Scores on Economizing Index Components
in 1968 and 1972, by Race

	1968		1972	
Index Component	White	Black	White	Black
Yearly alcohol expenditure (scored negatively)	$86.02	$134.61	$129.39	$204.56
Yearly cigarette expenditure (scored negatively)	$133.16	$133.53	$163.64	$137.00
Age of newest car	3.3	3.7	3.2	3.6
Number of days per week that family eats together	3.6	3.4	3.4	2.9

TABLE 2.13

Mean Scores on Real Earnings Acts
Index Components in 1968 and 1972, by Race

	1968		1972	
Index Component	White	Black	White	Black
Whether saved more than $75 by additions and repairs to housing (YES=2, NO=1)	1.38	1.22	1.51	1.33
Whether more than $75 saved on food grown (YES=2, NO=1)	1.13	1.11	1.15	1.06
Whether more than $75 saved in own car repair (YES=2, NO=1)	1.28	1.20	1.31	1.20
Whether does productive spare time activity (YES=2, NO=1)	1.39	1.33	1.44	1.30
Average	1.29	1.22	1.35	1.22

FIGURE 2.8

Estimated Economic Status Attainment Model,
With Economizing Index, for Whites

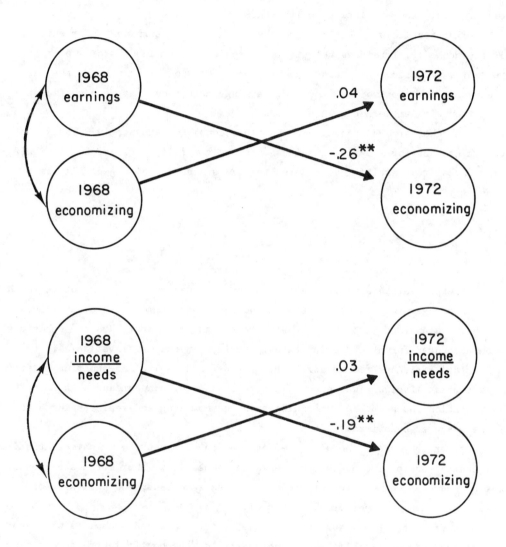

* path is significantly different from zero at 1%
probability level.

NOTE: Path coefficients come from the full status attainment
model. See Appendix Table 1 for complete estimation
of model.

the 1972 income measure are weak and insignificant. Paths going from the initial income measure to the 1972 index of economizing are strong, negative and highly significant. Families with the lowest initial income thus tend to economize the most over the five years. Economizing behavior itself does not relate in any significant way to changes in either labor earnings of the household head or the family's total income relative to its needs.

Similar results are obtained for the index of real earnings. For whites, initial income level relates negatively to change in the index scores over the five years. Coefficients are not as large for this index, though, as they are for economizing. For whites, the real earnings acts index has no significant association with either earnings measure.

For blacks, arrows running from initial economic status to 1972 indexes of economizing behavior and real earnings acts are generally negative but insignificant. Paths from initial index scores to 1972 status are also generally small and negative.

SUMMARY

The purpose of this investigation has been to determine the extent to which short run changes in economic status can be explained by measures of attitudes and behaviors and, conversely, to what extent changes in attitudes and behaviors can be accounted for by economic status. Various indexes are available in the Panel data. Efficacy, future orientation, trust and aspiration-ambition comprise the list of attitudinal indexes, while risk avoidance, connectedness to sources of information and help, money earning acts, economizing and real earning acts are the measured behavioral indexes.

In order to isolate the direct effects of these measures, we have statistically controlled for the background variables education, labor force experience, and test score. Two measures of economic status were used, and analyses for blacks and whites were performed separately.

In general, the short run associations of attitudes and behaviors with economic status were negligible. Only one-quarter of the coefficients representing these associations were statistically significant. The distribution of these significant paths among the racial groups, however, is quite interesting. Although the *size* of coefficients needed to attain statistical significance is considerably larger for blacks than whites (because of a smaller sample size), two-thirds of the significant paths pertain to the black subsample.

Furthermore, within the two racial subgroups, the measures of economic well-being had differential effects. Most of the significant effects for whites showed up for head's labor market earnings, while the majority of black effects were related to the total family income/needs measure. By decomposing this income/needs variable for blacks, we found that most of the effect of the attitude and behavior indexes operated through family income and *not* through changes in the needs standard. Of the components of family income, the labor income of the wife was often as important as the head's labor income. For the black subsample, then, the effects of the attitudes and behavior patterns of the head are not directly translated into labor market results; rather, they seemed to operate through the labor force activity of the wife.

Of the 36 possible recursive, dynamic systems examined in this chapter, three were found to be complete. For whites, efficacy was positively affected by the logarithm of earnings *and* positively affected the logarithm of earnings. A similar positive feedback system was found to be significant for blacks' total family income to needs and risk avoidance. A negative or dampening feedback system was found to be operating on blacks' future orientation from the logarithm of earnings. Those blacks scoring high on the future orientation in 1968 experienced greater increases in logarithm of earnings over the five-year period, while those with high earnings in 1968 experienced relative declines in future orientation.

Although these findings do not provide strong support for a culture of poverty or affluence theory, it must be recognized that we are able to observe changes only over a relatively short time period. Five years time is not sufficient to pick up the effects of economic status on attitudes and behavior if the process is intergenerational. Future studies should deal with longer time periods, if possible, or with the split-offs from original sample families.

Despite the fact that some attitudes and behavior patterns had statistically *significant* effects on income change, they did not have *powerful* effects. Not once was it found that an attitude or behavior affected a measure of economic status more than did education. Labor force experience and cognitive skills were also generally more important determinants of income than were the attitudinal and behavioral indexes. While additional research on this topic is clearly needed, we see little reason at this time to argue against the policy conclusions reported in Volume I.

References

Council of Economic Advisors, 1964 Economic Report of the President, Washington, D.C., Government Printing Office, 1964.

Dickinson, Katherine, "Investigation of the Attitudinal and Behavioral Indexes" working paper, Survey Research Center, University of Michigan, 1974.

Duncan, Otis Dudley, "Inheritance of Poverty or Inheritance of Race?" in Daniel P. Moynihan, ed., On Understanding Poverty Perspectives From the Social Sciences, Basic Books, New York, 1968, pp. 85-110.

Duncan, Otis Dudley, "Path Analysis: Sociological Examples", The American Journal of Sociology, Vol. 72, Number 1, July 1966, pp. 1-16.

Gurin, Gerald, Inter-City Negro Youth in a Job Training Project: A Study of Factors Related to Attrition and Job Success, Ann Arbor: Institute For Social Research, University of Michigan, 1968.

Gurin, Gerald and Gurin, Patricia, "Personal Efficacy and the Ideology of Individual Responsibility" in Burkhard Strumpel, ed. Economic Well-Being in a System of Social Indicators, forthcoming.

Joreskog, Karl G., "A General Method for Estimating a Linear Structural Equation System" in Arthur S. Goldberger and Otis D. Duncan, eds., Structural Equation Models in the Social Sciences, Seminar Press, New York, 1973, pp. 85-112.

Mincer, Jacob, Schooling, Experience, and Earnings, National Bureau of Economic Research, New York, 1972.

Morgan, James, et al, Five Thousand American Families -- Patterns of Economic Progress, Vol. I, Survey Research Center, University of Michigan, Ann Arbor, 1974.

Morgan, James, et al, A Panel Study of Income Dynamics: Tape Codes and Indexes, Vol. II, Survey Research Center, University of Michigan, Ann Arbor, 1972.

Moynihan, Daniel P., The Negro Family: The Case for National Action, Office of Policy Planning and Research, United States Department of Labor, March 1965.

Rossi, Peter H., and Blum, Zahava D., "Class, Status, and Poverty" in Daniel P. Moynihan, Ed. On Understanding Poverty: Perspectives From the Social Sciences, Basic Books, New York, 1968, pp. 36-63.

APPENDIX 2.1

A somewhat different view of the model estimated in this chapter is provided by the structural equations upon which it is based. These can be written
as follows:

(1) $\quad Y_1 = \gamma_{11}X_1 + \gamma_{12}X_2 + \gamma_{13}X_3 + U_1$

(2) $\quad Y_2 = \gamma_{21}X_1 + \gamma_{22}X_2 + \gamma_{23}X_3 + U_2$

(3) $\quad Y_3 = \beta_{31}Y_1 + \beta_{32}Y_2 + \gamma_{31}X_1 + \gamma_{32}X_2 + \gamma_{33}X_3 + U_3$

(4) $\quad Y_4 = \beta_{41}Y_1 + \beta_{42}Y_2 + \gamma_{41}X_1 + \gamma_{42}X_2 + \gamma_{43}X_3 + U_4$

where Y_1 and Y_3 are the 1968 and 1972 measures of economic status, Y_2 and Y_4 are
the 1968 and 1972 measures of an attitudes or behavior pattern index, X_1, X_2 and
X_3 are education, labor force experience and test score, respectively.

The coefficients of greatest interest are β_{32} and β_{41}. β_{32} can be interpreted as the effect on 1972 earnings of a unit change in the 1968 index score,
once 1968 earnings, education, experience and test score have been taken
into account.

Equation (3) can be rewritten as follows:

$$Y_3 - Y_1 = (\beta_{31} - 1)\, Y_1 + \beta_{32}Y_2 + \gamma_{31}X_1 + \gamma_{32}X_2 + \gamma_{33}X_3 + U_3,$$

so that β_{32} also can be interpreted as the effect of the index on *change* in economic status. When income/needs is used as the status variable, then this
change is measured as the *absolute* difference between 1972 status and some fraction of 1968 status. When the logarithm of earnings variable is used, then
relative status differences are measured.

TABLE A2.1(a)

Standardized Regression Coefficients (and Standard Errors) of Income Determination

Model for Efficacy Index

| | Dependent Variable | | | | | | | | | | | | | |
| | White | | | | | | | Black | | | | | | |
Independent Variable	1968 log earnings	1968 income/ needs	1968 index	1972 log earnings	1972 income/ needs	1972 index	1972 index	1968 log earnings	1968 income/ needs	1968 index	1972 log earnings	1972 income/ needs	1972 index	1972 index
Education	.54 (.03)	.38 (.04)	.21 (.04)	.14 (.03)	.17 (.03)	.06 (.04)	.09 (.04)	.39 (.07)	.44 (.06)	.03 (.08)	.20 (.06)	.21 (.07)	.18 (.08)	.22 (.08)
Labor force experience	.32 (.03)	.05 (.03)	-.02 (.04)	-.01 (.03)	.10 (.03)	.01 (.04)	.03 (.04)	.21 (.06)	-.02 (.06)	.07 (.07)	.05 (.05)	-.03 (.05)	.09 (.07)	.10 (.07)
Test score	.11 (.03)	.12 (.03)	.06 (.04)	.07 (.03)	.06 (.03)	.08 (.03)	.09 (.03)	.25 (.06)	.22 (.05)	.03 (.06)	.15 (.05)	.11 (.05)	.02 (.07)	.04 (.07)
1968 log earnings	--	--	--	.61 (.03)	--	.09 (.04)	--	--	--	--	.52 (.05)	--	.04 (.06)	--
1968 income/needs	--	--	--	--	.58 (.03)	--	.04 (.04)	--	--	--	--	.36 (.06)	--	-.05 (.07)
1968 index	--	--	--	.05 (.02)	.01 (.03)	.25 (.03)	.26 (.03)	--	--	--	.00 (.04)	.11 (.05)	.07 (.06)	.08 (.06)
R^2	.29	.18	.06	.54	.46	.11	.11	.24	.35	.00	.49	.36	.04	.04
Number of observations	891	891	891	891	891	891	891	321	321	321	321	321	321	321

TABLE A2.1(b)

Standardized Regression Coefficients (and Standard Errors) of Income Determination

Model for Future Orientation Index

Dependent Variable

Independent Variable	White							Black						
	1968 log earnings	1968 income/needs	1968 index	1972 log earnings	1972 income/needs	1972 index	1972 index	1968 log earnings	1968 income/needs	1968 index	1972 log earnings	1972 income/needs	1972 index	1972 index
Education	.54 (.03)	.38 (.04)	.10 (.04)	.15 (.03)	.17 (.03)	.03 (.04)	.02 (.04)	.39 (.07)	.44 (.06)	.21 (.08)	.19 (.06)	.18 (.07)	.03 (.08)	.03 (.08)
Labor force experience	.32 (.03)	.05 (.03)	-.17 (.04)	-.01 (.03)	.11 (.03)	.00 (.04)	-.00 (.03)	.21 (.06)	-.02 (.06)	-.01 (.07)	.05 (.05)	-.02 (.05)	.12 (.06)	.09 (.06)
Test score	.11 (.03)	.12 (.03)	.02 (.04)	.07 (.03)	.06 (.03)	.03 (.03)	.02 (.03)	.25 (.06)	.22 (.05)	-.08 (.06)	.15 (.05)	.12 (.05)	.12 (.06)	.11 (.06)
1968 log earnings	--	--	--	.62 (.03)	--	-.00 (.04)	--	--	--	--	.52 (.05)	--	-.12 (.06)	--
1968 income/needs	--	--	--	--	.58 (.03)	--	.01 (.03)	--	--	--	--	.38 (.06)	--	-.10 (.07)
1968 index	--	--	--	.00 (.02)	.02 (.03)	.46 (.03)	.46 (.03)	--	--	--	.08 (.04)	.10 (.05)	.36 (.05)	.35 (.05)
R^2	.29	.18	.05	.53	.46	.22	.22	.24	.35	.03	.50	.36	.15	.14
Number of observations	891	891	891	891	891	891	891	321	321	321	321	321	321	321

TABLE A2.1(c)

Standardized Regression Coefficients (and Standard Errors) of Income Determination

Model for Trust-Hostility Index

Dependent Variable

Independent Variable	White							Black						
	1968 log earnings	1968 income/ needs	1968 index	1972 log earnings	1972 income/ needs	1972 index	1972 index	1968 log earnings	1968 income/ needs	1968 index	1972 log earnings	1972 income/ needs	1972 index	1972 index
Education	.54 (.03)	.38 (.04)	.19 (.04)	.15 (.03)	.17 (.03)	.07 (.04)	.06 (.04)	.39 (.07)	.44 (.06)	.23 (.07)	.19 (.06)	.18 (.07)	.02 (.07)	.10 (.07)
Labor force experience	.32 (.03)	.05 (.03)	.06 (.04)	-.01 (.03)	.10 (.03)	.02 (.04)	.02 (.04)	.21 (.06)	-.02 (.06)	.20 (.06)	.04 (.05)	-.04 (.06)	.20 (.06)	.22 (.06)
Test score	.11 (.03)	.12 (.03)	.11 (.04)	.07 (.03)	.06 (.03)	.15 (.03)	.15 (.03)	.25 (.06)	.22 (.05)	.22 (.06)	.14 (.05)	.09 (.05)	.13 (.06)	.18 (.06)
1968 log earnings	--	--	--	.62 (.03)	--	-.01 (.04)	--	--	--	--	.52 (.05)	--	.11 (.06)	--
1968 income/ needs	--	--	--	--	.58 (.03)	--	.01 (.03)	--	--	--	--	.37 (.06)	--	-.08 (.06)
1968 index	--	--	--	.03 (.02)	-.00 (.03)	.38 (.03)	.38 (.03)	--	--	--	.05 (.04)	.13 (.05)	.33 (.05)	.33 (.05)
R^2	.29	.18	.06	.54	.46	.21	.21	.24	.35	.12	.49	.36	.22	.22
Number of observations	891	891	891	891	891	891	891	321	321	321	321	321	321	321

TABLE A2.1(d)

Standardized Regression Coefficients (and Standard Errors) of Income Determination Model for Aspiration-Ambition Index

Dependent Variable

Independent Variable	White							Black						
	1968 log earnings	1968 income/needs	1968 index	1972 log earnings	1972 income/needs	1972 index	1972 index	1968 log earnings	1968 income/needs	1968 index	1972 log earnings	1972 income/needs	1972 index	1972 index
Education	.54 (.03)	.38 (.04)	-.13 (.04)	.15 (.03)	.18 (.03)	-.09 (.04)	-.10 (.04)	.39 (.07)	.44 (.06)	-.02 (.08)	.20 (.06)	.22 (.07)	-.08 (.08)	-.05 (.08)
Labor force experience	.32 (.03)	.05 (.03)	-.13 (.04)	-.01 (.03)	.11 (.03)	-.12 (.04)	-.13 (.03)	.21 (.06)	-.02 (.06)	-.15 (.07)	.05 (.05)	-.03 (.06)	.09 (.07)	.06 (.06)
Test score	.11 (.03)	.12 (.03)	-.04 (.03)	.07 (.03)	.06 (.03)	-.06 (.03)	-.06 (.03)	.25 (.06)	.22 (.05)	.06 (.06)	.15 (.05)	.12 (.05)	-.00 (.06)	.01 (.06)
1968 log earnings	--	--	--	.62 (.03)	--	-.04 (.04)	--	--	--	--	.52 (.05)	--	-.10 (.06)	--
1968 income/needs	--	--	--	--	.58 (.03)	--	-.03 (.03)	--	--	--	--	.35 (.06)	--	-.17 (.06)
1968 index	--	--	--	-.03 (.02)	.04 (.03)	.33 (.03)	.33 (.03)	--	--	--	-.01 (.04)	-.07 (.05)	.34 (.05)	.33 (.05)
R^2	.29	.18	.02	.54	.46	.15	.15	.24	.35	.03	.49	.35	.14	.15
Number of observations	891	891	891	891	891	891	891	321	321	321	321	321	321	321

TABLE A2.1(e)

Standardized Regression Coefficients (and Standard Errors) of Income Determination
Model for Risk Avoidance Index

Dependent Variable

Independent Variable	White							Black						
	1968 log earnings	1968 income/ needs	1968 index	1972 log earnings	1972 income/ needs	1972 index	1972 index	1968 log earnings	1968 income/ needs	1968 index	1972 log earnings	1972 income/ needs	1972 index	1972 index
Education	.54 (.03)	.38 (.04)	.37 (.04)	.14 (.03)	.18 (.03)	.16 (.04)	.17 (.03)	.39 (.07)	.44 (.06)	.18 (.07)	.20 (.06)	.21 (.07)	.17 (.07)	.15 (.07)
Labor force experience	.32 (.03)	.05 (.03)	.11 (.04)	-.01 (.03)	.11 (.03)	.06 (.03)	.07 (.03)	.21 (.06)	-.02 (.06)	.12 (.07)	.05 (.05)	-.03 (.06)	.14 (.06)	.18 (.06)
Test score	.11 (.03)	.12 (.03)	.03 (.03)	.07 (.03)	.06 (.03)	.07 (.03)	.07 (.03)	.25 (.06)	.22 (.05)	.18 (.06)	.14 (.05)	.10 (.05)	.03 (.06)	.03 (.06)
1968 log earnings	—	—	—	.61 (.03)	—	.06 (.03)	—	—	—	—	.50 (.05)	—	.17 (.06)	—
1968 income/ needs	—	—	—	—	.58 (.03)	—	.04 (.03)	—	—	—	—	.34 (.06)	—	.20 (.06)
1968 index	—	—	—	.06 (.02)	-.02 (.03)	.52 (.03)	.53 (.03)	—	—	—	.05 (.04)	.10 (.05)	.28 (.05)	.29 (.05)
R^2	.29	.18	.12	.54	.46	.41	.41	.24	.35	.08	.49	.36	.22	.22
Number of observations	891	891	891	891	891	891	891	321	321	321	321	321	321	321

TABLE A2.1(f)

Standardized Regression Coefficients (and Standard Errors) of Income Determination

Model for Connectedness Index

Dependent Variable

Independent Variable	White							Black						
	1968 log earnings	1968 income/ needs	1968 index	1972 log earnings	1972 income/ needs	1972 index	1972 index	1968 log earnings	1968 income/ needs	1968 index	1972 log earnings	1972 income/ needs	1972 index	1972 index
Education	.54 (.03)	.38 (.04)	.15 (.04)	.15 (.03)	.18 (.03)	.04 (.04)	.07 (.04)	.39 (.07)	.44 (.06)	.28 (.07)	.20 (.06)	.21 (.07)	-.04 (.07)	-.00 (.07)
Labor force experience	.32 (.03)	.05 (.03)	.22 (.04)	-.01 (.03)	.11 (.03)	-.04 (.03)	-.03 (.03)	.21 (.06)	-.02 (.06)	-.03 (.07)	.05 (.05)	-.02 (.06)	.04 (.06)	.05 (.06)
Test score	.11 (.03)	.12 (.03)	.04 (.04)	.07 (.03)	.06 (.03)	-.05 (.03)	-.04 (.03)	.25 (.06)	.22 (.05)	-.00 (.06)	.15 (.05)	.12 (.05)	.08 (.06)	.10 (.06)
1968 log earnings	--	--	--	.62 (.03)	--	.03 (.03)	--	--	--	--	.51 (.05)	--	.04 (.06)	--
1968 income/ needs	--	--	--	--	.58 (.03)	--	-.04 (.03)	--	--	--	--	.36 (.06)	--	-.04 (.06)
1968 index	--	--	--	.02 (.02)	-.04 (.03)	.49 (.03)	.49 (.03)	--	--	--	.02 (.04)	.03 (.05)	.48 (.05)	.49 (.05)
R^2	.29	.18	.05	.53	.46	.24	.24	.24	.35	.09	.49	.35	.24	.24
Number of observations	891	891	891	891	891	891	891	321	321	321	321	321	321	321

TABLE A2.1(g)

Standardized Regression Coefficients (and Standard Errors) of Income Determination

Model for Money Earnings Acts Index

	Dependent Variable													
	White							Black						
Independent Variable	1968 log earnings	1968 income/ needs	1968 index	1972 log earnings	1972 income needs	1972 index	1972 index	1968 log earnings	1968 income/ needs	1968 index	1972 log earnings	1972 income/ needs	1972 index	1972 index
Education	.54 (.03)	.38 (.04)	-.01 (.04)	.15 (.03)	.17 (.03)	.04 (.04)	-.00 (.04)	.39 (.07)	.44 (.06)	.16 (.07)	.21 (.06)	.18 (.07)	.04 (.07)	.07 (.07)
Labor force experience	.32 (.03)	.05 (.03)	-.04 (.04)	-.01 (.03)	.11 (.03)	-.03 (.04)	-.05 (.03)	.21 (.06)	-.02 (.06)	.18 (.07)	.06 (.05)	-.05 (.05)	.16 (.06)	.16 (.06)
Test score	.11 (.03)	.12 (.03)	.06 (.04)	.08 (.03)	.06 (.03)	-.03 (.03)	-.04 (.03)	.25 (.06)	.22 (.05)	.13 (.06)	.16 (.05)	.09 (.05)	.20 (.05)	.21 (.05)
1968 log earnings	--	--	--	.62 (.03)	--	-.05 (.04)	--	--	--	--	.51 (.05)	--	-.02 (.05)	--
1968 income/ needs	--	--	--	--	.58 (.03)	--	.04 (.03)	--	--	--	--	.37 (.05)	--	--
1968 index	--	--	--	-.02 (.02)	.01 (.03)	.36 (.03)	.36 (.03)	--	--	--	-.05 (.04)	.18 (.05)	.50 (.05)	.50 (.05)
R^2	.29	.18	.01	.54	.46	.14	.14	.24	.35	.05	.49	.38	.36	.36
Number of observations	891	891	891	891	891	891	891	321	321	321	321	321	321	321

TABLE A2.1(h)

Standardized Regression Coefficients (and Standard Errors) of Income Determination

Model for Economizing Index

Dependent Variable

Independent Variable	White							Black						
	1968 log earnings	1968 income/ needs	1968 index	1972 log earnings	1972 income/ needs	1972 index	1972 index	1968 log earnings	1968 income/ needs	1968 index	1972 log earnings	1972 income/ needs	1972 index	1972 index
Education	.54 (.03)	.38 (.04)	.16 (.04)	.15 (.03)	.17 (.03)	.11 (.04)	.04 (.04)	.39 (.07)	.44 (.06)	-.21 (.07)	.21 (.06)	.21 (.07)	-.03 (.07)	-.02 (.07)
Labor force experience	.32 (.03)	.05 (.03)	.01 (.04)	-.01 (.03)	.10 (.03)	.02 (.04)	-.05 (.04)	.21 (.06)	-.02 (.06)	-.01 (.07)	.05 (.05)	-.02 (.06)	.07 (.06)	.08 (.06)
Test score	.11 (.03)	.12 (.03)	.05 (.04)	.07 (.03)	.06 (.03)	.05 (.04)	.04 (.04)	.25 (.06)	.22 (.05)	-.11 (.06)	.15 (.05)	.11 (.05)	-.03 (.06)	-.02 (.06)
1968 log earnings	--	--	--	.62 (.03)	--	-.26 (.04)	--	--	--	--	.52 (.05)	--	.05 (.06)	--
1968 income/ needs	--	--	--	--	.58 (.03)	--	-.19 (.04)	--	--	--	--	.35 (.06)	--	.01 (.06)
1968 index	--	--	--	.04 (.02)	.03 (.03)	.07 (.03)	.06 (.03)	--	--	--	.01 (.04)	-.05 (.05)	.43 (.05)	.42 (.05)
R^2	.29	.18	.03	.54	.46	.05	.03	.24	.35	.08	.49	.35	.20	.20
Number of observations	891	891	891	891	891	891	891	321	321	321	321	321	321	321

TABLE A2.1(i)

Standardized Regression Coefficients (and Standard Errors) of Income Determination

Model for Real Earnings Acts Index

Dependent Variable

Independent Variable	White							Black						
	1968 log earn-ings	1968 income/needs	1968 index	1972 log earn-ings	1972 income/needs	1972 index	1972 index	1968 log earn-ings	1968 income/needs	1968 index	1972 log earn-ings	1972 income/needs	1972 index	1972 index
Education	.54 (.03)	.38 (.04)	-.04 (.04)	.15 (.03)	.17 (.03)	-.01 (.04)	-.01 (.04)	.39 (.07)	.44 (.06)	.02 (.08)	.20 (.06)	.21 (.07)	-.09 (.08)	-.04 (.08)
Labor force experience	.32 (.03)	.05 (.03)	.06 (.04)	-.01 (.03)	.11 (.03)	.03 (.04)	-.04 (.03)	.21 (.06)	-.02 (.06)	.16 (.07)	.06 (.05)	-.00 (.06)	.03 (.07)	.05 (.07)
Test score	.11 (.03)	.12 (.03)	-.01 (.04)	.07 (.03)	.06 (.03)	.01 (.03)	.02 (.03)	.25 (.06)	.22 (.05)	-.03 (.06)	.15 (.05)	.11 (.05)	.04 (.07)	.08 (.07)
1968 log earnings	--	--	--	.63 (.03)	--	-.07 (.04)	--	--	--	--	.52 (.05)	--	.10 (.06)	--
1968 income/needs	--	--	--	--	.57 (.03)	--	-.11 (.03)	--	--	--	--	.38 (.06)	--	-.03 (.07)
1968 index	--	--	--	.02 (.02)	-.04 (.03)	.42 (.03)	.41 (.03)	--	--	--	-.04 (.04)	-.11 (.05)	.18 (.06)	.18 (.06)
R^2	.29	.18	.01	.54	.46	.19	.19	.24	.35	.02	.49	.36	.05	.04
Number of observations	891	891	891	891	891	891	891	321	321	321	321	321	321	321

TABLE A2.2

Mean Scores on Aspiration-Ambition Questions
in 1968 and 1972, by Race

Question	Code	1968 White	1968 Black	1972 White	1972 Black
Would you like more work?	YES = 2 NO = 1	1.12	1.22	1.18	1.25
Would you rather have a job you like that doesn't offer a chance to make more money or a job you don't like that does?	a job that offers more money = 5 a job that offers more money, gratification = 4 pro-con = 3 a job I like qualified = 2 a job I like = 1	1.75	2.31	1.44	1.86
Are you more often satisfied or dissatisfied with yourself?	most often dissatisfied = 5 generally dissatisfied = 4 pro-con = 3 generally satisfied = 2 more often satisfied = 1	1.68	1.35	1.60	1.36
Do you spend time figuring out ways to get more money?	always = 5 quite a bit = 4 pro-con = 3 very little = 2 never = 1	2.28	3.04	2.32	3.10

TABLE A2.3

Mean Scores on Money Earning Acts Questions
in 1968 and 1972, by Race

Question	Code	1968		1972	
		White	Black	White	Black
Head's annual hours worked	1000-9999	2432	2264	2399	2255
Wife's annual hours worked	0000-9999	569	967	591	1075
Are you self-employed or do you own a business?	YES = 1 NO = 2	.18	.07	.24	.08
Are there times when you are late getting to work?	NEVER = 2 OFTEN = 1	1.90	1.84	1.86	1.81
Are there times when you don't go to work at all even though you are not sick?	NEVER = 2 OFTEN = 1	1.98	1.95	1.98	1.90
Did you have any extra jobs or ways of making money besides your main job?	YES = 2 NO = 1	1.27	1.31	1.29	1.31

TABLE A2.4

Mean Scores on Connectedness to Sources of Information
and Help Questions in 1968 and 1972, by Race

Question	Code	1968		1972	
		White	Black	White	Black
When did you last attend a PTA meeting?	within the last year = 3 more than a year ago = 2 never = 1	2.42	2.39	2.29	2.31
How often do you go to church?	once a week or more = 3 once or twice a month = 2 very seldom, never = 1	1.96	1.81	2.39	2.28
How much TV do you watch?	0-8 hours/day	1.86	2.62	1.94	2.52
How often do you read a newspaper?	every day = 5 week days = 4 Sunday only = 3 occasionally = 2 hardly ever = 1 never = 0	4.48	3.99	4.42	3.98
How many people in the neighborhood do you know by name?	six or more = 3 three to five = 2 two or less = 1	2.71	2.60	2.82	2.56
Do you have any relatives who live within walking distance?	YES = 2 NO = 1	1.41	1.62	1.41	1.58
How often do you go to social clubs or organizations?	about every day = 3 once a week = 2 hardly ever, never = 1	1.43	1.33	1.43	1.36
How often do you to to a bar or tavern?	almost every day = 3 once a week = 2 hardly ever, never = 1	1.42	1.49	1.47	1.53
Do you belong to a labor union?	YES = 2 NO = 1	1.29	1.48	1.30	1.51

Chapter 3

THE CREDIT INCOME REBATE PLAN:
AN ALTERNATIVE INCOME MAINTENANCE PROGRAM
Richard Coe

INTRODUCTION

The welfare "system" in this country is beset with troubles. As administrators at all levels of government search for solutions to the various problems
in the welfare programs, inequities seem to multiply. In recent years the call
has increasingly been heard for a complete restructuring of the welfare system
before it destroys itself through waste and abuse. This paper analyzes a particular alternative income maintenance program originally proposed by Milton
Friedman. Designed to work within the framework of the Federal individual income
tax laws, this plan involves returning to the individual some percent of his unused exemptions and deductions in the form of a cash subsidy. (Hereafter, unused
exemptions and deductions will be called "credit income" for simplicity.)

The plan is analyzed in two different formats -- as a supplement to the existing welfare programs, and as a replacement for the existing public non-contributory welfare programs. For each of these formats a different percent of
credit income is assumed to be rebated to the individual. For the supplemental
program, a 14 percent rebate rate, equal to the marginal tax rate of the Federal
income tax at the lowest taxpaying income levels, was chosen. For the replacement programs two rebate rates were selected -- 50 percent, the rate proposed by
Friedman, and 25 percent, a rate which appeared to leave the total value of rebate payments roughly equivalent to the total value of existing non-contributory
welfare payments, both in cash and in kind.[1]

---

[1]It should be stressed at the outset that the data available from the survey of
5285 families in 1972 are not ideally suited for making aggregate national calculations of costs of various programs. The survey families were weighted along
several dimensions -- race, head's education, family income, distance to the
center of the nearest city of 50,000 and others -- in an attempt to make an efficient but non-random sample as representative as possible of the nation as a
whole. However, it is conceivable that certain dimensions which could affect
the aggregate costs of the programs discussed in the paper were not accounted
for by the weighting procedure. Therefore, while the survey contains the requi-

The results are illuminating. Virtually all of the most needy families would be covered by a credit income rebate plan, compared to only one-half of those who currently qualify for public welfare. If a credit income rebate plan with a 25 percent rebate rate were to replace the existing public non-contributory welfare programs (at approximately the same cost), average incomes of families in the lowest income decile would increase by 15 percent. However, this would occur at the expense of the families who currently qualify for welfare -- their average rebate would be only 37 percent of their current average welfare payments. If a 50 percent rebate rate were selected, average income of families in the lowest income decile would increase by 46 percent, with current welfare recipients receiving an average rebate equal to 75 percent of their current welfare payments. However, this would add substantially to the current welfare bill. Though the results are somewhat mixed, it appears that a credit income rebate plan has several advantages over alternative income maintenance programs and could be a solution to what is now succinctly termed "the welfare mess."

In addition to the analysis performed on the entire sample, a separate section examines the current position of elderly families in the distribution of income and how this would be affected by a credit income rebate plan. It finds that the elderly fare poorly at present when compared to the rest of the survey families, with average income roughly one-half that of the entire sample. The low-income elderly would improve their economic position considerably under a credit income rebate plan with a 25 percent rebate rate designed to replace existing welfare programs, with average income of elderly families in the lowest income decile increasing by 29 percent. However, as with the entire sample, elderly families which now manage to qualify for welfare would suffer a decline in welfare payments of approximately 44 percent. On balance, though, it would seem that a credit income rebate plan could significantly ease the economic burden of the elderly.

Finally, Appendices 3.1 through 3.5 cover certain selected topics related to the results presented in the main body of the paper.

---

site information (e.g., taxable income, transfer income by source, family size and age composition) to enable one to make accurate estimates of the effect of such programs on individual families, one would want to recalculate the aggregate costs of the program with a larger sample to insure the accuracy of the aggregate costs estimated here. For full details of the weighting method, see Morgan (1972).

ANALYSIS

I. Definitions and Data

This study is based on data collected by the Survey Research Center of the Institute for Social Research, the University of Michigan. The data were gathered from interviews with 5,285 families. From this data set two income definitions are used in assessing the effects of a credit income rebate plan. One is called "money income" and is equal to the sum of the cash receipts received by the family unit in a particular time period. This measure includes labor earnings, cash receipts from capital assets, and transfer income both public and private.[1] Income from realized capital gains, however, is not included.

"Money income" as an income base is deficient in that it takes no account of the needs which a particular family has to meet out of its cash receipts. A $10,000 money income is not the same thing to a family of four as it is to a family of two, as the income tax laws themselves recognize. In an attempt to take account of this factor, a measure of annual needs was calculated, based primarily on the food requirements of a family. A weekly food need was estimated for each individual in the family, based on age and sex. These weekly needs were then summed, multiplied by 52, and adjusted for economies of scale of family size to give the annual needs standard. Thus, some account is taken of the size of the family, as well as the age composition.[2] Money income was then divided by the annual need standard to form the second income base, money income/needs.

Table 3.1 gives the income decile breakpoints and the average income for each decile for both income measures.

II. The Credit Income Rebate Plan

In his book, _Capitalism and Freedom_, Milton Friedman briefly puts forward a plan for alleviating poverty.[3] He argues that many low-income families cannot take advantage of all the exemptions and deductions allotted them under the Federal individual income tax law because their income is too low. For example,

---

[1] In estimating public transfer income, a cash value was assigned to certain in kind payments, such as payments for utility bills and rent. This value is a component of money income.

[2] Full details of the development of the annual need standard can be found in Morgan (1972), pp. 303-304.

[3] Friedman (1962), pp. 191-195.

TABLE 3.1

Income Decile Breakpoints and Mean
Income Levels, All Families, 1972

Money Income

	Decile Upper Limits	Mean Income
Lowest	$ 2,700	$ 1,939
Second	4,392	3,685
Third	6,046	5,334
Fourth	7,745	7,121
Fifth	9,304	8,863
Sixth	11,395	10,772
Seventh	13,350	12,946
Eighth	16,219	15,620
Ninth	21,000	19,176
Highest	--	31,121
All	--	11,663

Money Income/Needs

	Decile Upper Limits	Mean Income
Lowest	1.12	.77
Second	1.59	1.35
Third	2.09	1.83
Fourth	2.60	2.33
Fifth	3.04	2.81
Sixth	3.57	3.29
Seventh	4.22	3.86
Eighth	5.06	4.57
Ninth	6.45	5.67
Highest	--	9.45
All	--	3.59

based on the provisions of the law in 1972, the head of a family with a non-income-earning spouse and two children could earn up to $4,300 before paying any tax. If the head had earned only $2,000 he would have had $2,300 worth of exemptions and deductions which he could not use. Friedman proposed that the government rebate some percent of this credit income to the family in the form of a cash subsidy. (In his book he calls for a 50 percent return. In other words, in the above example, the government would pay $1,150 to the family.)

The major advantages of such a program, according to Friedman, are 1) it would be directed at the most needy, 2) it would be income in cash rather than kind, 3) it would not interfere with the market as much as many current welfare measures do, 4) it would not eliminate incentives to work for those who receive such subsidies, since earned income would be taxed at the rebate rate rather than at 100 percent as in some current welfare programs, and 5) it would be more efficient to administer than the host of welfare programs now in existence in that it would fit directly into the current tax laws and could thus be administered by the Internal Revenue Service, thereby requiring a minimum of new regulations and subsequent bureaucracy. In addition to these advantages listed by Friedman, there is the further advantage that such a program would be a dignified welfare program, eliminating the demeaning aspects of many current welfare programs.

In light of these possible advantages it is somewhat surprising that a guaranteed annual income plan designed explicitly to fit directly into the current tax laws has not received much notice of late.[1] Recently proposed plans, such as the Family Assistance Plan, embody the essence of the Friedman proposal in that they call for a nationwide guaranteed annual base income and some rate of taxation of less than 100 percent on additional earnings, but the base income level is not tied directly to the provisions of the current tax law. Besides the possible advantage of administrative ease of a single set of regulations, there is the further advantage of legislative ease in giving tax relief to all those deemed needy. For example, the Tax Reform Act of 1969 aided many low-income families, but it did *not* help the very needy, i.e., those families so poor that they were paying no tax anyway. (This problem is further discussed in Section IV, with particular reference to the position of the elderly under the income tax law.) Under a credit income rebate plan the tax law changes of 1969 would have automatically helped these no-tax families by increasing their credit income and hence their rebate, as well as reducing the tax burden for families that were paying some tax. Under a guaranteed annual income plan not tied directly to the

---

[1] However, see David and Leuthold (1972) for a discussion of some of the aspects of Friedman's proposal.

tax law, a different set of legislative rules would have had to have been passed in order to benefit the no-tax families as well as relieve the tax burden on families whom Congress deemed were paying too much tax.

Thus it would seem that there are distinct advantages contained in a credit income plan compared to other welfare programs and proposals. The real question is how effective would such a plan be in aiding those families who are most needy. In order to answer this, the amount of credit income was estimated for each family in 1972. Based on the tax laws which allowed $750 for each exemption and a flat $1,300 low-income allowance, the following formulas were used to calculate the credit income of a family.[1]

1) CREDIT INCOME OF HEAD AND WIFE

Credit income = $2,050 + ((Exemptions - 1) x $750) -
taxable income of head and wife

2) CREDIT INCOME OF OTHERS

Credit income = ($2,050 x number of others) - taxable
income of others

The number of exemptions is equal to the number of dependents (including head and wife) plus any old-age allowances which are appropriate. The number of others eligible for credit income is calculated by subtracting from family size the number of dependents.[2,3] The positive amounts of these two formulas are

---

[1] It should be noted that these formulas take no account of the effect of unusually large deductions, which could result in higher-income families qualifying for a rebate.

[2] This procedure assumes that one aspect of the current tax law would be changed if a credit income plan were introduced. That is the provision which allows a person to claim himself as a dependent and also allows someone else to claim him as a dependent if that other person contributed 50 percent of his support. This provision is probably particularly beneficial to those families whose children are students (especially college students), since there is no income ceiling on what a student can earn and still be claimed as a dependent. Since more children of higher-income families attend college than children of lower-income families, the benefits of this provision probably accrue disproportionately to higher-income families. The estimation procedure used here assumes that if a person is claimed as a dependent by someone else, he cannot claim himself as a dependent. If such a change in the law were not made, the credit income plan would become much more costly than estimated in the paper, and a substantial portion of the benefits would accrue to higher-income families.

Also, this procedure may underestimate somewhat the amount of credit income of others in the family. Taxable income of others is coded as a single variable, thus aggregating the earnings of all members of the household other than the head and the wife. Thus, this variable may overstate the taxable income of those other members of the household eligible for credit income, and thus understate their amount of credit income. It is doubtful whether this introduces any serious error in the figures.

[3] Because of the general problem of the treatment of others in a family unit,

added to obtain family credit income. A straight addition of the two would not
be appropriate, since a head and wife with negative credit income would not can-
cel out the positive credit income of another member of the family who is an independent income earner.

These formulas enable one to calculate the annual base income a family with
no adjusted gross income would receive under a credit income rebate plan, depending on the rebate rate chosen and the number of exemptions a family can claim.
Table 3.2 shows the guaranteed annual income by number of exemptions for the
three rebate rates used in this study.

TABLE 3.2

Guaranteed Annual Income Under a Credit
Income Rebate Plan By Number of Exemptions
and Rebate Rate, 1972 Tax Law Provisions

Rebate Rate	Number of Exemptions					
	1	2	3	4	5	6
.50	$1025	$1400	$1775	$2150	$2525	$2900
.25	513	700	888	1075	1263	1450
.14	287	392	497	602	707	812

Using these formulas the distribution of credit income was then determined,
according to level of money income and money income/needs. The results are
shown in Table 3.3.[1] As is clear, the distribution of credit income is concentrated in the lower income deciles. More than 50 percent of the families who
have credit income are in the lowest two income deciles. It also is apparent
that most low income families have some credit income. Ninety-five percent of
the families in the lowest income decile qualify for some credit income, and 70
percent in the second lowest income decile. By contrast, five percent of the
families in the highest income decile have some credit income. Furthermore, the
average amount of credit income for the low-income families is not trifling --
approximately $2,500 for families in the lowest money income decile and $3,000
for families in the lowest money income/needs decile. Thus it would appear that
a credit income rebate plan can form the basis of an effective welfare program
both in terms of being directed at the most needy and of offering potentially
large benefits for those needy.

Appendix 3.2 discusses the distribution of credit income for the head and wife
only.

[1] For comparative distribution of current welfare payments, see Appendix 3.1.

TABLE 3.3

Distribution of Credit Income by Income Deciles,
All Families, 1972

Decile 1972 Money Income	Unweighted Number of Families with Credit Income	Weighted Percent of All Families with Credit Income	Weighted Percent of Families in Income Decile With Credit Income	Mean Credit Income
Lowest	623	30.1%	94.8%	$2,536
Second	448	22.4	70.4	2,900
Third	338	15.6	48.9	2,700
Fourth	212	11.0	34.7	2,584
Fifth	107	5.4	17.0	2,787
Sixth	91	4.8	15.0	2,644
Seventh	58	3.5	10.9	2,931
Eighth	41	3.0	9.6	2,171
Ninth	37	2.5	8.0	2,064
Highest	21	1.7	5.3	1,266
Totals:	1976	100.0%	31.5%	$2,636

Money Income/Needs

Decile 1972 Money Income/ Needs	Unweighted Number of Families with Credit Income	Weighted Percent of All Families with Credit Income	Weighted Percent of Families in Income Decile With Credit Income	Mean Credit Income
Lowest	910	30.2%	95.2%	$3,007
Second	407	21.6	68.0	2,760
Third	244	15.1	47.4	2,566
Fourth	147	10.6	33.4	2,513
Fifth	78	6.6	20.8	2,399
Sixth	71	5.9	18.7	2,006
Seventh	45	3.4	10.7	2,174
Eighth	33	2.7	8.5	1,794
Ninth	25	2.2	6.9	2,212
Highest	16	1.5	4.8	1,704
Totals	1976	99.8%	31.5%	$2,636

The first question to be answered, then, is how the distribution of income would be affected by a credit income rebate plan designed to supplement the existing welfare programs. A 14 percent rebate rate, which would in effect extend the current marginal tax rate of 14 percent to the lowest earnings level, was chosen. Table 3.4 shows what effect such a plan would have on the 1972 distribution of income. As one might expect from the figures in Table 3.3, the benefits of this plan fall primarily on the families in the lower income deciles. While aggregate average money income rose by one percent, average money income for families in the lowest money income decile increased by 17.7 percent. Average money incomes of families in the six highest deciles were essentially unchanged. Similar results were found when families were ranked according to their money income/needs ratios. It would seem, then, that even a modest credit income rebate plan would prove to be an effective supplemental income maintenance program in terms of extending significant benefits to the most needy.

But this is not really the point. Though a supplemental plan may be useful as a transitional program, it is not a solution to the welfare problem. As emphasized in the discussion at the beginning of this section, one would not merely want to supplement the current menagerie of welfare programs in order to realize the full benefits of a credit income rebate plan, but actually replace them. Consequently, one would want to know what changes in the current distribution of income would occur if existing public welfare payments were stopped and a credit income rebate plan were introduced.

In order to answer this question public noncontributory welfare payments are first subtracted from family money income. These payments include, for the head and wife, AFDC and ADC cash payments and payments in kind, and other payments by various welfare agencies for utilities, rent, clothing and miscellaneous. For other members of the family all transfer income, both public and private, is included in the amount subtracted from family money income. For 1972, survey data do not exist for two major categories of noncontributory welfare payments -- food stamps and free medical care -- and hence the effect of eliminating these programs cannot be calculated.[1] After these payments were sub-

---

[1] Data do exist on unemployment compensation, another form of noncontributory (at least legally) transfer income. However, these payments are not subtracted from family money income. The rationale is that the purpose of unemployment compensation programs is to provide a *temporary* buffer against the frictions of the labor market, which often prevent a worker who loses his job from immediately finding new employment in his occupation. Unemployment benefits are meant to cover the transitional period between jobs. Thus the purpose differs from that of a guaranteed annual income program, which is meant to benefit all low-income families -- those who work, who cannot work, or who will not work.

Also, it should be noted that no account is taken of farm price supports, min-

TABLE 3.4

Changes in the Distribution of Income
With Credit Income Rate, All Families, 1972

Rebate Rate = 14%

Money Income

Decile 1972 Money Income	Mean Income	Average Absolute Increase	Percent Increase
Lowest	$ 2,282	$343	17.7%
Second	3,977	292	7.9
Third	5,523	189	3.5
Fourth	7,249	128	1.8
Fifth	8,931	68	0.8
Sixth	10,828	56	0.5
Seventh	12,992	46	0.4
Eighth	15,650	30	0.2
Ninth	19,200	24	0.1
Highest	31,131	10	0.03
All	$11,781	$118	1.0%

Money Income/Needs

Decile 1972 Money Income	Mean Income	Absolute Increase	Percent Increase
Lowest	$ .91	.14	18.2%
Second	1.45	.10	7.4
Third	1.90	.07	3.8
Fourth	2.38	.05	2.1
Fifth	2.83	.02	0.7
Sixth	3.31	.02	0.6
Seventh	3.87	.01	0.3
Eighth	4.57	---	--
Ninth	5.67	---	--
Highest	9.46	.01	0.1
All	3.64	.05	1.4%

tracted, the credit income rebate was added to family money income. Table 3.5
shows the consequent changes in the 1972 distribution of income when a 50 percent
and a 25 percent rebate rate were assumed.

With a 50 percent rebate rate, the effect on the distribution of income was
dramatic. Average income of families in the lowest money income/needs decile increased by a hefty 42 percent, raising their average money income/needs ratio
above 1.00. Families in the second lowest decile experienced, on the average, a
16 percent increase in income. Families in the higher income deciles remained
virtually unaffected by the change. Overall, average money income/needs increased by 2.5 percent. However, it would appear that this program would add
roughly $13 billion to the welfare bill, a substantial amount.[1]

Such is not the case with a 25 percent rebate rate. Overall, average family money income decreases by $7.00, indicating that the total cash payments of
the program would be about the same as the value of the cash payments of income
in kind of the current welfare programs existing at all levels of government.
But though the aggregate payments would be roughly the same, the distribution of
payments would not. Average income of families in the lowest income decile (by
either ranking) would increase by about 15 percent, while that of families in
the second lowest decile would increase by three percent. On a money income
ranking, families in all other deciles would suffer a decline in average income,
but that decline never exceeds one percent. On a money income/needs ranking,
families in each of the four lowest deciles would experience an increase in average money income/needs ratio, while the position of families in the other deciles
remains essentially unchanged, on the average. It would seem, therefore, that a
credit income rebate plan with a 25 percent rebate rate in place of current welfare programs would be a feasible income maintenance plan, in terms both of costs
and of aiding the most needy.

Another approach to test the efficiency of a credit income rebate plan
against that of the current welfare programs is to assume that no government noncontributory transfer programs exist, and then compare the distribution of current welfare payments to those of a credit income rebate plan. To do this families were first ranked according to their money income and money income/needs
after current welfare payments were subtracted from family money income. Tables

---

imum wage laws and other forms of income maintenance, which Friedman argued
should be scrapped along with the more explicit welfare programs.

[1]Multiplying the $200 average increase in family money income by the approximate-
ly 65 million family units in the country yields a rough estimate of the additional cost of the program of $13 billion.

TABLE 3.5

Changes in the 1972 Distribution of Income With a
Credit Income Rebate Plan in Place of Existing
Public Noncontributory Welfare Programs,
All Families

Money Income

Decile 1972 Money Income	50 Percent Rebate Rate			25 Percent Rebate Rate		
	Mean Income	Absolute Change	Percent Change	Mean Income	Absolute Change	Percent Change
Lowest	$ 2,838	$899	46.3%	$ 2,237	$298	15.4%
Second	4,305	620	16.8	3,794	109	3.0
Third	5,610	276	5.2	5,280	−54	−1.0
Fourth	7,293	172	2.4	7,069	−52	−0.7
Fifth	8,943	80	0.9	8,824	−39	−0.4
Sixth	10,837	65	0.6	10,737	−35	−0.3
Seventh	12,948	2	0.0	12,868	−78	−0.6
Eighth	15,597	−23	−0.1	15,545	−75	−0.5
Ninth	19,123	−53	−0.3	19,082	−94	−0.5
Highest	31,088	−33	−0.1	31,071	−50	−0.2
All	$11,863	$200	1.7%	$11,656	$− 7	−0.06%

Money Income/Needs

Decile 1972 Money Income	50 Percent Rebate Rate			25 Percent Rebate Rate		
	Mean Income	Absolute Change	Percent Change	Mean Income	Absolute Change	Percent Change
Lowest	$1.09	.32	41.6%	$ .85	.12	15.6%
Second	1.57	.22	16.3	1.39	.04	3.0
Third	1.99	.16	8.7	1.87	.04	2.2
Fourth	2.42	.09	3.9	2.34	.01	0.4
Fifth	2.85	.04	1.4	2.81	--	--
Sixth	3.31	.02	0.6	3.28	−.01	−0.3
Seventh	3.89	.03	0.8	3.87	.01	0.3
Eighth	4.57	--	--	4.56	−.01	−0.2
Ninth	5.67	--	--	5.65	−.02	−0.4
Highest	9.42	−.03	−0.3	9.42	−.03	−0.3
All	3.68	.09	2.5%	3.61	.02	0.6%

3.6 through 3.9 show the comparative distributions of a credit income rebate plan with a 25 percent rebate rate and the existing noncontributory welfare programs. Two major points are illustrated by these comparative figures. One is that a credit income rebate plan would cover many more families than the existing welfare programs, especially at the lower income deciles. Virtually all families in the lowest income decile qualify for some credit income rebate. This contrasts sharply with the rather bleak performance of the current programs, which cover only roughly one-half of the families in the lowest income decile.[1] However, for those families that the current welfare programs do reach, the current payments, on the average, are substantial, at least when compared to the payment levels which would be received from a credit income rebate plan with a 25 percent rebate rate. This result, of course, follows directly from the fact that the credit income rebate plan with a 25 percent rebate rate would cost essentially the same as the current welfare programs but would cover many more families. For families who would be in the lowest money income/needs decile if there were no government welfare programs and which currently qualify for welfare, the average welfare payment is equal to $2,218. Under a credit income rebate plan with a 25 percent rebate rate, these same families, all of whom would qualify for some credit income rebate, would receive an average payment of $1,047. This is less than half of what they are currently receiving. With a 50 percent rebate rate, these families would receive an average rebate of $2,094. For all families who qualify for a credit income rebate in the lowest no-welfare money income/needs decile the average rebate payment would have been $830, if a 25 percent rebate rate were selected. (See Appendix C for more details of how families who received welfare in 1972 would have fared under a credit income rebate plan.)

These figures shed new light on the results shown in Table 3.5 which demonstrates that with a 25 percent rebate rate, a credit income plan in place of cur-

_____
[1] These comparative figures are somewhat unfair, since it is assumed that all individuals who qualify for a credit income rebate will actually receive it, while the figures for current welfare programs reflect only those who actually reported receiving benefits and not the number who qualify for benefits. As pointed out in Chapter 5, Volume I, there are some needy families who qualify for welfare, but for whatever reason do not receive any payments. However, it is doubtful whether this can account for any substantial portion of the large discrepancy between the number of needy families who qualify for a credit income rebate and who currently qualify for welfare. Indeed, further research is needed to discover whether those families with substantial credit income but not on welfare are in the South, live in rural areas, have substantial imputed income (especially rental income) that welfare authorities take into account, are simply discouraged from applying for welfare by the administrative complexities of the current welfare system, or just do not qualify for welfare due to local regulations.

TABLE 3.6

Distribution of Welfare Payments by Money Income
(Excluding Noncontributory Welfare Income) Deciles, 1972,
All Families

Decile of Income (excluding Non-contributory Welfare Income)	Unweighted Number of Current Welfare Recipients	Weighted Percent of All Welfare Recipients	Weighted Percent of Families in Decile	Mean Welfare Payment
Lowest	451	42.7%	45.5%	$2,166
Second	139	17.2	18.3	1,948
Third	95	13.0	13.9	2,426
Fourth	58	6.0	6.4	1,871
Fifth	41	4.7	5.0	1,398
Sixth	24	3.5	3.8	1,655
Seventh	20	3.3	3.5	1,585
Eighth	17	4.1	4.5	1,462
Ninth	15	2.8	2.9	1,363
Highest	10	2.6	2.7	2,037
All	870	100.0%	10.6%	$2,017

TABLE 3.7

Distribution of Credit Income Rebate
(Excluding Noncontributory Welfare Income) by Deciles, 1972,
All Families

Rebate Rate = 25%

Decile of Credit Income Rebate (Excluding Non-contributory Welfare Income	Unweighted Number of Credit In-come Rebate Recipients	Weighted Percent of All Credit Income Rebate Recipients	Weighted Percent of Families in Decile	Mean Credit Income Rebate
Lowest	764	31.3%	98.5%	$753
Second	415	23.2	73.0	642
Third	300	16.7	52.8	665
Fourth	181	9.7	30.6	593
Fifth	102	5.2	16.3	650
Sixth	76	4.2	13.2	624
Seventh	51	3.1	9.9	560
Eighth	35	2.8	9.0	487
Ninth	33	2.1	6.4	452
Highest	19	1.6	5.2	300
All	1976	100.0%	31.5%	$659

TABLE 3.8

Distribution of Welfare Payments by Money Income/Needs
(Excluding Noncontributory Welfare Income) Deciles,
1972, All Families

Decile of Income/ Needs (Excluding Noncontributory Welfare Income	Unweighted Number of Current Welfare Recipients	Weighted Percent of All Welfare Recipients	Weighted Percent of Families in Decile	Mean Welfare Payment
Lowest	561	51.1%	54.5%	$2,218
Second	115	15.5	16.7	1,764
Third	74	10.2	10.6	2,246
Fourth	43	6.9	7.4	1,694
Fifth	22	4.3	4.5	1,900
Sixth	19	3.6	3.8	1,367
Seventh	16	3.1	3.3	1,566
Eighth	7	2.0	2.1	1,240
Ninth	9	2.1	2.3	1,854
Highest	4	1.2	1.3	1,772
All	870	100.0%	10.6%	$2,017

TABLE 3.9

Distribution of Credit Income Rebate by Money Income/Needs
(Excluding Noncontributory Welfare Income) Deciles,
1972, All Families

Rebate Rate = 25%

Decile of Credit Income Rebate (Excluding Non-contributory Welfare Income	Unweighted Number of Credit Income Rebate Recipients	Weighted Percent of All Credit Income Rebate Recipients	Weighted Percent of Families in Decile	Mean Credit Income Rebate
Lowest	929	31.4%	99.3%	$830
Second	426	21.8	69.7	623
Third	231	15.2	47.2	627
Fourth	137	10.3	32.3	570
Fifth	78	6.8	21.6	559
Sixth	63	5.2	16.2	482
Seventh	43	3.2	10.2	555
Eighth	31	2.6	8.2	453
Ninth	24	2.2	6.8	505
Highest	14	1.2	3.9	347
All	1976	100.0%	31.5%	$659

rent welfare programs would increase the average income of families in the low-est income decile by 15 percent. This increase no doubt stems from the fact that many families presently not qualifying for welfare would experience a sig-nificant increase in income. This would not be a result of higher payments to those who were receiving welfare, as one might first suspect. These families more than offset the families in that decile who are on welfare and would suffer a decline in income. Many families now qualifying for welfare would probably be in a higher income decile anyway, as a consequence of their high transfer pay-ments, a component of family money income. The lower increases in income for the second lowest decile, and the decline in incomes in some higher deciles, are probably a result of less new families receiving payments and the families cur-rently on welfare suffering a substantial decline in payments received. While these changes in support levels for individual families can no doubt be par-tially explained by differences in the cost of living between regions, which would not be accounted for by a nationwide credit income rebate plan, they also reflect differences in eligibility requirements, standards of support and other aspects of various state programs now in existence.

It seems, therefore, that the choice between a credit income rebate plan and the existing array of noncontributory welfare programs is in reality a de-cision concerning the ultimate goal of a welfare system. At a given level of cost, should the nation have a program which extends some help to all the needy, or should we have a program which aids only some of the needy, but aids them substantially? Or, should we increase the welfare bill so that all the needy can be helped adequately? A credit income rebate plan appears to be an effi-cient method of reaching all the needy,[1] but precisely because of this it would require either an increase in the total welfare bill or a decrease in the pay-ments to families now receiving welfare.

This section has attempted to show the distributional impact of a credit in-come rebate plan. It appears that it would be an effective, efficient solution to the welfare problem. At the beginning of the section some general advantages of such a plan were mentioned.[2] Some of these advantages seem unarguable -- it would be a nondemeaning income maintenance program, it would have minimal inter-

---

[1] Though a credit income rebate plan appears to be an efficient method of reach-ing the needy, it might not be as efficient as current welfare programs in di-recting a higher percent of total welfare payments to the most needy. For a discussion of this point, see Appendix 3.4.

[2] For a brief general discussion of some of the major problems of any nationwide guaranteed annual income program, see Fried, et al. (1973), pp. 81-84.

ference with the market mechanism, it would be income in cash rather than kind.[1]
Though the data are not available from the Panel Study to estimate the administrative costs of such a program, it is hard to imagine that there would not be
substantial savings in administering this type of program as compared to the administrative costs of current welfare programs.[2] The real question is who would
be helped, and *how much*. The analysis in this section shows that virtually all
the needy would be helped by a credit income rebate plan. *How much* would be up
to us as a nation to decide.

III. The Elderly

Concern over the economic position of the elderly people in our society has
been widespread in recent years. The reason for this concern is well illustrated
by Table 3.10, which shows the distribution of income for elderly families (families with head aged 65 years or more). On the whole, the incomes of the elderly
are considerably lower than the incomes of the entire sample. In 1972 nearly 50
percent of the elderly families were in the two lowest money income deciles, with
only five percent in the highest two deciles. Average money income of the elderly was only 56 percent of that of the entire sample.

The position of the elderly appears to improve when money income/needs is
used as the income base rather than money income. In 1972, 35 percent of elderly families were in the two lowest deciles by this ranking measure, while 10 percent were in the two highest deciles. Average money income/needs ratio for the
elderly was 77 percent of that of the entire sample. Though this improvement
may reflect the actual economic position of the elderly, it is probably at least
partially due to the method used in constructing the need standard. The weekly
individual food standard is lower for persons aged 56 or more than for any other
age group except children less than ten years of age. Since the weekly food
standard (adjusted for economies of scale of family size) forms the basis of the
annual need standard, the need standard for elderly people would be lower than

---

[1]It is not clear, however, that everyone would consider this an advantage, as
many economists would.

[2]This is not meant to imply that there would be no problems in administering a
credit income rebate plan. Certainly some changes in the administration of the
current tax laws would have to be undertaken if such a plan were introduced.
Most notable of these would appear to be the timing of payments. Obviously,
welfare recipients could not wait until the end of the year to receive one lump-
sum-transfer payment.

Also, it should be made clear that certain important aspects of introducing such
a program have not been discussed, most notably work incentives and changes in
family size.

TABLE 3.10

Distribution of Income of Families With Head
Aged 65 Years or More, 1972

Money Income

Decile 1972 Money Income	Unweighted N	Weighted Percent of All Elderly Families	Mean Money Income
Lowest	194	26.6%	$1,967
Second	130	21.2	3,655
Third	91	15.4	5,345
Fourth	69	11.4	6,994
Fifth	47	7.8	8,835
Sixth	37	6.4	10,768
Seventh	20	3.3	12,750
Eighth	19	3.4	15,412
Ninth	12	2.1	19,657
Highest	14	2.3	38,793
All	633	100.0%	$6,559

Money Income/Needs

Decile 1972 Money Income/ Needs	Unweighted N	Weighted Percent of All Elderly Families	Mean Money Income/ Needs Ratio
Lowest	136	17.1%	.80
Second	114	17.4	1.35
Third	95	15.7	1.84
Fourth	74	13.0	2.36
Fifth	34	5.8	2.83
Sixth	45	7.5	3.30
Seventh	43	7.5	3.86
Eighth	38	6.7	4.57
Ninth	26	4.3	5.55
Highest	28	5.1	11.27
All	633	100.0%	2.78

that of a younger family of the same size. Hence the money income/needs ratio would be higher. This improvement, however, is probably partly illusory, since no adjustment has been made to reflect certain higher costs the elderly must face, primarily medical costs. On the other hand, no allowance has been made for imputed income. The elderly, being predominantly homeowners without mortgages, have substantial imputed rental income. While they are overhoused and cannot use this imputed income to pay for food and medical care, they are better off in terms of housing than most younger families with the same money income/needs ratio.

In general, though, it seems clear that the elderly fare poorly economically when compared to the rest of the sample. In recognition of this the Federal individual income tax laws have historically placed the elderly in a somewhat favorable position by allowing an extra exemption to persons aged 65 years and over and by not taxing Social Security payments, an important component of money income for the elderly. This has resulted in elderly families paying less of their money income in taxes than the average family with the same income. However, it has also prevented the lower income elderly from benefiting greatly from the liberalization of the personal exemption allowance and the minimum standard deduction, as occurred in 1969. Both of these points are illustrated in Table 3.11. This table shows the percent of money income paid as income tax, by the entire sample and by families with head aged 65 years or more, for the years 1969 and 1970. Presumably, the differences in the ratios for the two years are primarily the result of the 1969 tax law changes, which went into effect in 1970. As can be seen, elderly families in the same income deciles pay a lower percent of their money income in taxes than do all the families in that decile. Secondly, although the 1970 tax law changes lowered the tax burden on the lowest income deciles for the entire sample significantly, the effect on the elderly families in the lowest income deciles was slight.

As discussed in Section II, a credit income rebate plan would ensure that the benefits of any such liberalization of the tax law would accrue to the most needy as well as others. Combining this with the fact that the elderly are granted an extra exemption under current tax laws, and that Social Security benefits are not taxed, it becomes apparent that a credit income rebate plan could be especially beneficial to the elderly. Table 3.12, showing the distribution of credit income for the elderly, reinforces this point.[1] Virtually all the elderly families in the lower income deciles (most elderly families are in these

---

[1] See Appendix 3.1 for a comparative distribution of current noncontributory welfare payments for the elderly.

134

TABLE 3.11

Percent of Money Income Devoted to the
Federal Individual Income Tax, 1969 and 1970

All Families

Decile Money Income	1969	1970
Lowest	0.8%	0.1%
Second	3.0	2.5
Third	5.4	4.3
Fourth	7.3	6.8
Fifth	8.9	8.0
Sixth	10.2	9.4
Seventh	11.3	10.8
Eighth	12.3	11.6
Ninth	13.6	12.8
Highest	18.3	17.5
Number of Observations	3984	4338

Elderly

Decile Money Income	1969	1970
Lowest	0.0%	0.0%
Second	0.5	0.2
Third	1.6	1.6
Fourth	2.3	2.2
Fifth	5.5	4.3
Sixth	5.3	4.9
Seventh	8.2	8.1
Eighth	9.2	8.2
Ninth	10.7	11.3
Highest	18.9	13.7
Number of Observations	424	483

Taxes were estimated for each family (not reported
by them) by procedures described in the documentation
volumes. See Morgan (1973) p. 315.

TABLE 3.12

Distribution of Credit Income for Families
With Head Aged 65 Years or Over, 1972

Money Income

Decile 1972 Money Income	Unweighted Number of Elderly Families With Credit Income	Weighted Number of Elderly Families in Income Decile	Mean Credit Income
Lowest	194	100.0%	$3,017
Second	126	97.2	3,124
Third	77	85.6	2,697
Fourth	52	75.1	2,798
Fifth	26	55.6	3,122
Sixth	16	43.0	2,994
Seventh	11	52.3	4,005
Eighth	6	34.0	2,899
Ninth	4	31.0	3,311
Highest	1	8.9	2,050
Totals	513	79.8%	$2,993

Money Income/Needs

Decile 1972 Money Income/ Needs	Unweighted Number of Elderly Families With Credit Income	Weighted Number of Elderly Families in Income Decile	Mean Credit Income
Lowest	136	100.0%	$3,492
Second	114	100.0	3,281
Third	89	94.2	2,842
Fourth	68	93.1	2,669
Fifth	29	88.9	3,035
Sixth	30	68.8	2,359
Seventh	19	43.6	2,588
Eighth	14	35.4	2,049
Ninth	11	46.9	2,805
Highest	3	10.2	2,270
Totals	513	79.8%	$2,993

deciles) would qualify for some credit income rebate, and 80 percent of all elderly families would qualify.[1] The amounts would be large. For example, elderly families in the lowest money income/needs decile would have, on the average,
nearly $3,500 in credit income.

Tables 3.13 and 3.14 present the results for the programs discussed in Section II. As a supplemental program, a credit income rebate plan with a 14 percent rebate rate would increase average money income/needs for elderly families
by 5.4 percent as shown in Table 3.13. Elderly families in the lowest money
income/needs decile would experience a substantial 27.5 percent increase in average income, lifting that average above 1.00. Families in the second lowest
money income/needs decile would have average income raised by 15.6 percent.
Thus, as expected, a supplemental credit income rebate would significantly improve the economic position of the elderly.

As a replacement for existing public noncontributory welfare programs, a
credit income rebate plan would likewise significantly help the elderly, as
shown in Table 3.14. With a 50 percent rebate rate, average money income/needs
for all elderly families would increase by 15 percent, with each income decile
experiencing an increase in average income. The most needy experience the
greatest improvement -- an 84 percent increase in average income for families in
the lowest money income/needs decile. Of even greater interest are the results
when a 25 percent rebate rate is assumed. As mentioned earlier, this rate would
keep the amount of payments under a credit income rebate plan roughly equivalent
to those under current public noncontributory welfare programs. With such a
plan, elderly families in the lowest money income/needs decile would experience,
on the average, a 33 percent increase in their money income/needs; families in
the second lowest decile a 21 percent increase. Overall, such a program would
raise the average money income/needs for elderly families 5.8 percent. Thus it
would seem that a credit income rebate plan with a 25 percent rebate rate in
place of existing welfare programs would be a feasible plan to help ease the economic burden of the elderly.

However, as evidenced in Section II, these aggregate figures can hide considerable fluctuations in incomes for individual families. Following the same

---

[1] In fact, one might argue that *too many* elderly families would qualify for some
credit income rebate, especially in the higher income deciles. Appendix 3.5
briefly discusses a possible remedy for this potential problem -- making Social
Security payments a component of taxable income. This would prevent elderly
families with large Social Security payments from qualifying for any credit income rebate. This also raises the question of whether some fraction of imputed
rental income should be included in the income base used to calculate credit income, since many elderly people live rent-free in their non-mortgaged houses.

TABLE 3.13

Changes in the Distribution of Income
With Credit Income Rebate, Families With
Head Aged 65 Years or More, 1972

Rebate Rate = 14%

Money Income

Decile 1972 Money Income	Mean Income	Absolute Increase	Percent Increase
Lowest	$2,398	$431	21.9%
Second	4,089	434	11.9
Third	5,674	329	6.2
Fourth	7,294	300	4.3
Fifth	9,083	248	2.8
Sixth	10,952	184	1.7
Seventh	13,049	299	2.3
Eighth	15,553	141	0.9
Ninth	19,804	147	0.7
Highest	38,819	26	0.1
All	$6,900	$341	5.2%

Money Income/Needs

Decile 1972 Money Income/ Needs	Mean Income	Absolute Increase	Percent Increase
Lowest	$ 1.02	$.22	27.5%
Second	1.56	.21	15.6
Third	2.01	.17	9.2
Fourth	2.51	.15	6.4
Fifth	2.98	.15	5.3
Sixth	3.40	.10	3.0
Seventh	3.92	.06	1.6
Eighth	4.61	.04	0.9
Ninth	5.62	.07	1.3
Highest	11.29	.02	0.2
All	2.93	.15	5.4%

TABLE 3.14

Changes in 1972 Distribution of Income With
Credit Income Rebate Plan in Place of Existing
Public Noncontributory Welfare Programs,
Families With Head Aged 65 Years or More

Money Income

Decile 1972 Money Income	50 Percent Rebate Rate			25 Percent Rebate Rate		
	Mean Income	Absolute Change	Percent Change	Mean Income	Absolute Change	Percent Change
Lowest	$ 3,293	$ 1,326	67.4%	$ 2,539	$572	29.1%
Second	4,954	1,299	35.5	4,195	540	14.8
Third	6,241	896	16.8	5,664	319	6.0
Fourth	7,654	660	9.4	7,129	135	1.9
Fifth	9,370	535	6.1	8,936	101	1.1
Sixth	10,995	227	2.1	10,673	− 95	− 0.9
Seventh	13,002	252	2.0	12,479	−271	− 2.1
Eighth	15,488	76	0.5	15,242	−170	− 1.1
Ninth	19,917	260	1.3	19,660	3	−−
Highest	38,635	− 158	− 0.4	38,589	−204	− 0.5
All	$ 7,470	$ 911	13.9%	$ 6,873	$314	4.8%

Money Income/Needs

Decile 1972 Money Income	50 Percent Rebate Rate			25 Percent Rebate Rate		
	Mean Income	Absolute Change	Percent Change	Mean Income	Absolute Change	Percent Change
Lowest	$ 1.47	$.67	83.8%	$ 1.06	$.26	32.5%
Second	2.01	.66	48.9	1.64	.29	21.5
Third	2.36	.52	28.3	2.06	.22	12.0
Fourth	2.76	.40	16.9	2.49	.13	5.5
Fifth	3.14	.31	11.0	2.86	.03	1.1
Sixth	3.45	.15	4.5	3.28	−.02	− 0.6
Seventh	4.08	.22	5.7	3.97	.11	2.8
Eighth	4.64	.07	1.5	4.58	.01	0.2
Ninth	5.65	.10	1.8	5.52	−.03	− 0.5
Highest	11.29	.02	0.2	11.26	−.01	− 0.1
All	$ 3.20	$.42	15.1%	$ 2.94	$.16	5.8%

procedure as at the end of Section III in comparing the relative efficiency of the existing welfare programs and a credit income rebate plan with a 25 percent rebate rate, we find similar results for elderly families as for the entire sample, as Tables 3.15 through 3.18 indicate. A credit income rebate plan would cover many more elderly families (including all elderly families in the two lowest non-welfare money income/needs deciles) than existing welfare programs, but at a significantly lower average payment than received by elderly families who did manage to qualify for welfare in 1972.[1] The lesson is clear. A credit income rebate plan with a 25 percent rebate rate in place of existing welfare programs would increase the average income of elderly families by approximately five percent, but only at the expense of some fortunate families who now are covered by such welfare programs.

SUMMARY

This analysis attempts to evaluate some of the aspects of a particular income maintenance program -- one that would have the government return to the individual as a cash subsidy some percent of his unused exemptions and deductions allotted to him under the Federal individual income tax laws. We find that a plan of this sort would reach virtually all needy families. Furthermore, as a replacement for existing public noncontributory welfare programs, a credit income rebate plan would significantly increase the incomes of the lowest income families, especially the low income elderly. However, if the aggregate value of payments is kept roughly equivalent to that of the existing programs, families who currently receive welfare would suffer a substantial decline in payments. Despite this, a credit income rebate plan has several potential advantages over alternative income maintenance programs. Most notably, its coverage of needy families is greater, it is more efficient to administer and, unlike several existing welfare programs, it would not eliminate work incentives.

_____

[1] Appendix 3.3 discusses how current elderly welfare recipients would fare under a credit income rebate plan.

TABLE 3.15

Distribution of Welfare Payments by
No Welfare Money Income Deciles, 1972
For Families With Head Aged 65 Years or More

Decile 1972 No Welfare Money Income	Unweighted Number of Current Welfare Recipients	Weighted Percent of All Welfare Recipients	Weighted Percent of Elderly Families in Decile	Mean Welfare Payment
Lowest	68	52.3%	35.6%	$1,280
Second	19	17.3	12.2	1,657
Third	15	15.3	13.6	3,537
Fourth	5	5.8	8.2	2,192
Fifth	2	1.0	2.1	1,001
Sixth	3	3.4	8.9	1,952
Seventh	1	0.1	3.6	834
Eighth	2	2.3	10.8	1,553
Ninth	0	--	--	---
Highest	3	2.6	18.3	1,363
All	118	100.0%	16.0%	$1,771

TABLE 3.16

Distribution of Credit Income Rebate by
No Welfare Money Income Deciles, 1972
For Families With Head Aged 65 Years or More

Rebate Rate = 25%

Decile 1972 No Welfare Money Income	Unweighted Number of Credit Income Rebate Recipients	Weighted Percent of All Credit Income Rebate Recipients	Weighted Percent of Elderly Families in Decile	Mean Credit Income Rebate
Lowest	175	29.6%	100.0%	$810
Second	142	28.5	99.3	730
Third	87	19.7	87.0	769
Fourth	51	10.3	73.1	668
Fifth	24	4.9	52.0	686
Sixth	15	3.3	42.9	726
Seventh	9	1.7	42.8	508
Eighth	6	1.5	34.6	695
Ninth	3	0.6	23.5	818
Highest	1	0.2	8.9	513
All	513	100.0%	79.8%	$748

TABLE 3.17

Distribution of Welfare Payments,
by No Welfare Money Income/Needs Deciles,
Families With Head Aged 65 or More, 1972

Decile 1972 No Welfare Money Income/Needs	Unweighted Number of Welfare Recipients	Weighted Percent of All Welfare Recipients	Weighted Percent of All Elderly Families in Decile	Mean Welfare Payment
Lowest	73	57.9%	52.7%	$ 1,517
Second	15	16.5	14.8	2,279
Third	14	11.5	11.0	1,877
Fourth	4	4.2	5.4	2,516
Fifth	4	4.3	9.5	3,267
Sixth	2	2.1	5.0	733
Seventh	2	2.5	5.3	1,241
Eighth	1	1.0	2.9	1,968
Ninth	2	1.0	3.9	217
Highest	1	1.0	4.1	2,000
All	118	100.0%	16.0%	$1,771

TABLE 3.18

Distribution of Credit Income Rebate
by No Welfare Money Income/Needs Deciles,
Families With Head Aged 65 Years or More, 1972

Rebate Rate = 25%

Decile 1972 No Welfare Money Income/Needs	Unweighted Number of Credit Income Rebate Recipients	Weighted Percent of All Credit Income Rebate Recipients	Weighted Percent of All Elderly Families in Decile	Mean Credit Income Rebate
Lowest	137	21.5%	100.0%	$971
Second	112	21.7	100.0	807
Third	97	19.9	96.4	707
Fourth	62	14.0	91.3	593
Fifth	36	8.1	90.9	691
Sixth	24	5.1	63.4	517
Seventh	20	4.3	46.1	650
Eighth	12	2.6	30.8	441
Ninth	10	2.2	42.3	697
Highest	3	0.7	10.6	567
All	513	100.0%	79.8%	$748

References

David, Martin and Leuthold, Jane, "Formulas for Income Maintenance: Their Distribution Impact," in Boulding, Kenneth and Pfaff, Martin, eds., Redistribution to the Rich and the Poor: The Grants Economics of Income Distribution. Belmont, California: Wadsworth Publishing Company, 1972.

Fried, Edward R., et al., Setting National Priorities: The 1974 Budget. Washington, D. C.: The Brookings Institution, 1973.

Friedman, Milton, Capitalism and Freedom. Chicago: The University of Chicago Press, 1962.

J. K. Lasser's Your Income Tax. New York: Simon and Schuster, Inc., 1972.

Morgan, James N., et al., A Panel Study of Income Dynamics: Study Design, Procedures, Available Data. Ann Arbor: Survey Research Center, Institute for Social Research, 1972.

APPENDIX 3.1

DISTRIBUTION OF CURRENT WELFARE PAYMENTS

Tables A3.1A and A3.1B show the distribution of public noncontributory welfare payments by 1972 income deciles, for all families and for the elderly families in the sample. They are meant to provide a comparison to Tables 3.3 and
3.10 in the text. It should be noted that there is a correlation between the
amount of welfare payments a family receives and its income decile, since welfare payments are a component of family money income.

TABLE A3.1(a)

Distribution of Public Noncontributory
Welfare Payments, All Families, 1972

Money Income

Decile 1972 Money Income	Unweighted Number of Families Receiving Welfare	Weighted Percent of All Families Receiving Welfare	Weighted Percent of Families in Income Decile	Mean Welfare Payment
Lowest	237	23.5%	25.0%	$1,211
Second	190	19.9	21.2	1,896
Third	161	16.1	17.1	2,251
Fourth	94	10.6	11.2	2,455
Fifth	53	7.2	7.7	2,039
Sixth	46	5.4	5.7	2,329
Seventh	30	4.9	5.3	3,016
Eighth	27	5.4	5.7	2,226
Ninth	17	4.0	4.2	3,217
Highest	15	3.0	3.2	2,096
All	870	100.0%	10.6%	$2,017

Money Income/Needs

Decile 1972 Money Income/ Needs	Unweighted Number of Families Receiving Welfare	Weighted Percent of All Families Receiving Welfare	Weighted Percent of Families in Income Decile	Mean Welfare Payment
Lowest	413	32.7%	34.8%	$1,720
Second	174	21.1	22.4	2,050
Third	109	12.8	13.5	1,922
Fourth	62	9.9	10.5	2,094
Fifth	31	5.1	5.4	2,728
Sixth	34	7.5	7.9	1,871
Seventh	12	2.0	2.2	1,872
Eighth	15	3.6	3.9	1,799
Ninth	12	2.8	2.9	2,732
Highest	8	2.6	2.8	4,288
All	870	100.0%	10.6%	$2,017

TABLE A3.1(b)

Distribution of Public Noncontributory Welfare Payments,
Families With Head Aged 65 Years or More, 1972

Money Income

Decile 1972 Money Income	Unweighted Number of Families Receiving Welfare	Weighted Percent of All Families Receiving Welfare	Weighted Percent of Families in Income Decile	Mean Welfare Payment
Lowest	53	39.0%	23.2%	$ 786
Second	21	19.0	14.2	1,542
Third	15	13.3	13.6	1,890
Fourth	9	9.7	13.5	2,878
Fifth	6	5.9	12.0	2,763
Sixth	4	4.3	10.6	3,940
Seventh	4	3.9	18.4	4,324
Eighth	2	2.1	9.9	4,205
Ninth	1	1.0	9.8	2,580
Highest	3	2.6	18.3	1,363
All	118	100.0%	16.0%	$1,770

Money Income/Needs

Decile 1972 Money Income/ Needs	Unweighted Number of Families Receiving Welfare	Weighted Percent of All Families Receiving Welfare	Weighted Percent of Families in Income Decile	Mean Welfare Payment
Lowest	47	35.0%	32.8%	$ 809
Second	23	18.0	16.6	1,288
Third	14	11.7	12.0	1,807
Fourth	12	11.1	13.7	2,812
Fifth	5	6.2	17.3	4,669
Sixth	9	9.9	21.3	2,237
Seventh	0	---	---	---
Eighth	3	3.4	8.1	2,352
Ninth	3	2.3	8.8	4,733
Highest	2	2.3	7.1	1,207
All	118	100.0%	16.0%	$1,770

APPENDIX 3.2

DISTRIBUTION OF CREDIT INCOME FOR HEAD AND WIFE

As shown in Table 3.3 of the text, a credit income rebate plan would cover a nontrivial number of families in the higher money income/needs decile -- 4.8 percent of the families in the highest decile, 6.9 percent in the second highest. These figures might seem high, and one could reasonably object to a credit income rebate plan on these grounds. Actually, these figures reflect a more fundamental question, namely, what is the proper measure by which to judge a person's economic position? Should it be his own individual economic status or that of his family? For example, should a 22-year-old unemployed person, living at home with his high income parents, be considered well-off or not? There has been, and still is, considerable controversy over the answer to this question. Conventionally, however, the "family" has been considered the proper unit by which to measure an individual's economic position. Accordingly, family money income and family money income/needs are the ranking measures used in the text. However, a credit income rebate plan considers the individual alone (if not claimed as a dependent by someone else) to be the unit upon which to judge his economic status. As a result, many of the higher income families who qualify for a credit income rebate do so as a consequence of having some low income adult other than the head and wife (most likely an offspring of the head and wife) in the family unit. An idea of the magnitude of this effect can be obtained by comparing Appendix Table A3.2 with Table 3.3 in the text. As would be expected, the number of families in the higher income deciles which qualify for a credit income rebate by virtue of the head and wife's taxable income alone drops significantly.

TABLE A3.2

Distribution of Credit Income of Head and
Wife Only, All Families, 1972

Money Income

Decile 1972 Money Income	Unweighted Number of Families With Credit Income	Weighted Percent of All Families With Credit Income	Weighted Percent of All Families in Income Decile	Mean Credit Income
Lowest	622	34.5%	94.7%	$2,373
Second	443	25.3	69.5	2,584
Third	319	16.9	46.4	2,466
Fourth	172	10.4	28.7	2,450
Fifth	67	4.6	12.5	2,662
Sixth	57	3.4	9.5	2,484
Seventh	33	2.3	6.2	2,369
Eighth	15	1.3	3.5	2,752
Ninth	12	1.2	3.4	2,368
Highest	1	0.1	0.3	3,550
All	1,741	100.0%	27.5%	$2,473

Money Income/Needs

Decile 1972 Money Income/ Needs	Unweighted Number of Families With Credit Income	Weighted Percent of All Families With Credit Income	Weighted Percent of All Families in Income Decile	Mean Credit Income
Lowest	894	34.4%	94.6%	$2,657
Second	377	23.6	65.0	2,506
Third	199	15.2	41.8	2,430
Fourth	113	10.4	28.6	2,316
Fifth	52	5.5	15.1	2,298
Sixth	43	4.2	11.5	2,025
Seventh	29	2.8	7.6	2,322
Eighth	20	2.2	6.0	1,906
Ninth	11	1.3	3.6	2,379
Highest	3	0.4	1.1	2,035
All	1,741	100.0%	27.5%	$2,473

APPENDIX 3.3

CREDIT INCOME REBATES TO CURRENT WELFARE RECIPIENTS

Appendix Tables 3.3A through 3.3D show how current welfare recipients would be affected by a credit income rebate plan. With a 25 percent rebate rate, families who currently receive welfare would suffer a 63 percent decrease in welfare payments. For families in the lowest money income/needs decile, average rebate payments would be only 47 percent of their current average welfare payments. With a 50 percent rebate rate, these families would receive average rebate payments equal to 94 percent of their average welfare payments. But a 50 percent rebate rate would increase the welfare bill substantially. (Unless Social Security payments were made a component of taxable income. See Appendix 3.5.)

For elderly families who currently qualify for public noncontributory welfare payments, reductions in payments would not be as great. With a 25 percent rebate rate, average rebate payments are 56 percent of current welfare payments. More importantly, elderly families in the lowest money income/needs decile who currently qualify for welfare would receive, on the average, rebate payments equal to 74 percent of current welfare payments. With a 50 percent rebate rate, these same elderly families would experience a 47 percent increase in payments. Overall, elderly families who currently qualify for welfare would receive a 12 percent increase in payments, on the average, with a 50 percent rebate rate.

TABLE A3.3(a)

Distribution of Credit Income Rebate to Current
Welfare Recipients, by No Welfare Deciles, All Families, 1972

Rebate Rate = 25%

Money Income

Decile	Unweighted Number of Welfare Recipients Who Qualify For Rebate	Weighted Percent of Welfare Recipients in Decile Who Qualify For Rebate	Mean Rebate for Welfare Recipients Who Qualify	Mean Rebate For All Welfare Recipients	Percent of Mean Welfare Payment
Lowest	451	100.0%	$ 985	$ 985	45.5%
Second	125	90.3	875	790	40.6
Third	80	85.6	883	756	31.2
Fourth	31	62.5	704	440	23.5
Fifth	25	59.4	749	445	31.8
Sixth	15	60.9	792	482	29.1
Seventh	14	60.8	623	379	23.9
Eighth	8	51.5	582	300	20.5
Ninth	7	49.3	441	217	15.9
Highest	2	20.7	363	75	3.7
All	758	84.2%	$ 894	$ 753	37.3%

Money Income/Needs

Decile	Unweighted Number of Welfare Recipients Who Qualify For Rebate	Weighted Percent of Welfare Recipients in Decile Who Qualify For Rebate	Mean Rebate For Welfare Recipients Who Qualify	Mean Rebate For All Welfare Recipients	Percent of Mean Welfare Payment
Lowest	561	100.0%	$1,047	$1,047	47.2%
Second	89	86.2	768	662	37.5
Third	48	70.5	665	469	20.9
Fourth	24	59.3	599	355	21.0
Fifth	12	70.6	592	418	22.0
Sixth	10	58.4	407	237	17.3
Seventh	4	23.8	462	110	7.0
Eighth	4	51.6	573	295	23.8
Ninth	3	29.8	478	143	7.7
Highest	3	76.3	473	361	20.4
All	758	84.2%	$ 894	$ 753	37.3%

TABLE A3.3(b)

Distribution of Credit Income Rebate to Current
Welfare Recipients, by No Welfare Deciles, All Families, 1972

Rebate Rate = 25%

Money Income

Decile	Unweighted Number of Welfare Recipients Who Qualify For Rebate	Weighted Percent of Welfare Recipients in Decile Who Qualify For Rebate	Mean Rebate for Welfare Recipients Who Qualify	Mean Rebate For All Welfare Recipients	Percent of Mean Welfare Payment
Lowest	451	100.0%	$1,970	$1,970	91.0%
Second	125	90.3	1,749	1,579	81.1
Third	80	85.6	1,767	1,512	62.3
Fourth	31	62.5	1,408	880	47.0
Fifth	25	59.4	1,498	890	63.7
Sixth	15	60.9	1,584	964	58.2
Seventh	14	60.8	1,246	758	47.8
Eighth	8	51.5	1,164	599	41.0
Ninth	7	49.3	881	435	31.9
Highest	2	20.7	727	151	7.4
All	758	84.2%	$1,789	$1,506	74.7%

Money Income/Needs

Decile	Unweighted Number of Welfare Recipients Who Qualify For Rebate	Weighted Percent of Welfare Recipients in Decile Who Qualify For Rebate	Mean Rebate for Welfare Recipients Who Qualify	Mean Rebate For All Welfare Recipients	Percent of Mean Welfare Payment
Lowest	561	100.0%	$2,094	$2,094	94.4%
Second	89	86.2	1,536	1,324	75.1
Third	48	70.5	1,329	937	41.7
Fourth	24	59.3	1,199	710	41.9
Fifth	12	70.6	1,184	836	44.0
Sixth	10	58.4	813	475	34.7
Seventh	4	23.8	924	220	14.0
Eighth	4	51.6	1,145	591	47.7
Ninth	3	29.8	957	285	15.4
Highest	3	76.3	946	721	40.7
All	758	84.2%	$1,179	$1,506	74.7%

TABLE A3.3(c)

Distribution of Credit Income Rebate to Current Welfare Recipients,
By No Welfare Deciles, Families With Head Aged 65 Years or More, 1972

Rebate Rate = 25%

Money Income

Decile	Unweighted Number of Welfare Recipients Who Qualify For Rebate	Weighted Percent of Welfare Recipients in Decile Who Qualify For Rebate	Mean Rebate For Welfare Recipients Who Qualify	Mean Rebate For All Welfare Recipients	Percent of Mean Welfare Payment
Lowest	68	100.0%	$1,005	$1,005	78.5%
Second	19	100.0	1,104	1,104	66.6
Third	15	100.0	1,200	1,200	33.9
Fourth	5	100.0	673	673	30.7
Fifth	2	100.0	1,136	1,136	113.5
Sixth	3	100.0	751	751	38.5
Seventh	1	100.0	1,638	1,638	196.4
Eighth	1	57.0	850	485	31.2
Ninth	--	----	---	---	---
Highest	1	48.7	513	249	18.3
All	115	97.7%	$1,018	$ 994	56.1%

Money Income/Needs

Decile	Unweighted Number of Welfare Recipients Who Qualify For Rebate	Weighted Percent of Welfare Recipients in Decile Who Qualify For Rebate	Mean Rebate For Welfare Recipients Who Qualify	Mean Rebate For All Welfare Recipients	Percent of Mean Welfare Payment
Lowest	73	100.0%	$1,116	$1,116	73.6%
Second	15	100.0	1,106	1,106	48.5
Third	14	100.0	803	803	42.8
Fourth	4	100.0	864	864	34.3
Fifth	4	100.0	845	845	25.9
Sixth	2	100.0	247	247	33.7
Seventh	1	46.7 '	700	327	26.3
Eighth	1	100.0	513	513	26.1
Ninth	--	---	---	---	---
Highest	1	100.0	513	513	25.7
All	115	97.7%	$1,018	$ 994	56.1%

TABLE A3.3(d)

Distribution of Credit Income Rebate to Current Welfare Recipients,
By No Welfare Deciles, Families With Head Aged 65 Years or More, 1972

Rebate Rate = 50%

Money Income

Decile	Unweighted Number of Welfare Recipients Who Qualify For Rebate	Weighted Percent of Welfare Recipients in Decile Who Qualify For Rebate	Mean Rebate For All Welfare Recipients Who Qualify	Mean Rebate For All Welfare Recipients	Percent of Mean Welfare Payment
Lowest	68	100.0%	$2,011	$2,011	157.1%
Second	19	100.0	2,207	2,207	133.2
Third	15	100.0	2,400	2,400	67.9
Fourth	5	100.0	1,347	1,347	61.4
Fifth	2	100.0	2,273	2,273	227.1
Sixth	3	100.0	1,501	1,501	76.9
Seventh	1	100.0	3,275	3,275	446.6
Eighth	1	57.0	1,700	969	62.4
Ninth	--	---	---	---	---
Highest	1	48.7	1,025	499	36.6
All	115	97.7%	$2,036	$1,988	112.3%

Money Income/Needs

Decile	Recipients Who Qualify For Rebate	Weighted Percent of Welfare Recipients in Decile Who Qualify For Rebate	Mean Rebate For Welfare Recipients Who Qualify	Mean Rebate For All Welfare Recipients	Percent of Mean Welfare Payment
Lowest	73	100.0%	$2,232	$2,232	147.1%
Second	15	100.0	2,212	2,212	97.1
Third	14	100.0	1,606	1,606	85.6
Fourth	4	100.0	1,728	1,728	68.7
Fifth	4	100.0	1,690	1,690	51.7
Sixth	2	100.0	493	493	67.3
Seventh	1	46.7	1,400	654	52.7
Eighth	1	100.0	1,025	1,025	52.1
Ninth	--	---	---	---	--
Highest	1	100.0	1,025	1,025	51.3
All	115	97.7%	$2,036	$1,988	112.3%

APPENDIX 3.4

MORE ON THE EFFICIENCY OF A CREDIT INCOME REBATE
PLAN VERSUS THE CURRENT WELFARE PROGRAMS

A credit income rebate plan appears to be an efficient method of reaching virtually all the needy families, especially when compared to the performance of the existing welfare programs. However, there is one criterion of efficiency by which the current welfare programs seem to perform as well as, if not better than, a credit income rebate plan. This criterion is the percent of total welfare payments which are received by the most needy families. Based on the figures in Tables 3.6 through 3.9 in the text, Appendix Table 3.4A shows the percent of current welfare payments which are received by families in each income decile as compared to a credit income rebate plan. As can be seen, families in the two lowest money income/needs (excluding welfare payments) deciles receive 70 percent of current total welfare payments as compared to only 60 percent of total rebate payments. From these figures, one would have to conclude that the current welfare programs are more efficient in funneling a given amount of money to the most needy.

However, the figures for the credit income rebate plan are heavily influenced by the effect of elderly families. Most elderly families are eligible for a credit income rebate, and many are eligible for large amounts. Furthermore, many elderly families who are eligible do not rank so poorly on the money/income needs standard used in this study. These two reasons explain much of the relatively poor performance by a credit income rebate plan. Table B of this appendix shows the relative efficiency of the two programs when elderly families are excluded. Both programs direct 70 percent of the total money received by non-elderly families to those families in the two lowest money income/needs decile.

From these figures it remains unclear which program is more efficient in this respect. Two additional points should be mentioned. One, if Social Security payments or some fraction of imputed rental income were included in taxable income (see Appendix 3.5) as a reform to reduce the number of potentially non-needy families who would qualify for a credit income rebate, the performance of a credit income rebate plan would presumably improve significantly. The truly relevant figures one would want to compare are the percentages of budgeted costs which went to each income decile under the two programs. If the alleged savings in administrative costs of a credit income rebate plan are indeed real, then such a program might clearly be more efficient than the current welfare programs in directing a higher percent of total money spent on welfare programs to the most needy families.

TABLE A3.4(a)

Percent of Total Welfare Payments Received by
Each No Welfare Decile, for Current Welfare Programs
And a Credit Income Rebate Program, All Families, 1972

Money Income

Decile	Current Welfare Payments		Credit Income Rebates, 25 Percent Rebate Rate	
	Weighted Total Welfare Payments	Weighted Percent of Total	Weighted Total Rebate Payments	Weighted Percent of Total
Lowest	$14,720,000	45.9%	$11,075,000	35.7%
Second	5,336,000	16.6	7,022,000	22.6
Third	5,027,000	15.7	5,240,000	16.9
Fourth	1,791,000	5.6	2,714,000	8.7
Fifth	1,047,000	3.3	1,591,000	5.1
Sixth	930,000	2.9	1,230,000	4.0
Seventh	831,000	2.6	827,000	2.7
Eighth	946,000	2.9	636,000	2.1
Ninth	608,000	1.9	445,000	1.4
Highest	835,000	2.6	233,000	0.8
All	$32,072,000	100.0%	$31,015,000	100.0%

Money Income/Needs

Decile	Current Welfare Payments		Credit Income Rebates, 25 Percent Rebate Rate	
	Weighted Total Welfare Payments	Weighted Percent of Total	Weighted Total Rebate Payments	Weighted Percent of Total
Lowest	$18,021,000	56.2%	$12,281,000	39.6%
Second	4,343,000	13.5	6,385,000	20.6
Third	3,625,000	11.3	4,496,000	14.5
Fourth	1,872,000	5.8	2,762,000	8.9
Fifth	1,286,000	4.0	1,796,000	5.8
Sixth	791,000	2.5	1,174,000	3.8
Seventh	770,000	2.4	842,000	2.7
Eighth	389,000	1.2	554,000	1.8
Ninth	629,000	2.0	518,000	1.7
Highest	344,000	1.1	204,000	0.7
All	$32,072,000	100.0%	$31,015,000	100.0%

TABLE A3.4(b)

Percent of Total Welfare Payments Received by
Each No Welfare Decile, for Current Welfare Programs
And a Credit Income Rebate Program, Nonelderly Families, 1972

Money Income

Decile	Current Welfare Payments		Credit Income Rebates, 25 Percent Rebate Rate	
	Weighted Total Welfare Payments	Weighted Percent of Total	Weighted Total Rebate Payments	Weighted Percent of Total
Lowest	$11,823,000	48.4%	$ 5,928,000	39.8%
Second	4,095,000	16.8	2,559,000	17.2
Third	2,695,000	11.0	1,993,000	13.4
Fourth	1,245,000	5.1	1,232,000	8.3
Fifth	1,005,000	4.1	868,000	5.8
Sixth	641,000	2.6	713,000	4.8
Seventh	826,000	3.4	647,000	4.3
Eighth	791,000	3.2	413,000	2.8
Ninth	608,000	2.5	344,000	2.3
Highest	681,000	2.8	205,000	1.4
All	$24,416,000	100.0%	$14,908,000	100.0%

Money Income/Needs

Decile	Current Welfare Payments		Credit Income Rebates, 25 Percent Rebate Rate	
	Weighted Total Welfare Payments	Weighted Percent of Total	Weighted Total Rebate Payments	Weighted Percent of Total
Lowest	$14,315,000	58.6%	$ 7,790,000	52.3%
Second	2,760,000	11.3	2,606,000	17.5
Third	2,713,000	11.1	1,474,000	9.9
Fourth	1,427,000	5.8	979,000	6.6
Fifth	692,000	2.8	594,000	4.0
Sixth	728,000	3.0	609,000	4.1
Seventh	638,000	2.6	236,000	1.6
Eighth	287,000	1.2	307,000	2.1
Ninth	619,000	2.5	183,000	1.2
Highest	234,000	1.0	124,000	0.8
All	$24,416,000	100.0%	$14,908,000	100.0%

APPENDIX 3.5

SOCIAL SECURITY AS TAXABLE INCOME

As shown in the text, 80 percent of all elderly families qualify for a credit income rebate, including a considerable percent of those in the higher income deciles. (However, the small number of observations in these higher deciles make these estimates somewhat unreliable.) It would be reasonable to object to an income maintenance program on these grounds. Part of the problem is that Social Security payments are not taxable. This enables families with large Social Security payments (most likely elderly families) to qualify for welfare payments under a credit income rebate plan. Probably the easiest solution to this problem is to make Social Security payments a component of taxable income. (If this were done, one might also want to make Social Security contributions tax deductible.) Tables A3.5A through A3.5D show what effect this would have on the distribution of credit income. Overall, ten percent fewer families would be eligible for a credit income rebate, including 26 percent fewer elderly families. However, the number of families in the two lowest money income/needs deciles who qualify for a rebate would be virtually unaffected by such a change. Furthermore, such a reform would allow a higher rebate rate with no increase in the total value of welfare payments. If Social Security payments were included as taxable income and a 25 percent rebate rate were assumed, average family money income would decline by $80. If a 50 percent rebate rate were assumed, average income would increase by $50. This suggests that with a rebate rate somewhere in the neighborhood of 40 percent, a credit income rebate plan would cost roughly the same as current public noncontributory welfare programs. If so, then the problem of current welfare recipients suffering sharp declines in welfare payments under a credit income rebate plan would be considerably lessened. In addition, if this change in the tax laws were incorporated, elderly families would still benefit from the replacement of existing welfare programs with a credit income

rebate plan costing roughly the same. With Social Security payments as taxable
income and a 25 percent rebate rate, average income of elderly families decreases
by only $27. With a 50 percent rate, average income of the elderly increases by
$230. This would indicate that if the savings from including Social Security
payments as taxable income were translated into a rebate rate of approximately
40 percent, the economic position of the elderly would improve under a credit income rebate plan. Though this is all conjecture, it would seem to be a fruitful
area for further research.

TABLE A3.5(a)

Distribution of Credit Income with Social Security
Payments as a Component of Taxable Income, All Families, 1972

Money Income

Decile 1972 Money Income	Unweighted Number of Families with Credit Income	Weighted Percent of all Families with Credit Income	Weighted Percent of Families in Decile	Mean Credit Income
Lowest	615	35.7%	92.9%	$1,829
Second	397	22.5	58.6	1,997
Third	277	12.0	31.3	2,299
Fourth	172	9.3	24.2	2,070
Fifth	83	4.4	11.6	2,271
Sixth	78	4.4	11.5	2,273
Seventh	51	3.6	9.3	2,756
Eighth	37	3.1	8.1	2,229
Ninth	35	2.8	7.3	1,840
Highest	21	2.1	5.3	1,266
All	1766	100.0%	26.0%	$2,013

Money Income/Needs

Decile 1972 Money Income/ Needs	Unweighted Number of Families with Credit Income	Weighted Percent of all Families with Credit Income	Weighted Percent of Families in Decile	Mean Credit Income
Lowest	905	36.4%	94.7%	$2,516
Second	381	24.9	64.9	1,760
Third	193	13.3	34.5	1,531
Fourth	94	7.0	18.3	1,951
Fifth	53	5.0	12.9	1,850
Sixth	53	5.3	13.7	1,750
Seventh	29	2.3	6.1	1,663
Eighth	23	2.1	5.4	1,749
Ninth	20	2.1	5.3	1,734
Highest	15	1.7	4.4	1,431
All	1766	100.0%	26.0%	$2,013

160

TABLE A3.5(b)

Distribution of Credit Income with Social Security
Payments as a Component of Taxable Income, Families
With Head Aged 65 Years or More, 1972

Money Income

Decile 1972 Money Income	Unweighted Number of Families with Credit Income	Weighted Percent of all Families with Credit Income	Weighted Percent of Families in Decile	Mean Credit Income
Lowest	192	46.1%	98.7%	$1,804
Second	93	26.6	71.6	1,520
Third	35	10.1	37.2	1,731
Fourth	25	7.3	36.9	1,559
Fifth	12	4.0	29.6	2,472
Sixth	7	2.1	18.9	2,057
Seventh	7	2.1	35.3	3,711
Eighth	3	0.9	14.8	2,925
Ninth	3	0.8	21.2	3,177
Highest	1	0.3	8.9	2,050
All	378	100.0%	57.2%	$1,797

Money Income/Needs

Decile 1972 Money Income/ Needs	Unweighted Number of Families with Credit Income	Weighted Percent of all Families with Credit Income	Weighted Percent of Families in Decile	Mean Credit Income
Lowest	136	29.8%	100.0%	$2,382
Second	111	30.1	98.9	1,478
Third	58	16.6	60.5	1,170
Fourth	27	8.9	39.2	1,943
Fifth	14	4.3	42.9	1,674
Sixth	13	4.4	33.7	2,046
Seventh	6	2.0	15.1	1,560
Eighth	4	1.1	9.4	2,559
Ninth	7	2.3	30.6	1,842
Highest	2	0.5	5.4	2,243
All	378	100.0%	57.2%	$1,797

TABLE A3.5(c)

Distribution of Credit Income with Social Security Payments
as Taxable Income, By No Welfare Deciles, All Families, 1972

Money Income

Decile	Unweighted Number of Families with Credit Income	Weighted Percent of all Families with Credit Income	Weighted Percent of Families in Decile	Mean Credit Income
Lowest	760	37.7%	98.2%	$2,453
Second	369	23.9	62.0	1,549
Third	237	13.4	34.8	1,869
Fourth	134	7.0	18.1	1,814
Fifth	80	4.4	11.4	1,990
Sixth	62	3.6	9.4	2,105
Seventh	43	3.1	8.0	2,160
Eighth	31	2.8	7.5	1,844
Ninth	31	2.3	5.7	1,693
Highest	19	2.0	5.2	1,200
All	1766	100.0%	26.0%	$2,013

Money Income/Needs

Decile	Unweighted Number of Families with Credit Income	Weighted Percent of all Families with Credit Income	Weighted Percent of Families in Decile	Mean Credit Income
Lowest	927	38.0%	99.3%	$2,871
Second	400	25.2	66.5	1,494
Third	185	14.3	36.7	1,237
Fourth	80	6.1	15.9	1,702
Fifth	48	4.6	12.1	1,474
Sixth	46	4.4	11.3	1,769
Seventh	26	2.0	5.1	1,617
Eighth	22	2.1	5.4	1,925
Ninth	19	2.0	5.2	1,527
Highest	13	1.3	3.5	1,270
All	1766	100.0%	26.0%	$2,013

TABLE A3.5(d)

Distribution of Credit Income with Social Security Payments as
Taxable Income, by No Welfare Deciles, Families with
Head Aged 65 Years or More, 1972

Money Income

Decile	Unweighted Number of Families with Credit Income	Weighted Per-cent of all Families with Credit Income	Weighted Percent of Families in Decile	Mean Credit Income
Lowest	175	41.3%	100.0%	$2,130
Second	113	31.4	78.4	1,357
Third	42	13.7	43.6	1,824
Fourth	22	6.0	30.5	1,442
Fifth	10	3.2	24.6	1,968
Sixth	6	1.9	17.6	1,667
Seventh	4	1.0	18.8	1,190
Eighth	3	0.9	15.6	3,401
Ninth	2	0.4	12.6	2,985
Highest	1	0.3	8.9	2,050
All	378	100.0%	51.5%	$1,797

Money Income/Needs

Decile	Unweighted Number of Families with Credit Income	Weighted Per-cent of all Families with Credit Income	Weighted Percent of Families in Decile	Mean Credit Income
Lowest	137	30.0%	100.0%	$2,873
Second	109	30.0	98.9	1,450
Third	71	20.5	71.2	959
Fourth	21	6.9	32.6	1,493
Fifth	15	4.8	39.1	1,241
Sixth	8	2.5	22.8	1,805
Seventh	6	2.0	15.2	1,560
Eighth	3	0.9	7.8	2,293
Ninth	6	1.9	25.8	1,746
Highest	2	0.5	5.5	2,243
All	378	100.0%	51.5%	$1,797

Chapter 4

MARITAL DISRUPTION: SOME SOCIAL AND ECONOMIC CONSEQUENCES
Robert Hampton

INTRODUCTION

Recent analysis of the Panel Study of Income Dynamics has indicated that changes in family composition are a major factor in changing economic well-being of families. Some changes in family composition are fairly routine life cycle progressions such as births and children growing up and leaving home. However, some less routine alterations in family structure, such as departure of either the head or spouse from a household, merit special study. The primary concern of this chapter is with the impact of separation and divorce on husbands and wives.

Separations, like many other changes in family composition, involve an interrelated set of decisions by which people move toward a satisfactory equilibrium in family, job, and other social and economic relationships. An important item to bear in mind is that not all separations involve the irrevocable decision to terminate a marriage. Some separations, resulting from the institutionalization of a spouse or a job-related absence from the household are initially reported as temporary but become permanent, while in some cases separated couples are reunited in subsequent waves of the study.

A thorough investigation of the sequences of interrelated decisions concerning separations is beyond the scope of this study. Morgan has reminded us that any joint decision can be interpreted, studied, and predicted as though it were a set of conditional decisions in almost any order.[1] We can, for example, study decisions to change marital status and then, given the result of this decision, we can study decisions about living arrangements, labor force participation, and other economic behavior. Our purpose in this chapter is more limited -- to provide an overview of some factors which predict separation and some ways in which separation has an impact on the former spouses.

---

[1] Morgan (1974), p. 99.

This chapter is divided into two sections. In Section I the characteristics of those who become separated or divorced are compared with those who maintain a stable marriage. For this analysis, we restrict the sample to families with both husband and wife present at the beginning of the study, the vast majority of whom maintained stable marital bonds throughout the study. Thus we have not included the newly-formed families of split-offs. We also have excluded families where the head was over age 55, a group in which separations and divorce are quite infrequent.

Because we are interested in comparing the experiences of husbands and wives, we have further limited our analysis in Section II to couples for whom the separation is clearly related to a decision to terminate a marriage and for whom we have six complete interviews for each spouse.[1] The final decision regarding the inclusion or exclusion of a particular couple was often made only after consulting the interview schedules for marginal comments which might help to explain the reasons for the separation. By limiting our analysis in this way, we can see how each member fared over a length of time -- which could be quite short for those separating in the later years of the panel. We are able to determine which spouses remained separated, remarried others, or if the couple was reunited. Because we have narrowed the sample down to matched pairs of separated husbands and wives, we have only 133 couples. Given the relatively small sample size, highly detailed multivariate analysis is likely to result in cell sizes too small to be statistically reliable. Therefore, our major concern in Section II is to describe the situation of many of the separated couples in 1973.

ANALYSIS

I. Multivariate Analysis of Marital Stability

We have run two Multiple Classification Analyses to examine the characteristics of couples who remained together during the study versus those who were separated.[2] A great many characteristics may be associated with marital disruption. The variables included in our models are based upon a review of relevant literature with certain limitations imposed by our particular data set.[3] Since

[1] Another approach to this topic would be to look at men and women who either separated or divorced during this period irrespective of whether or not their spouse's record is intact for all six years.

[2] See Appendix D for methods of assessing significance of multivariate coefficients.

[3] The variables included in this analysis draw in part upon the work of Farley (1971), Bumpass and Sweet (1972), and Cutright (1971).

family instability among blacks has been the focus of considerable research and discussion by both researchers and policy makers, we have run a separate analysis for this group.

Using MCA, we can see what variables help to explain marital stability both before and after taking into account their intercorrelation with other independent variables. For example, we can see whether age, income, and education make separate contributions in predicting marital stability or whether they explain the same part of the variance.

In our models, the dependent variable is set equal to one if the marriage is disrupted between 1969 and 1973 and equals zero if no change in marital status occurs. The mean value of the dependent variable -- 8.3 percent and 8.5 percent for the entire sample and blacks, respectively -- is equal to the percent who were married in 1968 and had a subsequent divorce or separation. The results of the MCA for predicting changes in marital status in terms of family income and other characteristics appear in Table 4.1.[1]

Perhaps few sociological findings are better established than those indicating that marriages tend to be more stable among the well-educated, well-paid, white-collar workers than among the poorly-paid, less-educated, blue-collar workers. Phillips Cutright (1971) has argued that while occupation, education, and income all affect marital stability, income is the most important factor. Our data support this argument in that income turns out to be the most important determinant of marital stability in our model.

As shown in Table 4.2, the probability of marital disruption decreases rather dramatically with rising income levels. The decision to terminate a marriage is the outcome of the level of satisfaction with the marriage and the level of constraints that inhibit marital dissolution. The higher the income, the higher the level of economic and social constraints that inhibit hasty marital breakups. At higher income levels the loss of social status to both spouses stemming from separation and divorce may also be greater than that experienced by couples who are less well off. Likewise, we know that marital satisfaction

---

[1]Transitions from one kind of family composition to another are best studied for individuals rather than families. If one starts with those families at the end of the transition period, some appear more than once in the initial state. If one starts with the initial families, then a decision must be made about which branch to follow when they split. We elected the second alternative to avoid the double counting problems and followed the husbands once the split had occurred. The only variable affected by this decision is six-year average income.

TABLE 4.1

Gross and Net Explanatory Power of Independent Variables in Regression
to Predict Whether Married Couples Will be Separated or Divorced 1968-1973[*]
(For entire sample and blacks only; head under 55)

Predictors	Total Sample		Blacks Only	
	Eta^2	$Beta^2$	Eta^2	$Beta^2$
Six year average family income	.027	.031	.058	.069
Lag between marriage and birth of first child	.014	.012	.003	.025
Age of head - 1968	.018	.010	.068	.068
Race	.000	.007	---	---
Head's education	.005	.005	.022	.024
Home ownership	.019	.004	.003	.002
Size of largest city PSU	.001	.004	.029	.039
Wife working	.004	.004	.003	.000
Head's occupation	.011	.003	.034	.029
Family size	.003	.002	.013	.098
Wife's education	.002	.002	.027	.007
Age of youngest child	.004	.002	.045	.019
Head's age at marriage	.002	.002	.006	.003
Wife's age at marriage	.000	.000	.020	.007
Age of wife	.014	.001	.078	.013
R^2 (adjusted)	.043		.288	
Number of cases	2049		575	
Mean of dependent variable	.083		.085	
Standard deviation of dependent variable	.276		.279	

[*]The full sample consists of 2049 families in which both head and wife were present in 1968, the head was less than age 55 in 1968, and in which the head did not change during the 1968-1973 period. If for any of these families the 1968 wife was not present in succeeding years because of divorce or separation then the dependent variable was set equal to one and otherwise zero. In this full sample, 201 families were coded "one."

TABLE 4.2

Unadjusted and Adjusted Means for Selected Independent Variables from Regressions
Predicting Whether Married Couples Will Become Separated 1968-1973
(Total sample)

Predictors	Number of Cases (Unweighted)	Weighted Percent	Unadjusted Mean	Adjusted Mean
6 Year Average Income				
<$3000	47	0.7	.171	.217
$3000-4999	177	4.0	.169	.182
$5000-7499	377	11.4	.162	.166
$7500-9999	405	17.7	.125	.123
$10,000-14,999	623	36.2	.061	.061
$15,000 or more	420	29.4	.040	.036
Lag Between Head's Age and Birth of First Child				
First child born 2 or more years before marriage	331	15.4	.123	.101
First child 1 year before to 1 year after marriage	558	37.7	.070	.081
First child born 2 years after marriage	320	17.2	.033	.043
First child born 3 years after marriage	152	8.5	.070	.076
First child born 4 years after marriage	80	4.8	.070	.086
First child born 5-7 years after marriage	129	7.8	.115	.139
First child born 8 or more years after marriage	115	5.4	.024	.048
Age of Head				
<25	232	10.9	.146	.113
25-34	602	28.8	.115	.116
35-44	688	34.9	.072	.074
45-54	527	25.4	.034	.044
Race				
White	1383	88.6	.084	.091
Black	575	8.0	.085	.029
Spanish American	70	2.8	.064	.009
Other	21	.7	.000	.000
Head's Education				
0-8 years	515	16.9	.103	.095
9-11	420	17.1	.101	.092
12 years	582	32.3	.076	.078
13-15 years	263	15.9	.064	.067
16+ years	244	17.0	.068	.077
NA	20	.8	.227	.267
Home Ownership				
Own	1155	66.5	.057	.072
Rent	806	30.4	.140	.108
Neither	88	2.6	.049	.026

is positively related to income.[1,2]

Premarital births, along with births which occur very early in a marriage, raise the risk of marital disruption. We find a higher probability of marital disruption among couples where the first child was born prior to marriage than among couples where the first child was born later in the marriage. One exception to this is the relatively high probability of marital disruption among couples whose first child is born five to seven years after marriage. There is no simple explanation for the relatively high probability of disruption at this point in a marriage followed by a sharp decline in the probability of disruption among couples whose first child is born after the seventh year.

As we expected, marital stability is related to the age of both husband and wife in a bivariate context. Although husband's and wife's ages are interrelated, the husband's age is more closely related to a number of other factors in our model such as income and education, so it is not surprising to find that the wife's age does not make an independent contribution.

Most studies of marital stability have reported that whites are more likely to be found in stable marriages than blacks, irrespective of the measure of stability used.[3] We find virtually no black/white difference in marital stability in a bivariate context. However, when we consider other factors, we find that whites have a higher probability of marital disruption than blacks (see Table 4.2); that is, once income, home ownership, and family size differences are taken into account, all of which are relatively highly correlated with race, the percentage of black families experiencing divorce or separation is six percentage points less than for whites. This suggests that it is the economic characteristics of blacks[4] that lead to divorce and separation rates that are as high as or higher than those of whites. Once these economic characteristics are taken into account by regression, we find that the blacks' rate of marital disruption is *lower* than that for whites.

II. Marital Stability Among Blacks

Our model explains the marital stability of our subsample of black families

---

[1] Cutright (1973) has discussed the issue of marital satisfaction being a multidimensional phenomena involving more than one's feeling toward the spouse. It also includes job satisfaction and other tensions faced by the marital dyad.

[2] Part of this income relationship could be the <u>result</u> of a marital disruption rather than the <u>cause</u> of it. The effect of the disruption on income is examined in Section III.

[3] For example, see Farley and Hermalin (1971) and Sweet and Bumpass (1973).

[4] Racial differences in socioeconomic achievement and the effects of racial discrimination are well documented. For example, Duncan (1968) and Duncan, Featherman, and Duncan (1972).

much better than of all families in the sample. The fraction of variance of the dependent variable explained (R-squared) for the two groups is .288 and .043, respectively.

When we look at marital stability among blacks, we see that income is again the best predictor. This variable is more powerful in explaining differences in marital disruption among blacks than it is among the total sample. As with the entire sample, the rate of marital stability increases with income.

As can be seen by examining Table 4.3, the relationship between wife's age and marital disruption is quite strong in a bivariate context. However, once again when we consider differences in the age of husband, family income, and family size, wife's age adds very little explanatory power. Both before and after adjustment for other family characteristics, there is a strong negative relationship between husband's age and marital breakup. The probability of marital disruption decreases rather dramatically with the age of the black husband.

An interesting difference between the model which predicts marital disruption for the total sample and the model which predicts marital disruption among blacks is the change in importance of family size, city size, husband's education and occupation (see Table 4.1). Childless black couples and black couples with only one child have the lowest disruption rates, while families with seven or more members have the highest disruption rates. Small towns have lower disruption rates than larger cities, and husband's education and occupational status are inversely related to marital disruption (see Table 4.3).

In their analysis of data from the National Fertility Study, Bumpass and Sweet (1972) found that age at marriage was a predominant factor affecting marital stability. We find that neither the husband's nor the wife's age at marriage is an important predictor of marital disruption once the effects of other variables have been taken into account.

III. Marital Disruption and Family Well-Being

Using total family money income/needs as a measure of economic well-being, we examine in 1973 the relative status of the husbands and wives of the 133 couples that had experienced disruption over the six-year period. Table 4.4 shows that the former husbands are better off than their wives. Over twice as many husbands are in the top three income/needs deciles as wives. We also find that only 15 percent of the husbands are in the three lowest income/needs deciles, while about 34 percent of the wives are in this category.[1]

---

[1] The distribution of the 133 couples across *all* income categories is given in Appendix Table A4.1.

TABLE 4.3

Unadjusted and Adjusted Means for Selected Independent Variables from Regression
Predicting Whether Married Couples Will Become Separated 1968-1973
(Black couples only)

Predictors	Number of Cases (Unweighted)	Weighted Percent	Unadjusted Mean	Adjusted Mean
6 Year Average Family Income				
<$3000	39	5.0	.121	.181
$3000-4999	109	10.8	.244	.272
$5000-7499	180	23.9	.115	.087
$7500-9999	120	20.2	.059	.057
$10,000-14,999	105	28.7	.045	.033
$15,000 or more	22	11.5	.000	.043
Age of Head				
<25	57	11.2	.263	.231
25-34	182	30.4	.116	.143
35-44	171	32.9	.028	.028
45-54	165	25.5	.044	.025
Family Size				
2	49	18.7	.083	.026
3	62	13.1	.051	.008
4	83	17.9	.118	.130
5	91	18.0	.034	.053
6	64	10.0	.116	.128
7 or more	221	22.4	.108	.158
Size of Largest City in PSU				
500,000 or more	275	44.1	.101	.122
100,000-499,999	101	25.4	.046	.067
50,000-99,999	59	8.9	.127	.162
10,000-49,999	59	10.7	.050	.035
Less than 10,000	81	10.9	.042	.036
Age of Wife				
<25	107	19.8	.238	.145
25-34	205	35.2	.066	.065
35-44	181	31.5	.045	.084
45-54	77	13.0	.039	.056
Head's Education				
0-8 years	246	32.3	.102	.119
9-11 years	172	28.5	.118	.107
12 years	110	26.8	.057	.042
13-15 years	30	9.5	.008	.000
16+ years	8	0.2	---	---

TABLE 4.4

1973 Family Money Income/Needs by 1973 Paired Marital Status
of Separated Husbands and Wives

1973 Paired Marital Status	Number of Cases	Percent in Three Lowest Deciles		Percent in Three Highest Deciles		Rank Correlation, Tau C
		Husband's Family	Wife's Family	Husband's Family	Wife's Family	
Both single	76	14.7	36.9	60.5	20.0	.23
Husband remarried, Wife single	20	15.4	52.1	51.3	7.6	.53
Wife remarried, Husband single	11	11.2	5.1	89.9	86.2	.62
Both remarried	17	17.3	17.8	36.3	20.1	.52
Average	124	14.7	34.8	58.8	23.4	.50

MTR 7400

One reason for this difference is that when children are members of the separating families, they tend to remain part of their mother's family rather than their father's. In all except eight of the 108 original intact families with children, the children are part of their mother's household in 1973.

By focusing on total family money income to needs, one ignores the alimony and child support payments which many husbands may be paying. If we subtract these payments from the husband's family income and recalculate his well-being, we would expect to reduce the spread between the families of the husbands and wives interviewed in 1973. Interestingly enough, Table 4.5 shows that even after adjusting for these out transfers, husbands are still better off than their wives.

The economic status of the wives' families in 1973 would perhaps be more dismal if many of them did not receive some type of transfer income. Table 4.6 indicates that 46 percent of the wives' current families were receiving alimony or child support payments, and 13 percent were receiving ADC, AFDC, or some other welfare assistance. This latter figure is lower than expected, given both the economic status of the families and the fact that it is often argued that marital instability often leads to welfare dependency. It should be noted, however, that virtually none of the 1968 intact families (one percent) received any type of transfer income.

Housing, in particular home ownership, is a good indicator of a family's well-being; it contributes to it both in a physical and sociopsychological sense. In addition to the imputed (nonmoney) rental "income," homeowners build up equity which can be converted into other goods and services at some point in the future. As Table 4.7 suggests, in our subsample of separated husbands and wives we see that 56 percent of the original intact families were home-owners.[1] In 1973, however, only 31 percent of the husbands' families owned their homes. What we observe here is a reduction in the proportion of home-owners after the conjugal split-up, at least initially. We also see that slightly more wives than husbands own their dwelling units. One explanation for this latter occurrence is that, as best we can tell, the husbands tended to be the first ones to report their departure from their original households even when both spouses eventually moved. Some of the former wives undoubtedly intend to keep their homes, while in some cases where the marital breakup occurred be-tween the 1972 and 1973 interviews, many wives probably have not had sufficient

---

[1]Roistacher (1974) found 61.5 percent and 71.9 percent of the original families in this study were homeowners in 1968 and 1972, respectively.

TABLE 4.5

Husband's Family Money Income/Needs 1973,
Unadjusted and Adjusted for Alimony and Child Support Payments,
by 1973 Paired Marital Status

1973 Paired Marital Status	Number of Cases	Percent in Three Lowest Deciles		Percent in Three Highest Deciles	
		Unadjusted	Adjusted	Unadjusted	Adjusted
Both single	76	14.7	19.9	60.5	47.0
Husband remarried, Wife single	20	15.4	22.5	51.3	47.2
Wife remarried, Husband single	11	11.2	11.2	89.9	73.6
Both remarried	17	17.3	17.3	36.3	30.6
	124				
Average		14.7	19.4	58.8	47.5

Association between Marital Status and Adjusted Income/Needs, Cramer's V[*] = .25

Association between adjusted and unadjusted Income/Needs, TauB[*] = .88

[*]For an explanation of these terms, see the Glossary.

TABLE 4.6

Percent of Wives Receiving Alimony-Child Support and Welfare - ADC payments
by 1973 Paired Marital Status

1973 Paired Marital Status	Number of Cases	Alimony-Child Support	Welfare - ADC
Both single	76	49.8%	14.5%
Husband remarried, Wife single	20	76.6	13.1
Wife remarried, Husband single	11	0.0	1.8
Both remarried	17	11.3	12.7
	124		
Average		45.9%	12.8%

TABLE 4.7

Change in Housing Status 1968 to 1973 for Husbands and Wives
Experiencing Marital Disruption

Housing Status	Intact Family 1968	Husband's Family 1973	Wife's Family 1973
Own	56.1%	30.7%	39.7%
Rent	40.4	56.7	45.4
Neither	3.5	12.6	14.9
	100.0%	100.0%	100.0%

N = 124

Association between husband 1968 and 1973 housing status, Cramer's V = .36

Association between husband's 1973 and wife's 1973 housing status,
Cramer's V = .25

time to make housing adjustments. This, along with the fact that many of the
remarried wives   are in families where they own their homes, accounts for the
difference between the 1973 housing status of the former spouses.

Two additional items related to housing should be noted. In addition to
the decline in the proportion of homeowners, we note an increase in the proportion who are living in situations defined as neither owning nor renting. It appears as though many of the 1973 families have moved in with other relatives.
It is also worth noting that there is virtually no difference in the quality of
the families' 1972 housing (the last year this variable was measured) and the
quality of the families' 1968 housing.

Another indicator of a family's economic well-being is the amount of savings
or reserve funds they have (see Table 4.8). About 37 percent of our subsample of
1968 intact families reported savings greater than or equal to two-months' income.
Virtually the same proportion of husbands and wives in 1972 (the last year this
question was asked) reported two months or more savings. We do notice a slight
increase in the proportion of husbands' 1972 families reporting no savings.
This shift is not large enough, however, to indicate a major change in the savings picture of the husbands. What appears to be happening is that those families with two or more months income saved initially are able to maintain or re-
accumulate this savings even during the process of marital disruption, while
some of the families with less than two-months income saved found themselves
with virtually no savings by 1972.

Related to the discussion of marital disruption and the subsequent economic
well-being of the families is the issue of the effect of marital disruption on
labor force participation of wives. Do wives begin to work as a result of marital disruption or do they anticipate the impending split and begin to work prior
to it? Numerous references can be found to a supposed adverse effect of wives
working on marital happiness and marital stability. This is particularly difficult to study due to the large number of factors which enter into a wife's
decision to enter the labor force, some of which are independent of her marital
relationship.[1] We did find, however, that among all families, those with work-

---

[1]Sweet (1973) discusses some ways in which marital happiness and marital stability may be related: (1) Women who work may also be women who are prone to un-
happy marriages and marital instability, independent of their employment. (2)
Unhappily married women may seek escape from the confines of the family and
seek employment because they are unhappily married. (3) Unhappily married
women may be more likely to be employed and earning relatively large amounts of

TABLE 4.8

Change in Savings, 1968 to 1973, for Husbands and Wives
Experiencing Marital Disruptions

Savings	Intact Family 1968	Husband's Family 1973	Wife's Family 1973
No savings	29.5%	38.7%	31.2%
Savings equal to two or more months' income	37.4	37.2	37.7
Savings equal to less than two months' income	33.1	23.4	29.9

N = 124

Association between savings of 1968 intact family and 1972 family of husband, Cramer's V = .29.

Association between savings of 1973 husband's family and 1972 wife's family, Cramer's V = .42.

ing wives had a marital disruption rate four percentage points higher than
families with nonworking wives.

About two-thirds of the wives in our subsample were employed in 1968. This
proportion increases to more than four-fifths in 1973. We notice the biggest
shift among those former wives who are still separated in 1973. Thirty-seven percent of those who were working in 1973 were not working in 1968 (see Table 4.9).

IV.   Changes in Husband's Attitudes and Behaviors

Several indexes have been created for each year of this study, from 1968 to
1972. Three of them are indexes measuring attitudes: efficacy-planning, trust-
hostility, and ambition-aspiration. Six measure behavior: real earning acts,
money-earning acts, economizing, risk avoidance, connectedness, and horizon
proxies. Most of these indexes were formulated on an a priori basis, although
some contain questions which have been used in previous studies. Several of
these indexes have been further investigated and found to demonstrate considerable empirical validity.[1] These indexes were included originally with the belief
that observation on various types of "proper" behavior and self-rated attitudes
would show which ones result in improved economic well-being.

Marital breakup is one of many disruptions which can interrupt the normal
flow of events in a family's life cycle. While neither the attitudes nor behaviors measured in this study appear to have considerable effects on changes in
well-being, events such as marital disruption could have important attitudinal
and behavioral effects on the individuals involved. We have referred to marital
disruption as an event. It is, in reality, a process such that even though all
of the couples had not split in 1972, many who had not were well along the way.

Looking at the husbands' scores on the three attitudinal indexes, we find
no major changes in their distribution on either the trust-hostility or ambition-aspiration index. We do observe a rather large difference between their
1968 and 1972 scores on the efficacy-planning index (see Table 4.10). In 1968,
34 percent of the husbands received scores in the top two categories, but in
1972 only 13 percent were in these categories. The efficacy-planning measure
attempts to measure the respondent's attitudes in two domains: his sense of
personal efficacy and his perceived propensity to plan ahead. Could the overall

---

income in anticipation of the time when they will need to support themselves
and their dependents. These propositions are quite difficult to study in any
causal sense.

[1]See Dickinson (1972) for a thorough discussion of the empirical validity of the
indexes.

TABLE 4.9

Change in Wives Employment Status 1968 to 1973
(Women still separated)

		1973			
1968	Working	Looking for Work	Housewife	Other	Total
Working	63.1%	96.8%	33.9%	84.8%	62.1%
Not working	36.9	3.2	66.1	10.2	37.9
	100.0%	100.0%	100.0%	100.0%	100.0%
Number of Cases	62	5	23	6	
Percent	83.1	4.5	10.5	1.9	

Cramer's V = .26

Change in Wives Employment Status 1968 to 1973
(Women remarried)

	1973		
1968	Working	Not Working	Total
Working	89.9%	60.0%	80.4%
Not working	10.1	40.0	19.6
	100.0%	100.0%	100.0%
Number of cases	21	7	
Percent	80.3	19.7	100.0%

Cramer's V = .49

TABLE 4.10

Distribution of Husbands' Efficacy Planning Score, 1968 and 1972

Score on Efficacy Planning Index	1968	1972
0	3.6%	5.0%
1	9.8	12.3
2	16.4	26.6
3	16.5	26.0
4	19.0	16.7
5	21.0	5.7
≥ 6	13.8	7.7
	100.1%	100.0%

Number of cases = 133

Cramer's V = .32

Rank Correlation (Tau B) = .34

TABLE 4.11

Change in Husbands' Economizing, 1968 to 1972

Score on Economizing Index	1968	1972
1	8.4%	16.1%
2	21.7	33.9
3	30.3	21.4
4	25.7	20.9
5	11.5	7.4
6	1.2	0.0
	98.8%	99.7%

Number of cases = 124

Cramer's V = .25

Tau B = .31

change in scores of this index primarily involve changes in only one of these
components? After decomposing the index into its two dimensions, in general,
the respondent's score on the efficacy components changes very little. The major change occurs in the respondent's perceived propensity to plan ahead. We
cannot argue that the process of marital disruption "caused" the change in
"planning ahead" among our husbands; however, intuitively we can see how this
trauma to the family's life cycle could have a rather substantial effect on
one's feelings of ability to plan ahead. For many husbands, this is both a period of transition and a period of relative uncertainty.

In addition to attitudinal indexes, we also looked at a component of the
ambition-aspiration index specifically relating to the respondent's self-evalua-
tion. The question, "Are you more often satisfied or dissatisfied with your-
self?" was asked of our respondents from 1968 through 1972. It was our belief
that among men going through the process of marital disruption, some changes in
their level of satisfaction with themselves might be observed; however, our data
seem to indicate that no major change occurs.

Turning now to husbands' self-reported behaviors in 1968 and 1972, we find
no systematic variation in their scores on the risk-avoidance index. The former
husbands do not appear to be any more or less risk averse in 1972 than they were
in 1968. There is slight change in their distribution along the economizing
index in the direction of less economizing (Table 4.11).

We have already reported that husbands engaged in the process of family
disruption report a lower propensity to plan ahead in 1972 than in the initial
interviews; consequently, it is not surprising that the husbands also have lower
scores on the horizons measure in 1972 (Table 4.12). The horizons index is a
measure of planning behavior with the domain (children, job, etc.) clearly specified on several items. With a marriage in the process of being disrupted along
with children leaving the husband's household for that of the wife's, it is not
surprising that many husbands would no longer express explicit plans for their
children's education. Under these circumstances, it is also unlikely that they
would have explicit fertility plans.

The other behavioral index where changes in the husbands' scores are found
is entitled, "Connectedness to Sources of Information and Help." It is made up
of such diverse connections as PTA, church, television, newspapers, bars or taverns, voluntary associations, labor unions, and number of neighbors known by
name. To some extent the connectedness measure is one of social integration into the surrounding community. When we compare the husband's distribution in
1968 to 1972 on the connectedness index (Table 4.13), we find a relatively sharp

TABLE 4.12

Distribution of Husbands' Score on Horizons Scale, 1968 and 1972

Score on Horizon Index	1968	1972
1	0.1%	0.0%
2	5.8	4.9
3	19.8	29.4
4	20.1	35.5
5	17.2	19.1
6	23.3	9.2
$\geq$7	13.9	1.9
	100.2%	100.0%

Number of cases = 133

Cramer's V = .23

TABLE 4.13

Distribution of Husbands' Connectedness Score, 1968 and 1972

Score on Connectedness Index	1968	1972
0	0.7	0.0
1	0.0	1.3
2	2.8	0.3
3	4.9	3.5
4	15.6	27.7
5	13.2	26.4
6	26.1	17.7
7	18.2	15.7
8	10.3	6.4
9	8.2	1.1
	100.0%	100.1%

Number of cases = 133

Cramer's V = .34

Rank Correlation (Tau B) = .25

decline in the proportion with scores greater than five. In 1968, 63 percent reported scores in this range, but in 1972 we find only 41 percent with scores greater than five.

Part of the decline in husbands' connectedness can be attributed to a decreased amount of church attendance. More importantly, however, the lower scores on the connectedness measure reflect the movement from former households to new neighborhoods where the husbands perhaps know fewer people by name and are less likely to be within walking distance of relatives.

In addition to the behaviors discussed above, we find neither systematic variation in the husbands' frequency of attendance at bars or taverns nor in the amount of money spent on cigarettes and alcohol in 1968 and 1972.

V. Is There a Difference in Husbands' and Wives'
   Attitudes and Behaviors After Disruption?

Unfortunately for our purposes here, only husbands were interviewed in 1968; therefore, we have no way of knowing wives' attitudes at the beginning of this study. In order to have a measure of wives' attitudes in 1972, they had to be the head of their respective households; consequently, in order to compare attitudes and behaviors of husbands and wives, we had to further restrict our small subsample to those whose marriages had already been disrupted and where the wife had not remarried. Only 80 husbands and wives met this criteria.

Generally, the husbands' and wives' scores on the various attitudinal and behavioral indexes are quite similar. There are slight differences on the ambition-aspiration and trust-hostility indexes which appear to be sex-related rather than related to marital breakup.[1] The one behavioral difference is in the area of economizing (Table 4.14). Given the lower level of well-being experienced by these women after the marriage has been terminated, it is not surprising that they score higher on the economizing index than their husbands.

During the 1972 interview, we asked all respondents for their overall impression of the preceding five years. Among our subset of husbands giving a reference to their overall quality of life during this period, nearly 75 percent of them mentioned the change in family structure. Likewise, among our 80 former wives for whom we have attitudinal data, 52 percent of those referring to their quality of life mentioned family change. Marital disruption is not only a process which has economic repercussions for the family unit and disrupts its life cycle, but it was a dominant factor for both the former husbands and wives in their evaluation of the period between 1968 and 1972.

---

[1]Dickinson (1972) addresses the issue that some of the indexes tend to be more appropriate for males than for females.

TABLE 4.14

Distribution of Husbands' and Wives' 1972 Family Economizing Score
(Families where split has occurred and wife is head of new household)

Score on Econ-omizing Index	1968	1972
1	20.7%	0.3%
2	33.4	5.9
3	18.6	30.8
4	20.6	29.8
5	6.7	24.9
6	0.0	8.3
	100.0%	100.0%

Number of observations = 80

Cramer's V = .29

Rank Correlation (Tau B) = .34

SUMMARY

1. In studying which couples became either separated or divorced, the strongest
predictors are income (which has a negative effect on the probability of dissolution), timing of the first birth (the earlier the birth, the more likely is
separation or divorce), and husband's age (negative effect). Race was found to
have an effect in the opposite direction than predicted, in our model, with
whites having a higher adjusted rate of disruption than blacks. In our separate
analysis for blacks, the strongest predictors are income, husband's age, family
size (larger families had greater probabilities of dissolution) and city size
(larger cities had the highest dissolution rates).

2. In order to compare the experiences of husbands and wives after separation,
we studied 133 couples whose marriages had been disrupted and for whom we had
complete records. We found that the major impact of separation on the status of
the former spouses operated through economic rather than attitudinal variables.
Probably because children usually remain in the maternal family after a separation, the economic status of former husbands improves while that of the former
wives deteriorates. This result is especially pronounced for those wives who
do not remarry. An interesting finding in light of the supposition that separation leads to dependence is that only 13 percent of the former wives received
ADC, AFDC, or any other welfare assistance.

3. The former husbands express a lower preceived propensity to plan ahead and
a lower level of planning as measured by the horizons index in 1972 compared to
1968. In addition to this, the former husbands reported fewer money-earning
acts at the end of this period than they did initially.

4. In order to compare the attitudes and behaviors of husbands and wives, we
had to limit our sample to 80 cases and basically found little difference between the two groups. The one major difference was on the economizing measure,
with the former wives scoring higher than their former husbands.

References

Bumpass, Larry L. and Sweet, James A., "Differentials in Marital Stability:
   1970," American Sociological Review, 37, December 1972, pp. 754-766.

Cutright, Phillips, "Income and Family Events: Marital Stability," Journal
   of Marriage and the Family, 33, May 1971, pp. 291-306.

186

Cutright, Phillips and Scanzoni, John, "Income Supplements and the American Family," in The Family, Poverty, and Welfare Programs: Factors Influencing Family Instability, 1973, U.S. Government Printing Office, Washington, D.C.

Dickinson, Katherine, "Investigation of the Attitudinal and Behavioral Indexes," Working paper, Survey Research Center (University of Michigan), 1972.

Duncan, O. D., "Inheritance of Poverty or Inheritance of Race?" in Moynihan, D.P., ed., On Understanding Poverty, New York: Basic Books, 1968.

Duncan, O. D., Featherman, David and Duncan, Beverly, Socioeconomic Background and Achievement, New York: Seminar Press, 1972.

Farley, Reynolds, Growth of the Black Population, Chicago: Markham Publishing Company, 1970.

Farley, Reynolds and Hermalin, Albert I., "Family Stability: A Comparison of Trends Between Blacks and Whites," American Sociological Review, 36, February 1971, pp. 1-17.

Morgan, James N., "Family Composition" in Five Thousand American Families -- Patterns of Economic Progress, Volume I, Ann Arbor: Survey Research Center, Institute for Social Research (University of Michigan), 1974.

Roistacher, Elizabeth, "Housing and Home Ownership" in Morgan, James N., ed., Five Thousand American Families -- Patterns of Economic Progress, Volume II, Ann Arbor: Survey Research Center, Institute for Social Research (University of Michigan), 1974.

Sweet, James A., Women in the Labor Force, New York: Seminar Press, 1973.

Sweet, James A. and Bumpass, Larry L., "Differentials in Marital Instability of the Black Population: 1970," Discussion paper, Institute for Research on Poverty, 1973.

APPENDIX 4.1

TABLE A4.1

Total Family Money Income of 1968 Intact Families,
1973 Family of Husband and 1973 Family of Wife

Family Income	1968 Intact Family	1973 Family of Husband	1973 Family of Wife
< $5,000	18.0%	12.1%	21.2%
5,000 - 7,499	20.6	10.5	21.5
7,500 - 9,999	14.5	10.1	18.5
10,000 - 14,999	32.8	27.0	15.3
15,000 +	14.1	40.1	23.5
	100.0%	99.8%	100.0%

N = 124

Association between income of 1968 intact family and income of
husband's 1973 family: Tau B = .44, Cramer's V = .42

Association between income of 1973 family of husband and income
of 1973 family of wife: Tau B = .19, Cramer's V = .27

Chapter 5

INVOLUNTARY DISRUPTIONS OF "LIFE-CYCLE" PLANS
Everett Ehrlich

INTRODUCTION

The incidence of exogenous disruptions to a family's "life-cycle" plans is a matter of import to diverse areas of the social sciences. The phrase "life-cycle" itself comes from economic theory, which posits that savings and labor supply decisions are the product of a long-term plan that a household maintains and readjusts when crucial parameters on which it is based change (e.g., increases in the wage rate or price level).[1] Understanding to whom such disruptive events, or "shocks," occur would represent a significant inclusion in economic theory.

On a broader plane, life-cycle shocks play an important role in major social questions. Such shocks, for example, could prove to be a significant obstacle in achieving income mobility. Similarly, these shocks could be a strong intervening variable in the "culture of poverty" argument, in that exposure to exogenous traumatic events could have important attitudinal effects.

A "feeling of powerlessness" is an important aspect of this phenomenon. The H.E.W. report <u>Work in America</u>[2] gives "a career that has been blocked and chaotic" as one of the three major sources of worker dissatisfaction. It would appear that a model of the distribution of these disruptive events is clearly in order.

In this essay we will first construct an index that measures the extent to which the household head has been exposed to life-cycle disruptions. The simple correlation between this index and selected explanatory variables will then be examined. Finally, we will develop a predictive model of the shock index using standard multiple regression techniques.

---

[1] See Ando and Modigliani (1963), (1957), and (1960).

[2] Department of Health, Education and Welfare (1973).

ANALYSIS

I. Components of the Aggregate Shock Index

The sample used for this analysis consists of those members of the entire sample who either participated, or sought to participate, in the labor force for all six years interviewing was conducted. All households in the sample also had the same head for all years.

In creating the index of traumatic events, or shocks, seven components were used. These were:

1) *Firings*: respondents who reported one of the following for any one of six possible years were considered under this category: company folded, changed hands, strikes, lockouts, work ran out, laid off or fired.

2) *Unemployment*: respondents who reported being unemployed while seeking work for two or more weeks for any one or more of six possible years were considered unemployed.

3) *Underemployment*: respondents who reported being unable to find additional work for any one or more of six possible years were considered underemployed.

4) *Evictions*: respondents who reported relocating as a response to exogenous conditions were considered evicted for any of five possible years.

5) *Emergency expenditures*: respondents who reported their welfare significantly decreased by an unplanned involuntary expenditure were scored as such for any of five possible years.

6) *Unplanned children*: respondents who reported no intention of having children within the foreseeable future, but did within the next two years, were considered to have unplanned children in any of four possible years.

7) *Illness*: respondents who reported suffering from illnesses or accidents that forced them to remove themselves from the labor force for two or more weeks were considered to have endured an illness in any of six possible years.

Each component was then standardized by the number of years in which it could be measured, the result being an expression of an implicit "rate" of experiencing shocks, expressed in shocks per year.

These seven components each share the common characteristic of being exogenous to the set of decisions a family makes. The degree of severity associated with each event, measured both in terms of impact on the family's welfare and disruptive effect on the family's life-cycle plans, will of course vary from family unit to family unit. However, this differential impact should not obscure the fact that each component stands as an exogenous trauma or "shock" of a family's plans.

Within other ideological circles, there would be opposition to the inclusion of some of these components. While the events are the results of decisions made outside the family and its decision-making apparatus, it could be argued that they are responses to behavior over which the family *does* have control. In the case of eviction and emergency expenditures this argument is not immediately applicable. In other situations assumptions must suffice. It is assumed that the family rationally pursues health and family planning within the limits of its resources and access to knowledge. With respect to unemployment and underemployment, it is assumed that the respondent maintains a justifiable supply price to which he is entitled and that any failure to complete labor supply plans is the product of deficiencies in his opportunity set provided by the labor market.

The area of firings is probably one of greater disagreement. The "firings" are of two sorts. One is failure of the enterprise: the employer went out of business, died, the work was completed and the employees sent home, or a strike or lockout occurred. The second sort is job displacement of the individual per se, that is, getting "canned." With respect to the former, it is difficult to argue that the enterprise that hired the worker failed or was forced to relocate because of the failure of the employees to work hard enough or accept a wage low enough to make production possible. The second type, however, is a matter of debate. The Taylorist view of such firings is largely subscribed to within economics and, in essence, states that firings are a response to the worker's inability to conform to dictated behaviors on the job (resulting in disobedience, instigation, absenteeism, etc.), and that firing is a justifiable response.[1] One should view such an argument as inordinately biased in favor of the employer's "right to fire." Support of such an argument is equivalent to the belief that the employer has the right to specify the behavior of other individuals and, in turn, the production should be carried out for the sake of the employer's profits at the expense, if necessary, of the personal well-being of the employee; or, in simpler terms, that production should be considered an inalterably alienating experience. The contrary assumption is made in this chapter.

---

[1] See Taylor (1911).

II. Aggregate Index

The aggregate shock index is a simple sum of average yearly scores of components. The mean score of .61, therefore, implies that, on the average, members of the sample under study experienced three shocks in five years (see Table 5.1).

TABLE 5.1

Sample Statistics for Components of Shock Index
(expressed as events per year)

Component	Mean	Standard Deviation
Fired	.04	.107
Unemployed	.09	.187
Underemployed	.18	.241
Evicted	.02	.063
Emergency expenditure	.16	.208
Unplanned children	.02	.082
Illness	.10	.140
Aggregate Index	.61	.532

In Table 5.2 the correlations among components of the aggregate index and their item-total correlations are examined.[1]

III. Selected Explanatory Variables

For the purposes of observation, six explanatory variables that seemed intuitively plausible predictors were tested for mean shock index score for each of their values. The variables were: occupation (a one-digit skill code), education, family money income, race, feelings of efficacy, and a code measuring social class.[2]

---

[1] Cronbach's alpha, a measure of similarity analogous to percentage of joint variance explained, is equal to .3999.

[2] The social class code divides the sample into groups categorized by their relationship to the productive process. It uses as a basis for differentiation among groups, attributes to the respondent's work role: whether self-employed, whether involved in "productive" or "organizational" (bureaucratic) work, hierarchical position of the respondent's jobs (a proxy for latitude at work), and the respondent's asset income. Further documentation on the development and explanatory power of this variable is available in Appendix 5.1.

TABLE 5.2

Inter-correlations of Components of Shock Index

	Fired	Un-employed	Under-employed	Evicted	Emergency Expenditures	Unplanned Children	Illness
Unemployed two or more weeks	.40						
Under-employed	.13	.28					
Evicted	.06	.05	.04				
Emergency expenditures	.02	.04	.09	.05			
Unplanned children	.03	.10	.10	.02	.12		
Illness two or more weeks	.12	.17	.09	.05	.15	.05	
ITEM-TOTAL CORRELATION	.45	.64	.65	.20	.51	.30	.46

Table 5.3 presents simple correlation coefficients between selected independent variables and the components of the shock index. Unemployment, underemployment, and illness are most closely correlated with all predictors, probably owing to a large extent to their larger variance. No predictor demonstrates an exceptional propensity to explain one component over all others. Low scores on eviction and unplanned children appear to be a product of the rarity of those events.

Table 5.4 presents shock values by education group. The sizes of the first two groups make their scores slightly suspect but, nevertheless, the shock index seems to divide education into three groups: less than high school graduation, less than college graduation, and college or more. The differences within these groups are trivial. Such a result does little to support the "human capital" model of education as a process of self-investment. Rather, it suggests that education endows the individual with "credentials" as opposed to "skills," the former more compatible with the discontinuous nature of the payoff function.

Table 5.5 presents shock values for family money income. While the relationship between the two is not "smooth," that is, monotonic, it is not as discontinuous as the relationship between education and the shock index.

TABLE 5.3

Simple Correlation (r) between Explanatory
Variables and Components of Shock Index

	Social Class 1968	Education (in Years)	Family Money Income 1968	Occupation 1968	Race (whether black)	Feelings of Efficacy in 1968
Fired	−.10	−.13	−.12	−.13	.03	−.12
Unemployed two or more weeks	−.22	−.23	−.17	−.24	.04	−.15
Underemployed	−.24	−.28	−.23	−.28	.13	−.21
Evicted	−.05	−.02	−.08	−.08	.04	−.04
Emergency expenditure	−.13	−.11	−.06	−.12	.05	−.09
Unplanned children	−.08	−.04	−.09	−.08	.01	.01
Illness two or more weeks	−.19	−.24	−.20	−.21	.06	−.19
Aggregate index	−.32	−.35	−.29	−.36	.12	−.26

TABLE 5.4

Shock Index Scores for Education Groups
(expressed as events per year)

Education Level	Unweighted Number of Observations	Mean
0 - 5 years, illiterate	40	0.782
0 - 5 years, reading	59	1.000
6 - 8 years	212	0.860
9 - 11 years	200	0.860
High school graduate	195	0.556
Vocational training	110	0.540
Some college	126	0.538
College graduate	84	0.296
Post-college	50	0.306
TOTAL	1076	0.613

$Eta^2 = .151$

195

TABLE 5.5

Shock Index Scores for Income Groups
(expressed as events per year)

Income	Unweighted Number of Observations	Mean
$0 - 4,000	230	0.893
$4,001 - 6,000	184	0.739
$6,001 - 7,500	155	0.582
$7,501 - 9,000	112	0.708
$9,001 - 11,000	132	0.559
$11,001 - 13,000	84	0.554
$13,001 - 15,000	51	0.592
$15,001 - 18,000	68	0.417
$18,001 or more	60	0.241
TOTAL	1076	0.613

$Eta^2 = .106$

The effects of race are measured in Table 5.6. As expected, nonwhites experience life-cycle shocks more often than whites. It should be noted, however, that the Eta-square statistic is only .014 for this variable.

TABLE 5.6

Shock Index Score by Racial Group
(expressed as events per year)

Race Group	Unweighted Number of Observations	Mean
White	702	0.589
Nonwhite	374	0.787
TOTAL	1076	0.613

$Eta^2 = .014$

Feelings of efficacy is an index of the respondent's *feelings* as to whether he is in control of his life. Table 5.7 measures the mean value of shocks experienced by efficacy score. There appears to be a general correspondence between the two scores, but the overall predictive level is still low (.073).

TABLE 5.7

Shock Index Score by Efficacy*
(expressed as events per year)

Efficacy	Unweighted Number of Observations	Mean
0	24	1.051
1	15	0.836
2	93	0.913
3	83	0.825
4	125	0.689
5	159	0.661
6	141	0.547
7	161	0.530
8	126	0.556
9	149	0.450
TOTAL	1076	0.613

Eta^2 = .073

———

*Sense of personal efficacy based on six self-evaluating questions.

Table 5.8 gives the index score for each occupational skill group. The sample here divides itself essentially into two groups: white and blue collar workers. The overall predictive power of this division is .172.

The social class variable measures the Marxist conception of social class in today's economy. The sample divides itself into three groups in this instance: a privileged group consisting of the owners and high-level hierarchical workers of enterprises, a middle group of clerical and sales workers and small proprietors, and a last group consisting of craftsmen, foremen, operatives and laborers, or more mundanely, the working class. Results for the class variable are shown in Table 5.9.

TABLE 5.8

Shock Index Score by Occupation Group
(expressed as events per year)

Occupation Group	Unweighted Number of Observations	Mean
Professional, technical	126	0.351
Managers, proprietors	87	0.344
Self-employed, businessmen	45	0.430
Clerical/sales	135	0.476
Craftsmen/foremen	205	0.806
Operatives	232	0.872
Laborers	215	0.821
Miscellaneous, police	31	0.643

$Eta^2 = .172$

TABLE 5.9

Shock Index Score by Social Class*
(expressed as events per year)

Class Group	Unweighted Number of Observations	Mean
Capitalists	30	0.263
Managers	74	0.342
High-level hierarchy	112	0.362
White collar	134	0.474
Artisans	58	0.576
Middle-hierarchy	186	0.789
Low-hierarchy	434	0.845
Miscellaneous	48	0.795
TOTAL	1076	0.613

$Eta^2 = .163$

*See Appendix A for derivation of social class.

These data demonstrate that the shock index is "given out" in an identifiable way; we expect blue collar workers, poor people, and people with low education levels to experience these shocks more often. In the following section we construct a predictive model of the shock index.

IV. Predicting the Shock Index

By constructing a predictive model of the aggregate shock index we may examine the relative strengths of different groups of explanatory variables. It seems intuitive to suggest that any of a diverse set of factors could affect the probability of experiencing exogenous shocks, including "economic," "sociological" and "psychological" variables. The diverse data set enables us to test competing hypotheses as to the determinants of exogenous shocks. Five hypotheses suggest themselves as possible frameworks for understanding the shock index. Each, in turn, are tested through the incorporation of a set of variables in a multiple regression framework. The use of standard "significance tests" common to statistics discern among those relationships between explanatory variables and the shock index that are "weak" and "strong." The five sets of variables used are: demographic variables, classification measures, income, behavioral or personality measures, and measures of the economic environment. Let us examine each in detail.

The "demographic" hypothesis maintains that shocks are experienced by black people, women, and old people, as victims of institutional racism, sexism, and ageism in our society. Given that many employer decisions are made on the basis of "social credentials" such as race, sex, or age, this is an ostensibly plausible hypothesis. The third of these variables is less straightforward than the others in that it measures both age and *year born*. It therefore measures effects of "age" which could include effects dependent on historical change; for example, older people's attitudes could be "different" not only because they are *old*, but because they experienced the depression of the 1930's. With this forewarning, the demographic variables included are race, sex, and age.

A second hypothesis views the avoidance of shocks as a matter of income, which enables the individual to plan flexibly over a longer time horizon. Freedom from exogenous misfortune may, therefore, be purchased. Income can also be included in the analysis as the sum of three separate types of income, labor, transfer, and asset income. Labor income is the sum of all wages, salaries, and other remunerations received by the household. Transfer income is income unassociated with "factor payments," that is to say, it is a bequest of some sort. Both government income transfers, like unemployment compensation or ADC, and

personal transfers such as alimony or gifts are considered to be "transfers."
Asset income is the income returned to the respondent as a consequence of his
portfolio holdings.

Our analysis will incorporate income source into the model along with income level. This is necessary because we might find, for example, that summed
income could exhibit a significant relationship to avoidance of involuntary disruptions and furthermore find that all three types of income exhibited the same
relationship. However, if we find that only some of the income types demonstrate
the same relationship, we can show that the source of income affects the probability of fulfilling plans.

Another hypothesis is that freedom from shocks is governed by "class" and
"status;" that is to say, it is a privilege enjoyed by a certain socioeconomic
class or set of classes. Both education and social class serve as measures of
this phenomenon, as are inter-generational background measures (father's occupation and education).

A fourth hypothesis holds that personality traits and patterns of behavior affect the experience of shocks. Such an "attitudinal capital" argument would operate in one of several ways. A specific set of attitudes could
direct an individual to "try harder" to avoid traumatic events, or opt for more
risk averse choices in making decisions. It would be true, for example, that a
set of attitudes or behaviors lend themselves to the workplace and minimize the
risk of being fired. The behavioral/personality variables used to test the ac-
companying hypotheses are the already created indexes: sense of efficacy, aspirations expressed, horizon expressed, and connectedness to help.

A final hypothesis maintains that conditions in the individual's "economic
environment" determine the extent to which he is subjected to "shock" type
events. The three environmental variables are the unemployment rate, the distance of the individual to a large city, and the size of the nearest city. While
the shock index is constructed from data collected in interviewing years 1968-73,
the values for *all* three variable groups are taken from 1968, and if not available then, from the first year asked. This procedure avoids the problem of "circularity" in the data.

In the first estimation, shown in Table 5.10, age and race appear to be
significant predictors of the shock index. The black-white differential, .3342,[1]

---

[1]This "raw score" is obtained from the standardized coefficient by multiplying it
by the ratio of standard deviations of the shock index and the race variable.
The standardized coefficient is the regression coefficient obtained when
variable scores are expressed as the number of standard deviations away from
the variable mean.

200

implies one shock every three years. The number of shocks experienced per year declines .0059 each year as the individual gets older. Whether or not the household head was a woman appears to be insignificant in determining exposure to shocks.

TABLE 5.10

Standardized Regression Coefficients for Predictors
of Shock Index - Demographic Variables

Variable	Raw Score Coefficient	Standardized Coefficient	T-Ratio
Age	-.0059	-0.1180	3.9133*
Race (whether nonwhite)	.3342	0.1954	6.5461*
Sex (whether female)	-.0008	-0.0005	0.0149

SEE = .5200 R^2 = .0529

*Indicates significance at the .01 level.

Income is added in the second estimation presented in Table 5.11. The presence of income diminishes the strength of both age and race effects, as it is positively correlated (.17) with both. Nevertheless, race and age are still significant predictors, as is sex, in this instance. (It should be noted that this is a sample of household heads *only* and not of all women.) An interpretation of these results shows that women experience one shock less than the other members of their income group each ten years.

TABLE 5.11

Standardized Regression Coefficients for Predictors
of Shock Index - Demographic and Income Variables

Variable	Raw Score Coefficient	Standardized Coefficient	T-Ratio
Age	-.0034	-.0678	2.2414*
Race	.2852	.1662	5.6666**
Sex	-.1079	-.0633	2.0514*
Family income (in thousands of dollars)	-.0188	-.2260	7.2814**

SEE = .5079 R^2 = .0974

*Indicates significance at the .05 level.

**Indicates significance at the .01 level.

The income coefficient, $-.0188$, implies that the income needed for a white 42-year-old male to avoid traumatic events is roughly \$48,000.

With the predictive importance of income established we can determine if the composition of income is also significant. Dividing all income outside of capital gains into asset, labor, and transfer income, we know that for the individual's total income, y:

$$1) \quad y = y_A + y_L + y_T$$

and that $\quad 2) \quad y_L = y - y_A + y_T$

If we formulate the model such that for shocks, X,

$$3) \quad X = \beta_0 + \beta_1 y_L + \beta_2 y_A + \beta_3 y_T \, ,$$

we can substitute 2) and get:

$$4) \quad X = \beta_0 + \beta_1 y + (\beta_2 - \beta_1)y_A + (\beta_3 - \beta_1)y_T$$

and then estimate 4).[1] This is a procedure used in previous econometric studies with success.[2]

Using the results presented in Table 5.12 we calculate $\beta_2 = -.1817$ and $\beta_3 = .2160$. The regression coefficients for a thousand dollars of labor, asset, and transfer income are $-.0236$, $-.0434$, and $-.1481$ respectively. All three have the expected negative sign, and the asset income coefficient is larger than the labor income coefficient, another plausible result. The size of β_3 is unexpectedly large. Apparently an extra dollar of transfer income offers more protection against exogenous shock than an extra dollar of asset income. This could be explained in one of several ways. For one, since the sample is composed of respondents who participated in the labor force for all six interview years, the transfer income would be of the alimony-family gift type as opposed to unemployment compensation or ADC grants. These might well be effective in leading to efficacious planning and avoiding shocks. Similarly, the people receiving this form of income are probably poorer and experience more shocks, and therefore stand to avoid more shocks if they get additional resources.

Age and race coefficients do not change when the composition of income is substituted for income. The male-female headed household distinction becomes more important, however, as the raw score regression coefficient goes from $-.1079$ to $-.1432$.

---

[1] See Modigliani and Ando (1957).

[2] See Hymans and Shapiro (1974) and Taylor (1971).

TABLE 5.12

Standardized Regression Coefficients for Predictors
of Shock Index - Demographic and Types of Income Variables

Variable	Raw Score Coefficient	Standardized Coefficients	T-Ratio
Age	-.0041	-.0808	2.6665**
Race	.2842	.1662	5.6812**
Sex	-.1432	-.0840	2.6935**
Family income[a]	-.0236	-.2837	7.8947**
Asset income[a]	.0434	.1020	2.9838**
Transfer income[a]	.1481	.0677	2.2869*

SEE = .5048 R^2 = .1099

*Indicates significance at the .05 level.

**Indicates significance at the .01 level.

[a]Income variables are measured in thousands of dollars.

If "status" or "social class" has any meaning separate from the composition of income, it can be examined by incorporating these variables into the fourth estimation, the results of which are contained in Table 5.13.[1] Of the new predictors representing "status" or "class," social class and education are significant while the intergenerational measures (head's father's occupation and education) are not. Given the order in which these characteristics are determined for the individual, there is strong reason to believe that the father's measures operate through the child's.

The addition of class/status variables weakens the race variable's explanatory power. With demographic variables alone, the racial shift parameter is .3342. With income variables included it is reduced to .2852 and with class and income variables it is further reduced to .1693. This substantial second reduction is a demonstration, perhaps, that blacks have achieved more income mobility than social mobility or the attainment of social status. The addition

---

[1]It should be pointed out that the social class index is presented in linear fashion solely as a matter of convenience. The classes are scored in order of their mean scores on the shock index.

TABLE 5.13

Standardized Regression Coefficients for Predictors
of Shock Index – Demographic, Type of Income and
Class/Status Variables

Variable	Raw Score Coefficient	Standardized Coefficients	T-Ratio
Age	−.0073	.1449	4.7017**
Race	.1693	.0989	3.4135**
Sex	−.0550	−.0323	1.0548
Family income[a]	−.0099	−.1199	3.1060**
Asset income[a]	.0134	.0635	1.9084*
Transfer income[a]	.0422	.0583	2.0434*
Education in years	−.0288	−.1812	5.0667**
Head's father's education	−.0092	−.0257	0.0823
Father's occupation	−.0025	−.0081	0.2711
Social class	−.0459	−.1705	5.0400**

SEE = .4851 R^2 = .1810

*Indicates significance at the .05 level.

**Indicates significance at the .01 level.

[a]Income variables are measured in thousands of dollars.

of the new set of variables also reduces the male-female headed household parameter from −.1432 to −.0550 here. If women household heads do receive less shocks
than their male income peers, it could well be due to the fact that women probably
have more education and/or social "standing" than males in the same income class.
Such a hypothesis is defended in these results.

The predictive power of income is also significantly reduced. The regression coefficient that states the difference in shocks experienced with an additional thousand dollars of labor, asset, and transfer income are reduced to
−.0099, −.0134, and −.0422 respectively. Both a human capital theorist who views
earnings as a reward for self-investment and a Neo-Marxist who views the school
system as the taxonomer of the labor force would anticipate such a result, in
that income is an intervening variable between education and shocks.

In the fifth-estimation, personality measures are added to the regression.
These are:

1) Sense of efficacy; an index of the respondent's feelings towards his ability to make and implement plans,

2) Aspirations expressed; an index of the respondent's feelings towards taking new jobs, accepting challenges, and self-betterment,

3) Expressed horizons; an index of the specificity of the respondent's plans concerning labor market participation and family planning,

4) Connectedness to help; an index of the respondent's access to information through "traditional" channels such as bars, churches, relatives, newspapers, etc.

The inclusion of these personality measures appears to do little to alter the magnitudes of the demographic, race, or class/status effects. Complete results are presented in Table 5.14. They would lead us to accept that these demographic, race and class variables operate independently of personality factors. The only striking change is that the coefficient for thousands of dollars of asset income is reduced from $-.0134$ to $-.0018$. It is interesting to note that personality measures seem to alter the effect of income source more than the effect of income level.

With the exception of connectedness to help, all the behavioral measures appear to be significant predictors. The more efficacious a respondent feels himself to be, or the more specific his plans, the less likely he is to experience shocks. The more ambitious he is, the more likely he is to experience shocks. The sign problem is, perhaps, due to circularity in the index construction. Respondents are given higher scores on the aspiration index if they stated they planned to try for new jobs, would be willing to move for a moderate pay increase, or would rather have an unpleasant job that paid more. Such preferences or intentions could be those of somebody who has experienced shocks or anticipates such an experience. A similar possibility of circularity exists for the other significant indexes. In the case of efficacy, for example, points are awarded for "getting to carry things out as expected," a judgment potentially influenced by past experience of shocks.

The last group of variables due for inclusion and testing are "environmental" variables; the distance to the nearest large city (50,000 inhabitants or more), the size of the nearest city, and the county unemployment rate (see Table 5.15). The first two variables have interesting divergent signs; as one moves closer to a large city, fewer shocks are experienced, but as the size of that city increases, more shocks are felt. Using these coefficients, an individual who lives within five miles of a city of half a million or more has the same chance of experiencing shocks as an individual who lives more than 50 miles away from a town

TABLE 5.14

Standardized Regression Coefficients for Predictors
of Shock Index - Demographic, Type of Income,
Class/Status, and Personality Variables

Variable	Raw Score Coefficient	Standardized Coefficients	T-Score
Age	-.0056	-.1111	3.5622**
Race	.1481	.0866	3.0439**
Sex	-.0926	-.0543	1.7867*
Family income[a]	-.0071	-.0863	2.2769*
Asset income[a]	.0018	.0786	2.4191**
Transfer income[a]	.0280	.0453	1.6219
Education in years	-.0251	-.1582	4.4667**
Father's education	-.0099	-.0274	0.9022
Father's occupation	-.0026	-.0085	0.2927
Social class	-.0450	-.1673	5.0271**
Sense of efficacy	-.0365	-.1564	5.4407**
Aspirations	-.0408	.1336	4.3220*
Horizons expressed	-.0413	-.1084	3.6544**
Connectedness to help	-.0086	-.0280	1.0216

SEE = .4725 R^2 = .22607

*Indicates significance at the .05 level.
**Indicates significance at the .01 level.
[a] Income variables are measured in thousands of dollars.

TABLE 5.15

Standardized Regression Coefficients for Predictors
of Shock Index - Demographic, Type of Income, Class/Status,
Personality, and Economic Environment Variables

Variable	Raw Score Coefficient	Standardized Coefficients	T-Score
Age	-.0057	-.1129	3.6124**
Race	.1485	.0868	3.0237**
Sex	-.1019	-.0598	1.9634*
Family income[a]	-.0083	-.1008	2.6363**
Asset income[a]	.0034	.0864	2.6582**
Transfer income[a]	.0379	.0455	1.6336
Education in years	-.0251	-.1577	4.4555**
Father's income	-.0092	-.0255	0.8400
Father's occupation	-.0001	-.0003	0.0115
Social class	-.0453	-.1683	5.0459**
Sense of efficacy	-.0362	-.1551	5.4041**
Aspirations expressed	.0414	.1355	4.3950**
Horizons expressed	-.0426	-.1118	3.7707**
Connectedness	-.0081	-.0264	-.9623
Miles to city	.0302	.0821	2.2001*
Size of city	-.0321	-.1076	2.9175**
Unemployment rate	.0266	.0342	1.1990

SEE = .4708 R^2 = .2337

*Indicates significance at the .05 level.
**Indicates significance at the .01 level.

[a]Income variables are measured in thousands of dollars.

of 10-25 thousand inhabitants. These results could well be idiosyncratic owing to the high correlation between city size and distance to center affecting the results.

SUMMARY

In the course of this essay we have constructed an index of exogenously induced events that disrupt the household's life-cycle plans and developed a predictive model that tested five sets of plausible hypotheses. The index consisted of seven events: firings, unemployment, underemployment, evictions, emergency expenditures, unplanned children and major illness. The following major results were obtained:

1) "class/status" and "personality" variables are the best predictors of the shock index, although the latter could owe some part of its correlation to circularity in index construction.

2) Black people experience more disruptions, and women, fewer disruptions, than individuals identical to them in all other respects.

3) Income source is important in predicting shocks, as well as income level.

Further work in this area will concern itself with the impact of these shocks on the household's income, labor force participation, and attitudes and behaviors. The research will point out recursive relationships between shocks and predetermined variables such as family background and education, providing new insight into whether attitude changes are induced by economic events, and enabling us to better weigh the possibility of success of the purposive (self-help) strategy of income mobility.

APPENDIX 5.1

SOCIAL CLASS AS AN EXPLANATORY VARIABLE

Marx's theory of social classes is never presented formally in his writings. Much like the premise of a murder mystery, he begins such a discussion in Chapter 53 of Capital, Volume 3, but after a few preliminary remarks, Engels (who edited the second and third volumes of Capital from Marx's notes after his death) inserts: "Here the manuscript breaks off," and Marx's definition of "a class" is never found.

This leaves the social scientist in the position of trying to piece together Marx's thoughts and fill in with assertions when necessary. In this appendix we try to employ what appear to be Marx's central concepts to create a class taxonomy for the United States today.

I. Production and the Nature of Social Class

When Marx divides the population of capitalist society into "capitalists" and "proletarians," he does so on the basis of their ownership of capital, which determines their different *roles in the productive process*. To identify classes in contemporary society, we would therefore have to identify the possible roles people can play with respect to their participation in the production.

Let us use Marx's distinction first. Does the individual buy or sell labor? If the individual buys the labor of others, then he is a "capitalist," for that is what capitalists qua capitalists do since they own the stock of the economy's assets or, as Marx called them, "the means of production." If the respondent is employed by others, he is a "proletarian" in the classic Marxist sense of one who sells his labor. Two groups do neither: artisans or shopkeepers, proprietors or jobbers who are self-employed but do not buy labor, and

nonparticipants, in the form of students, regularly unemployed, retired or idle
rich.

II. Distinctions Within the Working Class

The working class, or proletariat, can be internally differentiated by the
different roles wage or salary earners can play at work. One such characteristic
is whether or not their work is productive. Marx employed the labor theory of
value not only because it was the common value theory of the day but because it
reflected a fundamental philosophic view of production. Something can only be
invested with value if it is transformed—if it becomes something else. In the
absence of such a transformation, no value could be produced. Therefore, commodities became invested with value when laborers transformed them (i.e., created
them out of component parts or raw materials, inputs).

But not all work involves making such transformations. Much work that goes
on within enterprises tends only to the bureaucratic and organizational functions
of the enterprise itself, payroll, correspondence, etc., and does nothing to
transfer inputs into commodities. Therefore, we can divide the group of all
workers into two bodies: "productive" and "organizational" workers.

Another important distinction of the modern productive process is "hierarchy."
The decision-making process at work is vertical and goes in one direction only.
Workers can either be supervised, or supervisors, or some combination of the two.
This entails measuring the worker's "hierarchial level." In creating the index,
a choice was presented between two possible proxies for this phenomenon. Occupational group was chosen over the respondent's feelings as to whether he had much
choice in the way he worked. Both productive and non-productive work is organized the same way. The only difference is that "managers" occupy the top of the
hierarchy for non-productive work and "professionals" or "technical workers"
occupy the top positions in the pyramid of productive work.

III. Coding the Class Structure

In presenting this outline, we have developed a definition of a class. A
group of individuals are defined as a class if they have similar relationship to,
and relationship within, the organization of production. Each has its own relation to its own system of production. To make the class structure outlined
here more comprehensible, it is presented in diagram form in Figure A5.1 This
section demonstrates how this typology can be recreated using the Panel Study
five-year family tape.

FIGURE A5.1

CLASS STRUCTURE OF THE UNITED STATES

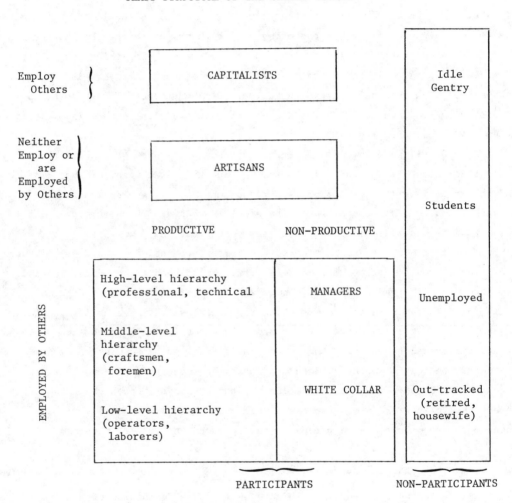

The sample used is a random half-sample of the population of nonfarm house-hold heads. Using the data available on each respondent, much of the information pertinent to class membership was present. This information included employment status, a one-digit occupational skill code, whether the respondent was self-employed, whether the respondent had an interest in an incorporated or unincorpo-rated enterprise, and the respondent's asset income. Of course, other material information that could have been used was absent: size of the enterprise, where the respondent works, the enterprise's role (if any) in international trade, or the individual's position in the hierarchy of production.

The absence of complete information on each respondent means that some amount of measurement error might be expected and that the class taxonomy will rely heavily on the occupational skill code. The following sections will demonstrate, however, that the social class variable as constructed still has great intuitive meaning and explanatory power.

The coding used to produce the class index was as follows:

1. *Big Capital*

            V2582 = 2,3
        and V2584 = 2,3
        and V2505 = 8
        and V2696 = 1,3
        and V2417 + V2423 greater than or equal to 75000
        and V2583 = 11 - 89

    (Managers, officials and businessmen who are self-employed, have asset incomes over $10,000, have an interest in an incorporated business, have social capital greater than $75,000, and work in the private sector.)

2. *Small Capital*

            V2582 = 2,3
        and V2584 = 2,3
        and V2505 = 2-7
        or V2696 = 1,3
        or V2417 + V2423 less than 75000
        and V2583 = 11-89

    (Managers, officials and businessmen who lack asset incomes over $10,000, and interest in an incorporated business, or social capital in excess of $75,000, and work in the private sector.)

    or

            V2582 = 1
        and V2584 = 2,3

    (Self-employed professionals)

3. *Proprietors*

    > V2582 = 2,3
    > and   V2505 = 0,1,9

    (Managers, officials and businessmen with insignificant asset
    income, or negative asset income.)

    or

    > V2582 = 5
    > and   V2584 = 2,3

    (Self-employed craftsmen)

4. *Administrators*

    > V2582 = 2
    > and   V2584 = 1

    (Managers and officials in the employ of others.)

    or

    > V2582 = 2,3
    > and   V2583 = 91-92

    (Managers, officials and businessmen in the public sector.)

5. *High Hierarchy*

    > V2582 = 1
    > and   V2584 = 1

    (Craftsmen and foremen in the employ of others.)

6. *Middle Hierarchy*

    > V2582 = 5
    > and   V2584 = 1

    (Craftsmen and foremen in the employ of others.)

7. *White Collar*

    > ·   V2582 = 4

    (Sales and clerical workers.)

8. *Low Hierarchy*

    > V2582 = 6,7

    (Operatives, laborers, service and farm workers.)

9. *Retired Gentry*

    > V2581 = 3,4
    > and   V2505 = 7,8

    (Retired, disabled, and housewives with asset income over
    $7500.)

10. *Out-tracked*

> V2581 = 3,4
> and V2505 = 0-6,9

> (Retired, disabled, and housewives without significant asset income.)

11. *Unemployed*

> V2581 = 2

> (Actively seeking work--not temporarily laid off.)

12. *Students*

> V2581 = 5

> (Student)

13. *Miscellaneous*

> (All other; unclassified; missing data, etc.)

Before any results are reproduced, it should be pointed out that there are *no* capitalists in the sample. This is not an astonishing finding, considering that the random component of the weighted sample being used totals about 1500, and it seems likely that there are not enough "big capitalists" in the United States to guarantee one's presence in the sample.

IV. Movement Between Classes

If social class is to be considered as an explanatory variable, then it must have some degree of "permanence," e.g., there should be a high probability that one's social class will be the same at two points in time. To investigate this problem, we compare class membership in 1968 and 1972.

Table A5.1 presents this comparison. The degree to which classes are "permanent" is best illustrated by the percentage of observations that lie along the diagonal--in this case, 71.01 percent. This figure, however, should be interpreted subject to the following qualifications:

1. Mobility is a *characteristic* of some classes; that is to say, there are some classes in which we expect movement in and out. This is true, for example, for the groups "proprietors" and "unemployed" in this study. Since proprietors includes shopkeepers and craftsmen who are self-employed and lack any assets, the high rate of failure of these enterprises would lead us to expect a large segment of this group to be turned over into wage labor classes. Similarly some individuals in the wage labor classes can be expected to enter the proprietor class in an attempt to secure upward economic mobility.

2. Measurement error in coding and reporting in the class taxonomy may create the appearance of mobility where there is none. This is particularly true of proprietors and small capitalists. Proprietors were defined as managers, officials, and entrepreneurs who were self-employed and reported asset income of $500 or less (including negative). This was the best possible measurement of shopkeepers, yet it probably entails some degree of measurement error in that individuals who should have been classified as "small capitalists" might report low asset incomes for personal reasons or quirks of accounting. Another measurement problem might exist in the case of administrators who report themselves under the employ of others when, in fact, they are officials of enterprises in which they own a significant share.

3. There is a significant amount of measurement error built into the Family Income Dynamics tape in which the data is stored. This takes the form of individuals who have not changed jobs in the period 1968-1972 but are assigned different values in the occupational skill code for these two years, upon which most of the class taxonomy is based.

To demonstrate this error, a comparison was made of 1968 and 1972 occupation code for those reporting no job change and the sum of the diagonal components, those correctly coded, was found to be 80.29 percent. There is, of course, the possibility of "on the job" promotions, which could account for different jobs without the respondent reporting changes in his job. If we assume that *all* cases in which 1972 skill code implied a "better" job than 1968 were generated by on-the-job promotions, then the coding is 92.22 percent consistent. In either case, measurement errors in this case exist to a significant extent.

When these different sources of error are taken into account, class does appear to have some degree of "permanence," enough to make it a meaningful explanatory variable. This degree of "permanence," or "immobility," requires more attention. If individuals are somehow channeled into these groups, then there must be active mechanisms of some sort that keep them within these groups. For example, "credentials" of different sorts, such as educational attainment or "social standing," might be prerequisites to entry into "higher" groups and such credentials might be allocated on the basis of previous credentials. On the other hand, the individual might perceive the transition from one group to another as futile on the basis of past experience or "popular knowledge," the experience of others. It could also be that individuals "cling" to their group in an attempt to rise within it, this being a more plausible strategy than moving through it. Understanding this "sorting" mechanism will provide a definitive picture of immobility and inequality in the economy.

TABLE A5.1

Class Mobility Among Five-Year Labor Force Participants

Class in 1972	Class in 1968								
	(A)	(B)	(C)	(D)	(E)	(F)	(G)	(H)	(I)
(A) Capitalists	64.3%	27.7%	3.3%	7.0%	0.0%	1.6%	0.0%	0.0%	0.0%
(B) Proprietors	14.8	42.9	9.8	3.3	6.0	2.9	4.0	5.8	0.0
(C) Administrators	8.2	8.0	70.1	7.6	2.5	11.9	0.5	0.0	0.0
(D) High-level hierarchy	2.9	3.2	4.2	78.6	1.3	4.1	0.1	17.2	7.7
(E) Middle-level hierarchy	0.0	2.0	0.7	2.3	74.4	4.3	13.8	26.1	3.1
(F) White collar	0.0	6.9	9.4	0.0	3.4	68.7	2.5	5.2	3.5
(G) Low-level hierarchy	5.8	5.8	2.6	1.2	9.8	6.4	76.2	29.9	24.5
(H) Unemployed	0.0	0.0	0.0	0.0	2.7	0.1	2.0	15.8	0.0
(I) Miscellaneous	4.0	3.4	0.0	0.0	0.0	0.0	0.8	0.0	61.2
TOTAL	100.0	100.0	100.0	100.0	100.0	100.0	100.0	100.0	100.0
Number of observations	30	58	74	112	186	134	434	17	31

V.   Comparison to Other Predictors

The question still remains as to whether comparable predictive power could be achieved using other theories of stratification.   In economics, the foremost alternative theory is "human capital" theory as advanced by Becker.[1]

Human capital theory posits that through self-investment workers can demand and receive a higher return for their labor, owing to the fact that their education or training makes them more "productive."   This theory should not, then, be responsible for making predictions in "social" areas, such as personality measures or demographic characteristics, but it should make predictions as to income, work enjoyability (these two variables combining to measure the actual "return" to labor) and, presumably, the efficacy-planning index, as it is a learned behavior.

To make such a comparison, a variable measuring education was used to explain the same income to needs ratio, the same job enjoyability responses, and the same index of feelings concerning efficacy and planning.   A comparison of the Eta-square (analagous to R^2) statistics is presented below.   It is noted that class, as derived from Marxist social theory, is in each case a better predictor than the human capital argument.   Not only is this true, but the notion of class extends itself into the area of social dynamics where human capital is yet to present itself.

Eta-square Statistics

	Class	Human Capital
Income/needs	.31	.19
Average hourly earnings	.18	.13
Job enjoyability	.58	.02
Efficiency/planning	.10	.09

Human capital theory does poorly by comparison.   The best possible explanation of this result is that human capital theory lacks what Marxist social theory has: an understanding of what the actual process of production is like.   Because Marx developed a model of how production in capitalist society is carried out, he was able to distinguish between the possible roles an individual could have in the economy.   It stands to reason that this would provide more explanatory power

---

[1]See Becker (1964).

than education or vocational training (the human capital argument), since the latter is merely *one* of the mechanisms that distributes people into the set of roles.

Marx argues against income or occupation as a substitute for class. By doing so, he suggests two competing hypotheses with which we can measure class explanatory power. Income is depicted by decile income group and occupation by a one-digit skill code. Table A5.2 presents the explanatory power of class, education, income and occupation in predicting dependent variables. The Eta-square statistics are derived by taking the mean of the dependent variable for each category of each predictor. Owing to the scarcity of computing resources, statistics were computed for selected dependent variables.

Income's comparatively lower explanatory power suggests Marx's assertion that it is obfuscatory. Occupation, as measured, does as well as class as an explanatory phenomenon. However, this does not refute class' explanatory power. On the contrary, the one-digit occupation code in many ways resembles class, in that as opposed to distinguishing between riggers and welders, the code distinguishes between the *group* of riggers and welders versus the *group* of managers and officials. It seems highly unlikely that substitution of a two-digit code would substantially improve explanatory power, and it would be in such a code that the true effects of occupation per se would be felt, as opposed to broad occupational groups. In fact, since the class taxonomy is derived to a large extent from the occupation skill code, it would seem that it draws upon this variable for much of its explanatory strength.

TABLE A5.2

Eta-Square Statistics for Dependent Variables
Viewed as "Determined" by Class

	Class	Education	Decile Y	Occupation
Job enjoyability	.58	.02	.15	.58
Income to needs	.31	.19	.25	.26
Average hourly earnings	.18	.13	.38	.23
I.Q.	.15	.22	.11	.15
Achievement motivation	.12	.12	.07	.08
Efficacy/planning	.10	.09	.07	.09
Late for work	.09	.03	.01	.03
Savings	.08	.09	.08	.06
Absenteeism	.03	.00	.00	.01

V.   Conclusions and Caveats

This essay is far from the last word in the area of social stratification. It has demonstrated, of course, that the particular social class taxonomy created here is capable of making respectable predictions of both economic variables and personality measures, and that those predictions "make sense."

The similarity of the "class" and "occupation" measures stems from the similarity of the two phenomena.   Kerr could be credited with developing a similar theory to Marx's in his discussion of "non-competing" groups in the labor market.[1] Blau and Duncan also present a stratification model based on occupation, although with an interval, as opposed to discontinuous, measure.[2]

If we ignore Marx's theories of social change, then his notion of class is similar to Mill's notion of "non-competing" groups. The common theme is that a limited opportunity set is presented to the individual with respect to his/her labor force participation: that society is segmented into groups by occupation. For the human capital theorist, the notion that hierarchy and productive versus non-productive work are the separating mechanisms is as absurd as is the notion that skill sorts the labor force out, in the eyes of the Marxist. The controversy can only be resolved by a data set that both accept as representative of the concepts both employ.

[1]See Kerr (1949).

[2]See Blau and Duncan (1967).

References

Ando, A., and Modigliani, F., "The Life Cycle Hypothesis of Saving," _American Economic Review_, Vol. 53, No. 1, March 1963, pp 55-84.

Becker, G., _Human Capital_, National Bureau of Economic Research, New York, 1964.

Blau, P., and Duncan, O. D., _The American Occupational Structure_, John Wiley and Sons, New York, 1967.

Cramer, J., "Births, Expected Family Size and Poverty," _Five Thousand American Families_, Volume II, Institute for Social Research, University of Michigan, Ann Arbor, 1973.

Department of Health, Education, and Welfare, _Work in America_, M.I.T. Press, Cambridge, Mass., March 1973.

Kerr, Clark, "Labor Markets: Their Character and Consequences," _Industrial Relations Research Association Procedings_, Dec. 1949, Vol. 2, pp 69-84.

Modigliani, F., and Ando, A., "Test of the Life Cycle Hypothesis of Saving," _Bulletin of the Oxford University Institute of Statistics_, May 1957, 19, pp 99-124.

Modigliani, F., and Ando, A., "The Permanent Income and Life Cycle Hypothesis of Saving Behavior: Comparison and Tests," in _Proceedings of the Conference on Consumption and Saving_, Vol. 2, Philadelphia, 1960.

Roistacher, E., "Residential Mobility," _Five Thousand American Families_, Vol. II, Institute for Social Research, University of Michigan, Ann Arbor, 1973.

Shapiro, H. and Hymans, S., "The Allocation of Household Income to Food Consumption," _Five Thousand American Families_, Vol. II, Institute for Social Research, University of Michigan, Ann Arbor, 1973.

Taylor, F. W., _The Principles of Scientific Management_, Harper, New York, 1911.

Taylor, L., "Saving Out Of Different Types of Income," _Brookings Papers on Economic Activity_, 2, 1971 Brookings Institute, Washington, D.C.

Chapter 6

CHILD CARE
Katherine Dickinson

INTRODUCTION

Recent interest in the child care arrangements made by working mothers prompted the inclusion of several questions on this subject in the sixth interviewing wave. Because the time available in the telephone interview was very limited, these questions were necessarily brief and objective. They concern mode of child care but not satisfaction with the quality of care. Nor did we ask whether respondents would use other methods of child care if available. We asked about only the most extreme type of breakdown of arrangements -- whether someone must stay home from work -- but not about other disruptions to the family.

The following two chapters present complementary analyses of child care methods. The first contains a bivariate analysis of the current arrangements for those mothers now working and the potential arrangements others might make if they chose to work. A note on the distribution of benefits which resulted from making child care costs tax deductible is also presented. The subsequent chapter contains a multivariate analysis of child care mode choice.

ANALYSIS

I. Mode and Cost of Child Care

The modes of child care used, distributed by sex, race and income of users, are shown in Tables 6.1, 6.2 and 6.3. Day care centers and nursery schools are currently used by only eight percent of the population of working mothers. Single women and those in the middle income range are somewhat more likely to use these facilities than others. A babysitter or friend is the most common single mode of child care, especially among the higher income groups.

Perhaps a surprising source of child care comes from the head or wife. In 24% of the families, either the parents have arranged their schedules so that

TABLE 6.1

Mode of Child Care by Sex of Head

	Male	Female	ALL
Day Care, Nursery	7.3%	11.0%	8.0%
Sitter, Friend	23.3	27.6	24.2
Head or Wife	29.0	3.6	23.9
Relatives Living with Family	8.4	15.5	9.8
Relatives Not Living with Family	16.2	22.4	17.4
Take Care of Selves	0.8	6.7	2.0
Public School	11.4	7.8	10.7
Other, Unspecified	3.5	5.4	3.9
	100%	100%	100%
	n = 897	n = 310	

TABLE 6.2

Mode of Child Care by Race

	White	Black	Other	ALL
Day Care, Nursery	7.9%	7.6%	13.5%	8.0%
Sitter, Friend	24.8	21.1	25.6	24.2
Head or Wife	26.3	14.4	16.3	23.9
Relatives Living with Family	8.8	13.6	13.5	9.8
Relatives Not Living With Family	16.0	24.0	17.0	17.4
Take Care of Selves	1.9	1.9	3.8	2.0
Public School	10.6	11.8	9.1	10.7
Other, Unspecified	3.7	5.4	1.1	3.9
	100%	100%	100%	100%
	n = 585	n = 578	n = 35	

MTR6041

TABLE 6.3

Mode of Child Care by Income Quintile

	Lowest 1st	2nd	3rd	4th	Highest 5th	ALL
Day Care, Nursery	6%	9%	11%	9%	3%	8.0%
Sitter, Friend	13	27	25	22	27	24.2
Head or Wife	17	15	23	29	27	23.9
Relatives Living with Family	15	12	9	8	10	9.8
Relatives Not Living with Family	30	26	18	14	12	17.4
Take Care of Selves	6	2	1	1	2	2.0
Public School	7	5	6	13	18	10.7
Other, Unspecified	6	4	7	4	1	3.9
	100%	100%	100%	100%	100%	100.0%
	n=142	n=340	n=523	n=272	n=182	

they work split shifts or, more rarely, the wife has work which she can do at home. Single women, of course, cannot make these split-shift arrangements and rely more heavily on other relatives either living in or outside of the family unit. Taken together, approximately half of the families use a child care method that involves some family member -- either a parent or other relative. This underscores the importance that family arrangements play in determining the economic well-being of its members.

We directed questions at families with children under the age of 12. In some families the children simply take care of themselves. This situation occurs mainly in single-parent homes in the lowest-income quintile, where there may be no economically feasible alternatives available. Finally, ten percent of the population rely on the public schools as a means of child care.

The cost of child care was collected on a weekly basis, but in order to compare the costs for those working differing amounts, the costs have been calculated on an hourly basis and are presented in Tables 6.4 and 6.5. There is some error introduced by dividing cost by hours since these two concepts may not correspond exactly: some hours of care may be free, for example. The eleven percent of the population calculated as paying $3 or more may well be a result of error.[1]

From these tables we see that nearly half the families report they do not pay anything for child care. This is not affected by our calculation procedure. Free care is somewhat more common among low-income families, but is very prevalent among those in the highest-income quintile as well.

Looking at the cost by mode of care (Table 6.5), we find that the source of free care is mainly family members living in the family unit, either the parents themselves or other relatives such as a grandparent or older sibling. Of course, free only means no regular money payment. Some reciprocity or return obligation may well be involved. A majority of families using other methods of care pay $1 an hour or less.

II. Breakdown of Child Care Arrangements

In the sixth wave we also asked the frequency of child care arrangement breakdown resulting in someone staying home from work. This type of breakdown, of course, only reflects loss of productivity in the market place and does not represent a measure of the disruption to the family or loss of quality in care, if such alternative arrangements are frequently made.

---

[1] This is underscored by the astonishing result that ten percent of those families in the two lowest income quintiles report payments of $3 or more per hour.

TABLE 6.4

Cost of Child Care by Income Quintile

	1st	2nd	3rd	4th	5th	ALL
None	60%	42%	43%	51%	54%	48.8%
< $.50/hour	19	24	19	16	9	16.6
$.50-.99/hour	9	23	19	14	16	17.1
$1.00-1.49	3	0.3	6	5	6	4.4
$1.50-2.99	0.3	1	0.5	2	4	1.9
$3.00 or more	9	10	12	13	11	11.1
	100%	100%	100%	100%	100%	100%
	n=142	n=340	n=523	n=272	n=182	

TABLE 6.5

Cost of Child Care by Mode of Care

	Day Care	Sitter	Head or Wife	Relative in Family	Relative Outside Family	ALL
None	4.6%	9.5%	91.8%	83.1%	45.9%	48.8%
<$.50/hour	45.2	27.3	.9	5.2	24.7	16.6
$.50-.99/hour	38.2	39.3	1.1	1.7	16.3	17.1
$1.00-1.49/hour	4.4	7.9	1.9	1.3	4.1	4.4
$1.50-2.99/hour	1.1	5.2	---	0.2	3.7	1.9
$3.00 or more	6.5	10.9	4.4	8.6	6.3	11.1
	100%	100%	100%	100%	100%	100%
	n=112	n=268	n=224	n=173	n=247	

MTR6041

Of the families responding to this question, three-quarters reported that the child care arrangements never broke down so completely that someone had to stay home from work. These figures contradict the hypothesis that working mothers must frequently miss work and thus are less productive. If such women are paid less on the assumption that this hypothesis is true, then prejudice exists.

Table 6.6 shows the reliability of the different modes of child care. Sitters and children taking care of themselves are the methods most likely to break down while family members inside the household -- either parents or other relatives -- are the most reliable means.

When we look at the frequency of breakdown by income (Table 6.7), we find that those in the lowest-income quintile miss work less frequently than others. Low-income families are not more likely to use more reliable means of child care (see Tables 6.3 and 6.6), but, perhaps, are simply unable to afford to miss work. Or they do not have jobs where lost time can be made up or covered by sick leave.

In order to find any subgroups of the population that experienced more frequent disruptions, the search program Automatic Interaction Detector was used with these data, treating the frequency of breakdown as a scale (never = 0, often = 4). The results of this program are shown in Figure 6.1. The families in which we find the greatest frequency of child care breakdown use the least reliable child care method -- baby sitters or the children looking after themselves. Those families who also live fifteen miles or more from the center of a city of 50,000, and where the mother works more than one-quarter time, and the youngest child is less than nine years old, have the highest incidence of missing work. But even within this group, breakdowns happen on the average of only once or twice a year.

III. Availability of Child Care for Those Not Working

We also asked a series of necessarily more subjective questions about the availability of child care if mothers not currently working wanted to take jobs. Nearly 68 percent of families questioned felt some arrangements could be made. Of the remaining families, half answered that child care definitely was not available, and the rest expressed uncertainty about whether such arrangements could be made. Single women and blacks were more uncertain about care than other families (see Tables 6.8 and 6.9).

There is a large difference in the type of care that families with non-

TABLE 6.6

Frequency of Breakdown of Child Care Arrangements by Mode of Care[*]

	Care	Sitter	Head or Wife	Relative in Family	Relative Outside Family	Selves	Public School	ALL
Often, twice or more a month	1.2%	2.1%	1.9%	---	4.1%	---	3.1%	2.2%
Once a month	1.4	4.5	---	---	3.1	---	---	2.0
Few times a year	9.9	14.9	3.2	4.0	8.0	11.4	3.7	8.4
Rarely, once or twice a year	11.1	10.7	10.5	3.0	8.8	28.5	11.6	9.9
Never	76.4	67.8	84.4	93.0	76.0	60.1	81.5	77.5
	100%	100%	100%	100%	100%	100%	100%	100%
	n=106	n=251	n=132	n=153	n=232	n=24	n=84	

* Excludes families where the frequency of breakdown was not ascertained.

TABLE 6.7

Frequency of Breakdown of Child Care Arrangements by Income Quintile

	Income Quintile					
	1	2	3	4	5	ALL
Often, twice or more a month	1.5%	2.3%	1.0%	1.1%	3.3%	1.8%
Once a month	1.5	2.2	2.3	1.1	1.4	1.7
Few times a year	3.6	8.7	9.7	5.6	5.5	6.9
Rarely, once or twice a year	5.8	7.8	8.0	9.9	6.7	8.0
Never	72.5	63.9	58.5	61.3	67.0	63.2
Not Ascertained	15.2	15.1	20.5	21.0	16.6	18.4
	100.1%	100.0%	100.0%	100.0%	100.0%	100.0%
	n=142	n=340	n=523	n=272	n=182	

MTR6041

228

FIGURE 6.1

Frequency of Child Care Breakdown

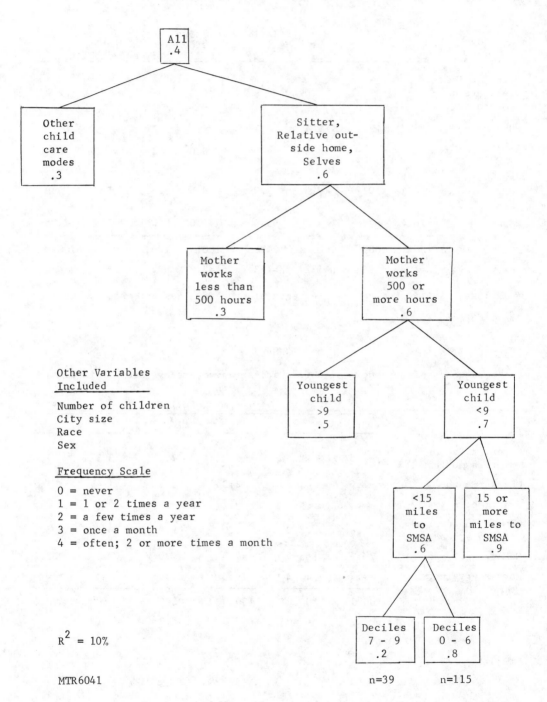

All
.4

Other child care modes
.3

Sitter, Relative out-side home, Selves
.6

Mother works less than 500 hours
.3

Mother works 500 or more hours
.6

Youngest child >9
.5

Youngest child <9
.7

<15 miles to SMSA
.6

15 or more miles to SMSA
.9

Deciles 7 - 9
.2

Deciles 0 - 6
.8

n=39   n=115

Other Variables
Included

Number of children
City size
Race
Sex

Frequency Scale

0 = never
1 = 1 or 2 times a year
2 = a few times a year
3 = once a month
4 = often; 2 or more times a month

R^2 = 10%

MTR6041

TABLE 6.8

Whether Child Care Available if
Mother Wanted to Work, by Sex of Head

	Male	Female	All
Yes	68.9%	53.6%	67.4%
No	14.2	15.3	14.3
Don't know	13.2	18.6	13.7
Not ascertained	3.7	12.5	4.6
	100.0%	100.0%	100.0%
	n=889	n=253	

TABLE 6.9

Whether Child Care Available if
Mother Wanted to Work, by Race of Head

	White	Black	Other	All
Yes	68.8%	58.9%	63.7%	67.4%
No	14.1	16.0	12.9	14.3
Don't know	12.8	18.8	18.1	13.7
Not ascertained	4.3	6.3	5.3	4.6
	100.0%	100.0%	100.0%	100.0%
	n=605	n=474	n=63	

MTR6041

working mothers perceive as available and the modes actually used by those who are working (see Table 6.10). Twenty-two percent feel they could use day care centers or nursery schools, while only eight percent currently have made such arrangements. Split-shift schedules or relatives within the family are mentioned much less frequently as potential methods of care than as actual methods used. Perhaps those who can easily make such arrangements are more likely to be working already than those who cannot. If the trend toward increasing numbers of working mothers continues, those who say they would rely on day care centers represent a large potential demand for such facilities in the future.

These families were also asked the probable cost of available care. The figures they gave are close to those actually being paid except that many fewer felt they could find free care.

Those who said they could not make arrangements for the children if the mother wanted to work were asked why they felt this way (see Table 6.11). Thirty percent said there was not child care available and another 20 percent mentioned that it would be too expensive. Nearly a quarter of the families did not answer the question directly but said that the mother should stay home with the children. Perhaps they are reflecting the belief that the existing facilities do not provide an adequate substitute in terms of quality of child care.

IV.   The Benefit of Child Care Deductions

Beginning in 1972, the cost of child care became tax deductible for wives or single parents working "substantially full time." In order to benefit from this change in the law, working women must work three-quarters time and file an itemized tax return rather than take a standard deduction. A recent project at the Survey Research Center which studied the itemization of 1972 tax returns provides insight into the possible benefits of this new law. Column 1 of Table 6.12 shows the proportion of families with working mothers who worked an average of thirty or more hours a week by income category. The second column shows the percentage of families with children who itemize their tax returns, estimated from the tax study. The product of these two numbers is then the proportion of families who can potentially benefit from child care deductions.

Only 18 percent of the families earning $6000 or less per year can realize a tax saving from this child care provision, and this income category contains over 12 percent of the families with working mothers. For most of the remaining groups, the proportion who can deduct child care expenses ranges from 40 to 45 percent.

TABLE 6.10

Mode of Child Care if Mother Wanted to Work
by Sex of Head

	Male	Female	All
Day care	22.1%	18.0%	21.8%
Sitter, friend	35.3	21.2	34.1
Head or wife	6.2	8.5	6.4
Relatives living with family	7.9	24.3	9.2
Relatives not living with family	19.4	18.7	19.3
Selves	0.9	3.6	1.1
Public School	3.5	2.9	3.4
Other, unspecified	4.8	2.9	3.3
	100.0%	100.0%	100.0%
	n=610	n=139	

TABLE 6.11

Why No Child Care Available if Mother Wanted to Work
by Sex of Head

	Male	Female	All
Special needs of children	2.8%	4.7%	3.0%
Transportation	0.2	1.5	0.3
Quality of care poor	7.8	8.2	7.8
No care available	30.3	30.9	30.4
Cost	18.6	31.4	20.0
Mother should stay home with children	25.8	0.5	23.0
Unspecified	14.6	22.8	15.6
	100.0%	100.0%	100.0%
	n=122	n=41	

TABLE 6.12

Benefit of Child Care Deductions to Working Mothers by Income

Total family income	Percent of families with mothers working at least 30 hours	Percent of families with children itemizing	Percent with potential benefits	Average tax savings per $100 child care expenditure
$0 - 5,999	75%	24%	18%	$ 0
$6,000 - 7,499	87	50	44	16
$7,500 - 9,999	75	55	41	19
$10,000-10,999	73	61	45	19
$11,000-12,499	74	53	40	19
$12,500-14,999	68	68	46	22
$15,000-17,499	71	61	43	22
$17,500-19,999	74	100	74	12*
$20,000-22,499	86	94	81	14*
$22,500 or more	70	81	57	18*

* The deduction cannot be more than $400 per month. The deduction itself is reduced by fifty cents for each extra dollar of income about $18,000, e.g.,

Income	Expense	Deductible
$18,000	$1,000	$1,000
18,000	5,000	4,800
19,000	1,000	500
19,000	5,000	4,300
20,000	1,000	0
20,000	5,000	3,800

MTR6041

The final column of Table 6.12 uses estimates of the marginal tax rate for families in each of the income brackets to calculate the tax savings of a $100 expenditure on child care. Because tax rates rise with income level, the dollar benefit does also, although at $18,000, the law provides that only half of the cost can be deducted. Thus, the average family in the lowest income bracket does not benefit from the tax law change because it pays no tax. Middle-income families benefit the most from the tax provision, although less than half of these families with working mothers can make any adjustment in their taxes for the cost of child care.

SUMMARY

This chapter has explored bivariate relationships between characteristics of child care mode and a variety of demographic characteristics of sample families. It was found that day care and nursery schools are not a popular child care mode, being used by only eight percent of the population of working mothers. In almost one-quarter of the families, care was provided by the head or wife through an arrangement like split shifts or work at home.

Half of the sample families do not pay for child care. Such free care has only a moderate negative correlation with family income.

Child care arrangements do not generally break down to the degree that a parent must stay home from work. Babysitters or having the children look after themselves were the least reliable modes in this regard.

Using some outside data, potential benefits of tax law changes which make child care costs tax deductible were analyzed. Since lower-income families do not itemize, most will not benefit from the change. Middle and upper-income families stand to benefit more.

Chapter 7

MODAL CHOICE IN CHILD CARE ARRANGEMENTS
Greg Duncan and C. Russell Hill

INTRODUCTION

The dramatic increase in the labor force participation rate of married women over the past half century is by now well known to even the most casual observer of economic and demographic trends. Even more striking, however, is the increase in the labor market participation of women with young children and the change in American family life that this trend implies. Two or three decades ago it was unusual for mothers to work outside the home, especially if they had young children. Now it is no longer unusual. In 1970, slightly more than half the mothers with school-age children and about one-third of those with children under six were in the labor force. This has not been the result of the breakup of families, for the largest part of this movement into the labor force has been by women living with their husbands.[1] The social and economic determinants of these secular trends are not of direct concern to us here and have, in any case, been adequately reviewed elsewhere.[2] It is clear, however, that this movement into the labor force by married women with children could not have occurred without the provision of some mode of child care either from within the family or external to it.[3] Future trends in the labor force participation of women with children will depend, in part, upon changes in the supply of and demand for these modes. It is important, then, to understand the determinants of child care mode choice. It is our purpose to describe and analyze these determinants with the data from the 1973 interviewing wave of the Income Dynamics Panel.

---

[1] Historical data on married women's participation rates are contained in U. S. Bureau of the Census (1972), Tables 346-348.

[2] A convenient summary of these determinants is contained in C. L. Schultz, et al. (1972), pp. 258-260.

[3] See, for example, James J. Heckman (1974).

ANALYSIS

I. The Choice of Mode

Like the decision regarding the mother's participation in the labor force, the choice of the mode of child care is best thought of as occurring within a family setting. That is, the economic and demographic characteristics of the family as a unit, as well as the characteristics of its individual members, are important inputs in the decision-making process. The decision itself is basically one of determining whether the child or children should be cared for within or outside the household and determining who should provide the care. The family's income, size and composition, its members' economic characteristics and personal tastes, together with exogenous (to the family) phenomenon, such as the provision of institutional day care centers or nursery schools, will ultimately determine the choice of mode.

As part of the 1973 survey of the Panel Study of Income Dynamics, a series of questions concerning the care of children was asked of families in which the wife worked in the labor market. The sample we analyze consists of 511 two-parent households in which both parents worked during 1972 and which included at least one child less than twelve years of age.[1] In order to ensure that the sample consisted of families that used some mode of child care on a relatively frequent basis, the analysis was also limited to those families who used some mode of child care at least ten hours per week.

The data distinguishes several different categories of child care. We have grouped these into three exhaustive and mutually exclusive modes on the basis of the location of care, its direct cost to the family, and whether it was provided institutionally or informally. The categories included in our three modes (FAMILY, SITTER and DAY CARE) and the proportion of the sample choosing each category are listed in Table 7.1.

The FAMILY mode includes at-home care provided by some family member at no direct cost to the family. There may be, however, an opportunity cost involved to the extent that this type of care requires withdrawal from the labor force by a member of the family and a consequent reduction in earnings.

The modal choice SITTER typifies relatively informal care (as compared with DAY CARE) provided by someone outside the family unit at some cost to the family. The cost may either be a direct charge or the implicit cost of support-

---

[1] We also expanded our sample to include one-parent households headed by a working female. Differences in modal choice between male and female headed families are discussed below.

TABLE 7.1

Description of Child Care Modes

Mode	Categories	Percent of sample* choosing category
1. FAMILY	a. Head and/or wife (wife does job at home; head and wife with split shifts, etc.)	15.7
	b. Relatives in family unit including siblings over 12 years of age	5.3
	c. Relatives not in family unit or friends of family if care is provided at no cost to family	10.8
		Total 31.8
2. SITTER	a. Babysitter, friend of the family and/or neighbor if there is some cost to family	36.9
	b. Relatives not in family unit if care is provided at some cost to family	16.0
	c. Public school	2.9
		Total 55.8
3. DAY CARE	a. Day care center	12.4
	b. Nursery school	Total 12.4
		Grand Total 100.0

*The sample consists of 511 two-parent households in which both parents worked during 1972 and at least one child was less than twelve years of age.

238

ing a public school.

DAY CARE represents the institutional mode provided outside the family unit. A recent survey of day care centers has classified them into the following groups by type of care: custodial centers where food, shelter and adult supervision are provided but nothing more; educational centers where educational services are provided in addition to the custodial; and developmental centers which provide all of the above plus health and family counseling and parent participation.[1] Unfortunately, our data are not detailed enough to enable us to distinguish among these types of centers. The cost of institutional care to the family will also vary among the three types with the developmental centers, for example, being supported almost entirely by public subsidy and provided at zero cost to the participating families.[2] In our sample, only a little over two percent of the families who used the DAY CARE mode reported free child care while the average hourly cost for those who paid was 63 cents compared to an average hourly cost of 70 cents for those who used the SITTER mode.

A useful way of characterizing the family's decision of mode choice is to view the process as dependent upon the interaction of factors affecting the supply and demand for child care. In this chapter we will describe these several factors and ultimately propose a model of modal choice, which is essentially a reduced form of this system of supply and demand.

SUPPLY OF CHILD CARE FACILITIES

The choice of child care mode is dependent, in part, upon the availability of the modes. Family arrangements are made easier in large families because older children may care for younger ones. Also, arrangements with relatives are made easier if they live within the household or in the immediate neighborhood. The supply of child care within the family thus depends upon past fertility and mobility decisions.

As measures of these decisions, the number of children in the family and the dichotomous variable of whether the family reported moving within the past year are used. Greater numbers of children should increase the supply and choice of family arrangements. Recent mobility would probably decrease the supply of relatives available for child care and thus be associated with a decrease in the choice of family arrangements.

Interest in and support for nursery schools and day care facilities have not been constant across all geographic areas. Nursery schools are more preva-

---

[1] This survey (the Westinghouse Survey of Daycare Facilities) is discussed in Schultz, et al. (1973).

[2] See Schultz (1973).

lent in urban than in rural areas.[1] There are regional differences as well.
Among three year old children, nursery school enrollments are highest in the
West and South. For four year olds, the West is still the region with the highest enrollment, followed by the North and then the South.[2] No national data
have been compiled on the distribution of day care centers but it seems unlikely
that it would differ greatly from the distribution of nursery schools, particularly with regard to concentration in urban areas. These geographic differences
in the supply of day care and nursery schools are indicated by (1) a four-cate-
gory region variable and (2) a five-category measure of city size.

The availability of sitters should be reasonably independent of the factors which affect the supply of other child care modes. An exception is perhaps
the mobility measure, since those living in an area for a very short time may
not have had enough time to find reliable sitters. Consequently, families reporting a move within the past year may be less likely to choose sitters (or
make family arrangements).

DEMAND FOR CHILD CARE ARRANGEMENTS

The three child care arrangements available to families with working mothers differ in both time and money costs and in the quality of child care they
provide. Because of these differences, the demand for the various modes can be
expected to be related to various characteristics of the family.

We begin with the obvious point that the demand for the child care mode is
dependent upon the ages of the children. The institutional arrangements of nursery school and day care are often restricted to children within the 3-5 year
age range. Families with all children outside of this range will be much less
likely to make nursery school and day care arrangements.

The three child care modes have different prices attached to them. Accordingly, the choice of mode is dependent upon the family's ability to pay, which
is measured by both total family money income and the number of children in

---

[1]Census figures show that the proportion of three and four year olds attending
nursery schools in urban areas is between two and three times the rural enrollment rate. See U. S. Bureau of the Census (1973), Table 3, p. 34.

[2]The exact enrollment rates are as follows:

	Percent Enrolled	
	3 Year Olds	4 Year Olds
North	6.2	16.8
South	7.7	15.2
West	11.2	22.5

U. S. Bureau of the Census (1973), Table 3, pp. 54, 64, 74.

the family.[1] The FAMILY mode is the least expensive, averaging less than five cents per hour. Almost ninety-five percent of the families making child care arrangements within the family reported paying nothing at all for them.[2] The prices for the SITTER and DAY CARE modes are quite similar, averaging 70.2 and 63.1 cents per hour, respectively. Very few families (less than three percent) report free sitting, day care or nursery school arrangements. Because of these price differences, families least able to pay for the child care might, ceteris paribus, choose family arrangements. Thus, the proportion making family arrangements should relate negatively to income level and positively to the number of children.[3]

Time taken away from work in the labor market imposes a (time) cost on the family. It takes time to make child care arrangements and to deal with breakdowns in these arrangements. Consequently, the opportunity or time cost of different modes will be an important determinant of the modal choice. Arrangement-time cost will probably be least for day care centers and nursery schools since they have regular schedules that are seldom altered. The time needed to arrange for a sitter or family child care will vary considerably. Some families may need to make almost daily adjustments to the child care schedules to suit the changing availability of sitters whether they are outsiders or family members, while other families will be able to make arrangements which are as reliable as nursery schools or day care centers.

A final time cost to child care arrangements comes when the arrangements break down and the work schedules of one or both parents are upset. One question in the Panel interview provides some information on this: "In the past year how many times did someone have to stay home from work to take care of the children (child) because these arrangements broke down?" Surprisingly, family arrangements are not the least reliable. Almost 80 percent of the families making child care arrangements within the family reported that they never broke down. About 65 percent of those with sitters and 70 percent using day care or

---

[1] A variable we would like to use as a predictor of modal choice is price per unit of quality which families pay for child care. This is, unfortunately, not available in the data. Nevertheless, predictors which are measured in our data such as age and number of children, and recent mobility have been shown by Heckman to be significant predictors of the quality-adjusted price of family arrangements.

[2] "Payment" in this case is a direct money transfer and neglects such nonmoney transactions as reciprocal child care arrangements during nonworking hours or payments in the form of free meals or housing.

[3] Recall that a positive association between family arrangements and the number of children in the household is also expected from supply considerations.

nursery school child care replied that they never broke down. A slightly different view is afforded by observing the proportion of families reporting that child
care arrangements broke down monthly or more often. Here day care-nursery
schools were the most reliable with less than three percent of their users experiencing a monthly breakdown, while 4.5 percent and 7.3 percent of those making
family and sitter arrangements reported a monthly breakdown.

The wage rate of the mother is used as a measure of the value of the time
spent making the child care arrangements. Since day care and nursery schools
are the most reliable and regular and thus probably the least time consuming, it
is expected that for equal quality of care, families in which the mother has the
highest wage rates will opt for the day care-nursery school arrangements. The
time costs of the other modes are ambiguous.

A final difference among the modes is the quality of child care they provide. We have no direct information on "quality" but it seems clear that there
will be both intra-modal differences and different perceptions of quality care
among the modes for our sample of families. To the extent that quality care positively influences the cognitive and affective abilities of the children, institutional arrangements, particularly nursery schools, will probably provide the
highest quality care. Family arrangements are often made with older siblings or
other relatives and are likely to be little more than custodial. The quality of
hired sitters will differ considerably since it is possible to have either a
situation with one sitter caring for several children with little chance of individual attention or a highly qualified sitter whose sole responsibility is interaction with a single child. In any case, whether "quality" is perceived to be
associated with parental awareness and control of the way their children are
cared for or by the developmental outcomes of various modes, attitudes concerning
quality are clearly related to the educational attainment of the parents.[1]

In previous work we have found that the education of the parents is related
both to the quantity of parental time devoted to preschool child care and to the
subsequent educational attainment of the children.[2] In this chapter the tastes
of the parents for the quality of child care are measured in part by parental
educational attainments. Since the years of schooling that husband and wife receive are often quite similar and the inclusion of both measures would introduce
considerable multicollinearity, an *average* education measure of the parents is
used. However, because the differences in the educational attainments of the

---

[1]This point is also made in Nelson and Krashinsky (1974).

[2]See Hill and Stafford (1974) and Duncan (1974).

parents may also be important, a variable measuring the difference between the schooling levels of the father and mother is also included and allowed to take on any functional form.

It is expected that high parental education levels will be associated with a decreasing proportion of child care arrangements within the family. Since the quality of most nursery school-day care facilities are likely to be greater than those of sitters, higher education levels should, in general, increase the proportion of parents choosing the nursery schools and day care centers. The emphasis placed in this relationship is not great, however, since some babysitters offer considerably higher quality child care than any nursery school or day care center.

Other family characteristics may relate to the tastes and preferences of the parents regarding their choice of mode of child care. Religious affiliation, for example, has been found by Hill and Stafford[1] to relate to parental time inputs to preschool children and by Hause[2] to be an independent factor which affects the post-school earnings of the children. Consequently, a categorical measure of religious preference is included. Race of head is also included among our predictors in order to discover whether, independent of other locational and personal characteristics, black and white families differ in their modal choice. Finally, while most of our analysis is concentrated on families in which a working male is present, we report some results which distinguish between male and female headed families.

II. Statistical Methods

As with most other statistical analysis, we wish to relate a dependent variable to a set of independent variables. Usual statistical techniques such as least-squares multiple regression are, however, inappropriate for our purpose because they use a dependent variable which is measured on an interval scale. The 'child care mode' dependent variable for this analysis is not interval but rather is scaled nominally:[3] It consists of three mutually exclusive categories with no natural order among the categories.

---

[1] Hill and Stafford (1974).

[2] Hause (1972).

[3] A useful distinction among levels of measurement has been developed by S. S. Stevens (1946). An interval (sometimes called continuous or cardinal) scale is composed of a set of categories which have equal distances between them -- e.g. dollars, years, miles, tons, and so on. Thus, income, prices and quantities are variables which can usually be measured on an interval scale. A second level of measurement is an ordinal scale. It applies when the mutually exclusive

The most commonly used statistical analysis technique for a nominally scaled dependent variable is multiple discriminant function analysis (MDF).[1] The MDF technique requires that independent variables be measured on interval scales and that the relationships among independent variables themselves are linear. These restrictions are quite severe. Consequently, a similar although more flexible technique is used here, the Multivariate Nominal Scale Analysis (MNA), which was developed by Andrews and Messenger.[2] MNA relates a nominally scaled dependent variable to a set of independent variables measured on nominal, ordinal and interval scales where the relationship among these independent variables may be either linear or nonlinear.

It is useful to conceive of the MNA technique as a series of dummy variable multiple regressions. The trichotomous dependent variable, child care mode, which consists of the categories (FAMILY, SITTER, DAY CARE) can be decomposed into three separate 1,0 variables: (1) family = 1, else = 0, (2) sitter = 1, else = 0, (3) day care = 1, else = 0. Each of these three dichotomous variables is technically measured on an interval scale (there is only one interval) and thus each can be related to independent variables with more conventional statistical techniques such as least squares regression.[3] MNA is simply a series of parallel multiple regressions with dichotomous dependent variables and categorical independent variables. In addition to the usual information provided by the three separate regressions, a series of bivariate and multivariate statistics for the three regression equations taken together are calculated. The most notable of these additional statistics is a generalized R^2 for the system of equations.

The independent variables in the system of equations of MNA can be scaled

---

categories of a variable have an order to them but do not necessarily have equal distances between them. The third level of measurement is the nominal. Nominal scales (sometimes called categorical) consist of sets of mutually exclusive categories which have no order at all. Region of the country is a commonly encountered variable measured at the nominal level. Child care mode is a second example because the categories (FAMILY, SITTER, DAY CARE) are mutually exclusive and have no natural order.

[1] Expositions of multiple discriminant function analysis are common among applied statistics textbooks. See, for example, Overall and Klett (1972).

[2] See Andrews and Messenger (1973). Much of the discussion of this section draws from their explanation of the technique.

[3] The least squares regression model is not entirely appropriate for the analysis of a dichotomous dependent variable because of heteroscedasticity and predictions outside the 0,1 range. Various transformations of the dependent variable like the logit or probit have appeared in the literature but they have not been incorporated into the MNA technique. See Andrew and Messenger, pp. 46-48.

at the nominal, ordinal or interval level because each is converted into a set
of dummy variables. Use of dummy variables in ordinary least squares regression
presents some complications because one subgroup from each predictor must be
omitted to avoid perfect multicollinearity.[1] Estimated coefficients in the included subclasses of a predictor show the extent to which each subclass differs
from the omitted category. The MNA technique, like the dummy variable regression program Multiple Classification Analysis,[2] presents coefficients on *all*
subgroups of each predictor and shows the extent to which they differ from the
mean value of the dependent variable.

The importance of an independent variable in predicting each of the categories of the dependent variable is given by the beta coefficient. The square
of the beta coefficient is the sum of squares attributable to a predictor (after
adjustments have been made for other predictors) relative to the total sum of
squares. This beta coefficient is analogous to the standardized regression coefficient[3] in usual numerical regression except that it has no sign attached to
it. This absence of sign is due to the fact that each independent variable in
MNA is composed of a set of subclasses, each of which may differ in distribution
across the dependent variable. There is considerable flexibility in allowing
for nonlinearities between predictors and dependent variables.

III. Results

The empirical model to be estimated with the Multivariate Nominal Scale
Analysis technique relates the three category dependent variable (FAMILY, SITTER,
DAY CARE) to the following set of categorical independent variables: the number
of children in the family, age of youngest child, whether the family moved in
the past year, city size, region of the country, family income quintile, mother's
wage rate, average education of the parents, difference in education of parents
(father's minus mother's), religion and race. It is assumed that an additive
(but not necessarily linear) relationship exists among the independent variables.[4]

---

[1] See Suits (1957).

[2] Andrews et al. (1973).

[3] Andrews et al. (1973), p. 49.

[4] The validity of this additivity assumption was investigated with a computer algorithm which systematically searches for interactions among predictors of a
categorical dependent variable. This technique, called THAID, is documented in
Morgan and Messenger (1973). The algorithm finds binary splits of the popula-

Since the MNA technique converts the three-category dependent variable into three separate dichotomous variables and then regresses each of them on the
same set of independent variables, it is instructive to first examine the fraction of the variance in each of the dependent variables that is explained by the
set of independent variables. These are given in Table 7.2. Regardless of the
adjustment for degrees of freedom, the SITTER child care mode is not as well
predicted by the independent variables as are the FAMILY and DAY CARE modes.
This may be due to the residual nature of this category and its resultant heter-
ogeneity.

TABLE 7.2

Unadjusted and Adjusted R^2's From the Three
Dichotomous Dependent Variable Regressions

Dependent Variable	R^2	R^2_A
Whether FAMILY	.20	.14
Whether SITTER	.13	.07
Whether DAY CARE	.21	.16

Since the three dichotomous dependent variables can also be combined into a
single trichotomous variable that is predicted by the set of independent variables, it is possible to calculate a generalized R^2 for the entire system of equations.[1] This generalized R^2 is the ratio of the sum of explained sums of squares
to the total sum of squares. It can be interpreted as a variance-weighted average of the three individual R^2's. For the child care regressions, this generalized R^2 equals .172. In addition, the MNA algorithm provides another summary
statistic which helps to evaluate the predictive power of the set of independent
variables: The Multivariate Theta Statistic. This is defined as the proportion
of families correctly classified as to child care mode choice ... "using a decision rule of predicting each family as being in that dependent variable category
having the maximum forecast value for that family."[2] For our sample of two-par-

tion on explanatory variables which have the greatest differences in the *distribution* across the categories of the dependent variable. When the "best" binary
split is found, then the population is actually divided into two groups. The
importance of all the independent variables in explaining the distributional
differences across categories of the dependent variable is then assessed within
these two population subgroups. When the program was applied to the child care
dependent variable with all of the independent variables mentioned above, *no* important interactions were found. An additive model thus appears to be appropriate.

[1] See Andrews and Messenger (1973), p. 33.

[2] Andrews and Messenger (1973), p. 33.

ent families, 64.6 percent of the families could be correctly classified by the model. In other words, the set of independent variables used here enables us to correctly classify an additional 8.8 percent of the sample beyond what could have been accomplished knowing only that the SITTER mode comprised 55.8 percent of the sample.

The importance of an independent variable in predicting child care mode depends upon two conditions. First, the variable must be able to explain a substantial amount of the variance of the dependent variable after the effects of other predictors have been taken into account. Second, the relationship between the dependent variable and the subclasses of a single independent variable must vary in a systematic and interpretable manner.

The relative importance of the independent variables in explaining each of the categories of the dependent variables is given by its beta square. This is the sum of squares attributable to the predictor relative to the total sum of squares. The beta square of each of the independent variables in the three regressions is given in Table 7.3[1] which shows that similar variables are important in the FAMILY and SITTER equations but differ from the independent variables which explain the DAY CARE mode. The number of children in the family and the wage rate of the mother are the most important in the FAMILY and SITTER equations, while region, average education of the parents, religion and several other, different predictors are the most important in the DAY CARE equation.

The relationship between the categories of a single independent variable and the dependent variable are given by the regression adjusted coefficient on each category. This indicates how they differ from the overall mean value of each of the dependent variables. The relationship between predictor categories and dependent variables can also be given by the regression-adjusted proportion of the sample in each predictor subclass choosing each of the three child care modes. For example, in the "number of children" variable, there is an adjusted fraction of all one-child families choosing family, sitter and day care arrangements. These fractions sum to one. A second category of this variable is composed of two-children families and these will also have adjusted fractions choosing the three modes which sum to one. A similar situation holds for families in the

---

[1]No test of statistical significance for the beta square is provided by the program. It is possible, however, to rerun the regressions and omit a single predictor and then perform an F-test on the partial R^2 of that predictor. In the absence of high multicolinearity, the partial R^2 and beta square are quite similar. Experimentation has shown that the beta square must be in the .010-.015 range before the corresponding partial R^2 attains statistical significance at the five percent probability level.

TABLE 7.3

Relative Importance of Each of the Independent
Variables in Predicting the Three Child Care Modes

Dependent Variable

Whether FAMILY		Whether SITTER		Whether DAY CARE	
Predictor	Beta^2	Predictor	Beta^2	Predictor	Beta^2
Number of children	.067	Number of children	.058	Region	.048
Mother's wage	.047	Mother's wage	.040	Average education of parents	.040
Religion	.017	Average education of parents	.013	Religion	.033
Region	.016			Age of youngest child	.029
Average education of parents	.015			Moved in past year	.025
				City size	.022
				Family income	.012
				Mother's wage	.012
				Difference in education of parents	.012
Difference in education of parents	.008	Income	.007	Number of children	.004
City size	.008	Age of youngest child	.007	Race	.001
Age of youngest child	.005	Religion	.006		
Family income	.003	Income	.006		
Moved in past year	.001	Moved in past year	.006		
Race	.000	Difference in education of parents	.005		
		Region	.001		
		Race	.001		

other categories of this independent variable. The unadjusted and adjusted fractions of the sample in subclasses of all the independent variables choosing the three modes is given in Appendix Table A7.1. The remainder of this discussion focuses upon results for the most important of the independent variables.

One way to see how the subclasses of an explanatory variable relate to the dependent variable is to plot the regression-adjusted proportion of the sample in each subclass opting for the three child care modes. This is done for the "number of children" variable in Figure 7.1.[1] This figure illustrates, as indicated by Table 7.3, that the "number of children" variable distinguishes families making sitter arrangements from those obtaining child care within the family but makes little difference among those using day care centers or nursery schools.[2]

The relationship between number of children and choice of family arrangements instead of sitter child care is positive and monotonic (as expected) but is also decidedly nonlinear. It makes little difference whether a family has one, two, or three children. The regression-adjusted proportion of families making sitter arrangements falls in the 55-60 percent range. Families with four or more children, however, are much less likely to choose a sitter. Only about 25 percent of these large families use sitters for child care. An increased number of children reflects both a decreased ability to pay for child care and the increased chance that older siblings will be able to care for younger ones. Both of these arguments lead to expectation of more frequent choice of FAMILY arrangements instead of the other two modes. The observed nonlinearity between number of children and FAMILY mode choice, however, tends to support the supply interpretation rather than the ability-to-pay explanation. The typically small age intervals between children within a family makes the chance that an older

---

[1]The triangular coordinate graph of Figure 7.1 is commonly used to plot points in three dimensions when the coordinates of the point must sum to 100. Since the population is divided among three mutually exclusive and exhaustive categories of child care, the percentage of the population opting for each mode must sum to 100. The graph has three axes. The lower left corner represents a group of families that opt exclusively for family child care arrangements. The point at the top of the diagram is for groups with 100 percent sitter arrangements, while the lower right hand corner stands for a group choosing only day care-nursery school child care. Points within the graph represent groups with heterogenous child care choices.

[2]A comparison of the vertical position of the subgroups show how they differ in the proportion making sitter arrangements. The prevalence of family child care can be seen by comparing the subgroups along a line that runs from the lower left hand vertex to the middle of the opposite side of the triangle. The day care-nursery school axis runs from the lower right hand vertex to the middle of the opposite side.

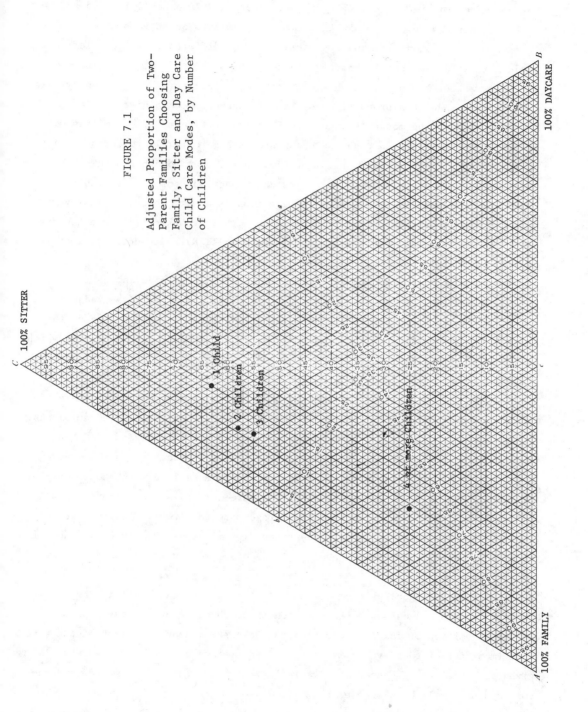

FIGURE 7.1

Adjusted Proportion of Two-
Parent Families Choosing
Family, Sitter and Day Care
Child Care Modes, by Number
of Children

sibling is old enough to care for a younger one much more likely in families with four or more children. An ability-to-pay interpretation should lead to a more constant increase in choice of FAMILY mode as family size increases.

A second important explanatory variable which differentiates families making child care arrangements with sitters instead of using other family members is the wage rate of the mother. This wage reflects, in part, the opportunity cost of her time. Adjusted proportions of families choosing each of the three modes by categories of the mother's wage rate is shown in Figure 7.2. Families with mothers earning less than $1.50 per hour are much more likely to choose family arrangements. The remaining groups of families cluster together with a much greater use of sitters. While the adjusted proportions for this variable do fluctuate considerably, the general implication is clear: holding other variables constant, working mothers who bear the highest cost for time spent away from the labor market choose a child care mode (SITTER) which does not require extended use of their own time.

A third important explanatory variable of child care mode choice is the average education level of the parents. This education effect (when adjusted for income level and the other explanatory variables) reflects the concern of the parents for the quality of the arrangements. The distribution of families which differ by parental education level is shown in Figure 7.3. There is a strong relationship between education and choice of the nursery school or day care center form of child care. Families with parents averaging up to six years of education have a very small chance of choosing these institutional arrangements. The adjusted proportion of those families choosing these modes is less than five percent. Families with parent education levels which exceed the sixth grade level but do not average more than high school are more likely to choose day care or nursery school. The greatest use of day care-nursery school arrangements is made by families in which the parents average more than twelve years of schooling: for these families the adjusted proportion is almost 25 percent. The relationship between education and choice of the other two child care modes is much more ambiguous.

Several additional predictors are able to differentiate families choosing nursery schools and day care centers from those choosing other modes. The adjusted proportion of families choosing the DAY CARE mode by category of the five most important of these variables (other than average education of parents) is given in Table 7.4. These variables reflect a mixture of supply and demand factors and each will be discussed briefly.

Marked regional differences appear in the choice of the DAY CARE mode.

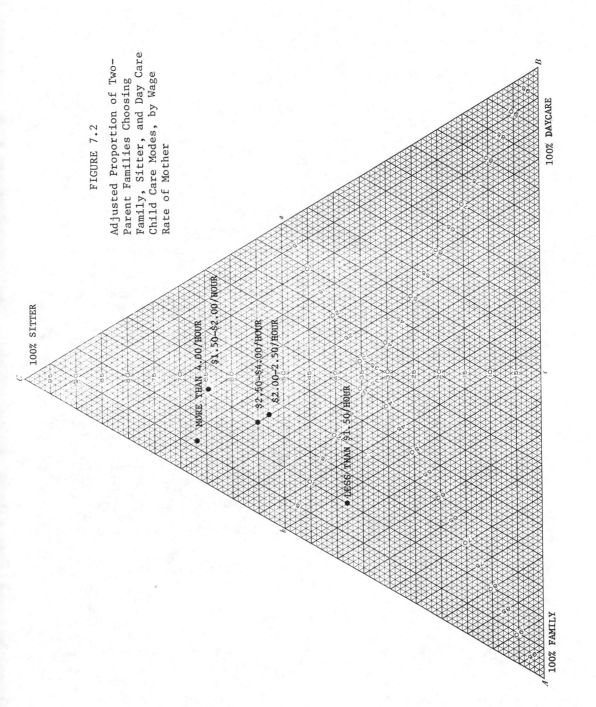

FIGURE 7.2

Adjusted Proportion of Two-
Parent Families Choosing
Family, Sitter, and Day Care
Child Care Modes, by Wage
Rate of Mother

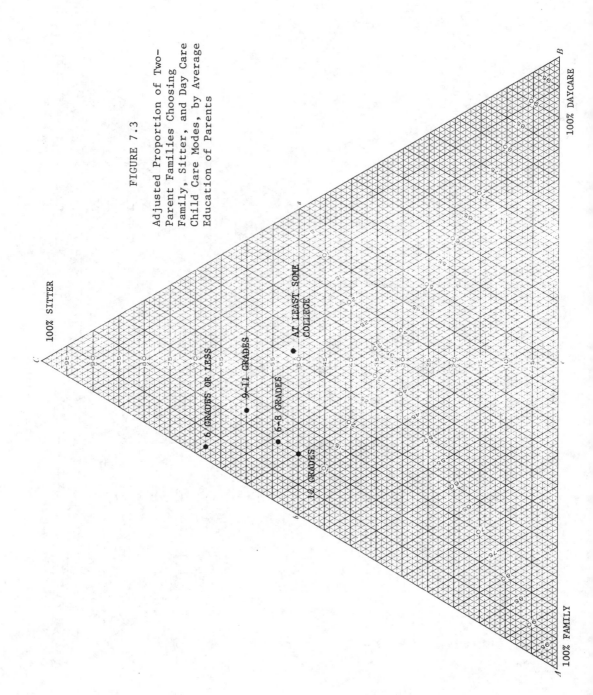

FIGURE 7.3

Adjusted Proportion of Two-
Parent Families Choosing
Family, Sitter, and Day Care
Child Care Modes, by Average
Education of Parents

TABLE 7.4

Adjusted Proportion of Families Choosing Nursery
School or Day Care Center Arrangements,
by Category of Independent Variables

Independent Variable	Number of Observations	Adjusted Percent Choosing Day Care-Nursery School
Region		
Northeast	46	9.5
North Central	114	2.2
South	277	19.4
West	74	14.5
Religion		
Baptist	224	18.1
Other Protestant	163	13.6
Catholic	69	1.2
Other	55	7.5
Age of youngest child		
< 3 years	232	8.2
3-6 years	168	19.9
7-12 years	111	8.4
Moved in past year		
Yes	176	20.5
No	335	9.1
City size		
500,000 or more	160	16.6
100-500,000	114	14.3
50-100,000	56	16.4
10-50,000	82	11.1
Less than 10,000	99	3.3

Families in the South and West are much more likely to choose this mode than are families in the Northeast and North Central regions. These differences, especially those for the West and North Central, are confirmed by the census enrollment data cited earlier. The low proportion of families in the Northeast choosing nursery schools and day care centers is somewhat unexpected but because it is based on fewer than fifty observations it cannot be considered a very reliable result.

Religious differences in child care choice are also quite apparent. Catholics are much less likely to choose the DAY CARE mode than are families having other religious preferences, and the proportion of Catholic families choosing the FAMILY mode is about .45, while Baptist and other Protestant families make this choice only 31 and 27 percent of the time, respectively. This finding of increased use of family arrangement by Catholic families is not totally unexpected. Hill and Stafford[1] found that Catholic mothers (regardless of labor force status) allocate more housework time to preschool children than do Protestants.

The relationship between the age of the youngest child and choice of nursery school or day care center is strong, with families in which the youngest child is between the ages of three and six being more than twice as likely to choose this mode than are families with the youngest children outside of this age range. This association is expected and presumably reflects, in part, the age-of-child restrictions imposed by the nursery school and day care centers available to the two-parent households in our sample.

The remaining two variables listed in Table 7.4 reflect differences in supply conditions for the three child care modes. Recent mobility considerably increases the chance of choosing day care centers or nursery schools. This fact is presumably associated with the smaller number of friends and relatives that mobile families can use for child care arrangements. City size is also associated with the choice of child care mode, with families in the larger cities much more likely to choose day care centers or nursery schools than families in smaller towns or rural areas. These results are confirmed by census data presented earlier which showed that enrollment rates of preschool children in nursery schools were much higher in urban than in rural areas.

Several of the remaining variables are interesting because of their *inability* to differentiate among families choosing the different child care modes. Race is the weakest variable in each of the three equations. There are virtually no differences in the adjusted proportions of black and white families choos-

---

[1] Hill and Stafford (1974), p. 337.

ing each of the child care modes. There are also few differences among the child care choice of families in different income quintiles after parental education, mother's wage rate, and the remaining variables have been taken into account. Finally, when our sample was expanded to include families headed by a working mother, the regression-adjusted proportions choosing among the three modes differed very little between male and female headed families. The beta-squared for the dichotomous variable "sex of head" was only .005, .001 and .003 for the FAMILY, SITTER and DAY CARE regressions respectively.

SUMMARY

Over 80 percent of the two-parent families in our sample chose some relatively informal, noninstitutional mode of child care while the mother and father were at work. Does this fact imply the failure of recent governmental and private efforts to supply and promote institutionalized child care? We believe the answer to this is a somewhat evasive "not entirely" because several of the most important factors which affect the choice of the DAY CARE mode are outside the control of government. First of all, the evidence presented here is consistent with the observation recently made by Heckman: most working women don't use formal modes of child care because the availability of older children, friends and relatives lowers the perceived price per unit of quality of the informal FAMILY and SITTER modes relative to that of the formal DAY CARE mode.[1] A variety of subsidy schemes have been proposed[2] which would lower the price of the formal modes. However, they lose some of their appeal since our ability-to-pay variable, family income, was not important in explaining modal choice after several other variables are held constant. Differences in the perception of what determines high quality care -- measured here by the educational attainment and religious affiliation of the parents -- are important determinants of the choice of child care mode, and these preferences are only changed slowly, if at all, by governmental and private sector action. Nevertheless, our analysis indicates that the choice of DAY CARE is heavily dependent upon several supply determinants such as region of residence and size of city, which reflect, in part, differential levels of governmental and private support for formal child care arrangements. To the extent, then, that there is a public role in promoting the use of institutionalized child care, our analysis implies that it is almost entirely one of achieving some type of population-adjusted regional and urban-rural parity in the supply of these services.

---

[1] Heckman (1974), pp. S144-S145.

[2] See, for example, the discussion in Schultz, et al., (1973).

References

Andrews, Frank M. and Messenger, Robert C., _Multivariate Nominal Scale Analysis_, Ann Arbor: Institute for Social Research, 1973.

Andrews, Frank M., Morgan, James N., Sonquist, John A. and Klem, Laura, _Multiple Classification Analysis_ (2nd Edition), Ann Arbor: Institute for Social Research, 1973.

Duncan, Greg, "Educational Attainment" in James N. Morgan et al. _Five Thousand American Families -- Patterns of Economic Progress_, Vol. I, Ann Arbor: Institute for Social Research, 1974.

Hause, J. C., "Earnings Profile: Ability and Schooling," _Journal of Political Economy_ (May/June, 1972), Part II.

Heckman, James J., "Effects of Childcare Programs on Women's Work Effort," _Journal of Political Economy_ (March/April, 1974), Part II.

Hill, C. R. and Stafford, F. P., "Time Inputs to Children" in James N. Morgan, ed. _Five Thousand American Families -- Patterns of Economic Progress_, Vol. II, Ann Arbor: Institute for Social Research, 1974.

Morgan, James N. and Messenger, Robert C., _THAID, A Sequential Analysis Program for the Analysis of Nominal Scale Dependent Variables_, Ann Arbor: Institute for Social Research, 1973.

Nelson, Richard R. and Krashinsky, Michael, "Public Control and Economic Organization of Day Care for Young Children," _Public Policy_ (Winter, 1974).

Overall, J. E. and Klett, C. J., _Applied Multivariate Analysis_, New York: McGraw-Hill, 1972.

Schultz, C. L. et. al., _Setting National Priorities: The 1973 Budget_, Washington, D. C.: Brookings Institution, 1972.

Stevens, S. S., "On the Theory of Scales of Measurement," _Science_, 103, 1946, pp. 677-680.

Suits, D. B., "Use of Dummy Variables in Regression Equations," _Journal of the American Statistical Association_, 52, 1957, pp. 548-551

U. S. Bureau of the Census, _Statistical Abstract of the United States: 1972_, Washington, D. C.: Government Printing Office, 1972.

U. S. Bureau of the Census, 1970 _Census of Population -- Subject Reports: School Enrollment_, Washington, D. C.: Government Printing Office, 1973.

APPENDIX 7.1

TABLE A7.1

Unadjusted and Adjusted Proportion of Families Choosing Each of the Child Care Modes, by Category of Independent Variables

Independent Variable	Unweighted Number of Observations	Proportion Choosing: FAMILY Unadjusted	FAMILY Adjusted	SITTER Unadjusted	SITTER Adjusted	DAY CARE Unadjusted	DAY CARE Adjusted
RACE							
Non black	296	30.2	32.0	57.3	55.1	12.5	13.0
Black	215	40.3	30.7	48.0	60.0	11.7	9.6
1972 FAMILY INCOME QUINTILE							
Lowest	21	48.7	43.8	35.6	45.7	15.7	10.5
Fourth	104	37.9	34.0	52.1	54.3	10.1	11.7
Third	167	31.0	31.6	54.9	55.0	14.1	13.3
Second	138	29.8	30.4	53.5	52.8	16.7	16.9
Highest	81	29.6	31.1	64.4	62.6	6.0	6.4
CITY SIZE							
500,000 or more	160	34.7	32.9	54.0	50.5	11.3	16.6
100,000-500,000	114	28.5	29.5	54.6	56.2	16.9	14.3
50,000-100,000	56	27.0	30.4	57.0	53.2	16.1	16.4
10,000-50,000	82	28.9	27.0	60.6	61.9	10.5	11.1
Less than 10,000	99	38.2	39.1	54.4	57.8	7.4	3.1
NUMBER OF CHILDREN							
One	211	21.4	22.2	61.1	63.2	17.5	14.5
Two	137	28.6	31.4	61.4	58.6	9.9	10.0
Three	75	40.0	34.0	52.5	55.5	7.5	10.5
Four or more	88	64.3	61.0	28.0	25.3	7.7	13.7
AGE OF YOUNGEST CHILD							
Less than 3	232	31.7	31.1	58.6	60.7	9.7	8.2
3 - 6	168	28.2	28.8	50.3	51.4	21.5	19.9
Over 6 years	111	36.8	36.9	59.2	54.7	4.1	8.4
MOTHER'S WAGE RATE							
Less than $1.50 per hour	91	56.2	52.5	34.4	37.4	9.4	10.1
$1.50-$2.00	102	28.7	20.4	61.7	65.4	9.6	14.2
$2.00-$2.50	93	27.0	30.1	55.4	54.4	17.7	15.5
$2.50-$4.00	149	27.4	29.5	56.6	55.4	16.0	15.2
More than $4.00 per hour	76	23.7	26.8	69.4	66.9	6.9	6.3
MOVED IN LAST YEAR							
No	335	33.0	32.6	57.9	58.3	9.1	9.1
Yes	176	28.9	29.8	50.7	49.7	20.4	20.5

TABLE A7.1
(continued)

| Independent Variable | Unweighted Number of Observations | Proportion Choosing | | | | | |
| | | FAMILY | | SITTER | | DAY CARE | |
		Unadjusted	Adjusted	Unadjusted	Adjusted	Unadjusted	Adjusted
RELIGION							
Baptist	224	31.8	30.8	50.1	51.1	18.2	18.1
Other Protestant	163	25.9	27.0	61.5	59.4	12.6	13.6
Catholic	69	44.9	44.4	52.5	54.5	2.5	1.1
Other	55	31.7	31.3	59.9	61.1	8.4	7.5
REGION							
Northeast	46	43.5	35.9	55.2	54.5	1.4	9.5
North Central	114	35.3	39.9	61.2	57.9	3.5	2.2
South	277	26.2	26.7	53.5	53.9	20.3	19.4
West	74	31.2	27.8	53.0	57.7	15.9	14.5
AVERAGE EDUCATION OF PARENTS							
6 grades or less	80	39.2	29.3	55.1	68.2	5.7	2.6
7 - 8 grades	144	38.7	35.8	50.6	54.5	10.7	9.6
9 - 11 grades	126	26.6	28.5	60.4	60.1	13.0	11.4
12 grades	87	40.7	40.1	49.3	49.9	10.0	10.0
Some college	74	17.5	24.4	63.2	51.7	19.3	23.9
DIFFERENCE IN EDUCATION OF PARENTS (FATHER'S MINUS MOTHER'S)							
2 or more levels*	87	35.0	32.4	54.9	52.3	10.0	15.3
1 more level	96	24.9	24.8	64.9	62.1	10.2	13.2
Same level	162	33.1	35.1	55.0	57.0	11.8	7.9
1 less level	94	32.5	36.3	53.3	52.1	14.2	11.6
More than 1 fewer levels	72	32.3	27.6	51.2	54.6	16.5	17.8
TOTAL	511	31.8	--	55.8	--	12.4	--

*Education "levels" are defined as follows:
  0. No education, cannot read or write
  1. 0-5 grades
  2. 6-8 grades
  3. 9-11 grades
  4. 12 grades
  5. 12 grades plus non-academic
  6. College, no degree
  7. College degree
  8. Advanced degree

NOTE: All results are calculated using weights which adjust for differential sampling and response rates.

Chapter 8

RESIDENTIAL MOBILITY: PLANNERS, MOVERS AND MULTIPLE MOVERS

Elizabeth Roistacher

INTRODUCTION

The importance of residential mobility and the suitability of the panel data for its investigation led to two chapters on the subject in Volume II of <u>Five Thousand American Families</u>. One focuses on planned and actual moves over the first five panel years from 1968-1972. Job and housing-related voluntary moves and involuntary mobility are distinguished. The second chapter focuses on local (intra-county) residential mobility between 1969 and 1971 and treats it as a resolution of housing disequilibrium. It was concluded in this chapter that initial housing stress does *not* predict these kinds of moves very well, and considerations about the journey to work fares even worse.

Two chapters in this volume also use the data to study still other aspects of the mobility process. In Chapter Nine Greg Duncan and Sandra Newman look only at families that had expressed the *expectation* of a job or housing-related move in 1970 and attempt to explain whether or not these families actually do move in the subsequent three years. In this chapter we examine the issue of plans and actual mobility, predicting each of these in terms of the economic and demographic characteristics of families living in the 24 largest Standard Metropolitan Statistical Areas (SMSA's); we then include plans in a model to predict mobility and to see what factors beyond plans explain it.[1]

In addition, we examine the characteristics of families who are multiple

[1]In the chapter by Duncan and Newman, fulfillment of moving plans for voluntary movers is examined. Here, the analysis includes all types of planned moves, whether voluntary or not. However, since the category of involuntary mobility is quite small, the behavior of voluntary movers will dominate the analysis.

Fulfillment is the intersection of plans and moves. The current chapter examines each of these dependent variables separately and then includes plans as a predictor of mobility as a control device in studying those with *and* without plans.

movers; that is, who have moved more than once during the sample period. These
analyses of residential mobility have interesting results among the black population: Black families move at the same rate as white families with similar
characteristics, although their expectations of moving are lower. However,
their multiple moving rates are substantially lower than those of white families.
The results also show higher annual mobility rates among welfare recipients.

ANALYSIS

I. Age and Family Size as Predictors of Residential Mobility

Age and family size are indicators of several reasons for which families
move. Most families move for voluntary reasons, either to alter employment or
housing situations.[1] If we view the probability of moving in terms of the probability of a family finding new housing or employment opportunities which are
better than the current situation, then we can expect each move to reduce the
probability of future moves by reducing the gap between the best possible alternative and the current situation. However, a move for a new job might expand
alternative employment and housing opportunities and therefore *increase* the
probability of another move for employment or housing. Having children in school
or owning a home are also age-related and tend to reduce the probability of
moving.[2] Hence, age and family size are really replacing more detailed information about the opportunities for improving housing or employment.

To the extent that one is concerned with *predicting* mobility, using age and
family size or a set of life cycle variables which combines marital status, age
of head, and age and number of children would be appropriate. If we were interested in the effects of certain policies which alter mobility, such as the impact
of education which leads to improved job opportunities, it would be important to
relate mobility more directly to the reasons for moving rather than indirectly
through demographic correlates.[3] Since the present concern is the prediction of

---

[1] See Roistacher (1974). Only 14 percent of movers between 1971 and 1972 reported
an involuntary reason for moving.

[2] Past mobility itself is not included as a predictor in the models in this chapter because it is too highly age-correlated and because its relationship with
future mobility can be uncovered only in a more complex model which takes account
of shifts in opportunities induced by a past move.

[3] This is similar to the approach in the next chapter.

residential mobility, we focus on the demographic variables.

II. The Relationship Between Plans and Actual Mobility

The general theory underlying our analyses of plans and actual mobility is that the same variables determine both; that is, people plan to and actually move for the same reasons -- these reasons being correlated with family characteristics. The implementation of moving plans depends on the intensity of the plan, with intensity being a function of the same family characteristics which predict plans to move. Hence, given a life cycle theory of plans to move,[1] we should find that younger heads have higher probabilities of planning to move and hypothesize that these higher probabilities reflect a greater commitment or greater intensity of moving plans among younger heads. Younger heads should, therefore, have greater probabilities of implementing their moving plans than families with older heads. A good test of such a theory of plan intensity or commitment would require scaling the responses of individuals to the "plans to move" question to see if intensity is correlated with the life cycle variables.[2]

The correlation of plans and mobility with the same set of predictors is compatible with a variety of other hypotheses. For instance, those variables which predict whether or not a family has moving plans may also be correlated with the availability of opportunities to satisfy such intentions. Or, young heads may have a general plan of moving to a larger dwelling, while more established families with older heads may have some very specific ideas of where and to what kind of dwelling they would like to or plan to move. (The desire to move is not necessarily the same thing as planning to move.[3]) Thus, the younger heads may be likely to find a satisfactory means of implementing their plans, while older heads may find fewer opportunities which meet their specifications and may have lower implementation rates. If a younger family is more likely to

---

[1]An informal test of the life cycle theory can be made in terms of age and family size. More formally, age, marital status, number and ages of children can be combined with life-cycle variables.

[2]This is done in the Duncan-Newman chapter using a two-point scale of intensity as a predictor of plan fulfillment.

[3]One might imagine a sequence of desires, plans, and actual mobility. Desires are less likely than plans to be suppressed by family economic or market constraints, and plans less likely than actual moves. For an analysis of the desire to move, see Newman (1974). .

be moving for job-related reasons than for housing-related reasons,[1] then again we might find the housing demands of the younger household less specific than the demands of the household moving for purely housing consumption reasons.

There is an element of circularity in the hypothesis that precise specification of demands reduces the probability of implementing plans. For example, an older respondent with very specific housing demands may report no *plans* to move because he feels that the market will provide very few opportunities for satisfying his requirements.

An alternative theory suggests that the factors which determine whether or not the move actually takes place are external to the original reasons to move, and there are countervailing forces which prevent implementation. For example, the prospect of a new job induces the family to plan a move, but this is offset by a degree of commitment to the current community. Such a countervailing factor may well be correlated with the demographics which induce a family to move, so that it may be difficult to distinguish empirically between a theory of conviction versus countervailing forces. However, if the countervailing forces are randomly distributed, then we expect to find no systematic relationship between unexplained differences in planned and actual mobility.

Before examining the similarity of relations of prospective and actual mobility to the explanatory variables, we examine each of them as dependent variables in separate regressions.

III. Plans to Move

In each year of the Panel Study, families were asked, "Do you think you might move in the next couple of years?"[2] We have used the response to this question as a dichotomous dependent variable, "plans to move," in a Multiple Classification Analysis with the predictors being the economic and demographic characteristics of the families. The analysis is restricted to the 24 largest SMSA's.[3] 1971 plans are analyzed in terms of 1971 income and 1972 family

---

[1] See Volume II, Chapter Two, for comparisons of job-related and housing-related movers.

[2] It could easily be argued that this question may elicit a different response than the question, "Do you plan to move in the next couple of years." An answer to "Do you think you might move" could fall somewhere between a desire and a plan to move.

[3] The reason for selecting the large metropolitan areas, a representative subsample of a full national sample, was partly convenience, and partly to eliminate the rural-urban movements which have been well studied and are a rather special subset of moves.

characteristics.[1] The gross and net explanatory power of the predictors appear in Table 8.1, and the unadjusted and adjusted moving expectations appear in Table 8.2.[2] Thirty-six percent of the families reported that they might move in the next couple of years.

Not owning a home is the most important predictor of plans to move. Although past tenure is itself determined by the family characteristics which predict mobility, whether the family owns or rents is likely to have an impact on the mobility decision above and beyond its relationship to family characteristics. There are probably fewer forces mitigating against a move for renters, who do not have to bother with selling their current dwelling in order to move to a new dwelling. One might ask whether past ownership (tenure) is not simply a reflection of the basic effects of age, family size, income and the rest. A measure of its independent effect is the partial R-squared which is equal to .08, indicating that inclusion of tenure reduces our ignorance by eight percent.

The next strongest predictor is the age of head of household. (See Table 8.1) The younger the head of household, the higher the probability that there is some plan to move (Table 8.2).

After accounting for differences which can be explained by age, family size remains an important predictor of moving plans. Small families more frequently have plans to move than larger ones. Perhaps, for relatively young heads, the anticipation of family expansion motivates the plan to move. Small families with older heads may want a smaller dwelling unit because children have grown up and left home. The only exceptions to this general pattern are very large families (seven or more) who have extremely high rates of planning to move, probably as a response to overcrowding.

By taking account of age, family size, and prior ownership, we reduce the estimated effect of income and education substantially. Their remaining influence has obvious interpretations such as making a move economically possible and extending time horizons so more replanning is done. None of the other included

---

[1] 1971 income is reported by the respondent in the 1972 interview. Future income rather than current income may be a better indicator of plans and mobility; we do recognize that people move in anticipation of changes when we include 1972 family size. Of course, anticipatory decisions are likely to be based on more than just next year's changes in income and family size. We have chosen 1971 income rather than 1972 income because people are probably less able to predict an income change than a family size change.

[2] See Appendix C, Volume I, for an explanation of Eta and Beta.

264

TABLE 8.1

Gross and Net Explanatory Power of Independent Variables*
in Regressions to Predict Plans to Move in 1971
(24 largest SMSAs; same head both years)

Predictor	Gross Effect (Eta^2)	Net Effect ($Beta^2$)
1971 tenure	.156	.102
Age	.144	.062
Family size	.027	.010
1971 income	.021	.007
Education	.027	.007
Welfare income in 1971	.003	.002
Reserve funds	.014	.006
Sex of head	.001	.003
Race	.001	.003
R^2 (adjusted)		.24

Number of observations   1947

Mean of dependent variable   .36

Standard deviation of
  dependent variable   .48

*Variables are as of 1972 unless otherwise specified.

MTR 2328

TABLE 8.2

Unadjusted and Adjusted Means for Selected
Independent Variables from Regressions
Predicting Plans to Move in 1971
(24 largest SMSAs; same head both years)

Predictors	Unadjusted Mean	Adjusted Mean	Weighted Percent	Number of Unweighted Cases
Overall Mean	.36			
1971 Tenure				
Own	.20	.23	58	803
Rent	.57	.53	40	1093
Neither	.80	.66	3	51
Age of Head				
< - 25	.78	.57	8	206
25 - 34	.58	.51	20	425
35 - 44	.31	.36	22	461
45 - 54	.25	.32	22	435
55 - 64	.27	.30	16	291
65 - 74	.18	.20	9	95
75 or older	.09	.07	4	34
Family Size				
One	.50	.42	20	316
Two	.33	.37	23	359
Three	.38	.36	16	308
Four	.33	.33	17	286
Five	.31	.32	13	265
Six	.18	.23	6	161
Seven or more	.38	.43	6	252
Some Welfare Income in 1971				
No	.35	.36	93	1565
Yes	.47	.44	7	382
Race				
White	.36	.37	82	947
Black	.36	.30	14	925
Other	.44	.34	3	57
Not ascertained	.30	.38	1	18

MTR 2328

variables are powerful predictors of plans to move,[1] although there is a significant difference in the planning rates of welfare and nonwelfare recipients.[2]
For families receiving welfare payments, the likelihood of having plans to move
is greater than it is for nonwelfare families, even controlling for income and
other family characteristics. This could reflect dissatisfaction with housing
conditions, a phenomenon which has been found in a study of mobility among New
York City welfare recipients.[3]

Blacks are less likely to have moving plans than are white families once we
have controlled for differences in other family characteristics and tenure.
This could reflect expectations of facing housing market discrimination (either
segregation which would keep them out of certain markets or price discrimination
which would force them to pay more for equivalent housing than white families).
This is an example of the perceived availability of housing reducing moving
plans, as discussed earlier.

IV. Actual Moves

A Multiple Classification Analysis was run with the dichotomous dependent
variable being whether or not the family had actually moved in the past year.
This analysis includes all families who actually moved, both those who had previously reported a plan and those who had not.[4] The results of this regression
appear in Tables 8.3 and 8.4.[5] In all, 17 percent of the families moved between
1971 and 1972.[6]

Moves, both planned and actual, are largely explained by the same predictors. The young, the renters, and those with small families are more likely to

---

[1] The reserve funds variable is a categorical variable for whether or not the
family currently has or has had at least two months' income saved in the past
five years. It is included as a proxy for wealth or permanent income.

[2] An approximate F-test on the Beta-squared indicates statistical significance at
95 percent confidence level.

[3] See Roistacher (1969).

[4] The chapter by Duncan and Newman looks only at the actual mobility of those
families who had previously reported a plan.

[5] See Volume II, Chapter Two, for a similar model based on movers over a five-
year period.

[6] This figure is lower than Census estimates of about 20 percent, since it does
not include newly-formed families.

TABLE 8.3

Gross and Net Explanatory Power of Independent Variables*
in Regressions to Predict Residential Mobility 1971–1972
(24 largest SMSAs; same head both years)

Predictor	Gross Effect (Eta^2)	Net Effect	
		(Beta^2) Without Plans	(Beta^2) With Plans
1971 tenure	.066	.066	.031
Age of head	.138	.081	.051
Family size	.031	.028	.022
Reserve funds	.043	.009	.010
Education	.018	.008	.009
1971 income	.021	.009	.012
Sex	.001	.009	.007
Race	.004	.008	.009
Some welfare income in 1971	.011	.004	.002
Planned to move	.166	--	.086
R^2 (adj)		.239	.286

Number of observations   1947

Mean of dependent variable   .17

Standard deviation of
  dependent variable   .37

*Variables are as of 1972 unless otherwise specified.

MTR 2328

TABLE 8.4

Unadjusted and Adjusted Means for Selected
Independent Variables from Regressions
Predicting Residential Mobility 1971-1972

Predictor	Unad-justed Mean	Adjusted Mean Excluding Plans To Move	Adjusted Mean Including Plans To Move	Weighted Percentage	Number of Unweighted Cases
Overall mean	.17				
1971 Tenure					
Own	.05	.09	.11	58	803
Rent	.32	.27	.24	40	1093
Neither	.53	.39	.33	3	51
Age of Head					
< - 25	.50	.36	.32	8	206
25 - 34	.32	.29	.26	20	425
35 - 44	.15	.20	.20	22	461
45 - 54	.07	.11	.12	22	435
55 - 64	.05	.06	.07	16	291
65 - 74	.05	.03	.06	9	95
75 or older	.06	.01	.07	4	34
Family Size					
One	.28	.26	.25	20	316
Two	.19	.19	.19	23	359
Three	.20	.19	.19	16	308
Four	.11	.11	.12	17	286
Five	.08	.07	.08	13	265
Six	.07	.08	.11	6	161
Seven or more	.17	.15	.14	6	252
Sex of Head					
Male	.16	.19	.19	75	1252
Female	.20	.10	.11	25	695
Race					
White	.16	.18	.17	82	947
Black	.22	.14	.16	14	925
Other	.12	-.01	-.01	3	57
Not ascertained	.06	.11	.11	1	18
Welfare Income 1971					
No	.16	.16	.16	93	1565
Yes	.31	.25	.24	7	382
Plans to Move 1971					
No	.05		.09	64	1151
Yes	.37		.31	36	796

MTR 2328

move. Very large families are also inclined to move.

Family size explains actual moves better than plans, while age and prior ownership explain plans better than moves. Owning a home apparently inhibits planning to move more than it stops actual moving. Both the sex and race variables become *more* important in explaining actual moves when adjusted by regression.

It is interesting to note the parallel downward shift in the age and family size effects when we observe actual versus prospective mobility. (See Figures 8.1 and 8.2.) These shifts suggest a significant amount of inertia in the implementation of plans. Of course, since our question on plans asks about a period of a "few years," plans not implemented in the first year may be implemented in the second or third year.

Although the welfare variable has relatively low net explanatory power, this variable is significant in explaining differences in moving rates. As was the case for moving plans, the moving rates of welfare families are significantly higher than the rates of those families not receiving welfare even when controlling for differences in the other independent variables such as age and income. Welfare recipients have an adjusted moving rate of .27, while nonwelfare families have a rate of only .16. The difference in the adjusted probabilities of welfare and nonwelfare families having moving *plans*, on the other hand, is smaller. This suggests that welfare families tend to move either involuntarily or on very short notice (to themselves). The higher moving rate of welfare families is consistent with the previously cited study of welfare mobility in New York City in which it was found that welfare families were twice as likely to move as nonwelfare families.[1]

In the mobility analysis presented in Roistacher (1974) no significant welfare effect was discernible. The lack of an effect in that context is probably due to the inclusion of families outside the 24 largest SMSA's in which the welfare housing situation, as well as the administration of welfare payments, is likely to be quite different from the largest metropolitan areas.

Although blacks had fewer moving plans than whites, adjusted moving rates are almost identical for blacks and whites. The unadjusted moving rate of blacks is much higher than that of whites, but this is eliminated by the adjustments for age, income, family size, and welfare status, all of which are correlated with race for this urban population. Blacks may be confronted with short-notice involuntary moves or may have shorter planning horizons; either of

---

[1]See Roistacher (1969).

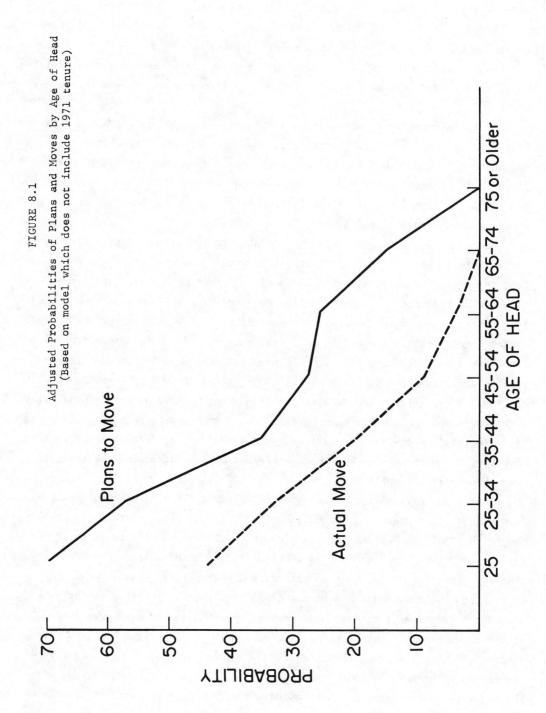

FIGURE 8.1

Adjusted Probabilities of Plans and Moves by Age of Head
(Based on model which does not include 1971 tenure)

FIGURE 8.2

Adjusted Probabilities of Plans and Moves by Family Size
(Based on model which does not include 1971 tenure)

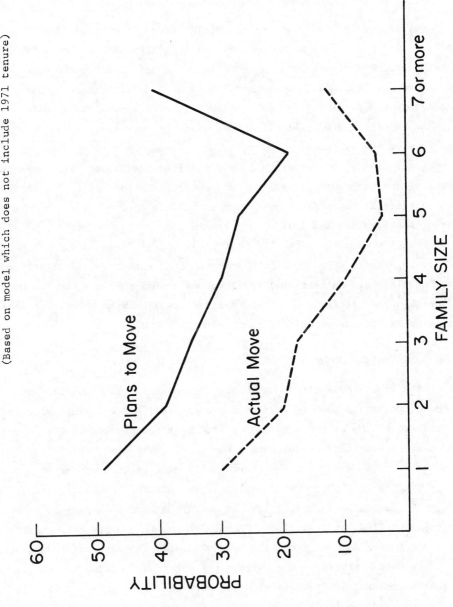

these situations would explain the reduction in black/white differences when we go from plans to actual moves.

V. Including Plans as a Predictor of Mobility

By including the family's 1971 moving plans in our model to predict a move between 1971 and 1972, we can observe what factors account for differences between plans and moves. Moving plans is the single strongest predictor of whether or not a family actually moves (see Table 8.3). Although this variable itself is determined primarily by age, family size, and tenure, these same variables remain important predictors of actual mobility above and beyond their ability to predict moving plans.

Inclusion of moving plans in the model to predict mobility does not represent a model of behavior; we include plans to see the net effect of family characteristics once plans have been taken into account. The fact that age of head, family size, and 1971 tenure remain important supports our earlier theory of intensity of plans being the best predictor of implementation. However, the other hypotheses discussed are also consistent with these findings. So although moving plans are quite a good predictor of actual mobility, we can substantially improve our predictions of which families are likely to move if we have information on family characteristics as well.

VI. Multiple Movers

The Panel Study allows us to observe repeated moves by the same family. Of course, we record no more than one move per year since we interview the family once a year. Moreover, although we lose very few respondents, the probability of a mover remaining in the sample may be slightly lower than that of nonmovers, and this would be particularly true in the case of repeated movers.

Families could move repeatedly for two distinct sets of reasons. Families might be moving on to better jobs or better housing as a part of increasing economic well-being over time. There also may be a group of poorer families who are forced to move because they continually inhabit substandard housing.

In this analysis we look within the group of families who have moved in order to observe which families moved more than once in the period of 1968 to 1972, compared to families who moved only once. We use the same set of predictors that we employed in the earlier analyses of prospective and actual mobility. The analysis is restricted to families with the same head in all five years, living in the 24 largest metropolitan areas, and who moved at least once.

Of all these families who moved at least once between 1968 and 1972, 35 percent are repeated movers. The life cycle variables are again the important predictors of multiple mobility, just as they were of prospective and actual mobility (see Tables 8.5 and 8.6). Our model is conditional on the family having moved once, and yet we find that, even having removed a good deal of the variance in age and family size, these two variables still remain crucial predictors that a family will move again.

The possession of reserve funds, which is included in these mobility models to pick up a component of wealth or permanent income, seems relatively important in distinguishing repeated movers. In particular, families who currently have at least two months' income saved are *less* likely to be multiple movers than families with smaller amounts of current savings. This could not be a spurious reflection of an age effect since the regression adjustment for age increases the apparent effect of reserve funds.

Black families are much less likely to be repeated movers than are white families, both before and after regression adjustment. Discriminatory treatment in the housing market, faced during a previous move, could have a negative impact on repeated mobility as well as on moving plans (see Figure 8.3).

Although it was expected that urban welfare families would, because of being repeatedly confronted with unsatisfactory housing situations, have higher probabilities of multiple moves than nonwelfare recipients, the data indicate this is not the case (see Figure 8.4). Regardless of whether or not we adjust for income and other family characteristics, there is virtually no difference in the probability of welfare and nonwelfare families being multiple movers. The absence of a welfare effect in our model of repeated movers and in the model in Volume II may be a result of the model being restricted to families in which the head is the same all five years. The earlier models in this chapter in which we did find higher plans and actual mobility rates for families receiving welfare included families in which the head is the same for only a two-year period. Families with less stability in the head of household may tend to be more mobile than those with the same head for a long period of time.

SUMMARY

Age, family size, and prior ownership of a home are the primary determinants of (and deterrents to) both plans to move and actual mobility. Moreover, when these independent variables plus plans to move are used to explain actual mobil-

TABLE 8.5

Gross and Net Explanatory Power of Independent Variables*
in a Regression to Predict Multiple Moves 1968-72
(Movers Only)
(24 largest SMSAs; same head 1968-72)

Predictor	Gross Effect (Eta^2)	Net Effect (Beta^2)
Age of head	.100	.120
Family size	.057	.079
Reserve funds	.042	.059
Race	.016	.028
1971 family income	.020	.019
Education of head	.033	.018
Sex of head	.000	.001
Some welfare income in 1971	.000	.000

R^2 (adj)	.22
Number of observations	647
Mean of dependent variable	.35
Standard deviation of dependent variable	.48

*Variables are as of 1972 unless otherwise specified.

MTR 2317

TABLE 8.6

Unadjusted and Adjusted Means for Selected Independent Variables
from a Regression Predicting Multiple Moves 1968-72
(Movers Only)
(24 Largest SMSAs; same head 1968-72)

Predictor	Unadjusted Mean	Adjusted Mean	Weighted Percentage	Number of Unweighted Cases
Age of Head				
< 25	.78	.69	3	21
25 - 34	.52	.54	29	197
35 - 44	.28	.32	30	185
45 - 54	.26	.23	19	138
55 - 64	.32	.30	12	103
65 - 74	.10	.06	4	12
75 or older	.00	-.16	3	8
Family Size				
One	.50	.52	17	104
Two	.38	.47	22	102
Three	.46	.43	13	78
Four	.35	.25	17	93
Five	.18	.15	18	112
Six	.32	.33	6	75
Seven or more	.19	.24	8	110
Race				
White	.37	.38	74	250
Black	.31	.28	21	395
Other	.14	.05	4	22
Not ascertained	.66	.65	1	7
Welfare				
No	.35	.36	89	505
Yes	.35	.33	11	169

MTR 2317

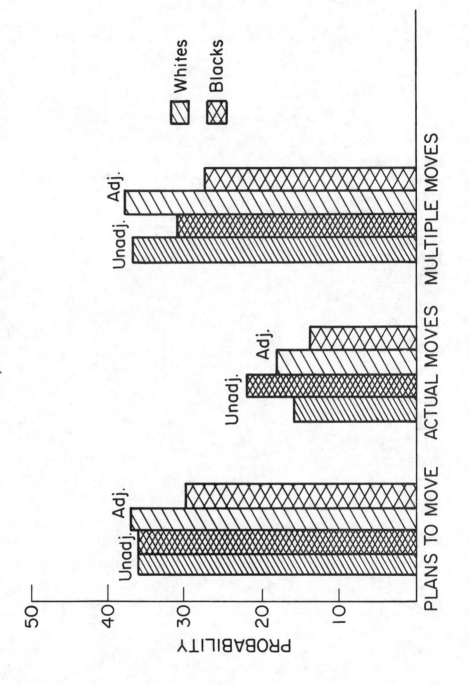

FIGURE 8.3

Unadjusted and Adjusted Probabilities of Plans, Actual Moves,
and Multiple Moves for Blacks and Whites

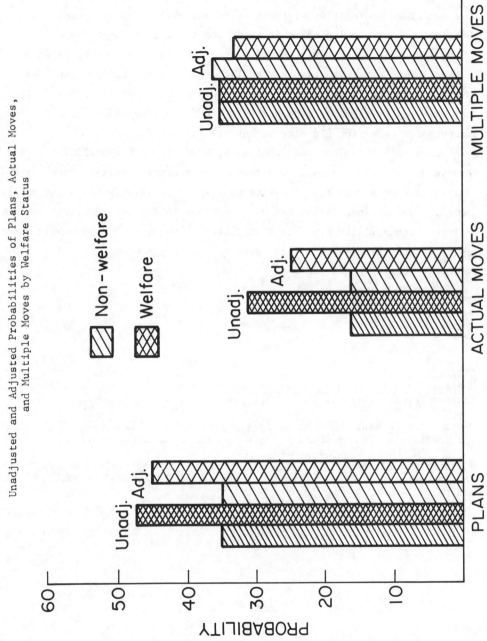

FIGURE 8.4

Unadjusted and Adjusted Probabilities of Plans, Actual Moves,
and Multiple Moves by Welfare Status

ity behavior, age, family size, and prior home ownership status still make a net contribution. This is consistent with a model where people gradually settle down to a satisfactory location as their needs and ability to pay change less, and the fit of their housing to their needs and ability to pay improves.

Although no other variables have strong explanatory power, we do find some interesting results with respect to black families and welfare families. Blacks have lower probabilities of planning to move and of multiple moves; this suggests that they may have faced housing market discrimination during some previous move, discouraging them from planning or actually moving again.

Welfare families, on the other hand, have higher probabilities of planning to move and of actually moving, although the repeated mobility rates of welfare families are no higher than those of nonwelfare families. Plans and mobility among the welfare population may be a response to the poor quality of housing that they occupy, although this should lead not only to higher mobility rates but also to higher repeated mobility rates unless they are able to move out of unsatisfactory housing situations.

References

Roistacher, Elizabeth "Residential Mobility" in James Morgan, ed. Five Thousand American Families - Patterns of Economic Progress, Volume II (Ann Arbor: Institute for Social Research, 1974), pp. 41-79.

Newman, Sandra "The Residential Environment and the Desire to Move," Institute for Social Research, Ann Arbor, 1974, (unpublished manuscript).

Roistacher, Elizabeth "The Intra-City Mobility of Welfare Households," Housing and Development Administration, The City of New York, 1969 (unpublished manuscript).

Chapter 9

PEOPLE AS PLANNERS: THE FULFILLMENT OF RESIDENTIAL MOBILITY EXPECTATIONS

Greg Duncan and Sandra Newman

INTRODUCTION

A residential move may be viewed as the end result of a sequence of decisions made by a household. The sequence begins with a desire to move, proceeds to crystallized intentions or plans and, finally, to the move itself.[1] Of course, the *desire* to change residences may not result in an actual move; some households encounter obstacles which prevent actual mobility. In a similar manner, not all households *expecting* to make a residential move translate these expectations into actual moves -- plans may be changed, delayed or cancelled.

In this paper we examine the link between the latter stages of the mobility process -- mobility expectations and actual moves. Our major objectives are to understand conditions under which moving expectations are converted into actual moves and to identify factors which prevent the fulfillment of mobility inclinations.

Because residential mobility can affect family well-being, it is clearly important to understand why some families can fulfill their expectations while others cannot. Moves made for housing-related reasons enable families to adjust housing to changes in family composition, circumstances and preferences, while job-related moves permit workers to take advantage of better economic opportunities. On a more aggregate level, moves help equilibrate labor and housing markets. Job-related moves adjust labor supply to demand changes brought about by changes in technology and industrial growth; housing-related mobility both causes and results from changes in demand for and supply of housing.

If mobility expectations and behavior are sequential stages in a process, then a first task is to account for the expectations themselves before turning to behavior.[2] Thus, in Section I we begin by looking at the 1970 mobility expectations of Panel families. Because housing and job needs are distinct motiva-

---

[1] See Rossi (1955), p. 102.

[2] Rossi (1955), p. 68.

tions in geographic mobility, we analyze housing and job-related mobility expectations separately.

In the second section, we examine the *actual* mobility behavior of those families that had reported, in 1970, the expectation of either a housing or job-related move. We look at information from the three subsequent interviews (1971-73) to see whether or not the family actually moved. The effects of several sets of variables (measured in 1970) on actual mobility are hypothesized and bivariate relationships are noted. Section III presents the framework and results of a multivariate analysis of the fulfillment of mobility expectations for families that had expected housing or job-related moves. The fourth section discusses the importance of measuring the intensity of mobility expectations. Results are presented from an analysis of fulfillment of mobility expectations when a measure of intensity is included. The fifth and final section summarizes results and speculates about possible policy implications.

ANALYSIS

I. Determinants of Mobility Expectations

If moves are, for the most part, rational, deliberate, and planned, it should be possible to ask people if they expect to move and receive meaningful answers.[1] In the Panel Study of Income Dynamics, respondents were asked, "Do you think you might move in the next couple of years?" If the response to this question was affirmative, the open-ended question, "Why might you move?" was then asked. Reports of moves which are primarily intended to change the future earnings stream of the family are combined into a category and called *productive* moves. Most productive moves are made to take new jobs although some are transfers and a few are made to attend school or to participate in training programs.[2]

Residential changes that are motivated by housing or locational considera-

---

[1] A discussion of questioning respondents about their mobility expectations may be found in Lansing and Barth (1964b).

[2] About 72 percent of respondents reported expecting to move for a new job, compared with 21 percent for a transfer and six percent to attend school or training program. As coded, this productive category includes moves to get closer to work. We have gone through each interview where the expectation of a productive move was expressed and have recoded those cases into the consumptive move category described below.

tions constitute a second category of residential shifts and are termed *consump-tive* moves.[1] The adequacy of space within the dwelling, the physical or social attractiveness of the neighborhood or the distance to work are some of the ways in which mobility facilitates an adjustment in a family's "bundle of housing services." Roughly three-quarters of the responses, however, relate specifically to the house rather than aspects of the neighborhood or community environments.

Some respondents also reported that they expected to make involuntary residential moves. Involuntary moves occur in response to such outside events as eviction, loss of dwelling through demolition or fire, and so on. In this paper we focus only on the voluntary reasons for mobility.

In all, about 22 percent of all families in 1970 reported that they expected to move for voluntary productive or consumptive reasons.[2] The percent of productive move expectations, however, is dwarfed when compared to the fraction of expectations for consumptive reasons -- four percent versus eighteen percent. This uneven distribution is, of course, not surprising, since there is substantial evidence that the majority of *actual* moves are motivated by consumptive rather than job-related reasons. Rossi, Foote and others have found that approximately three-fifths of residential moves represent efforts to find more satisfactory housing.[3] Using Panel Study data, Roistacher found that consumptive moves are almost three times as prevalent as productive moves.[4]

Past research points to a fairly consistent set of independent variables to explain mobility expectations. Demographic characteristics such as the age of the household head and the family's stage in the life cycle, and housing characteristics such as whether the dwelling is owned or rented and how adequately it accommodates the family have often been discussed as useful predictors of aggregate prospective mobility.[5]

---

[1] "Consumptive" is used here in the economic rather than the tubercular sense of the word.

[2] The sample analyzed in this section consists of all families with the same head for each of the years 1970-73. The analysis of productive expectations includes all of these families, while a random half-sample is used in the consumptive expectations analysis.

[3] See Rossi (1955) and Foote, et al. (1960), Chapter 6.

[4] See Roistacher (1974), pp. 1-41.

[5] See Rossi (1955); Foote, et al. (1960); Lansing, et al. (1964a); Lansing and Barth (1964b); Butler et al. (1969); Gist and Fava (1964); Newman (1974).

This past research on prospective and actual mobility, however, has failed to distinguish job-related from housing-related moves. Because most residential changes are efforts to find more satisfactory housing, variables discussed in the existing literature are, by and large, dominated by consumptive moves. To the extent that different factors motivate productive and consumptive moves, predictors found to be important in explaining expectations of one category of moves will not be identical to those which are important for the other category.

In addition to this conventional set of predictors, we also examined other independent variables for effects on mobility expectations. These additional variables fall into three domains: 1) locational characteristics; 2) friendship, kinship and social ties; and 3) job ties.

The size of the city or town in which the residence is situated, a locational variable, may have differential effects on the expectations of productive and consumptive moves. On the one hand, because larger places offer more job opportunities than smaller towns, the expectations of productive moves should be lowest in large places and highest in smaller areas. On the other hand, past research suggests that people find the residential environments of large metropolitan areas less attractive than those in outlying places.[1] Thus, for consumptive moves, the reverse relationship may prevail.

It might also be expected that people with friendship, kinship, social and job ties within an area are less inclined to move. Friendship ties can be measured in the Panel data by the number of neighbors living nearby that the respondent knows by name, kinship ties by the number of relatives living nearby, social ties by the frequency with which the respondents attend social clubs in the area, and job ties by the length of time the respondent has worked at the present job. These factors are hypothesized to deter the formulation of both productive and consumptive mobility expectations.

Finally, different hypotheses regarding the effect of the hours spent travelling to work on the expectation of moving may be advanced. Considerations of convenience and accessibility to job locations should motivate workers with long commuting times to pick residential locations closer to their places of employment. However, if people attach relatively little importance to the journey to work compared with the advantages of residential locations in outlying areas at some distance from work centers, an insignificant or negative relationship between time spent commuting to work and expectations of residential mobility may result.

---

[1] See Dillman (1972), Newman (1974), and Lansing, et al. (1964a).

To describe families who expect to move for consumptive or productive reasons and to detect differences between these two groups of families, we performed bivariate and multivariate analyses with two dichotomous dependent variables. The first dependent variable equals one if the family reports the expectation of a consumptive move and zero otherwise; the second is equal to one if respondents expect a productive move and zero if they do not. The simple associations (Eta^2) between these variables and the predictors of mobility expectations, and the relative importance ($Beta^2$) of the various predictors in accounting for mobility expectations can then be examined and compared. We will turn first to the results for families who reported expectations of consumptive moves and then present results for productive move expectations.

The results of the bivariate and multivariate analyses for consumptive expecters are listed in descending order of relative importance in Table 9.1.

Home ownership is clearly the most important predictor of consumptive move expectations. After the effects of all other variables have been taken into account, renters are almost three times as likely to report a consumptive move expectation as are home owners.[1,2]

The age of the oldest child, the next most important variable, has been used here as a measure of family life cycle stage. Figure 9.1 shows the unadjusted and adjusted proportions of families expecting to move for consumptive reasons by the categories of the age of oldest child variable. Families with an oldest child under six years of age in the household have the highest probability of expecting to move for consumptive reasons. These families tend to be in early stages of the life cycle and are often still expanding. Thus, it is not surprising that this characteristic is associated with expectations of a housing-related move.

The relationship between education and consumptive move expectations is also strong. Previous research suggests that anticipatory mobility is positively related to the level of educational attainment.[3] As shown in Figure 9.2, the plots of both adjusted and unadjusted proportions are not strictly consistent with these previous findings. The peak on both curves occurs not at a high level of

---

[1]The simple and regression adjusted proportions of families expecting a consumptive move by category of independent variable are given in Appendix Table A9.1.

[2]As Rossi notes, "Without exception, previous residential mobility studies have shown that renters are considerably more mobile than owners." (p. 68).

[3]See Foote, et al. (1960), p. 51.

TABLE 9.1

Simple Association (Eta^2) and Relative Importance (Beta^2)
of Predictors in Explaining Consumptive Move Expectations

Variable	Eta^2	Beta^2
Home ownership	.072	.046
Age of oldest child	.033	.012
Education of head	.022	.011
Job tenure	.028	.009
Actual-required number of rooms	.027	.007

Number of observations: 3994

Other variables included in the regression: age, sex, race, money
income/needs, hours of travel to work, city size, number of neighbors known by name, number of relatives near and social club
attendance.

TABLE 9.2

Adjusted and Unadjusted Proportion of Families
Expecting to Move for Consumption Reasons,
by Measure of Crowding

Actual-required room category	Unadjusted class mean	Adjusted class mean
2-3 less rooms than required	.17	.19
1 less room than required or actual=required	.25	.20
1 extra room	.27	.22
2-3 extra rooms	.13	.14
4+ extra rooms	.13	.17

MTR 7096

FIGURE 9.1

Adjusted and Unadjusted Percent of Families Expecting to Move
for Consumptive Reasons, by Age of Oldest Child

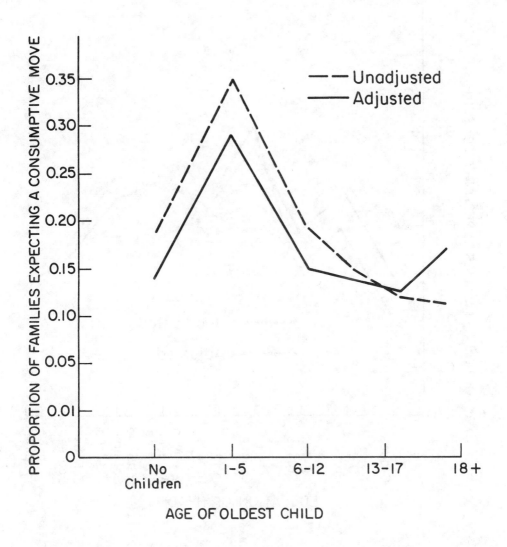

AGE OF OLDEST CHILD

MTR 7093

FIGURE 9.2

Adjusted and Unadjusted Percent of Families Expecting to Move
for Consumptive Reasons, by Education of Head

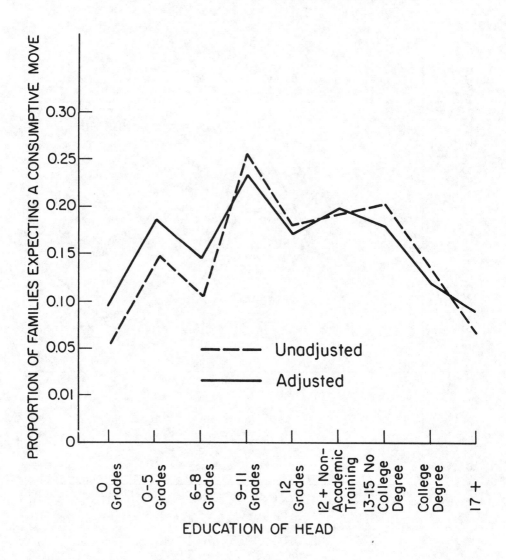

MTR 7093

educational attainment but at a relatively low level -- some high school but no high school diploma. In addition, the curves drop somewhat at the relatively higher educational levels.

The adjusted and unadjusted relationship between job tenure and the expectation of consumptive moves indicates that the greatest probability of such an expectation occurs when the family head has worked at the present job for less than one year (unadjusted = 30%, adjusted = 24%). This probability does not decline as job tenure increases, however. Instead, while consumptive move expectations decrease in the one-to-three-year category, a slight increase presents itself when the worker has been employed at the current job for four to nine years. Length of time at one job is correlated with length of time at one residence. The relationship of the latter variable to inclinations of a consumptive move is more coherent theoretically and its utility in analyzing these expectations has been demonstrated before.[1] Because length of residence was not controlled in the analysis, though, job tenure may be capturing a substantial amount of its explanatory power.

An interpretation similar to that of the oldest child variable can be proposed for the pattern of effects shown by the crowding variable (actual-required number of rooms) on consumptive move expectations.[2] According to the results listed in Table 9.2, families with somewhat less than sufficient space or those with slightly more space than needed are most likely to expect a consumptive move. While those with substantial excess space are least likely to anticipate a move, it is surprising that even when variables such as race and income are taken into account, the most underhoused families are *not* the most likely to expect to make a consumptive move. Perhaps the perception of the lack of alternative options inhibits the formulation of expectations.

Interestingly, none of a large group of additional variables including sex, race, money income/needs, size of place, time spent travelling to work, and friendship, kinship and social ties, was found to be significantly related to the expectation of consumptive mobility in either a bivariate or a multivariate context. It has been hypothesized, for example, that inclinations toward changing

---

[1] See Newman (1974), Butler, et al. (1969), Zehner and Chapin (1974).

[2] In computing required rooms a base of two rooms (exclusive of bathrooms) was allowed for head and wife or for a single head. One additional room was allocated for each single person age 18 or above, one room for a married couple other than head and wife, and one room for every two children of the same sex under age 18. Children under age 10 were paired regardless of sex if this reduced the room requirements.

residences are diminished when households have developed strong interpersonal ties in their residential areas.[1] In addition, location theorists have emphasized the importance of commuting time, costs and overall convenience in the residential location decisions of households.[2] Our analysis does not lend support to these hypotheses.

Following the framework just utilized in presenting the results for consumptive move expectations, we turn now to the findings for families expecting to make a productive move. Accordingly, Table 9.3 lists the simple associations and relative importance of variables in descending order of importance.

Age of head is the most important and significant predictor of productive move expectations. Furthermore, its adjusted and unadjusted pattern of variation, shown in Figure 9.3, is consistent with that found by other researchers. In particular, it has been noted that:

> Individuals aged between 20 and 24 are more likely than any others to move during a given year...Mobility gradually decreases with each year of age...The relationship between age and mobility operates not only among those who have moved but among those who plan to move.[3]

The largest proportion of respondents reporting the expectation of a productive move in the Income Dynamics Study are also younger than 25 years -- 13 percent in unadjusted form and 12 percent when other variables are taken into account. The shape of the curves indicates that expectations of productive mobility decline steadily with age.[4]

Education is also an important predictor of productive move expectations. Not surprisingly, the probability of anticipating a residential shift for

---

[1] Kennedy (1950).

[2] Lansing, et al. (1964), pp. 37-42; Alonso (1964).

[3] Foote, et al. (1960), p. 146.

[4] As noted earlier, age of head was not important for the prediction of consumptive move expectations. Interestingly, the bivariate relationship between consumptive move expectations and age of head is significant. Its pattern is not monotonic, as it is for productive move expectations, but rather decreases until age 55 and then increases slightly for the 55-65 age group (probably representing housing adjustments undertaken in response to reduced family size). Once other variables are accounted for, however, the importance of age is greatly reduced and little variation can be discerned among different age groups. This differential importance of age of head in the multivariate analysis of expectations of consumptive and productive move expectations suggests that because life cycle factors are most prominent in the explanation of consumptive expectations, age of oldest child captures the greatest amount of explanatory power as it is a better measure of family life cycle than is age of head alone. In contrast, life cycle does not seem to be as important for productive move expectations.

TABLE 9.3

Simple Association (Eta^2) and Relative Importance (Beta^2) of Predictors
in Explaining Productive Move Expectations

Variables	Eta^2	Beta^2
Age of head	.038	.046
Education of head	.027	.017
Job tenure	.008	.007

Number of
 observations: 1996

Other variables included in the regression:
   sex, race, age of oldest child, money income/needs,
   whether own, actual-required number of rooms, city
   size, number of neighbors known by name, number
   of relatives near and social club attendance.

290

MTR 7093

FIGURE 9.3

Adjusted and Unadjusted Percent of Families Expecting to Move for Productive Reasons, By Age of Head

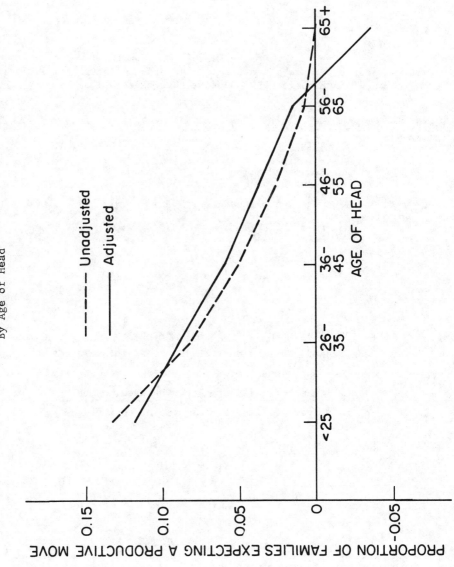

productive reasons tends to increase as level of education increases. Accounting for the intercorrelation between education and the other independent variables does not change this relationship.

In a similar manner, the results for job tenure are expected: the longer one has worked at one job, the less likely a change of residence for job-related reasons is likely to occur.

Once more, a large number of additional variables do not relate significantly to the expectations of productive moves. Among these variables are measures of friendship, kinship and social ties, hours of travel to work, city size, crowding within the house, home ownership status, money income/needs, and the demographic characteristics of age of oldest child, and sex and race of head. It is interesting that all of the house/locational variables included in both analyses are significant in relation to consumptive expectations but insignificant for productive expectations.

Although the relative importance of the size of place or urbanization variable is not large for families expecting to undertake either consumptive or productive moves, its pattern of effects is interesting. In Figure 9.4, the adjusted mean percents of productive and consumptive move expectations for each size of place are plotted. As the graph indicates, the curves behave very differently. A much larger probability of move expectations for housing or locational reasons is associated with living in larger places while the smallest probability of move expectations for productive reasons is found in such locations.

II. Determinants of Actual Mobility

The analysis of the previous section has shown that about one-fourth of all families in any one year report the expectation of a residential move. Most of those who expect to move do so for housing-related reasons. Families that expect to move for voluntary reasons differ from the population as a whole in several dimensions. First, they are younger. While the average age of all household heads exceeds 45 years, the mean ages of family heads that reported the expectations of consumptive and productive moves are about 40 and 33, respectively. Second, families expecting both kinds of moves tend to rent rather than own a home. Young children are more likely to be present in families that expect consumptive moves. Finally, the education attained by heads of households that expect productive moves is higher than average.

In this section, we look only at families who in 1970 reported that they expected to move for either productive or consumptive reasons. Our primary aim is to identify the determinants of whether or not these families fulfill their ex-

FIGURE 9.4

Adjusted Proportion of Families Expecting to Move
for Productive and Consumptive Reasons,
by Size of Place of Residence

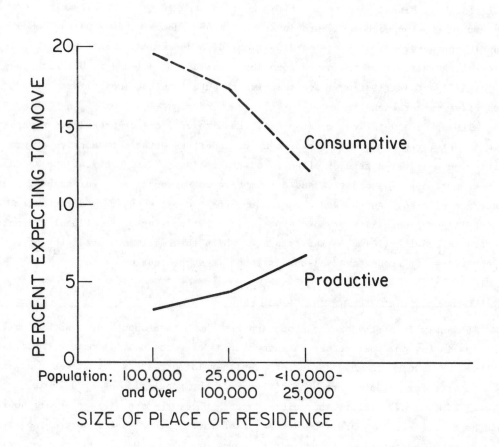

pectations and actually move for the reasons stated. The longitudinal nature of
the sample is well suited to examine this question, since families are observed
for three years after stating their mobility expectations.

Regardless of the reason given for expecting the voluntary move, fewer than
half of the families actually do move. Table 9.4 shows the mobility outcomes for
those who in 1970 had expected to move for either productive or consumptive reasons. Forty-two percent of productive expecters actually moved; 39 percent of
the families who reported consumptive expectations moved. In addition, most of
these moves occurred during the first year after the intention was stated. This
result is consistent with the findings of previous mobility research which shows
that the planning period for both productive and consumptive movers is quite
short.[1]

Among the families that did not move during the three-year period, less than
one-third *delayed* the move.[2] Table 9.4 also shows that the delayers are more
prevalent among families expecting to move for consumptive rather than productive
purposes.

Slightly less than ten percent of the families that had expected to move for
consumptive reasons actually moved for involuntary reasons. Since this paper
focuses on voluntary mobility, families actually moving for involuntary reasons
are eliminated from subsequent analysis.

Among families that expect to make a voluntary move, only a minority actually do move. What are the characteristics of this minority and how does it differ
from the majority of families who expect to move but fail to do so? To answer
this question we constructed an expectations fulfillment variable and related it
to a set of explanatory variables. It is a dichotomous variable, taking the
value of one if the family actually moved for the stated reason within the three-
year period after expressing the mobility expectation. Its value is zero if such
a move did not occur. While this scaling sacrifices the knowledge of the timing
of the move or the status of plans for those who had not moved, additional analysis has shown that these distinctions add little to the results for the dichotomous dependent variable.[3]

---

[1]Lansing and Mueller (1967) found that one-third of respondents who had moved recently seriously considered their move one month or less, while an additional
third deliberated between one and six months.

[2]Delayers are those who continued to expect to move for the same reason for each
of the three years but didn't actually move in any of these years.

[3]In this additional analysis, a mobility outcome variable was constructed from
the columns of Table 9.4 and then related to various predictors. Significance
tests were then performed on column differences. The largest differences were

TABLE 9.4

Mobility Outcomes for Families Expecting to Move in 1970

Reason for Expected Move	Number of Observations	Outcome						
		Moved for Stated Reason			Did Not Move for Stated Reason			
		Moved in 1971	Moved in 1972	Moved in 1973	Moved Involuntarily	Delay in Plans	Dropped or Changed Plans	Total
Productive	157	31.7%	6.1%	3.8%	0.0%	8.2%	50.2%	100.0%
Consumptive	875	24.8	9.4	5.1	9.4	16.2	35.2	100.0

Several groups of factors can be distinguished for an analysis of the determinants of mobility among the group of families that expected, in 1970, to undertake a voluntary move: economic ties, family and community ties, housing characteristics, income and needs, social-psychological variables, and demographic characteristics.

In their analysis of long distance productive moves, Lansing and Mueller examined the relationship between mobility and two economic ties -- home ownership and pension plans -- and found that both had small negative effects.[1] The sale of a home involves expenditures of time and money and these costs may be expected to act as deterrents to the fulfillment of mobility expectations for home owners. Confounding this simple association between home ownership and mobility are the additional characteristics of home owners which relate to residential mobility, such as their age. Thus, the simple association between home ownership and mobility rates is not only the result of economic ties. Unadjusted expectation fulfillment rates given in Table 9.5 for productive and consumptive movers indicates that, nevertheless, renters are almost twice as likely to fulfill moving expectations as are homeowners.

Coverage by a pension plan is an additional economic tie that could hinder the mobility of families expecting a productive move. Under some plans, employees receive benefits only if they remain with the company until retirement. Other plans, however, contain vesting provisions and might not impede mobility as much. While a direct measure of pension plan arrangement is not available in the Panel data, both job tenure and union membership status can be used as proxy variables. Longer tenure should be associated with lower mobility rates for families expecting a productive move. Similarly, prevalence of pension plans among union members should result in a negative relationship between union membership and actual moves. In addition to measuring pension plan availability, however, job tenure and union membership are associated with other job aspects that might hinder productive mobility. Job seniority not only provides pension rights but also privileges, freedoms and additional "nonpecuniary" work rewards. Social ties with co-workers will also increase with tenure and union membership.

The unadjusted fulfillment rates by job tenure and union status are given in Table 9.6. They support the notion that both variables retard mobility among those expecting a productive move. They have a weaker and more erratic relationship for families expecting a consumptive move.

---

found when movers were contrasted with nonmovers. Divisions by the year moved or by reason for not moving made little difference.

[1] Lansing and Mueller (1967), p. 174.

TABLE 9.5

Fulfillment Rates of Families Who Expected to Move
for Productive and Consumptive Reasons,
by Home Ownership Status

	Fulfillment rates for families expecting a productive move	Fulfillment rates for families expecting a consumptive move
Own home	29.3%	38.0%
Do not own home	51.4	62.0
Number of observations	157	796

TABLE 9.6

Fulfillment Rates of Families Who Expected to Move
for Productive and Consumptive Reasons,
by Job Tenure and Union Membership Status

	Fulfillment rates for families expecting a productive move	Fulfillment rates for families expecting a consumptive move
Job tenure		
Not employed	46.1%	42.7%
Less than one year	49.3	49.5
1 - 4 years	40.8	45.8
5 - 10 years	32.1*	31.8
More than 10 years	34.4*	35.7
Union Status		
Union member	30.6	44.3
Not union member	43.7	39.8

*Result based on fewer than 25 cases

MTR 7093

The social ties a family develops at a particular residential location may impede the fulfillment of mobility expectations. Further, these ties may be more important for those considering a consumptive rather than a productive move, since the existing social ties are often an important part of housing consumption itself. The data allow the construction of a family and community ties index which consists of components relating to church, bar or social club attendance, the number of neighbors known, whether relatives live nearby and, finally, for families with children in school, whether or not the parents recently attended PTA meetings. The simple relationship between the index and fulfillment is presented in Table 9.7. Higher scores on this index are associated with lower actual mobility among those expecting to move for consumptive reasons while the index has an ambiguous relationship with residential moves for those expecting a productive move.

The adequacy of space within the dwelling unit -- either too little or, in rare cases, too much -- is often the motivation for consumptive moves. Mobility rates for families who in 1970 were either under- or over-housed and expected to move for consumptive reasons should be higher than those for families with housing which was more adequate for their needs. As shown in Table 9.8, the unadjusted fulfillment rates are highest among families that expected to move for consumptive reasons and had fewer rooms than required by their family size and composition. That families with surplus rooms had the lowest fulfillment rates (for consumptive expecters) may result from the intercorrelation between surplus rooms and other variables, such as home ownership and income. The multivariate analysis presented below should help to disentangle these effects.

Although it was shown in Section I that income and family size have little relationship to the *expectation* of a productive or consumptive move, there are reasons to believe that these two variables may effect the *actual* mobility of those expecting to make a voluntary move. Moving entails several direct costs, but because most moves are local, the *average* direct cost of moving is not large.[1] Long distance moves, however, are likely to involve considerable direct expense. Since consumptive moves are predominantly local (more than four-fifths are intra-county) and relatively inexpensive, income and family size should have little effect on the fulfillment rates of those who expect consumptive moves. Productive moves, on the other hand, tend to be made over longer distances, with almost half of all productive moves crossing county lines. The higher direct costs of productive moves, then, may make income and family size important factors for

---

[1] In Lansing and Mueller (1967), p. 258, these direct costs were estimated to be about $225 in 1962.

TABLE 9.7

Fulfillment Rates of Families Who Expected to Move
for Productive and Consumptive Reasons,
by Family and Community Ties

Family and community ties index score	Fulfillment rates for families expecting a productive move	Fulfillment rates for families expecting a consumptive move
0-4	39.6%	43.5%
5-7	51.3	41.7
Over 7	16.5	30.4

TABLE 9.8

Fulfillment Rates of Families Who Expected to Move
for Productive and Consumptive Reasons,
by Actual Required Number of Rooms

Actual minus required number of rooms	Fulfillment rates for families expecting a productive move	Fulfillment rates for families expecting a consumptive move
< 0	34.0%	59.0%
0 - 3	49.1	43.5
More than 3	32.6	29.5

MTR 7093

actual fulfillment rates. Furthermore, a period of unemployment may be experienced by those people who make a productive move for some reason other than a job transfer. The loss of income due to unemployment can easily exceed the direct costs of moving. In contrast, the likelihood of unemployment occurring because of a consumptive move is remote. Because indirect and direct costs of moving should be lower for consumptive movers, income should have much less of an effect on the fulfillment of consumptive mobility expectations.

The unadjusted fulfillment rates by income level and family size listed in Table 9.9 do not show a monotonic pattern for families expecting to move for either job-related or housing reasons. While fulfillment rates are highest at both ends of the income scale for the former group of families, families that expected to move for consumptive reasons have high fulfillment rates if they are in the middle income category. This lack of an income relationship may be attributed to the effects of other variables which are associated with income. Home ownership, for example, increases with income level and may depress actual fulfillment rates at the upper end of the income scale. As is the case for other variables described in this section, final judgment on the income variable should be made only after results of the multivariate analysis have been examined.

With the exception of the low fulfillment rates of single-person families, the percent of families moving declines steadily as family size increases. This relationship holds for families that expected to move for either productive or consumptive reasons.

Several demographic characteristics belong in a model of mobility, partly because they can be expected to have direct effects on fulfillment rates and partly because multivariate analysis of other independent variables is more useful if the effects of these demographic characteristics are taken into account. Three such characteristics are included in our model -- age, race, and sex. The simple relationship between fulfillment rates and these three variables appears in Table 9.10.

While it was shown earlier that the probability of expecting either productive or consumptive moves declines with age, Table 9.10 shows that age has a similar relationship to the fulfillment of expectations only for the consumptive movers.

The effects of sex and race on fulfillment depend critically on the reason for the move. Female heads of households fulfill productive expectations more frequently than male heads; males, however, have twice the consumptive mobility rates of females. The sex difference for productive movers is based on a small number of observations. Estimated differences in consumptive fulfillment rates

TABLE 9.9

Fulfillment Rates of Families Who Expected to Move
for Productive and Consumptive Reasons,
by Income and Family Size

	Fulfillment rates for families expecting a productive move	Fulfillment rates for families expecting a consumptive move
Family income quintile		
Lowest	46.8%	38.6%
Fourth	39.0	41.3
Third	41.6	49.7
Second	30.6	37.5
Highest	49.0	34.6
Family size		
One	38.3	27.1
Two	61.4	44.4
Three	41.4	56.9
Four	34.8	38.1
Five or more	32.7	35.2

TABLE 9.10

Fulfillment Rates of Families Who Expected to Move
for Productive and Consumptive Reasons,
by Age, Race and Sex

	Fulfillment rates for families expecting a productive move	Fulfillment rates for families expecting a consumptive move
Age		
< 25	49.7%	61.8%
25 – 34	37.8	48.7
35 – 44	41.2	30.4
45 – 54	33.4	34.2
55 – 64	44.2*	26.1
65 and over	--	27.9
Sex of head		
Male	40.7	45.1
Female	47.4*	25.7
Race		
White	42.7	38.8
Non white	27.6	52.1

*Result based on fewer than 25 cases

MTR 7093

by sex are more reliable and could be attributed to the effects of other variables. They may also stem from discriminatory treatment that women receive in housing credit markets.

Whites are much more likely to carry out productive move plans than nonwhites, while whites are *less* likely to make consumptive moves than are nonwhites. Multivariate analysis will show that these racial differences are not significant.

Two final determinants of actual mobility for those expecting to move which will be examined here are education and personal efficacy. Both of these variables measure a sense of personal effectiveness that other researchers have related to a variety of outcome variables.[1] Education also correlates with access to information and thus it should have additional importance, especially for families making long distance, productive moves.[2] The simple relationship between efficacy, education and mobility for families expecting to move appears in Table 9.11. Efficacy has a positive effect on the fulfillment of both productive and consumptive move expectations; education's effect is monotonic only for the fulfillment of productive expectations.

The numbers presented in this and all previous tables in this section are fulfillment rates which are unadjusted for the effect of other predictors. Education's "true" effect on fulfillment, for example, can be estimated only after the effects of other variables associated with education (e.g., efficacy and income) have been taken into account. Multivariate analysis is required and is the subject of the next section.

III. Multivariate Analysis on the Fulfillment
     of Mobility Expectations

The determinants of mobility for families with expectations of productive and consumptive moves are best examined in a multivariate context. Linear regression will be used with the dichotomous fulfillment variable regressed on the set of independent variables discussed in the previous section. Some, but not all, of the independent variables are expressed in dummy variable form. A linear relationship is assumed between the remaining predictors and the dependent variable in order to preserve the small number of degrees of freedom afforded by the 157 families that expected to move for productive reasons.

The standardized regression coefficients estimated for each of the independent variables are given in Table 9.12. The entire set of independent variables

---

[1] See, for example, Gurin and Gurin (1974).

[2] This argument is presented in Bowles (1970), p. 357.

TABLE 9.11

Fulfillment Rates of Families Who Expected to Move
for Productive and Consumptive Reasons,
by Efficacy and Education

	Fulfillment rates for families expecting a productive move	Fulfillment rates for families expecting a consumptive move
Efficacy		
Low	28.1%	35.6%
Medium	44.9	39.1
High	45.7	48.7
Education		
0 - 11 grades	36.3	37.5
High school graduate or some college	38.9	44.9
College graduate	47.6	37.0

MTR 7093

TABLE 9.12

Standardized Regression Coefficients of Predictors
of Actual Mobility -- for Families Expecting
a Productive or Consumptive Move

Predictor	Coefficients for Families Expecting a Productive Move	Coefficients for Families Expecting a Consumptive Move
Whether own home	$-.28^{**}$	$-.12^{**}$
Job tenure	$-.09$	$.01$
Union member	$-.06$	$-.00$
Family and community ties	$-.09$	$-.04$
Total family income	$.35^{**}$	$-.04$
Family size	$-.11$	$-.07$
Actual - Required Room < 0	$-.09^{**}$	$.11^{**}$
Actual - Required > 3	$-.19$	$-.03$
Whether female head	$.13$	$-.20^{**}$
Whether non-white	$-.14$	$.08^{**}$
Age	$.09$	$-.18$
Efficacy	$.21^{**}$	$.06$
Education	$-.02$	$-.04$
$\bar{R}^2$	$.121$	$.128$
Number of observations	157	739

**Significantly different from zero at the 1% probability level.

MTR 7096

explains almost identical amounts of the variation in the fulfillment of productive and consumptive expectations. The estimated population variance explained ($\bar{R}^2$) for families expecting a productive move is .121, while for families with consumptive expectations the $\bar{R}^2$ is .128. What is most interesting about the regression, however, is not the overall explanatory power of the model but rather the extent to which the importance of various predictors depends upon the motivation for the move.

Total family income is the most important determinant of actual mobility among families expecting a productive move but has virtually no effect on the fulfillment of consumptive expectations. The income coefficient, when translated into dollar terms,[1] has the following interpretation: after the effects of all other variables have been taken into account, among families expecting a productive move, each additional $1000 of family income is associated with a 2.6 percent increase in the probability that a family will actually move. The importance of the income variable for those expecting and fulfilling productive moves is consistent with the cost explanation advanced earlier. Because direct and indirect moving costs are substantially higher in productive moves, as contrasted with consumptive moves, income should be more important for productive movers.

The detrimental effect of family size on mobility is also consistent with this cost explanation, although neither the coefficient for those expecting to make productive or consumptive moves is statistically significant.

Since the sample of families examined here for fulfillment of mobility expectations includes a higher fraction of renters than does the population as a whole, it is interesting that the home ownership variable still has a significant negative effect on actual mobility for families that had expected to move for both productive and consumptive reasons. The magnitude of the effect depends upon the stated reasons for expecting the move. Home ownership depresses fulfillment rates only half as much for those who had expected consumptive moves as compared with those expecting productive moves. When the effects of other variables are controlled statistically, those families that expected to move for productive reasons are 27.3 percent less likely to actually move if they own a home, while families anticipating consumptive moves have actual mobility rates that are 12.1 percent lower if they are home owners.[2]

---

[1] A standardized coefficient can be converted into raw score form if it is multiplied by the ratio of the standard deviation of the dependent variable to the standard deviation of the independent variable. The means and standard deviations of all variables in the analysis are presented in Appendix Table A9.2.

[2] These percentage differences are estimated from raw score (not standardized) coefficients and therefore differ from those presented in Table 9.12.

Job tenure is also associated with lower fulfillment rates for families
expecting productive moves but has no effect on consumptive mobility. Neither of
these effects, however, is statistically significant. The final "economic ties"
variable, union membership, is not important for either group of families.

While the index of family and community ties has a small, negative effect
on fulfillment, its coefficient is not significantly different from zero.

The association between fulfillment rates and the extent to which the
family is under- or over-housed depends upon the reason for the mobility expectation. Families expecting to move for consumptive reasons who did not have
as many rooms as required by their family size were significantly *more* likely to
move. Crowded housing thus seems to be a significant "push" factor for families
expecting consumptive moves; being over-housed, however, has little effect.[1]

The effects of the crowding variable on families that expect to move for
productive reasons are quite different. The fulfillment rates for families with
inadequate space do not differ significantly from the rates of families that
have a small number of surplus rooms. Once this surplus exceeds three rooms,
however, the rate of fulfillment drops markedly.

Interactions are also found among several demographic characteristics and
the reasons for moving. Among families that expect a consumptive move, those
with female heads have fulfillment rates that are almost 25 percentage points
less than those of male-headed families. The reader should bear in mind that
this estimate is obtained after the effects of income, education, age, and all
the other variables have been taken into account. Differential treatment for
men and women in housing credit markets is a possible explanation that was advanced earlier, although we have no direct evidence on this issue.

Blacks have lower fulfillment rates than whites among families that expect
a productive move, and higher fulfillment rates among families stating the expectation of a consumptive move. However, neither of these coefficients is statistically different from zero at the five percent level.

Even though the older families that had not expected a consumptive move were
eliminated from the analysis in this section, the age variable still has a sig-

---

[1] Although not central to our special interest in factors which enable families to
fulfill their mobility expectations, the finding that, among families expecting
and fulfilling consumptive moves, dwelling unit adjustment considerations are
mentioned about three times as often as neighborhood or community environment
characteristics is interesting. This may suggest that many urban-suburban moves,
for example, stem more from the need to find suitable housing than from the need
to find amenity-rich environments. This notion is supported by other research
such as Greenbie (1969) and Newman (1974). It was not directly relevant to
our purpose and was not tested here.

nificant, negative effect on the mobility rates of those expecting consumptive moves. Each additional year is associated with a one-half percent drop in fulfillment rates of these families. The age effect on the fulfillment rates of families expecting a productive move is small, positive, and insignificant.

Sense of efficacy has a strong, positive, and significant effect on the fulfillment rates of those expecting a productive move, even when its intercorrelation with education has been taken into account. It has a small and insignificant effect on the actual moves of families that in 1970 had expected to move for consumptive reasons. This suggests that efficacy works for a certain kind of behavior but not another. Those expecting a productive move -- to get a new job or to transfer locations but remain with the same employer -- are aided by this personality trait. Families expecting a move to adjust housing consumption, on the other hand, are not significantly affected by it.

The final variable included in the analysis -- education -- did not significantly affect the fulfillment rates of either group of families.

IV.   A Note on the Intensity of Expectations

A potential flaw in the preceding analysis is the absence of control on the intensity with which families expect to move. As Rossi has stated:

> At any point in time, a survey of households will find
> some that are at the point of moving, others feeling
> vaguely that they would like to do so, and still others
> can be found who are firmly wedded to their present res-
> idences. Inclinations towards mobility will be found to
> vary along a continuum.[1]

The effect of explanatory variables on the fulfillment of mobility expectations will be masked if a strong association exists between these predictors and the intensity of mobility expectations. To illustrate, consider the effect of education on expectations and fulfillment of expectations. Suppose that highly educated people are perfectly accurate in assessing their probability of making a productive move. For a group that says its chances of making such a move are one in four, for example, 25 percent actually do move. Similarly, among families that say their chance of moving is 90 percent, nine out of ten will actually make the move.

If the responses of the highly educated people to the question "Do you think you might move in the next couple of years?" are coded either "yes" or "no", the detail of the intensity or probability of expectations is lost. Those with a probability greater than some level are coded "yes" and all others are coded "no".

---

[1]Rossi (1955), p. 66.

The analysis of Sections II and III focused on the group of families that answered the expectations question affirmatively. Those who had a 75 percent probability of moving were not differentiated from families that were absolutely certain that they would move. The effect of education on mobility comes from comparing the *average* probability of moving for the highly educated family heads (which equals the *actual* mobility rate in this example) with the actual mobility of less educated families, and the fact that the highly educated can forecast future mobility perfectly will not be discovered.

Ideally, this problem would be avoided if the subjective probability of future mobility could be ascertained from all respondents. Developing the actual questions to elicit this probability (if, in fact, any exist) is beyond the scope of this paper.

We can, however, shed some light on the extent to which the "intensity effects" of independent variables confound their true effects on the fulfillment of moving expectations. Below, we summarize the results of additional coding and analysis which we did on the 157 families who reported in 1970 that they expected to move for productive reasons.

By examining actual interviews, it became clear that "yes" responses to the question of productive move expectations could, in fact, be subdivided into two different codes representing different levels of the intensity of expectation. Although the questionnaire did not ask about expectation intensity directly, this intensity could easily be inferred from responses in most questionnaires. Into the low intensity code went responses such as, "Now that you mention it, yes I might move," and "If a job opportunity comes up we will move." The high intensity code contains responses on definite planned moves. There was, of course, a gray area of responses where the intensity was more difficult to ascertain, but it was small and we are confident that this dichotomous coding of intensity captures a substantial amount of the differences. About two-thirds of the families were coded as having a high intensity of expectation while the remaining third were in the low intensity category.

The extent to which this intensity variable relates to the set of independent variables described in Section II can be seen in a multiple regression of the intensity variable on the independent variables. Results from this regression are presented in Table 9.13. Several of the predictors do, in fact, have a significant relationship with this intensity variable. In general, the variables that are important predictors of intensity are also important in explaining fulfillment. Income and home ownership are significant independent variables for both dependent variables. The index of family and community ties has a signifi-

TABLE 9.13

Standardized Coefficients of Independent Variables
Predicting the Intensity of Mobility Expectations--
for Families Expecting a Productive Move in 1970

Predictor	Standardized Coefficient
Whether own home	-.35**
Job tenure	.01
Union member	.08
Family and community ties	-.25**
Total family income	.24*
Family size	-.02
Actual – Required < 0	-.01
Actual – Required > 3	-.08
Whether female head	-.00
Whether non-white	-.15
Age	.02
Efficacy	.08
Education	.02
$\overline{R}^2$	.137
Number of observations	157

*Significantly different from zero at the 5% probability level
**Significantly different from zero at the 1% probability level

MTR 7096

cant, negative effect on the *intensity* of expectation -- although it is not a powerful predictor of fulfillment.

This intensity variable can further be used to give better estimates of the effects of the independent variables on fulfillment. To do this, the fulfillment regression (the results of which are given in Table 9.12) was rerun including the intensity variable as an additional predictor. Results from this regression (with the coefficients of Table 9.12 reproduced for comparative purposes) are given in Table 9.14.

Although there is a statistically significant increase in the $\bar{R}^2$ when intensity is included, the *size* of the increase (from .12 to .15) is hardly dramatic. Variables found to be important when intensity is the dependent variable decrease somewhat in importance when fulfillment is the dependent variable. The effects of home ownership on mobility drops the most: the standardized coefficient falls from .28 to .20. Income remains the most significant predictor of the fulfillment of expectations when the intensity variable is added. A slight downward adjustment, however, does occur. Without controlling for intensity, each additional $1000 of income is associated with a 2.6 percent increase in the probability of moving. When the intensity variable is added, this estimated income effect is 2.2 percent.

While some coefficients do change when the intensity of expectation is taken into account, the relative importance of the various sets of predictors in the productive mobility fulfillment model does not change. Income is still the most important determinant of the actual mobility of families expecting to move for productive reasons. Home ownership, efficacy, and whether there are more than three surplus rooms maintain their rank as the second, third, and fourth most important independent variables. Variables found to be significantly different from zero in the regression which did not include the intensity variable are still statistically significant when the variable is added, although the level of significance for the home ownership and efficacy variables drops from the one percent to the five percent level.

In sum, our *post hoc* measurement of intensity of voluntary mobility expectations appears to have only a minor effect on the prediction of the fulfillment of these mobility expectations. It is difficult, however, to speculate about the extent to which better measurement of intensity would produce greater adjustments or whether these conclusions would also hold for fulfillment of consumptive mobility plans.[1]

---

[1]Two notes on these adjustments are in order. First, adjustments could also be expected in the estimated importance of predictors of *expectations* them-

TABLE 9.14

Standardized Regression Coefficients of Predictors
of Actual Mobility With and Without Intensity of
Expectations -- For Families, Reporting in 1970, the
Expectation of a Productive Move

Predictor	Estimated Standardized Coefficients	
Whether own home	$-.28^{**}$	$-.21^{*}$
Job tenure	$-.09$	$-.10$
Union member	$-.06$	$-.05$
Family and community ties	$-.09$	$-.04$
Total family income	$.35^{**}$	$.30^{**}$
Family size	$-.11$	$-.11$
Actual – Required < 0	$-.09_{*}$	$-.09_{*}$
Actual – Required > 3	$-.19^{*}$	$-.18^{*}$
Whether female head	$.13$	$.13$
Whether non-white	$-.14$	$-.11$
Age	$.09$	$.09$
Efficacy	$.21^{**}$	$.20^{*}$
Education	$-.02$	$-.03$
Intensity of expectation	$-$	$.20^{*}$
$\bar{R}^2$	$.121$	$.153$
Number of observations	157	157

*Significantly different from zero at the 5% probability level

**Significantly different from zero at the 1% probability level

MTR 7096

SUMMARY

In this paper, we have identified several variables that relate to the actual mobility of families expecting to make a residential move. Furthermore, it appears that the effects of these variables depend upon the reasons for the expected move. We now speculate on the implications of these results both for the fulfillment of job-related (productive) mobility expectations and for housing-related (consumptive) moves.

The results for the fulfillment of productive mobility expectations lend support to the hypothesis that many intended job-related moves are not undertaken simply because they are too costly. These expenses arise for at least two reasons. First, because job-related moves tend to occur over long distances, they tend to involve substantial direct moving costs. Second, because productive moves are made primarily for the purpose of finding a new job, they may involve a substantial period of unemployment for the job seeker. That these costs are important is suggested by our finding that income had the greatest effect on actual productive mobility. It is estimated that an additional $1000 of family income is associated with an increase in fulfillment rates of about two and one-half percent. Increased family size decreases fulfillment. Each additional family member decreases fulfillment rates by almost three percent. This estimated effect of family size is substantial although not significant at the five percent probability level.

Less direct evidence in support of this cost hypothesis stems from finding that home ownership is a significant deterrent to the fulfillment of productive move expectations. After the effects of income, education, age and other factors have been taken into account, home owners have fulfillment rates that are less

---

selves. In Section I of this paper, the expectation of a move was scaled dichotomously. The ideal scale would be a continuous probability ranging from zero to one hundred percent. To see whether better measurement of the intensity dependent variable changed results of the expectation model of productive movers, we scaled a new dependent variable as follows: the expectation variable equals zero if the family did not expect a productive move, one if the family expected a productive move with high intensity and 0.5 if the family had a low intensity expectation of a productive move. This rescaling had a negligible impact on the estimated effects of predictors in the expectations model of Section I.

Second, while some coefficients did change with the addition of an intensity variable which was scaled in the crude, dichotomous form, it is not necessarily true that more refined scaling would cause further large adjustments. Surprisingly little of the explanatory power of a continuous variable is lost when it is collapsed to a small set of dummy variables. See Lansing and Morgan (1973), p. 275.

than half those of renters. While part of this effect may be due to other, excluded characteristics of home ownership, the time and money expenses incurred in the sale of a home may very well contribute to these lower rates.

If, in fact, the direct and indirect costs of moving impede labor mobility, policies aimed at facilitating job-related moves seem to be indicated. Relocation allowances, for example, have been successfully implemented in several European countries. Some of the experimental, pilot mobility assistance projects undertaken in the United States during the mid-sixties were also evaluated as useful and practical tools in facilitating moves that might not have occurred otherwise.[1]

Variables found important for the actual mobility of families expecting a consumptive move are quite different from the predictors of productive mobility. While income, for example, is the most important determinant of job-related mobility, it has an insignificant *negative* effect for consumptive mobility. Efficacy is a second variable with a significant effect on job-related moves but is of no importance for the fulfillment of housing-related mobility expectations.

The only variable found to be significant for both types of moves is home ownership status. The negative association between owning a home and fulfilling consumptive mobility expectations is less than half the size of its association with productive mobility rates.

Other variables, however, did affect consumptive fulfillment. A family that did not have as many rooms as its family size required was significantly more likely to fulfill its mobility expectations than if it had sufficient space. Age had an important negative effect on fulfillment even when the effects of other variables were taken into account.

The significance of the crowding and age variables extends previous findings that young, expanding families in early stages of the life cycle are also highly mobile households by suggesting that these families are also more effective in carrying out their expectations.

It was also found that households headed by a woman were much less likely to fulfill consumptive mobility expectations than male-headed families. These differences could not be attributed to the effect of income, family size, education or any other variables included in our analysis. Many unmeasured characteristics of the families, their living situation and the obstructions to mobility they en-

----

[1] See Brandwein (1969).

counter, could contribute to this sex difference. Without additional data and analysis, however, we refrain from ungrounded speculation. Further research is clearly needed to explain and perhaps suggest policies to eliminate these differences.

References

Alonso, William, Location and Land Use. Cambridge: Harvard University Press, 1964.

Bowles, Samuel, "Migration as Investment: Empirical Tests of the Human Investment Approach to Geographic Mobility," Review of Economics and Statistics, November 1970.

Brandwein, Seymour, "Pilot Mobility Assistance Experience: Assessment and Recommendations," background paper, National Manpower Advisory Committee, June 1969.

Butler, Edgar, et al., Moving Behavior and Residential Choice: A National Survey. Washington: National Cooperative Highway Research Report No. 81, 1969.

Dillman, Don, "Population Distribution Policy and People's Attitudes: Current Knowledge and Needed Research," a paper prepared for the Urban Land Institute, October 15, 1973.

Foote, Nelson, et al., Housing Choices and Housing Constraints. New York: McGraw Hill Book Company, 1960.

Gist, Noel and Fava, Sylvia, Urban Society, New York: Thomas Y. Crowell Company, 1964.

Greenbie, Barrie, "New House or New Neighborhood? A Survey of Priorities Among Homeowners in Madison, Wisconsin," Land Economics, Vol. 45 (August) 1969, pp. 359-365.

Gurin, Gerald and Gurin, Patricia, "Personal Efficacy and the Ideology of Individual Responsibility" in Burkhard Strumpel, Economic Well-being in a System of Social Indicators, forthcoming.

Kennedy, Robert W., "Socio-psychological Problems of Housing Design," in Leon Festinger, et al., Social Pressures in Informal Groups. New York: Harper and Brothers, 1950.

Lansing, John D. and Morgan, James N., Economic Survey Methods. Institute for Social Research, University of Michigan, Ann Arbor, 1971.

Lansing, John, et al., Residential Location and Urban Mobility. Ann Arbor: Institute for Social Research, 1964a.

Lansing, John and Barth, Nancy, Residential Location and Urban Mobility: A Multivariate Analysis. Ann Arbor: Institute for Social Research, 1964b.

314

Lansing, John and Mueller, Eva, The Geographic Mobility of Labor. Ann Arbor: Institute for Social Research, 1967.

Newman, Sandra, The Residential Environment and the Desire to Move. Ann Arbor: Institute for Social Research, 1974.

Roistacher, Elizabeth, "Residential Mobility," in James N. Morgan, Five Thousand American Families -- Patterns of Economic Progress. Ann Arbor: Survey Research Center, 1974, Vol. II, pp. 41-78.

Rossi, Peter, Why Families Move. Glencoe: The Free Press, 1955.

Zehner, Robert and Chapin, F. Stuart, Across the City Line: A White Community in Transition. Lexington: D. C. Heath-Lexington Company, 1974.

APPENDIX 9.1

TABLE A9.1

Unadjusted and Adjusted Mean Proportions of Families Expecting Productive Moves and Consumptive Moves, by Categories of Independent Variables

Independent Variable	Productive Move Expectations			Consumptive Move Expectations		
	Number of cases	Unadjusted	Adjusted	Number of cases	Unadjusted	Adjusted
Near Neighbors Known	$\beta^2 = .0002$			$\beta^2 = .0008$		
None	159	.056	.035	88	.294	.198
1-5	842	.049	.040	420	.251	.195
6+	2993	.043	.046	1488	.152	.169
Relatives Near	$\beta^2 = .007$			$\beta^2 = .000005$		
No	2111	.062	.059	1064	.178	.175
Yes	1883	.020	.024	932	.170	.174
How Often Attend Clubs	$\beta^2 = .000002$			$\beta^2 = .004$		
Never; hardly ever	2941	.042	.044	1459	.166	.160
Occasionally – 4 days a week or more	1043	.050	.044	537	.194	.209
Whether Own	$\beta^2 = .002$			$\beta^2 = .046$		
No	1915	.069	.055	974	.310	.283
Yes	2079	.030	.038	1022	.099	.114
Job Tenure	$\beta^2 = .007$			$\beta^2 = .009$		
Not working	990	.040	.074	492	.134	.151
< 1	565	.081	.047	281	.300	.238
1-3 years	787	.061	.034	413	.197	.163
4-9 years	694	.034	.022	339	.215	.222
10+	958	.026	.039	471	.107	.143
Education of Head	$\beta^2 = .017$			$\beta^2 = .011$		
Can't read	158	.002	.027	99	.053	.103
0-5 years	220	.002	.030	116	.150	.180
6-8 years	817	.011	.027	426	.112	.152

TABLE A9.1 (continued)

Independent Variable	Productive Move Expectations			Consumptive Move Expectations		
	Number of cases	Unad-justed	Adjusted	Number of cases	Unad-justed	Adjusted
9-11 years	854	.030	.032	424	.252	.238
12 years	717	.039	.028	337	.186	.171
12 + non-academic training	309	.038	.043	151	.191	.192
13-15 years (no degree)	474	.064	.049	225	.215	.186
16 years	265	.117	.107	127	.147	.131
17+	136	.114	.106	66	.078	.091
Decile of Total Money Income/Needs		$\beta^2 = .002$			$\beta^2 = .003$	
0 -1.30	1220	.026	.026	651	.154	.143
1.31-2.11	904	.045	.048	444	.200	.196
2.12-2.95	678	.056	.053	337	.188	.164
2.96-4.20	622	.051	.052	300	.169	.173
4.21+	570	.042	.041	264	.163	.197
Actual-Required Number of Rooms		$\beta^2 = .0007$			$\beta^2 = .007$	
2-3 less than needed	360	.040	.052	200	.171	.195
1 less than needed or actual=required	751	.054	.051	378	.250	.202
1 extra room	838	.055	.048	427	.277	.220
2-3 extra rooms	1429	.037	.039	698	.126	.142
4+ extra rooms	616	.045	.047	293	.138	.178
Age of Head		$\beta^2 = .046$			$\beta^2 = .003$	
< 25	457	.134	.119	234	.309	.190
< 35	806	.082	.088	373	.273	.200
< 45	909	.050	.058	474	.171	.197
< 55	797	.026	.037	392	.124	.153
< 65	601	.008	.015	321	.138	.159
65+	424	.000	-.030	202	.079	.147

TABLE A9.1 (continued)

	N	β² = .0006		N	β² = .00006	
Sex of Head						
Female	1070	.028	.034	544	.189	.169
Male	2924	.049	.047	1452	.171	.176
Race of Head		β² = .0002			β² = .0002	
Non-white	1470	.023	.037	766	.211	.161
White	2524	.048	.045	1230	.169	.177
Age of Oldest Child		β² = .001			β² = .012	
No children	757	.084	.056	350	.188	.141
< 6	448	.085	.039	217	.355	.280
< 12	490	.057	.037	254	.191	.154
< 18	601	.050	.048	308	.135	.137
> 18	1698	.011	.041	867	.131	.179
Size of Place		β² = .007			β² = .006	
100,000+	2376	.039	.032	1143	.216	.198
25,000-100,000	640	.043	.046	369	.156	.176
<10,000-25,000	978	.058	.071	484	.104	.127
Hours Spent Travelling to Work for Household Head		β² = .007			β² = .003	
No journey to work	1180	.045	.064	584	.148	.195
< .25 hour	929	.065	.055	453	.161	.146
< .50 hour	959	.035	.027	486	.203	.189
< 1.0 hour	103	.008	.003	50	.169	.109
> 1.0 hours	823	.030	.028	423	.193	.168

(Adjusted) R^2 = .076   (Adjusted) R^2 = .119

$\bar{Y}$ .044 $\bar{Y}$ .175

Standard deviation of Y   .206   Standard deviation of Y   .380

MTR 7093

TABLE A9.2

Means and Standard Deviations of
Predictors of the Fulfillment
of Mobility Expectations

| | Population | | | |
| | Families expecting a consumptive move | | Families expecting a productive move | |
Predictor	Mean	Standard Deviation	Mean	Standard Deviation
Family and community ties	5.1	2.1	5.3	2.1
Whether own home	.37	.48	.45	.50
Job tenure (years)	5.5	7.5	4.6	6.7
Union member	.35	.46	.16	.37
Efficacy planning	3.6	1.6	3.9	1.7
Actual-required < 0	.12	.33	.14	.35
Actual-required > 3	.28	.45	.31	.46
Whether black	.18	.38	.07	.26
Whether female	.21	.41	.12	.33
Family income	9,783	6,436	10,561	6,479
Family size	3.2	1.8	3.2	1.8
Age of Head	40.4	15.3	33.3	9.5
Education	4.3	1.8	5.5	1.8

Chapter 10

A NOTE ON THE SHORT AND LONG-RUN EQUITY OF
THE FEDERAL INDIVIDUAL INCOME TAX
Richard Coe

INTRODUCTION

The Federal individual income tax is the largest source of revenue for the
Federal government, accounting for an estimated 44.2% of total Federal budget receipts in 1973. Because of its leading role in Federal government finance, it
has received considerable attention from social science researchers, particularly
economists. This note, consisting of two parts, devotes additional attention to
this tax. Part I examines the vertical equity of the tax, both in the short run
(a one-year time period) and the long run (a six-year time period). The conclusions are not surprising. The tax is found to be progressive in both the
short and the long run, although for low-income families the percent of their
income that is paid in taxes is greater when viewed over a six-year time horizon
than a one-year horizon. Part II examines the horizontal equity of the tax,
again in both the short and the long run. It is found that at the extreme income deciles families fall closely into the same tax/money income quintile, but
for the middle income deciles families with the same income pay widely varying
percents of that income for the tax. This is likewise not surprising, since
families with the same income differ in age, size and the amount of transfer income, all of which would affect the amount of income taxes a family would pay.

ANALYSIS

I. Basic Concepts

Two income definitions are used to assess the burden of the Federal individual income tax. One is called "money income" and is equal to the sum of the cash
receipts received by the family unit in a particular time period. This measure
includes labor earnings, cash receipts from capital assets, and transfer income,

both public and private.[1] Income from realized capital gains, however, is not included.[2]

"Money income" as an income base is deficient because it takes no account of a family's needs. A $10,000 money income is not the same thing to a family of four as it is to a family of two, as the income tax laws themselves recognize. In an attempt to take account of this, a weekly food need was estimated for each individual in the family, based on age and sex. These needs were summed, multiplied by 52 to give an annual food needs standard, adjusted for economies of scale of family size, and multiplied by approximately three (depending on family size) to give an annual needs standard. Thus some account is taken of the size of the family, as well as the age composition.[3] Money income was then divided by the need standard to form the second income base, "money income/needs."

These income bases were then measured for different time periods and different population subgroups to assess the impact of the tax. For the short-run analyses one-year measures of the two income bases were used, and included all the families in the sample in that year. For the long-run analyses a six-year time period was used. Both money income, deflated by the Consumer Price Index (1967=100), and money income/needs were averaged over the six years to form the long-run income bases. Furthermore, the sample was restricted to only those families who had the same head and wife over the entire six-year period. This was done to eliminate the effect of marriage, divorce, death and other startling events which so alter the make-up of a family as to make it essentially a new one.

Tables 10.1-10.4 show, for the relevant time periods, the income decile breakpoints and the average income for each decile, for both income bases and both groups of the sampling population.

---

[1] In estimating public transfer income, a cash value was assigned to certain in kind payments, such as utility bills and rent. This value is a component of money income.

[2] In a series of computer runs realized capital gains income was imputed to each family, based on the taxable income of the head and wife, the income from capital of the head and wife, and data from Internal Revenue Service (1971). When this component of income was added into the income base, the results of the analysis changed insignificantly. Thus it seems safe to ignore, in the aggregate, this part of family income.

[3] Full details of the development of the annual need standard can be found in Morgan (1972), pp. 300-4.

TABLE 10.1

Lower Bound on Income Deciles
(All Families)

Decile	Money Income		Income/Needs	
	1967	1972	1967	1972
Lowest	$ 0	$ 0	0	0
Second	2256	2700	.75	1.12
Third	3642	4392	1.10	1.59
Fourth	5200	6046	1.46	2.09
Fifth	6534	7745	1.79	2.60
Sixth	7700	9304	2.14	3.04
Seventh	9132	11,395	2.55	3.57
Eighth	10,717	13,350	3.05	4.22
Ninth	12,712	16,219	3.67	5.06
Highest	16,019	21,050	4.61	6.45
Number of Observations	3426	5285	3426	5285

TABLE 10.2

Mean Income Levels by Income Deciles
(All Families)

Decile	Money Income		Income/Needs	
	1967	1972	1967	1972
Lowest	$ 1508	$ 1939	0.545	.77
Second	2936	3685	0.924	1.35
Third	4413	5334	1.267	1.83
Fourth	5882	7121	1.013	2.33
Fifth	7127	8863	1.961	2.81
Sixth	8440	10,772	2.382	3.29
Seventh	9947	12,946	2.805	3.86
Eighth	11,639	15,620	3.333	4.57
Ninth	14,275	19,176	4.082	5.67
Highest	22,212	31,121	6.663	9.45
Average	$ 8841	$11,663	2.679	3.59

TABLE 10.3

Lower Bound on Income Deciles
for Families with Same Head and Wife

	Money Income			Income/Needs		
Decile	1967	1972	6-Year Average	1967	1972	6-Year Average
Lowest	$ 0	$ 0	$ 0	0	0	0
Second	2204	3100	2633	.81	1.17	1.07
Third	3654	5000	4167	1.19	1.72	1.56
Fourth	5200	7100	5826	1.55	2.24	1.98
Fifth	6500	9012	7199	1.89	2.75	2.41
Sixth	7700	11,050	8630	2.24	3.24	2.84
Seventh	9100	13,131	10,002	2.66	3.79	3.27
Eighth	10,717	15,638	11,618	3.15	4.45	3.76
Ninth	12,700	18,700	13,774	3.77	5.32	4.51
Highest	16,034	23,350	17,561	4.83	6.75	5.63

Number of
 Observations = 3203

TABLE 10.4

Mean Income Levels by Income Deciles
For Families with Same Head and Wife

Decile	Money Income			Income/Needs		
	1967	1972	6-Year Average*	1967	1972	6-Year Average
Lowest	$1487	$2089	$ 1787	.56	.82	.79
Second	2924	4000	3388	.99	1.44	1.32
Third	4426	5989	4989	1.37	1.97	1.78
Fourth	5838	8099	6490	1.71	2.49	2.20
Fifth	7086	10,070	7908	2.06	2.99	2.62
Sixth	8406	12,180	9328	2.44	3.51	3.05
Seventh	9921	14,425	10,770	2.89	4.11	3.51
Eighth	11,619	17,137	12,609	3.45	4.84	4.11
Ninth	14,298	20,744	15,315	4.21	6.02	5.00
Highest	22,480	33,621	23,606	7.08	10.38	8.16
Average	$ 8865	$12,850	$ 9622	2.68	3.86	3.26

*
Deflated by Consumer Price Index, 1967 = 100

II. Vertical Equity of the Federal Individual Income Tax

SHORT RUN

In the research devoted to the Federal individual income tax particular attention has been paid to the vertical equity of the tax, that is, whether the
tax is progressive, regressive or proportional. This concern stems not only from
the important role this tax plays in the Federal revenue structure but also from
the fact that the law is purposefully legislated to be progressive. All previous
studies have found that, when viewed over a one-year time horizon, the tax is indeed progressive. This study is no exception, as Table 10.5 indicates.[1] Employ-
ing the conventional assumption that the individual taxpayer bears the full
burden of the tax, it was estimated that families in the lowest money income
decile in 1967 paid less than 1% of their income in taxes while families in the
highest money income decile paid better than 15% of their income in taxes. Pro-
gression proceeds throughout the income deciles. In 1972 similar results were
found, with families in the lower income deciles paying a lower percent of their
income for the tax than in 1967, in spite of rising incomes. This was a result,
no doubt, of the Tax Reform Act of 1969, which increased the personal exemption
and introduced the low-income allowance, which in effect increased the minimum
standard deduction.

When money income/needs was used as the income base, the tax was likewise
found to be progressive throughout the income scale; that is, the percent of
money income paid in taxes increased as a family's money income/needs ratio increased. It is also interesting to note that at the lower income deciles there
was virtually no change in the incidence pattern between 1967 and 1972 when this
income base was used. This is in sharp contrast to the changes in the tax burden
between 1967 and 1972 when money income was used as the income base. A possible
explanation of this is that the tax law changes of 1969, while helping low money
income/needs families, did not help them as much as families with a low money income but correspondingly lower needs. This point will be discussed at greater
length in Section III.

---

[1]It should be stressed at this point that the Federal income paid by the survey
families was *estimated*, rather than a response to a survey question. This estimation was based on a family's taxable income, number of dependents, age of
head and wife, the minimum standard deduction or a 15% deduction (whichever yielded the lowest taxable base), and the relevant tax taken from the IRS
tax tables. Thus unusually large deductions, preferential income such as realized capital gains, tax loopholes, or just plain cheating are ignored in the
estimates. Hopefully, this will not affect the results in any significant
manner.

TABLE 10.5

Percent of Money Income Paid to the Federal Individual
Income Tax, by Income Deciles, All Families

Decile	Money Income		Income/Needs	
	1967	1972	1967	1972
Lowest	.8	.2	.3	.3
Second	2.4	1.7	1.4	1.5
Third	4.7	3.8	3.7	3.8
Fourth	6.5	5.7	5.9	6.0
Fifth	8.0	7.6	7.3	8.4
Sixth	8.8	9.2	9.0	9.2
Seventh	10.1	10.3	10.0	10.4
Eighth	10.7	11.6	11.0	11.6
Ninth	11.8	12.6	12.3	13.5
Highest	15.7	18.2	16.4	18.9
All	10.7	11.6	10.7	11.6
Number of Observations	3426	5285	3426	5285

Despite this possibility, however, it is clear that the provision regarding additional dependents in the current tax law are at least sufficient to maintain the progressive nature of the tax when some provision is made for family size in the income base. This is to be contrasted with a tax system which makes no allowances for additional dependents. Such a tax system would presumably be less progressive when money income/needs are used as the ranking measure than when money income alone is used. Since no pattern of decreased progressiveness emerges from these figures, it would appear that the provisions in the current tax law are indeed sufficient.

LONG RUN

It is becoming an issue of increasing controversy whether one year is the appropriate time period to judge the equity of a particular tax. It is argued that often a family's income level in a particular year does not reflect the family's normal income position, and consequently, one should be more concerned with the equity of the tax over a longer time span which would presumably better reflect the actual economic position of the family. Though this debate is currently centered over the proper time period to judge the incidence of the property tax, it is nevertheless of interest concerning all taxes, if one feels that a measure of permanent income is more appropriate in determining the equity of a tax.

To determine the incidence of the Federal income tax over a longer time horizon, estimated annual tax payments and money income (both deflated by the Consumer Price Index, 1967=100) were averaged over six years for families with the same head and wife during those six years. The percent of average money income which went to pay the average annual tax was then calculated for each income decile, with both six-year average money income and six-year average money income/ needs used as the income base. The percent of money income paid in taxes was calculated for two one-year periods, 1967 and 1972, in order to compare this subgroup of the sample with the findings for the entire sample. As can be seen in Table 10.6, the one-year figures for these families are equivalent to those for all families (see Table 10.5). However, the results show that the percent of money income paid in taxes increases when six-year average income is used as the base, particularly at the lower income deciles.[1] The reason for this is straight-

---

[1]Though the tax burden does increase for low-income families when viewed over a six-year period, the tax is still progressive throughout the income deciles. This result is in contrast to the results reported in Chapter Eight, Volume II, which shows the tax to be regressive at the lowest income decile. This regressiveness was found to be the result of a programming error.

TABLE 10.6

Percent of Money Income Paid to the Federal Individual Income
Tax by Income Deciles, Families With Same Head and Wife

Decile	Money Income			Income/Needs		
	1967	1972	6-Year Average	1967	1972	6-Year Average
Lowest	.7	.1	.9	.3	.2	.8
Second	2.1	1.1	3.2	1.8	1.8	3.0
Third	4.7	3.4	5.7	4.3	4.3	5.6
Fourth	6.2	5.9	7.2	6.2	6.6	7.5
Fifth	8.0	7.9	8.7	8.0	8.4	9.1
Sixth	8.7	9.6	10.0	9.3	9.3	10.2
Seventh	10.0	10.3	11.0	10.1	10.7	11.2
Eighth	10.7	11.8	11.9	11.2	12.0	12.3
Ninth	11.7	12.9	12.7	12.4	13.7	13.7
Highest	16.0	18.9	18.1	16.8	19.6	18.7
All	10.7	11.9	11.8	10.7	11.9	11.8

forward. Incomes vary during the years, especially for lower income families.[1]
In any given year a number of families will earn less than their normal income
and will thus fall into a lower income decile for that year. But in the long
run incomes will average out to their normal level. This will result in families
in the lower income deciles for the six-year period having, in every year, a
higher average income than the families who fell in that decile for any particular year. (The converse argument can be made with respect to families at the
higher income deciles, though the fluctuations in income probably are not pro-
portionally as severe as at the lower income deciles.) Table 10.7 shows the
average money income in 1967 and 1972 for families with the same head and wife,
ranked according to six-year average money income rather than one-year money income. Comparing these figures with those in Table 10.4, it can be seen that in
both years the lower seven income deciles based on a six-year time period had a
higher average money income than the lower seven income deciles based on a one-
year time span. On the other hand, the two higher income deciles had a lower
average money income in both years. As a result, the percent of money income
paid in taxes in any year will be higher for the lower income deciles and lower
for the higher income deciles when ranked on a six-year basis rather than a one-
year basis, as a comparison between Table 10.6 and Table 10.8 shows.

It should also be noted from Table 10.6 that the same curious results occur as found in Table 10.5 concerning the use of money income/needs as the income
base. In 1967 the use of money income/needs as a ranking device instead of money
income apparently improved the position of the families in the lower deciles.
But in 1972 the position of the families in the lowest income decile when ranked
by money income/needs was actually worse than when ranked by money income, though
the tax remained progressive. When viewed over the entire six-year period, the
use of either income measure as a ranking device had little effect on the incidence pattern of the tax, except to alter somewhat the burden on the highest
income deciles. These results reinforce the conclusion that the provisions in
the tax law concerning additional dependents are sufficient to maintain the progressive nature of the tax, even when an income measure is used that accounts
for family needs.

---

[1]See Chapter I, Volume I, for a detailed discussion of changes in income
measures during the first five years of the survey.

TABLE 10.7

Mean Income Levels by Six-Year Average Money
Income Deciles, Families With Same Head and Wife

Decile	6-Year Average Money Income	
	1967	1972
Lowest	$1,775	$2,441
Second	3,285	4,522
Third	5,069	6,356
Fourth	6,036	8,652
Fifth	7,365	10,599
Sixth	8,636	12,508
Seventh	10,006	14,612
Eighth	11,339	17,156
Ninth	13,894	19,979
Highest	21,216	31,632
All	8,865	12,850

TABLE 10.8

Percent of Money Income Paid to the Federal Individual
Income Tax by Six-Year Average Money Income Deciles,
Families With Same Head and Wife

Decile	6-Year Average Money Income	
	1967	1972
Lowest	1.4	.7
Second	3.6	2.7
Third	6.4	4.7
Fourth	6.9	6.5
Fifth	8.3	8.2
Sixth	9.3	9.8
Seventh	10.4	10.6
Eighth	10.5	12.1
Ninth	11.4	12.7
Highest	15.8	19.0
All	10.7	11.9

III. Horizontal Equity

SHORT RUN

In studying the equity of a particular tax it is of interest to know whether families in the same economic position are treated similarly by the tax. By conventional standards a tax is considered equitable (horizontally) if families receiving the same level of income pay roughly the same amount of tax and, conversely, is considered inequitable if families receiving the same level of income pay widely differing amounts of tax.

To assess the horizontal equity of the Federal individual income tax the percent of money income which each family paid in taxes was calculated. Families were then divided into five roughly equal groups according to tax/income ratios. The distribution of families in each income decile across tax/money income groups was then determined, with the results shown in Tables 10.9 and 10.10.[1]

When families are ranked on the basis of their money income, three points stand out in the figures. First, the tax performs well in families at the extremes of the income distribution since most of the families in those income deciles are in the same tax/money income quintile. For example, in 1972, 94.5% of the families in the lowest income decile paid no tax, and thus fell in the lowest tax/money income quintile. At the other end of the income distribution, nearly 80% of the families in the highest income decile were in the highest tax/ money income quintile. This upper quintile, however, conceals considerable differences in tax/money income ratios among the families in that quintile, as evidenced by the large standard deviation of the tax/income ratio for families in that income decile, as shown in the bottom panels of Tables 10.9 and 10.10.

Second, the effects of the 1969 liberalization of the tax laws show up markedly. In 1967, 82.5% of the families in the lowest income decile paid no tax. In 1972 that percentage had risen to 94.5%, notwithstanding the rise in personal incomes over that period. The effect of these tax law changes was apparently felt throughout the income distribution, as the percent of families which paid no tax increased in each income decile except the highest. In all, 25% of the families in the sample paid no tax in 1972, compared to 19.2% in 1967. The Eta-squared statistic, which shows the extent to which the ten income deciles account

------

[1] It should be reemphasized at this point that the tax payments for each family were estimated. Also, income from realized capital gains is not included in the income base, and naturally no taxes on this source of income were estimated. Thus, one should view these figures as a minimum estimate of the variations in tax/money income ratios.

TABLE 10.9

Percent of Families in Each Income Decile by
Tax/Money Income Quintiles, All Families

| | | 1967 Money Income -- Tax/Money Income Ratios | | | | | |
| | | .0002 | .0713 | .0996 | | | Standard |
Decile	Zero	-.0712	-.0995	-.1213	.1214+	Mean	Deviation
Lowest	82.5	15.5	2.0	--	--	.007	.017
Second	57.7	27.2	10.2	4.8	--	.022	.034
Third	31.1	37.3	18.9	9.1	3.6	.046	.042
Fourth	12.1	40.0	30.2	10.3	7.4	.064	.039
Fifth	4.7	30.1	39.8	16.5	8.8	.080	.041
Sixth	1.2	24.1	36.5	31.0	7.1	.088	.031
Seventh	1.0	10.6	30.3	32.9	25.2	.101	.028
Eighth	--	8.3	22.9	44.8	24.0	.106	.025
Ninth	0.5	5.7	9.8	36.9	47.1	.117	.026
Highest	0.7	1.8	3.4	13.5	80.7	.146	.042
All	19.2	20.1	20.4	20.0	20.3	.078	.053

$$\text{Eta}^2 = .605$$

| | | 1967 Income/Needs -- Tax/Money Income Ratios | | | | | |
| | | .0002 | .0713 | .0996 | | | Standard |
Decile	Zero	-.0712	-.0995	-.1213	.1214+	Mean	Deviation
Lowest	87.5	12.3	0.3	--	--	.004	.013
Second	59.9	37.8	2.3	--	--	.012	.020
Third	30.4	57.7	10.4	1.5	--	.034	.029
Fourth	15.3	50.7	29.8	4.2	--	.056	.031
Fifth	7.6	21.4	66.0	4.7	0.3	.071	.029
Sixth	3.7	8.9	62.3	23.1	2.0	.087	.033
Seventh	1.7	8.1	19.2	64.9	6.1	.099	.024
Eighth	2.7	6.3	6.2	59.8	25.0	.108	.028
Ninth	1.2	1.6	3.9	28.6	64.7	.123	.022
Highest	0.6	2.3	2.9	5.7	88.5	.148	.042
All	19.2	20.1	20.4	20.0	20.3	.078	.053

$$\text{Eta}^2 = .712$$

TABLE 10.10

Percent of Families in Each Income Decile by
Tax/Money Income Quintiles, All Families

		1972 Money Income -- Tax/Money Income Ratios					
Decile	Zero	.0003 -.0743	.0744 -.1071	.1072 -.1333	.1334+	Mean	Standard Deviation
Lowest	94.5	5.5	--	--	--	.001	.006
Second	68.0	26.9	5.1	--	--	.016	.026
Third	43.2	33.1	16.1	7.6	--	.038	.042
Fourth	24.3	38.6	22.7	12.8	1.6	.056	.045
Fifth	10.0	33.4	28.1	17.6	10.9	.076	.045
Sixth	5.6	20.6	33.5	31.1	9.1	.092	.039
Seventh	2.8	11.0	35.4	38.8	12.0	.103	.033
Eighth	1.2	8.4	23.9	39.5	26.9	.115	.031
Ninth	0.6	5.0	15.9	34.3	44.2	.126	.029
Highest	--	1.8	6.2	13.6	78.4	.165	.052
All	25.0	18.4	18.7	19.5	18.3	.078	.061

$$Eta^2 = .640$$

		1972 Income/Needs -- Tax/Money Income Ratios					
Decile	Zero	.0003 -.0743	.1744 -.1071	.1072 -.1333	.1334+	Mean	Standard Deviation
Lowest	92.4	7.3	0.3	--	--	.002	.008
Second	62.6	37.2	0.1	--	--	.012	.019
Third	36.7	53.5	9.4	0.4	--	.033	.030
Fourth	24.5	34.8	39.2	1.6	--	.053	.037
Fifth	12.7	11.6	60.3	15.1	0.4	.080	.037
Sixth	8.8	13.2	42.4	34.3	1.3	.088	.037
Seventh	5.7	11.7	19.8	55.2	7.5	.100	.038
Eighth	3.9	9.7	8.5	55.4	22.5	.113	.035
Ninth	1.9	3.5	3.8	25.6	65.1	.133	.029
Highest	1.0	2.0	3.2	7.5	86.3	.169	.052
All	25.0	18.4	18.7	19.5	18.3	.078	.061

$$Eta^2 = .689$$

for the variation in tax/money income ratios for the entire sample, was .604 in 1967, indicating that 60.4% of the variance in tax/money income ratios was "explained" by the grouping of families into income deciles. By 1972, this fraction had risen to 64.0%, a slight increase.

The third point shown in these figures is that in the middle income deciles there is considerable variation in the percent of a family's money income that is paid in taxes. For instance, in the fifth income decile in 1972 roughly 10% of the families paid no tax, 33% paid between .03% and 7.5% of their income in taxes, 28% between 7.5% and 10.7%, 18% between 10.7% and 13.3%, and 11% paid 13.3% or more of their income in taxes. This fact by itself is not particularly surprising. As noted above, the Federal individual income tax is not designed so that every family with the same money income pays the same amount of tax. Provisions in the tax law are such that larger families, families with older heads and/or wives, and families with larger percents of their money income in the form of government transfer payments pay a lower tax.

One way of viewing these various provisions of the tax law which lower the tax burden for particular families with the same money income as others is that Congress does not consider money income as the proper measure by which to rank families according to ability to pay. Instead, some account must be taken of the needs of a family, and needs vary with family size, age and so on. If so, then a ranking of families by an income measure which takes into account the needs of a family should lower the intra-decile variations in the tax/money income ratios.

Tables 10.9 and 10.10 show the intra-decile variations of tax/money income ratios when families are ranked according to the money income/needs measure. Again the results are mixed. In 1967 a ranking of families by money income/needs increased the percent of families in the lowest income decile which paid no tax as compared to a ranking by money income alone, a result one would expect, given the tax laws. As shown in the top row of Tables 10.9 and 10.10, the mean tax/money income ratio fell from .007 to .004 for the lowest income decile.[1] Money income/needs deciles are able to account for significantly more of the variation in tax/income ratio, 71.2%, compared to 60.5%, for money income deciles. One would also expect this result, since the money income/needs measure attempts to take account of family size, as do the tax laws. However, in 1972 the percent of families in the lowest income decile which paid no taxes increased when families were ranked according to money income/needs, and the mean tax/money income ratio increased. Overall, the ranking of families by income/needs

---

[1]One might wonder why the results in Tables 10.9 and 10.10 do not match the results given in Table 10.5, concerning mean tax payments as a percent of income

had less effect in 1972 than in 1967, as the Eta-squared only rose from .640 to .689. Furthermore, compared to 1967, the intra-decile variation increased somewhat, as the Eta-squared fell from .712 to .689. However, these changes are small and could be stochastic rather than real.

A possible explanation for these results is that the tax law changes which went into effect in 1970 did not benefit the high-income families with high needs as much as the low-income families with correspondingly low needs. For example, a family of four with head and wife between 36 and 55 years old and with a son and a daughter both between 13 and 15 years old would have an annual need standard of $4290. If family money income were $4800, family money income/needs would equal 1.12. If all this income were taxable, the family would have paid $264 in taxes in 1967, equal to 5.5% of family income. In 1972 this family would have paid $74 in taxes, a reduction of 72%. Their tax/money income ratio would have fallen to 1.5%. This can be compared to a single male, aged 36-55, with money income equal to $2421, all taxable. His annual need standard would equal $2105, and his money income/needs would equal 1.15, higher than the above family of four. In 1967 this individual would have paid $227 in taxes, equal to 9.8% of his money income. In 1972, after the liberalization of the tax laws, he would have paid $51 in taxes, a 77.5% reduction. Thus, it appears possible that the changes in the tax laws benefitted the low-income/low-needs family more than the family with a higher income but even higher needs, and this may explain the somewhat puzzling results found when changing the income ranking measure. This is not to say, of course, that the changes did not benefit the most needy families. That the percent of families in the lowest money income/needs decile which paid no taxes increased between 1967 and 1972 and that the mean tax/money income ratio decreased are ample evidence that the most needy families were aided

---

for a given income decile. The reason for the differences is that Table 10.5 presents the ratio of two means, while Tables 10.9 and 10.10 give the mean of a ratio. Mathematically, the percentages in Table 10.5 can be represented by the formula:

$$\frac{(T_1 + T_2 + \ldots + T_N)/N}{(Y_1 + Y_2 + \ldots + Y_N)/N}$$

where T_i is the tax payment for the ith family and Y_i is the money income for the ith family. The percentages in Tables 10.9 and 10.10 can be represented by the formula:

$$(\frac{T_1}{Y_1} + \frac{T_2}{Y_2} + \ldots + \frac{T_N}{Y_N})/N$$

by the tax law changes. The point is that low money income families benefitted significantly *independent* of their needs. However, it is not clear that this phenomenon can explain the increase in intra-decile variations (on a money income/ needs ranking) in tax/money income ratios which apparently occurred between 1967 and 1972. In the above example, if the single man had had money income of $2358 (all taxable), giving him the same money income/needs ratio as the family of four, the percent of his money income paid in taxes would have decreased from 9.3% in 1967 to 1.9% in 1972. When compared to the decrease from 5.5% to 1.5% for the family of four, one would have to conclude that the tax law changes *decreased* intra-decile variations in tax/money income ratios. Thus, the results remain unclear.

LONG RUN

As with the vertical equity of a tax, it is possible to argue that a one-year time period is not the appropriate time period to judge the horizontal equity of a particular tax. Though there may be considerable variation in the tax payments made by families in the same income decile in a one-year period, these variations may average out over a longer time horizon so that all families in the same long-run economic position are treated roughly equally by the tax. It is thus of interest to see if lengthening the time period has any significant effect on the intra-decile variations in tax/money income ratios.

Tables 10.11, 10.12 and 10.13 show the intra-decile variations in tax/money income ratios for families with the same head and wife during the entire six-year survey period. Tables 10.11 and 10.12 for the individual years of 1967 and 1972 are almost identical to Tables 10.9 and 10.10, indicating that this subgroup of families is similar to the entire sample. Table 10.13 shows the horizontal equity of the tax when viewed over the entire six-year period.[1] The major point illustrated by these figures is that there is little change from a one-year period in the distribution of tax/money income ratios within the income deciles. The extent to which the income deciles account for variations in tax/income ratios (as shown by Eta^2) changes little when a six-year, rather than a one-year, income measure is used. The major exception to this is the fact that far more families pay some income tax over the entire six-year period than in any single year. This is hardly surprising, given the variability of income, especially at the lower income deciles. While in any given year a substantial number of families may have

---

[1] In estimating the annual Federal individual income tax payments for families, no account was taken of the averaging provisions embodied in the law, concerning both unusually high incomes or losses in a particular year. It is improbable that such omissions would seriously affect the distribution shown in the table.

TABLE 10.11

Percent of Families in Each Income Decile by Tax/Money Income Ratios,
Families With the Same Head and Wife

Decile		1967 Money Income -- Tax/Money Income Ratios					
	Zero	.0002 -.0709	.0710 -.0990	.0991 -.1212	.1213+	Mean	Standard Deviation
Lowest	83.6	14.8	1.7	--	--	.006	.016
Second	58.9	27.7	9.4	3.9	--	.021	.032
Third	29.7	38.2	19.3	9.0	3.7	.047	.042
Fourth	12.3	42.1	29.4	10.4	5.8	.062	.038
Fifth	4.5	29.6	38.8	17.6	9.5	.080	.040
Sixth	1.3	25.5	34.2	31.7	7.3	.087	.031
Seventh	1.0	10.3	32.3	32.7	23.7	.100	.027
Eighth	--	8.3	21.9	45.7	24.1	.106	.025
Ninth	0.5	5.3	10.5	36.7	47.1	.117	.026
Highest	0.7	0.9	3.4	13.7	81.2	.147	.043
All	19.2	20.2	20.1	20.2	20.3	.077	.053

$Eta^2 = .613$

Decile		1967 Income/Needs -- Tax/Money Income Ratios					
	Zero	.0002 -.0709	.0710 -.0990	.0991 -.1212	.1213+	Mean	Standard Deviation
Lowest	86.7	13.3	--	--	--	.004	.011
Second	52.0	45.3	2.6	--	--	.015	.021
Third	24.6	60.9	12.8	1.7	--	.041	.029
Fourth	14.6	42.6	39.9	3.0	--	.059	.031
Fifth	5.5	15.4	71.2	7.2	0.7	.077	.033
Sixth	3.2	8.0	48.2	36.2	4.4	.091	.027
Seventh	2.0	7.7	14.5	70.0	5.8	.100	.026
Eighth	2.4	4.8	5.8	56.3	30.6	.110	.025
Ninth	1.4	2.2	3.4	23.1	69.9	.123	.023
Highest	0.7	2.3	2.1	4.2	90.7	.153	.042
All	19.2	20.2	20.1	20.2	20.3	.077	.053

$Eta^2 = .722$

TABLE 10.12

Percent of Families in Each Income Decile by Tax/Money Income Ratios,
Families With the Same Head and Wife

		1972 Money Income -- Tax/Money Income Ratios					
Decile	Zero	.0003 -.0794	.0795 -.1095	..1096 -.1347	.1348+	Mean	Standard Deviation
Lowest	96.6	3.4	--	--	--	.001	.006
Second	76.0	22.4	1.6	--	--	.011	.022
Third	46.0	32.3	13.2	8.5	--	.034	.042
Fourth	19.1	45.8	19.2	7.4	8.5	.059	.046
Fifth	9.5	35.9	28.5	19.8	6.3	.078	.042
Sixth	4.4	15.8	46.8	26.8	6.2	.096	.035
Seventh	0.9	17.6	34.0	36.4	11.1	.103	.118
Eighth	1.8	7.1	21.6	44.0	25.6	.118	.030
Ninth	--	4.5	15.8	33.8	45.9	.129	.026
Highest	--	1.7	5.2	9.5	83.5	.172	.052
All	25.4	18.7	18.6	18.7	18.7	.080	.063

$Eta^2 = .677$

		1972 Income/Needs -- Tax/Money Income Ratios					
Decile	Zero	.0003 -.0794	.0795 -.1095	.1096 -.1347	.1348+	Mean	Standard Deviation
Lowest	94.6	5.1	0.3	--	--	.001	.008
Second	61.4	38.4	0.2	--	--	.012	.019
Third	37.4	56.6	6.0	--	--	.034	.031
Fourth	25.6	30.3	42.6	1.4	--	.057	.039
Fifth	13.7	14.5	64.8	7.0	--	.078	.037
Sixth	9.2	16.1	40.0	34.0	0.6	.089	.038
Seventh	6.3	10.1	16.2	60.9	6.5	.103	.037
Eighth	3.6	9.9	8.6	51.2	26.7	.116	.036
Ninth	2.1	3.6	5.0	21.9	67.3	.135	.031
Highest	0.8	1.8	2.5	9.9	85.0	.175	.052
All	25.4	18.7	18.6	18.7	18.7	.080	.063

$Eta^2 = .694$

TABLE 10.13

Percent of Families in Each Income Decile by Tax/Money Income Ratios,
Families With Same Head and Wife

| Decile | | Six-Year Average Money Income -- Tax/Money Income Ratios | | | | | |
	Zero	.0001 -.0680	.0681 -.1044	.1045 -.1304	.1305+	Mean	Standard Deviation
Lowest	70.2	26.4	3.4	--	--	.008	.019
Second	30.5	53.6	10.2	5.7	--	.030	.035
Third	10.0	51.4	24.5	8.1	6.0	.056	.041
Fourth	3.6	39.4	32.6	17.0	7.4	.072	.040
Fifth	1.8	24.3	41.8	24.0	8.1	.087	.036
Sixth	0.1	12.5	39.7	36.7	10.9	.100	.029
Seventh	--	8.6	30.2	40.5	20.6	.110	.030
Eighth	0.7	1.9	20.2	43.1	34.0	.119	.024
Ninth	--	1.3	14.1	36.4	48.1	.127	.021
Highest	--	0.8	3.5	9.8	85.9	.168	.044
All	11.7	22.1	22.1	22.2	21.9	.088	.056

$Eta^2 = .653$

| Decile | | Six-Year Average Money Income -- Tax/Money Income Ratios | | | | | |
	Zero	.0001 -.0680	.0681 -.1044	.1045 -.1304	.1305+	Mean	Standard Deviation
Lowest	64.2	35.7	0.1	--	--	.006	.012
Second	30.2	64.4	4.6	0.5	0.2	.025	.025
Third	11.2	55.4	32.2	1.2	--	.050	.030
Fourth	5.4	22.1	67.4	5.1	--	.071	.031
Fifth	1.4	16.5	56.9	23.9	1.3	.088	.029
Sixth	2.8	8.1	31.7	52.6	4.7	.101	.029
Seventh	1.0	8.6	11.7	69.4	9.2	.110	.028
Eighth	0.5	6.5	7.1	49.8	36.1	.120	.028
Ninth	0.5	2.2	5.5	15.6	76.2	.135	.024
Highest	0.7	1.4	3.2	4.6	90.1	.170	.046
All	11.7	22.1	22.1	22.2	21.9	.088	.056

$Eta^2 = .728$

incomes so low as not to pay any tax, it is probable that over a longer time period their incomes will increase in at least one year to such a level that they will be subject to some tax liability.

SUMMARY

The Federal individual income tax was found to be progressive when viewed over both a one-year time period and a six-year time horizon, although the tax burden on low-income families increased when measured over a six-year period as compared to a one-year period. Except at the extremes of the income scale, considerable variation in the amount of taxes paid was found for families with the same income, even after some account was taken of the needs a family must meet. As with the vertical equity of the tax, little change was found in the horizontal equity of the tax when viewed over a six-year time period as compared to a one-year time period.

References

Internal Revenue Service, Statistics of Income - 1969, Individual Income Tax Returns, Washington, D.C., 1971.

Morgan, James N., A Panel Study of Income Dynamics - Study Design, Procedures, Available Data, Volume I, Ann Arbor: Institute for Social Research, 1972.

Chapter 11

SOME EQUITY ASPECTS OF GASOLINE PRICE INFLATION
Greg Duncan

INTRODUCTION

Rising gasoline prices and possible gas tax increases impose the greatest and least avoidable burdens on those who depend upon their cars to get to work. Some drivers may reduce the impact by car pooling, using public transportation, or even changing residence or jobs. Data from the sixth wave of the Income Dynamics Panel provide current information on two important aspects of the gasoline price inflation: first, the distribution of the probable burden of price increases by income level[1] and second, the availability of public transportation as an alternative for those drivers affected most by the rising prices.[2]

ANALYSIS

About two-thirds of the heads of families in the sample traveled to their jobs in one way or another. The remaining third either did not work or did not travel to work. Of heads who traveled to work, automobile travel was the most popular mode; none of the alternatives to driving was used by as many as ten percent of them (see Table 11.1).

---

[1] Robin Barlow has pointed out that complete discussion of equity aspects would cover the distribution of capital gains and dividends of oil stocks generated by the inflation. This information is not available from Panel families.

[2] Future waves of the Panel will be invaluable in studying the behavioral responses of families to the extraordinary increase in gasoline prices. Indeed, the seventh wave not only replicated past questions but also asked about total annual passenger miles.

TABLE 11.1

Travel Mode Used by Heads of Households
in Getting to Work, Spring, 1973

80.2% drove automobiles alone or with other family members

7.8% rode in public transportation vehicles such as buses or trains

5.1% rode in car pools

4.2% walked

2.5% used other unspecified means of travel

Those most directly affected by rising gasoline prices are those driving to work alone or in car pools. The extent to which they are affected depends upon the actual distances they drive and the availability of alternatives which lessen the burdens. Alternatives are considered in greater detail below. At this point we look only at the situation as of spring, 1973 and assume that the family heads continue to travel to work as they did at that time. In the following tables it is further assumed that the small number of car poolers incur half the driving expenses per mile of those who drive but do not car pool. Thus, their travel distances are calculated to be half those of other drivers.

The burdens placed by rising gasoline prices on a family depend upon the family's ability to pay for them. Two measures of "ability to pay" are used here. The first is total family money income—the sum of labor, capital, and transfer income of all family members. The second is family income relative to a needs standard which accounts for the size of the family, and the age and sex of family members.

Several indications of the probable burdens of rising gasoline taxes can be gleaned from Table 11.2, which tabulates the head's daily mileage in his journey to work by family income quintile. The numbers in the table are proportions of *all* families in the various mileage-income categories; all numbers within the table sum to 100 percent.

Perhaps the most surprising fact that emerges from the data in Table 11.2 is that more than two-fifths of all family heads are not directly affected by rising gasoline prices. They neither drive nor use a car pool to get to work—either because they do not work or because they get to work in some other way. Most of the unaffected families are in the lower income quintiles. About three-eighths (16.4/42.9) of those unaffected families are in the lowest family income quintile; slightly over one-quarter are in the second quintile.

TABLE 11.2

Proportion of All Families by Mileage
and Family Income Quintile Categories*

Daily Driving Mileage of Head's Travel to Work	1972 Family Income Quintile					
	Low 5th $0- 4499	4th/5th 4500- 7999	3rd/5th 8000- 11,899	2nd/5th 11,900- 17,099	Top 5th 17,100 & over	Total
0, doesn't work, doesn't drive to work	16.4	11.4	6.5	4.2	4.4	42.9
1-5	1.3	2.5	2.5	2.4	2.4	11.2
6-10	0.5	1.2	2.3	2.5	2.0	8.6
11-15	0.6	1.7	2.4	2.8	2.8	10.4
16-30	0.5	1.7	3.5	4.5	4.2	14.3
Over 30 miles	0.6	1.5	2.9	3.5	4.1	12.6
Total	19.9	20.0	20.1	19.9	20.0	100.0

*Car poolers are assumed to drive half the time.

Those families with heads driving the greatest distances are concentrated
at the upper end of the income scale. Of all families with heads whose daily
journey to work involves driving 30 miles or more, almost one-third come from the
highest quintile while only about five percent of them are in the lowest income
quintile.

That a greater proportion of high income families are likely to be affected
by rising gasoline prices does not mean that the *burden* of the inflation increases with income. The distribution of burdens *within* each income class is
markedly unequal. Over 80 percent of the families in the lowest quintile are unaffected by the rising prices. Less than five percent of these poor families
fall into the heaviest burden category of daily mileage in excess of 30 miles.
But the burden for this latter group of families is large indeed, which can be
seen if a simple set of assumptions is applied to the data of Table 11.2.

Suppose that a family head drives exactly 30 miles to and from work on each
of five days a week, driving 50 weeks of the year, and his car averages 12 miles
per gallon of gas. It is impossible to predict the extent to which gasoline
prices will rise due to market forces and possible additional taxes, but an in-

crease of 30 cents per gallon is probably not unreasonable. The impact of this
increase on a family with an income at the median of the lowest two income quintiles (i.e., with family income of $4500), given these assumptions, will amount
to about $188 per year--or 4.2 percent of that family's annual income. Heads
driving 10 or 20 miles per day with this family income will be burdened proportionately less, of course, but the impact will still amount to 1.4 percent and
2.8 percent of total family income, respectively. Thus, while most low income
families escape the burden completely, a few have to allocate a significant
fraction of their income to pay for the price increases. It is rare for price
inflation to have such an unequal impact upon families with similar means. Recent
rising food prices, for example, have imposed a more equal burden on lower income
families, but this is not the case for gasoline price inflation.

Heads of high-income families traveling to work are more likely to be affected by rising gasoline prices, but the fraction of income that needs to be
allocated for the increased prices is less. While four-fifths of the lowest income quintile families are unaffected, only about one-fifth of the highest income
quintile families escape these effects. Heads of families with incomes at the
break point between the bottom two quintiles and driving 30 miles daily will
spend over four percent of their incomes on a price increase of 30 cents per gallon; heads of families at the median of the upper two quintiles (i.e., with family
income of $17,100) driving the same distance will spend about one percent of their
income on it.

The assumption that the distance and mode of travel to work remain unchanged
from the situation in the spring of 1973 is not totally valid. Family heads who
form car pools can cut the burdens imposed by rising gasoline prices by one-half
or more. Some are able to use public transportation while others may move closer
to work or change jobs.

The data also provide some information on the alternative of public transportation for those family heads most likely to be affected. Specifically, the
following questions were asked of all family heads:

Is there public transportation within walking distance of (here) your house?

Is it good enough so that a person could use it to get to work?

Notice that whether the respondent thought the public transportation was good
enough to get to *his* workplace was not asked; rather, the question is less specific and asks about whether "a person" could use it to get to work.

The proportion of family heads responding affirmatively to both of these questions for the various mileage-income groups is shown in Table 11.3. In general, there is little correspondence between income level and public transportation availability. Families in the lowest two income quintiles are only slightly more likely to report its availability than are families in the upper three quintiles. If we focus on those most likely to be affected by rising gasoline prices -- that is, those driving a considerable distance to work each day -- the prospects for lower income families worsens. If heads driving at least ten miles daily are distinguished from all other heads, public transportation is *least* available for those families in the lowest income quintile (Table 11.4). These percentages are all quite similar and there appears to be no association between public transportation availability and income level for those families most likely to be affected by rising gasoline prices.

A final look at the probable burdens of rising gasoline prices is provided by changing the definition of ability to pay through the adjustment of the total family income for family size, and the sex and age of family members. Table 11.5 presents this information. The format of this table is identical to that of Table 11.2 with the exception that the columns are composed of quintiles on family income/needs rather than family income alone. Results for the two tables do not differ dramatically, although there is a tendency for probable burdens to fall more heavily on families at the bottom of the distribution of income/needs. While about 80 percent of the lowest income quintile families are unaffected, only 70 percent of the families in the bottom income/needs quintile are in a similar situation. Roughly twice as many of the lowest quintile families have heads who drive at least ten miles daily to get to work if income/needs is used to measure ability to pay instead of using only family income.

SUMMARY

Rising gasoline prices affect more families at the upper end of the income distribution because they are more likely to be headed by those who drive considerable distances to work. While most low income families do not have heads who drive or car pool to get to work, a small proportion are in this situation. For this small number of families, the burdens imposed by rising prices are large indeed. Furthermore, lowest income families are not more likely to have the alternative of public transportation available to them. This availability seems independent of income level for those families most likely to be affected

TABLE 11.3

Proportion of Families by Income and Miles to Work
Reporting Public Transportation Good Enough to Get to Work

Daily Driving Mileage of Head's Travel to Work	Family Money Income Quintile				
	Low 5th	4th/5th	3rd/5th	2nd/5th	Top 5th
0, doesn't work, doesn't drive to work	38.9	46.1	40.0	39.2	42.7
1-5	22.0	40.0	34.1	27.1	35.8
6-10	15.0*	39.4	36.5	40.2	36.2
11-15	33.4*	40.9	31.0	40.3	36.7
16-30	30.8*	35.1	33.4	29.3	38.7
Over 30 miles	20.5*	23.3	19.6	19.6	21.3
Total	36.2	41.9	33.7	32.3	35.2

*Figure based on fewer than 50 cases.

TABLE 11.4

Proportion of Family Heads Driving at Least 10 Miles Daily
Who Report Public Transportation is Good Enough to Use to Get to Work

Income Quintile	Percent Reporting Good Public Transportation	Number of Observations
Lowest quintile	28.0%	126
4th quintile	33.4	339
3rd quintile	28.2	478
2nd quintile	29.0	488
Highest quintile	31.8	410

TABLE 11.5

Proportion of All Families by Mileage
and Family Income/Needs Quintile Categories[*]

| Daily Driving Mileage of Head's Travel to Work | 1972 Family Income/Needs Quintile | | | | | |
	Low 5th 0-1.58	4th/5th 1.59-2.59	3rd/5th 2.60-3.56	2nd/5th 3.56-5.05	Top 5th 5.06+	Total
0, doesn't work, doesn't drive to work	14.5	10.6	6.9	5.8	5.2	42.9
1-5	1.6	2.2	2.5	2.9	2.1	11.2
6-10	0.9	1.7	2.0	1.8	2.2	8.6
11-15	1.0	1.7	2.2	2.6	2.8	10.4
16-30	1.0	1.9	3.4	3.7	4.3	14.3
Over 30 miles	1.1	1.9	3.0	3.2	3.4	12.6
Total	20.1	20.0	20.0	20.0	20.0	100.0

[*]Car poolers are assumed to drive half the time.

by rising prices.

The tremendous inequality of burden among the lower income strata families, the absolute size of the burdens for those most affected, and the small absolute number of families so burdened suggests that temporary schemes for lessening the burdens on low-income families may be feasible.[1] Gas payment subsidies or a tax credit plan might be ways in which the small number of heavily burdened families could be given assistance. The delineation of those "heavily burdened" is, of course, somewhat arbitrary, but if it is taken to be those families in the lowest two income quintiles with heads who must drive at least ten miles daily to get to work, then only 6.6 percent of all families, or about 4.3 million in all, would be involved. If those from the lowest quintile only are taken, the number of families falls to about 1.1 million.

---

[1] The reader should keep in mind that results presented here relate to heads of households and not wives. No information has been gathered on the mode and distance of the wife's journey to work. Earlier waves collected some data on the *costs* of their journey and they confirm that extensive commuting costs are very closely related to income. Virtually none of the families in the lowest income quintiles have wives who incur substantial commuting costs. Data from another Survey Research Center study in the winter of 1973 on total family miles driven to work shows the same strong, positive correlation with income.

Chapter 12

CORRELATES OF A RISK AVOIDANCE INDEX
Al Arterburn

INTRODUCTION

The concept of risk avoidance has received a considerable amount of attention in the literature of economics. Most of it, however, has been confined to
observation and theoretical explanation of the behavior of business firms and
wealthy individuals in the uncertain world of entrepreneurial and financial
portfolio decision making. This chapter attempts to investigate an aspect of
risk avoidance that, although it relates to well-being of families, has been
largely neglected in the literature.

The type of risk avoidance that we look at here concerns efforts made on
the part of family heads to avoid abrupt and unexpected deterioration in the
family's standard of living. We conduct our investigation in three stages: in
Section I we construct a measure of the risk-avoiding activities of family
units; in Section II we determine the differences in risk aversion across demographic and situational variables; and in Section III we analyze the effects of
differing patterns of risk-avoiding behavior on measures of family welfare.

ANALYSIS

I. Index Construction

Ideally, the concept of risk avoidance should be considered an attitude or
state of mind of the decision maker(s) and should be measured as such. But in
the absence of reliable data on such matters for a broad cross section of the
population, perhaps the concept of risk avoidance is best measured by the actions of decision makers when confronted with a situation involving risk.

The particular method for the measurement of risk in this study consists
of the construction of an index, the Index of Risk Avoidance, in which a family
is credited with points if its head acts to avoid undue risks in a specified

situation. A family's score on the Risk Avoidance Index is determined in the following manner:

All family automobiles insured	2 points
Some automobiles insured but one or more autos not insured	1 point
No autos insured but auto ownership	0 point
Family does not own an auto	1 point
Head uses seat belts all of the time	2 points
Head uses seat belts some of the time	1 point
Head does not use seat belts but does drive an auto equipped with seat belts	0 point
Family does not own a car or family car is not equipped with seat belts	1 point
Family currently has savings greater than two months' income	2 points
Family presently has some savings (less than two months' income) or has had savings totaling two months' income at some time in recent past	1 point
Family has no savings now and no substantial savings in the past	0 point
Whole family covered by medical insurance (either purchased or freely available through VA, medicaid, etc.)	2 points
Some members of family not covered (or if the only member of a one-person family is covered)	1 point
Family head does not have access to any form of medical insurance	0 point

Of the approximately 5,000 families interviewed in the Panel Study of Income Dynamics, the risk avoidance score was computed for each of the five interview years 1968 to 1972 for 3,503 families. The remaining cases were excluded because of the failure to ascertain information on one of the relevant questions or, more commonly, because the family unit changed heads at least once over the five-year period. A five-year average risk avoidance score was thus computed for the included families. Of a possible average score of eight, the mean is 5.60 and the standard deviation is 1.31. Of the 3,503 families, the highest average score achieved is the maximum of eight, while the lowest is 0.50.

A casual inspection of the components of the devised index reveals the lack of independence between a family's income and its ability to score highly on the index. For example, a family with a high income, other factors being equal, is in a more advantageous position to purchase extensive medical or automobile insurance and accumulate savings than is a family with a lower income. In other words, a high level of income enables one to purchase the luxury of greater certainty. Therefore, it must be recognized that the index, as constructed, is biased in the sense that it is easier for the wealthy to achieve a higher score.

The index is also biased in favor of a high score for families headed by males, as a male usually earns more than a female with a similar background. Similar biases exist with respect to region of residence (Southerners earn less), age (a 45-year-old earns more than a 25-year-old), education, and so forth. These and other biases must be taken into account in the interpretation of the analysis that follows.

II. The Determinants of Risk Avoidance

In order to determine the differences in risk avoidance behavior across the spectra of several demographic and situational variables, two methods of analysis are used. The first is the method of least-squares regression. The most obvious handicap one encounters in using this method of analysis is the necessity of having to assume linear relationships between the dependent variable and the various independent variables. The second method of analysis, Multiple Classification Analysis, to a certain extent circumvents this problem. MCA, in essence, is a variation of linear regression in which all of the explanatory variables are categorized and then each category is represented by a dichotomous or dummy variable in a regression.[1] In this way the necessity of assuming linear relationships with the dependent variable is eliminated. Unfortunately, however, the usefulness of MCA itself is limited by its inability to be subjected to precise tests of statistical significance. The two methods of analysis are thus complementary in nature.

To determine the differences in risk avoidance activities among respondents, the analysis is conducted simultaneously on the entire sample and that part (2,372 cases) in which the family head was fully employed for the duration of the period of the study. This division in the analysis is desirable for two reasons. The first is the obvious dependence, as a result of the construction

---

[1] For a detailed description of the MCA method of analysis, see Andrews et al., (1973).

of the index, of the ability to avoid risk on money income and thus on employment status. The second is to provide greater flexibility in the use of the
findings of the study.

Tables 12.1 and 12.2 present various statistics showing the relationship
between the Risk Avoidance Index and eleven demographic and background variables.
The first two columns show the results of the eleven independent variables, each
regressed individually on the Index of Risk Avoidance. Seven of the variables
(average income, family size, age of head, education of head, sentence completion
test score, job seniority and head's father's education) have a natural ordering,
while the remaining four (race, sex, occupation and region of current residence)
have no such natural ranking and thus enter the regression equation in the form
of dichotomous or dummy variables. The race and sex dummy variables assume unit
values when the respondent is nonwhite and female, respectively.

In the absence of a theory as to the distribution of risk avoidance behavior across occupational and industrial lines, an occupation-industry dummy was
constructed to have unitary value when the respondent was employed in a manufac-
turing or construction capacity (both supervisory and skilled and unskilled labor)
or when the respondent listed his occupation as "farmer" or "farm laborer." The
region-of-current-residence variable utilized three dummy variables, representing North Central, Southern, and Western residences as opposed to a Northeastern
one. The risk avoidance and average income variables are five-year averages
(1967 to 1971), while all other variables are as reported by the respondent in
the 1972 interview.

The fourth and fifth columns give the multiple regression coefficients and
a measure of the explanatory power of each predictor when added to all the others
(the partial correlation coefficient squared).[1] The third and sixth columns give
measures of the explanatory power of each predictor when all are introduced as
sets of categories, and no linearity need be assumed. Ten occupational classes
rather than a dichotomy are used in that analysis. Column three gives the square
of the correlation ratio, the proportion of the variance explained by the sub-

---

[1] Significant effects are indicated by asterisks. For those who desire the
actual t-ratios there is a simple relationship between the partial correlation
and t:

$$t^2 = (\frac{R^2}{1-R^2}) (n-2)$$

For the beta-squares there is an analogous approximation to the F-ratio:

$$F = (\frac{\beta^2}{1-\beta^2}) (\frac{N-K-1}{K-1})$$ where there are K-classes in the predictor.

TABLE 12.1

Bivariate and Multivariate Regression Results
(For 3503 Families With Unchanged Heads)

Variable	Bivariate			Multivariate		
	Coef-ficient	R^2 Linear	Eta^2	Coef-ficient	Partial R^2 (From Linear Regression)	$Beta^2$ (From MCA)
Average income	.00008**	.210	.310	.00004**	.042	.219
Family size	.00172	.001	.069	-.0608**	.008	.020
Age of Head	.0005	.000	.019	.0177**	.045	.091
Education of Head	.2722**	.174	.196	.1465**	.044	.026
Race	-1.2042**	.092	.089	-.4424**	.017	.004
Sex of Head	-.9312**	.077	.076	-.6475**	.045	.006
Test score	.2122**	.140	.151	.0770**	.021	.009
Occupation of Head	.1063	.001	.153	.0356	.000	.095
Job seniority	.1612**	.073	.077	.0821**	.021	.046
Head's father's education	.1812**	.044	.064	.0469	.004	.003
Region of Residence:						
North Central	.0293	.000	.023	.0590	.000	.001
South	-.4378**	.014	.023	-.1173**	.004	.001
West	-.0130	.000	.023	.0074	.000	.001

$$R^2 = .391 \qquad R^2 = .481$$
$$\text{Constant} = 3.02$$

**denotes significance at the .01 level.

TABLE 12.2

Bivariate and Multivariate Regression Results
(For 2372 Families With Fully Employed, Unchanged Heads)

	Bivariate			Multivariate		
Variable	Coef-ficient	R^2 Linear	Eta^2	Coef-ficient	Partial R^2 (From Linear Regression)	Beta^2 (From MCA)
Average income	.00007**	.178	.290	.000034**	.040	.131
Family size	-.0464**	.005	.080	-.0562**	.009	.024
Age of Head	.0141**	.018	.030	.0101**	.010	.016
Education of Head	.2380**	.149	.171	.1411**	.044	.033
Race	-.9412**	.063	.056	-.3491**	.011	.001
Sex of Head	-.6593**	.030	.027	-.5843**	.026	.001
Test score	.1726**	.092	.108	.0506**	.009	.005
Occupation of Head	-.1012	.001	.153	.0401	.000	.037
Job seniority	.1704**	.049	.055	.1109**	.025	.020
Head's father's education	-.1582**	.040	.047	.0460**	.004	.003
Region of Residence:						
North Cent.	-.0417	.000	.021	-.0176	.000	.001
South	-.4000**	.014	.021	-.1563**	.003	.001
West	-.0026	.000	.021	.0240	.000	.001

$$R^2 = .322 \qquad\qquad R^2 = .419$$
$$\text{Constant} = 3.58$$

** denotes significance at the .01 level.

class means on that predictor, and column 6 gives a measure analogous to the normalized regression coefficient, for a predictor scaled according to the co-efficients estimated by dummy-variable regression (beta-squared). It is a good approximation of the marginal power (partial correlation squared) of such a pre-dictor, provided the other explanatory variables are as highly correlated with the risk avoidance score as they are with the predictor in question (see gloss-ary).

In view of the powerful effect of income, we look first to see whether the multivariate analysis, adjusting for correlations of income with other variables, still leaves anything else important in explaining risk avoidance. Not only does everything that was significant in the bivariate analysis remain signifi-cant, but family size and age, which were not significant for the whole sample of families with same heads, become significant when adjusted for income and other differences. There are, of course, reductions in the coefficients esti-mating the size of the effects of most of the other variables.

For both age and family size, the adjusted coefficients are higher at least in part because the adjustments make the effects more nearly linear. A look at the categorical predictor coefficients in columns 3 and 6 (eta^2 and beta^2) shows that the family size effect is smaller after adjustments for intercorrelations have been made. Also, only when the not fully employed are included do the ad-justments make age seem *more* powerful. (We shall see shortly that this is be-cause those over 65 are substantially better risk avoiders if one considers their low income and education.)

Comparing columns 2 with 3 and columns 5 with 6 it is possible to see where the main non-linearities exist in the relationships. When the eta-squared is larger than the bivariate R^2 then there are non-linearities in the bivariate re-lationship. Large beta-squared relative to partial R-squared indicate non-lin-earities in a multivariate context. Non-linearities show up for income, family size, age, but not for the rest of the variables.

To see more clearly both the non-linearities and the kinds of adjustments that the multivariate analysis makes in the relationships, we turn to Figures 12.1 through 12.7 and Tables 12.3 through 12.6. They are based on the Multiple Classification Analysis (dummy variable regression) and provide a picture of the shapes of each effect, unadjusted, and adjusted by regression for correlations with the other predictors.

The patterns of unadjusted and adjusted means by income category are quite similar, showing that the strong effect of higher income in inducing or allowing more avoidance of undue risks is largely unaffected by adjustment for other things. The extent that the lines diverge is probably caused, particularly for the employed population, by correlations with education, seniority, and test scores (Figure 12.1).

The effect of family size is clearly non-linear, with single person families avoiding risk less than slightly larger families and the very large families scoring the lowest on the index (Figure 12.2).

The increase of risk avoidance with age is startlingly uncovered after it is adjusted for correlations with income and education, particularly when the non-employed are included (Figure 12.3). Among those 65 and older, risk avoidance is absolutely lower, but, relative to the income, education, etc. of those people, much higher than expected. Among the very young, also, risk avoidance is adjusted upward substantially when adjustments are made for income and seniority.

Education and test scores are correlated with each other and with income, and the regression substantially reduces the estimated effect of both of them (Figures 12.4 and 12.5).

The importance of dealing with the non-employed population appears in Figure 12.6 where the main effect of "seniority" is to distinguish them, avoiding more risk rather than less, when one takes account of their advanced age and/or lower income.

Figure 12.7 shows how adjustments for correlations among the predictors, leave little or no effect of head's father's education, even if it does remain statistically significant with such a large sample. Tables 12.3 and 12.4 show the same dramatic reduction of apparent race and sex effects.

Occupation is an important variable when coded in ten categories, and it retains a great deal of importance even in the multivariate context, (Table 12.5). The adjustments reduce the apparent superiority of the first two classes -- professionals and managers. But they also increase those of clerical and sales workers and farmers so that they appear as risk averse as the professionals and managers.

Finally, the propensity for Southerners to avoid risk less is shown by the regression to be largely a reflection of lower incomes, Table 12.6 showing once again how a small effect can remain significant with a large sample.

The large difference in R-squared and eta-squared for the average income variable in Table 12.1 suggests a non-linear relationship between average income and risk avoidance. To account for this, a variable measuring squared average income was introduced in the regression equations. As expected, both income and its square are highly significant, the former in the positive direction, the latter in the negative. The negative sign on the coefficient of the squared term

FIGURE 12.1

Risk Avoidance, by Average Income

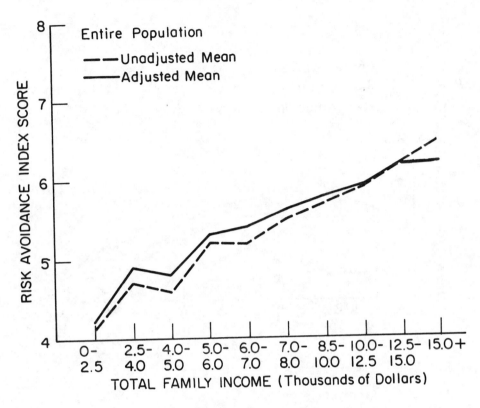

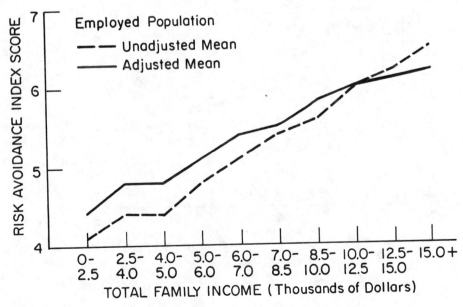

FIGURE 12.2

Risk Avoidance, by Family Size

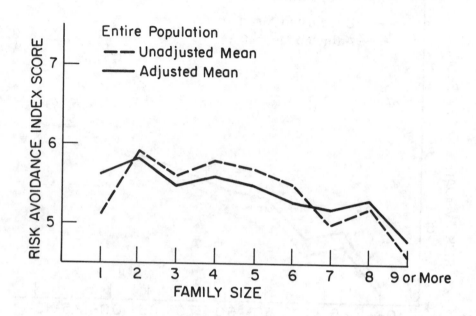

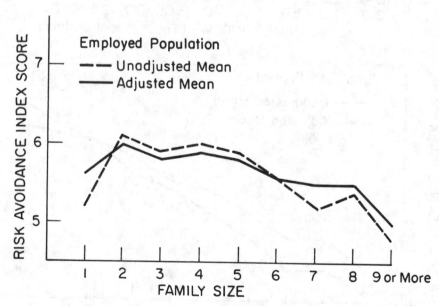

FIGURE 12.3

Risk Avoidance, by Age of Head

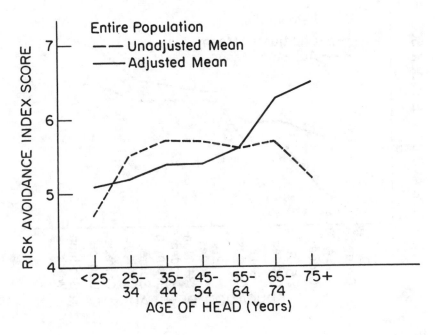

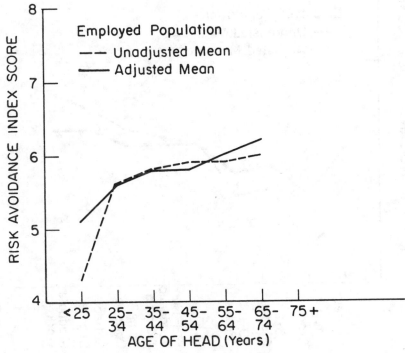

FIGURE 12.4

Risk Avoidance, by Education of Head

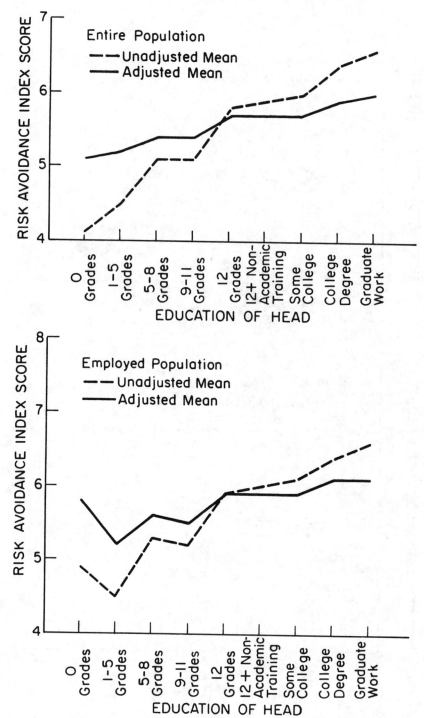

FIGURE 12.5

Risk Avoidance, by Test Score

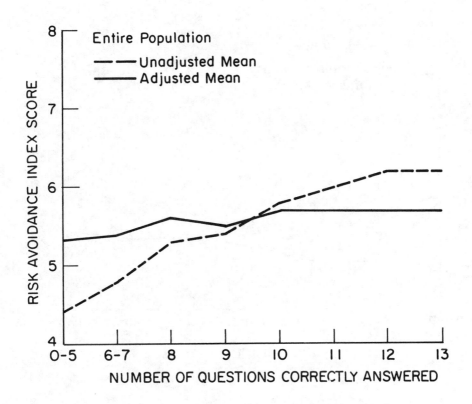

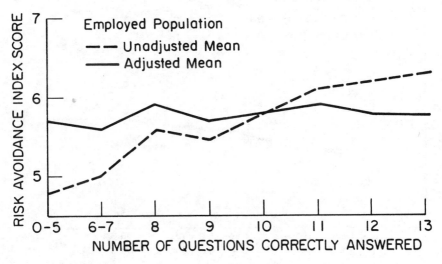

FIGURE 12.6

Risk Avoidance, by Job Seniority

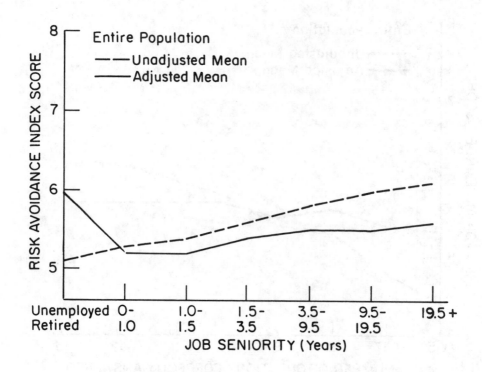

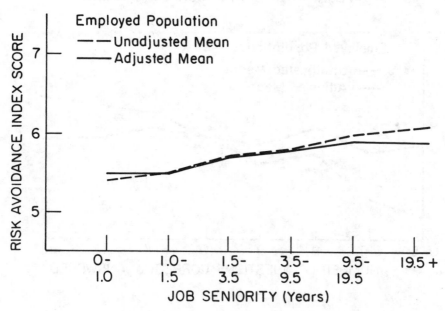

FIGURE 12.7

Risk Avoidance, by Education of Head's Father

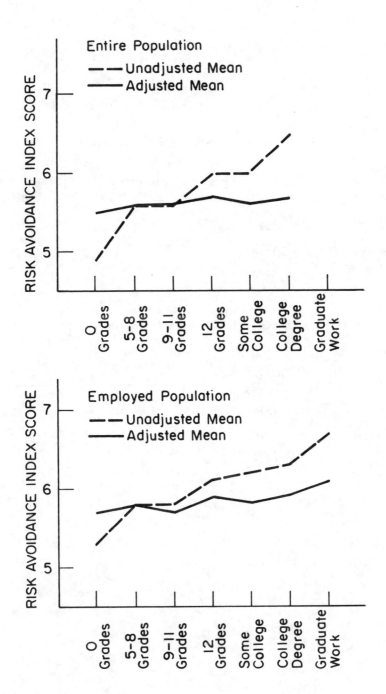

TABLE 12.3

Risk Avoidance and Race - Whole Population

Class	Cases	Unadjusted Mean	Adjusted Mean
White	2229	5.75	5.63
Non-white	1274	4.59	5.39
	3503		

Risk Avoidance and Race - Employed Population

Class	Cases	Unadjusted Mean	Adjusted Mean
White	1554	5.90	5.82
Non-white	818	5.04	5.69
	2372		

TABLE 12.4

Risk Avoidance and Sex of Head, Whole Population

Class	Cases	Unadjusted Mean	Adjusted Mean
Male	2605	5.75	5.65
Female	898	4.59	5.38
	3503		

Risk Avoidance and Sex of Head, Employed Population

Class	Cases	Unadjusted Mean	Adjusted Mean
Male	2025	5.87	5.81
Female	347	5.24	5.72
	2372		

TABLE 12.5

Risk Avoidance and Occupation of Head: Whole Population

Class	Cases	Unadjusted Mean	Adjusted Mean
1. Professional, technical and kindred workers	333	6.28	5.90
2. Managers, officials and proprietors	223	6.42	5.98
3. Self-employed businessmen	149	5.69	5.60
4. Clerical and sales workers	312	5.91	5.99
5. Craftsmen, foremen and kindred	470	5.75	5.79
6. Operatives and kindred workers	453	5.33	5.74
7. Laborers, service workers and farm laborers	469	4.72	5.71
8. Farmers and farm managers	76	5.48	5.83
9. Miscellaneous	40	6.19	6.09
0. Not in labor force or unemployed	978	5.12	4.96
	3503		

Risk Avoidance and Occupation of Head: Employed Population

Class	Cases	Unadjusted Mean	Adjusted Mean
1. Professional, technical and kindred workers	291	6.34	5.91
2. Managers, officials and proprietors	220	6.42	5.97
3. Self-employed businessmen	144	5.70	5.58
4. Clerical and sales workers	272	5.98	5.99
5. Craftsmen, foremen and kindred workers	454	5.76	5.77
6. Operatives and kindred workers	434	5.35	5.69
7. Laborers, service workers and farm laborers	406	4.77	5.66
8. Farmers and farm managers	68	5.53	5.90
9. Miscellaneous	35	6.26	6.05
0. Not in labor force or unemployed	48	4.24	4.08
	2372		

TABLE 12.6

Risk Avoidance and Region of Current Residence

Whole Population

Class	Cases	Unadjusted Mean	Adjusted Mean
Northeast	621	5.71	5.59
North Central	883	5.74	5.66
South	1460	5.29	5.54
West	534	5.73	5.63
Other	5		
	3503		

Risk Avoidance and Region of Current Residence

Employed Population

Class	Cases	Unadjusted Mean	Adjusted Mean
Northeast	426	5.92	5.82
North Central	576	5.89	5.81
South	1031	5.53	5.76
West	337	5.93	5.82
Other	2		
	2372		

indicates that incremental income for a high-income family has less effect on risk avoidance than does the same increment for a lower-income family. That is, a $5,000 income increase for a $45,000/year family will affect that family's behavior less than it will affect the behavior of a family with an average income of $5,000. This phenomenon may be due in part to the existence of a maximum achievable index score of eight in conjunction with the probable high score achieved by the wealthy family without the income increment.

It is interesting to note that the inclusion of the income-squared term increases the percentage of the total variation in the Risk Avoidance Index explained by the group of independent variables from 39.1 percent to 42.5 percent when the entire sample is considered and from 32.2 to 35.7 for the employed sample.

ANALYSIS OF RESIDUALS

In an effort to eradicate the effect of income completely, a two-stage regression analysis is employed. To do this we first regress risk avoidance exclusively on income and income-squared and use the parameters from this regression to obtain for each family a predicted value of risk avoidance based solely on that family's income. The predicted value is then subtracted from the actual score to obtain the part that income is incapable of explaining. This difference is then regressed on the remaining explanatory variables both individually and collectively. These operations are performed in Tables 12.7-12.9. It is true, of course, that any correlation between income and the other explanatory variables makes these second-stage estimates biased downward. This procedure thus provides a strict test on the importance of the remaining explanatory variables.

It is apparent in Tables 12.8 and 12.9 that age, education, and test scores affect risk avoidance beyond their effects through income. Each, however, loses part of its explanatory power when attention is restricted to the employed sample. On the other hand, the income-dependent effect of job seniority is *more* pronounced among the employed heads.

It is evident, too, that beyond all income effects large families and those headed by nonwhites and/or females tend to be less risk averse than the rest of the population. Table 12.9 indicates that this appears to be true even when education, test scores, and job seniority effects are considered. The smaller effect for employed females could be explained by the realization that it is the better-educated female head with fewer dependents who finds it most advantageous to enter the work force.

That Southern families tend to score lower on the Risk Avoidance Index

TABLE 12.7

Risk Avoidance Regressed on Average Income

and

$(\text{Average Income})^2$

(14a) $\hat{RA} = 4.23 + .000166^{**}$ (average income) $- .000095^{**} \dfrac{(\text{average income})^2}{1000}$
    (31.00) (17.82)

$R^2 = .279$

(14b) $\hat{RA} = 4.23 + .000159^{**}$ (average income) $- .000023^{**}$ (average income)^2
    (24.18) (15.28)

$R^2 = .254$

**denotes confidence in the .01 level.

TABLE 12.8

Risk Avoidance Residuals Regressed on All Remaining
Predictors, Simultaneously
(for all 3503 families with unchanged heads)

C = -1.45 $R^2 = .174$

| | Coefficients | |
Variable	Bivariate	Multivariate
Family size	-.1321**	-.1004**
Age of head	.0135**	.0168**
Education of head	.1041**	.0809**
Race	-.7512**	-.3101**
Sex of head	-.2024**	-.3600**
Test score	.0977**	.0579**
Occupation of head	-.0932	.0239
Job seniority	.0050	.0184*
Head's father's education	.0909**	.0389**
Region of residence:		
North Central	.0908	.0861
South	-.1725**	.0895
West	.0473	.0068

*denotes significance at the .05 level.

**denotes significance at the .01 level.

TABLE 12.9

Risk Avoidance Residuals, Regressed on All Remaining Predictions
for 1972 Families with Fully Employed, Unchanged Heads

C = -.921 R^2 = .101,

| | Coefficient | |
Variable	Bivariate	Multivariate
Family size	-.0893**	-.0804**
Age of head	.0093**	.0045**
Education of head	.1062**	.0751**
Race	-.4576**	-.1821*
Sex of head	.0091	-.1637*
Test score	.0776**	.0277*
Occupation of head	-.0196	.0626
Job seniority	.0993**	.0847**
Head's father's education	.0892**	.0418**
Region of residence:		
North Central	.0076	.0026
South	-.1619**	.0748
West	.0156	.0074

*denotes significance at the .05 level.

**denotes significance at the .01 level.

appears to be explained by the income, race and education variables since the *adjusted* coefficient representing Southern residence is insignificant.

III.   The Effects of Risk Avoidance

After examining differences in risk avoidance behavior across the population, we now use the index to predict certain economic and social events to see whether the index affects family well-being. Specifically, in what follows we measure the predictive ability of the index on four variables: (a) changes in income; (b) the degree of income stability; (c) unforeseen misfortunes of a nontrivial nature (measured by an Index of Disruptions in Life-Cycle Plans); and (d) the degree of self-satisfaction reported by the family head.

CHANGES IN INCOME

Since income change is a function of many variables, including most of our previously used explanatory variables, it is reasonable to subject the Risk Avoidance Index to a more meaningful test by regressing it on differences between actual changes in income between 1967 and 1972 and the changes in income predicted by the other variables. In other words, we regress the changes in income not explained by the other variables on risk avoidance. The procedure involves three steps:

(1) Δ Income = Income (1972) - (1967)

(2)   Expected (Δ Income) = f [average income,
(average income)^2, education, etc.]

(3)   Unexplained Δ Income = [Δ Income - Expected
(Δ Income)] = g (risk avoidance)

The third step of this procedure is performed in Table 12.10. The coefficient is negative (significant at the .01 level of confidence), indicating that a high level of risk avoidance is associated with a *smaller* income advance over the six-year period. Translated into dollar terms, the coefficients mean that if Family A achieves a one-point-higher score on the index than does Family B, one would expect its income to increase by an amount of $215 less than the increase in B's income.

INCOME INSTABILITY

As a measure of income instability we use an adjusted version of income variance. The variance of any variable X is given by the formula:

$$\text{Variance } (X) = \sum_{i=1}^{n} (X_i - \bar{X})^2 / n-1, \text{ where } \bar{X} \text{ is the mean of } X.$$

We adjust the income variance by dividing by the average income in recognition of

TABLE 12.10

Unexplained Changes in Income Regressed
on Risk Avoidance

	Constant	Coefficient	T-Ratio	R^2
Same Heads	657.24	−215.23**	2.60	.002
Same Fully Employed Heads	896.58	−351.66**	2.88	.004

**denotes significance at the .01 level.

the fact that an income rise or decline of $5,000 from one year to the next represents much greater income instability for a family with an average income of $5,000 than it does for a family with an average income of $30,000. Thus Adjusted Income Variance =

$$\sum_{i=1967}^{1972} (\text{Income (i)} - \text{Average Income})^2 /5 \div \text{Average Income}.$$

Adjusted Income Variance is regressed on the Index of Risk Avoidance alone and together with the other independent variables in Table 12.11. Risk avoidance appears to affect income instability positively when used individually to predict Adjusted Income Variance (although significant only when the whole population is considered) and negatively when included with the host of other regressors. But, since its partial R-squared is .001, it is doubtful that risk avoidance activities have much effect on income instability.

LIFE CYCLE DISRUPTIONS

Next the Risk Avoidance Index is tested as a predictor of unforeseen misfortunes. The Risk Avoidance Index is regressed against an index originated by Everett Ehrlich[1] and constructed in a manner similar to the Risk Avoidance Index. This index measures the extent to which families experience the following misfortunes: getting fired from a job, being underemployed, being evicted from a place of residence, having to make unexpected emergency expenditures for any reason, and experiencing two or more weeks of illness in a given calendar year.[2]

As can be seen from Table 12.12, the score on the Risk Avoidance Index is a highly significant predictor of family environmental shocks. The negative sign preceding the risk avoidance coefficient indicates that families with higher scores experience fewer shocks.

SELF-SATISFACTION

Finally, we use the Risk Avoidance Index to predict the family head's degree of self-satisfaction. The dependent variable is derived from the head's answer to a question asking whether he/she is most often satisfied or dissatisfied with himself/herself. The response is scored in the following manner:

More often satisfied	5 points
More often satisfied, qualified	4 points
Sometimes satisfied, sometimes not	3 points

---

[1] See Chapter 5 of this volume.

[2] The original index also contained a component based on the number of unplanned children; that component is deleted in this chapter.

TABLE 12.11

Adjusted Income Variance Regressed on Risk Avoidance
and Other Predictors
(for 3503 families with unchanged heads)

C = 1209.7 R^2 = .172

Variable	Coefficient	T-Ratio
Risk avoidance	-85.8296**	4.46
Average income	.0730**	9.70
(Average income)^2	.0003*	1.97
Family size	-6.0306	.48
Age of head	-7.7137**	4.78
Education of head	-41.3848**	3.07
Race	-14.2435	.21
Sex of head	-17.8607	.27
Test score	-10.9504	1.06
Occupation of head	21.2047	.37
Job seniority	-57.8112**	5.33
Head's father's education	22.2235	1.53
Region of residence:		
North Central	-61.1210	1.11
South	94.2027	1.67
West	22.3079	.35

*denotes significance at the .05 level.
**denotes significance at the .01 level.
***bivariate coefficient of Risk Avoidance Index = 52.04**, and its
    t-ratio = 3.23 and R^2 = .003.

TABLE 12.12

Index of Disruptions In Life-Cycle Plans
Regressed on Risk Avoidance and Other Independent Variables
(for 3503 families with unchanged heads)

C = 1.41 $R^2 = .193$

Variable	Coefficient	T-Ratio
Risk avoidance***	-.0606**	8.52
Average income	.0001	1.19
(Average income)^2	.0000	.56
Family size	.0292**	6.32
Age of head	-.0077**	12.85
Education of head	-.0276**	5.54
Race	.0666**	2.72
Sex of head	-.0711**	3.19
Test score	-.0069	1.82
Occupation of head	.0987**	4.77
Job seniority	-.0038	.94
Head's father's education	-.0105*	1.97
Region of residence:		
North Central	-.0521**	2.58
South	-.0831**	4.00
West	-.0223	.96

*denotes significance at the .05 level.
**denotes significance at the .01 level.
***bivariate coefficient of Risk Avoidance Index = -.0956**, and its
t-ratio = 16.41, and $R^2 = .071$.

TABLE 12.12
(continued)

(for 2372 families with fully employed, unchanged heads)

C = 1.68 R^2 = .271

Variable	Coefficient	T-Ratio
Risk avoidance***	-.0806**	8.94
Average income	-.0001**	3.83
(Average income)^2/1000	.0000*	2.16
Family size	.0300**	5.55
Age of head	.0012	1.17
Education of head	-.0370**	5.98
Race	.0920*	2.97
Sex of head	-.0482	1.39
Test score	-.0155**	3.09
Occupation of head	.0652**	2.90
Job seniority	-.0770**	12.11
Head's father's education	-.0060	.91
Region of residence:		
North Central	-.0402	1.62
South	-.1159**	4.51
West	-.0453	1.56

*denotes significance at the .05 level.
**denotes significance at the .01 level.
***bivariate coefficient of Risk Avoidance Index = -.1576**, and its
     t-ratio = 20.00 and R^2 = .146.

More often dissatisfied, qualified   2 points
More often dissatisfied   1 point

The risk avoidance prediction of this variable is shown in Table 12.13. As can be seen, a high level of risk avoidance predicts greater self-satisfaction only when the whole population is considered. In other words, a high level of risk avoidance predicts a greater level of self-satisfaction, especially among heads who are not in the labor force or not fully employed. But as the fraction of total variation explained is very small, the increased satisfaction attributable to the achievement of risk avoidance is probably quite small.

SUMMARY

An index of risk avoidance designed to measure family efforts to avoid undue risk has been constructed from components of insurance on a family's automobiles, use of seat belts, possession of savings reserves and the extent of health insurance coverage. This index was then subjected to statistical analysis to determine how behavior aimed at avoiding risks differs across various population groups. Furthermore, an attempt was made to determine some consequences of different patterns of risk avoidance behavior. We found that:

  (a) Average income is the most powerful predictor of risk avoidance score. The relationship between the two variables is slightly U-shaped.

  (b) Education, test score, job seniority and occupation were also found to influence risk avoiding behavior positively, independent of their effects through their correlations with income.

  (c) Nonwhites, females and heads of large families were found to be slightly less risk averse than the rest of the population.

  (d) The more risk averse were found to experience slightly smaller income advances over the period of the study but no appreciable difference in income stability.

  (e) Those who scored high on the index experienced fewer disruptions in life cycle plans and, if not in the labor force, experienced greater self-satisfaction.

References

Andrews, Frank M., Morgan, James N., Sonquist, John A. and Klem, Laura, Multiple Classification Analysis, 2nd edition, Ann Arbor: Institute for Social Research, 1973.

TABLE 12.13

Extent of Self-Satisfaction of Family
Head Regressed on Risk Avoidance
and Other Variables

(for 3,503 families with unchanged heads)

C = 2.57 R^2 = .033

(32a) Variable	Coefficient	T-Ratio
Risk avoidance	.0720**	2.89
Average income	-.0000	.90
(Average income)^2	.0000	1.21
Family size	-.0064	.39
Age of head	.0057**	2.74
Education of head	-.0299	1.74
Race	.0 39	.87
Sex of head	-.3461**	4.50
Test score	.0173	1.31
Occupation of head	.1406	1.93
Job seniority	.0543**	3.85
Head's father's education	-.0247	1.33
Region of residence:		
North Central	.1742*	2.47
South	.2390**	3.31
West	.1996*	2.46

*denotes significance at the .05 level.

**denotes significance at the .01 level.

***bivariate coefficient of Risk Avoidance Index = .0896**, and its
t-ratio = 4.64, and R^2 = .007.

TABLE 12.13
(continued)

(for 2,372 families with fully-employed, unchanged heads)

C = 1.98 R^2 = .028

(32b)	Variable	Coefficient	T-Ratio
	Risk avoidance	.0236	.78
	Average income	.0000	.09
	(Average income)^2	.0000	.58
	Family size	-.0115	.63
	Age of head	-.0011	.35
	Education of head	-.0303	1.49
	Race	.1417	1.39
	Sex of head	-.3717**	3.27
	Test score	.0016	.09
	Occupation of head	.1485*	1.98
	Job seniority	-.0722**	3.35
	Head's father's education	-.0240	1.10
	Region of residence:		
	North Central	.1889*	2.30
	South	.1990*	2.34
	West	.2819**	2.93

*denotes significance at the .05 level.

**denotes significance at the .01 level.

***bivariate coefficient of Risk Avoidance Index = .0271, and its
t-ratio = 1.09, and R^2 = .001.

Chapter 13

SUMMARY OF WORKS IN PROGRESS

This section contains three reports on work in progress sufficiently far along to justify spelling out procedures and preliminary findings. The report on food expenditures by Benus, Kmenta and Shapiro represents a very sophisticated set of procedures both in the possible models envisaged and in the procedures for selecting the best one. It takes advantage of the substantial sample size to let the data speak and to allow for rather complex interaction effects. This is done with an independent part-sample. The final assessment of the best-selected model on the other (fresh) data will be reported later when it is finished. The unit of analysis is a family in any one of four years, treating the sample as 4 x N observations. Since a family's consumption expenditures may be influenced by past experiences, the five-year average income and the direction of income change are introduced as explanatory variables. In addition, the analysis includes an estimate of the price level for food and several other main expenditures in that county or state for that year. (Those data have been incorporated into the data file as we merged the seventh year of interview data into it.)

The main policy-relevant finding, yet to be tested on the remainder of the data, is that almost all of the income generated through food subsidy programs is actually spent on food and *not* diverted to other uses.

The report on "unjustified" differences between women's and men's wages by Michael Conte uses wage "norms" calculated from male earnings. These differences are corrected for male deviations which also appear when other variables are added to the analysis.

The report on job change, one year and five year, by Greg Miner, provides some illuminating comparisons of change over shorter and longer periods. The longer period provides more variance to explain (more changes) and better correlations with the explanatory factors. There are also initial results of who plans to change jobs.

THE DYNAMICS OF HOUSEHOLD BUDGET
ALLOCATIONS TO FOOD EXPENDITURES

Jacob Benus
Research Economist
Stanford Research Institute

Jan Kmenta
Harold T. Shapiro
Department of Economics
University of Michigan

I.

The empirical analysis of the determinants of family food consumption, particularly the relationship between a household's income and its food budget, is one of the oldest branches of quantitative economics. "Engel's Law" concerning the income elasticity of household food expenditures was one of the first empirical regularities isolated from economic data. Stigler[1] has presented an excellent historical survey of the initial pioneering work in this area and Houthakker,[2] on the occasion of the one-hundredth anniversary of "Engel's Law," published an extensive comparative survey of the empirical results obtained in a large number of different countries. Both of these studies were completed in the mid-1950's, coincident with the publication of the landmark cross-sectional study of family budgets by Prais and Houthakker.[3] Since that time new studies have continued to examine this area in order to exploit both the increased understanding of quantitative techniques, as well as the availability of new data bases. The current study is in this latter tradition. Our purpose here is to take advantage of a new and unusually rich body of data along with some recent developments in econometrics in order to further our understanding of the determination of household food budgets.

Almost all previous studies of the determinants of household food consumption have been based either on cross-sectional or aggregate time series observations. The cross-sectional studies have been characterized (often necessarily) by the assumption that all households in the sample are operating in the same

---

[1] Stigler (1954).

[2] Houthakker (1957).

[3] Prais and Houthakker (1955).

market making it impossible to study the effect of price variation on the family food budget. Further, such data sets could not be used to generate any insight into the dynamics of household budget allocation and to distinguish short-run versus long-run behavior patterns. It was generally believed, however, that the results from cross-sectional studies yielded information on long-run behavior, leaving the analysis of time series data to reveal information on the short-run behavior of households. The studies based on aggregate time series are inherently subject to a different set of limitations in that, for example, they could not shed any light on such important "household specific" questions as the effect of family composition on food expenditures or on the economies of scale in food consumption.

In the present study we are able to relax many of the important limitations of both the cross-sectional and aggregate time series by basing our analysis on an extensive set of panel observations, i.e., observations of a sample of households over a number of time periods. Such a data set permits us to study simultaneously the dynamic adjustment of household food budgets to changed conditions, as well as both the "household specific" effects noted above and the effects of changing prices on food expenditures. The actual data underlying this study are drawn from the Panel Study of Income Dynamics, a data set collected by the Survey Research Center at The University of Michigan.[1] This panel contains budget and other data on five thousand United States households over a period of five years. Although the panel data contains observations both on the original set of households and the new households formed by this group (splitoffs), we have used only those observations on the original households in order to be able to study behavior patterns over the entire five year period.

Our model of household behavior (set out in detail below) distinguishes between various sources of income, family composition and various price effects, and allows for the dynamics of adjustment in household behavior. Further, with regard to functional form, we make use of the procedure suggested by Box and Cox[2] to determine the appropriate degree of curvature. With respect to estimation procedures, the variance-covariance matrix of disturbances is specified in

---

[1] This is the second study to use this set of data for the analysis of household food expenditures. An initial study, Hymans and Shapiro (1974), in Volume II of Five Thousand American Families, was designed to reveal the "equilibrium" or "normal" level of household expenditure patterns from simple five year averages of all the data. Our approach, on the other hand, is designed also to extract from the data the available information on the short-run dynamic response of households to various stimuli of interest.

[2] Box and Cox (1964).

386

accordance with the assumed nature of these pooled cross-section and time-series observations. In addition, the size of our data set allows us to separate carefully the hypothesis searching and hypothesis testing phases of our study. Our procedure is to separate our sample into two *independent* subsamples using one for exploring various behavioral relationships ("data mining") contains approximately one-quarter of the households in the sample, leaving three-quarters of the sample for the hypothesis testing phase. The first stage of our research, therefore, involves extensive interaction between *a priori* model building and data analysis of the evidence in the first quarter sample with the objective of formulating a model of household expenditures to be tested on an independent set of data.

The present paper is in the nature of a detailed progress report containing the results of the first stage of work. Section II presents a derivation of the basic model underlying our study, as well as the results of our empirical analysis on the initial one-quarter sample. A final section outlines the general procedures followed in testing the hypothesis developed in Section II and a number of concluding comments.

II.

In formulating our model, we start with the linear expenditure system which was proposed by Stone[1] and which can be expressed as follows:

$$(1) \qquad P_j X_j = c_j P_j + b_j (Y - \sum_{r=1}^{n} c_r P_r)$$

where P=price, X=quantity consumer, and Y=current income. All subscripts refer to individual commodities. We change the parameters in this function to allow for constancy of *some* prices and to specialize its reference to a particular household with members of different ages.[2] In an equilibrium situation in a particular time period t, we have

$$(2) \qquad C_t^* = \alpha_0 + \sum_{k=1}^{H} \alpha_k N_{kt} + \beta Y_t + \sum_{q=1}^{Q} \gamma_q P_{qt}$$

where now C_t^*=equilibrium expenditure on food of a particular household and N_{kt}= number of household members in the kth age category. Since, in general, the collective decision unit is the household and not a single family member, the above model aggregates over all household members and does not allow for each member to have his or her own parameters reflecting his or her own specific utility function. The term Y_t, therefore, represents total household income in

---

[1] Stone (1954)

[2] See Muellbauer (1974) for a discussion on the effects of household composition.

period t. The model as specified in (2) has to be modified and extended in a number of ways to approach a reasonable reflection of reality and to facilitate testing of interesting hypotheses. In the first place, it may be presumed that the consumer's decisions with respect to food consumption may be influenced by the type of income he receives. An obvious reason for this presumption is the observation that some income is received in the form of food stamps but other kinds of income may also be regarded with some distinction by the consumer. To the extent that different types of income can be associated with a different degree of "permanency," our disaggregation of income may also be viewed as a concession to the permanent income hypothesis. With this modification, our model becomes

$$(3) \quad C_t^* = \alpha_0 + \sum_{k=1}^{H} \alpha_k N_{kt} + \sum_{m=1}^{M} \beta_m Y_{mt} + \sum_{q=1}^{Q} \gamma_q P_{qt}$$

As the next modification we consider the possibility that the consumer may react differently to an income increase than to an income decrease. We perceive the consumer as having certain tastes that have been acquired as a result of past expenditures associated with past levels of income. As consumer income increases he may move to a higher level of food expenditure (even if not instantaneously) but, when the consumer's income decreases, he may be unlikely to change his standard of food consumption by the same amount.[1] This hypothesis can be formulated by introducing a dummy variable into (3) as follows:

$$(4) \quad C_t^* = \alpha_0 + \sum_{k=1}^{H} \alpha_k N_{kt} + \sum_{m}^{M} \beta_m Y_{mt} + \sum_{m}^{M} \delta_m Y_{mt} Z_{mt} + \sum_{q}^{Q} \gamma_q P_{qt}$$

where $Z_{mt} = 1$ if $Y_{mt} \geq Y_{m,t-1}$

=0 otherwise.

So far we have been concerned only with the determination of equilibrium expenditure. In reality, however, adjustments to equilibrium are not instantaneous but are delayed by habit, time needed for gathering information, etc. One way of taking this delay into account is by adopting a "habit persistence" or "partial adjustment" model of the form[2]

$$(5) \quad C_t - C_{t-1} = \phi(C_t^* - C_{t-1}) + \epsilon_t \qquad (0 < \phi \leq 1)$$

---

[1] The idea of a differentiated response to different directions of change of income was originally formulated in Duesenberry (1949). It could also be applied to changes in prices.

[2] Originally formulated in Nerlove (1958).

388

where C_t=actual household food expenditure in period t. Substituting for C_t^* from (5) into (4) and rearranging terms, we get the following expression for household food expenditures

$$(6) \quad C_t = \alpha_0^* + \phi^* C_{t-1} + \sum_{k=1}^{H} \alpha_k^* N_{kt} + \sum_{m}^{M} \beta_m^* Y_{mt} + \sum_{m}^{M} \delta_m^* Y_{mt} Z_{mt} + \sum_{q}^{Q} \gamma_q^* P_{qt} + \varepsilon_t$$

where $\phi^* = 1 - \phi$, $\alpha_k^* = \phi \alpha_k$, $\beta_m^* = \phi \beta_m$, etc.

The above model (equation 6) reflects a simple aggregation over all members of a given household and thus does not allow for any kind of economies (or diseconomies) of scale in expenditure. If there are economies of scale in food expenditure, then as the number of household members increases, the expenditure on food *per member* decreases. One way of formulating this hypothesis is to allow expenditure to be a quadratic function of the number of household members of each age group rather than a simple linear function as outlined above. The hypothesis of economies of scale in food consumption, for example, would require that the coefficients attached to the square terms be negative. Finally, to account for possible effects on food expenditure of factors which were common to all households but specific to each time period under consideration we extend out model by the introduction of period-specific dummy variables. With all of the above modifications the food expenditure equation for the ith household and the tth period becomes

$$(7) \quad C_{it} = \alpha_0^* + \phi_i^* C_{i,t-1} + \sum_{k=1}^{H} (\alpha_{ik}^* N_{ikt} + \theta_{ik}^* N^2_{ikt})$$

$$+ \sum_{m=1}^{M} \beta_{im}^* Y_{imt} + \sum_{m=1}^{M} \delta_{im}^* Y_{imt} Z_{imt}$$

$$+ \sum_{q=1}^{Q} \gamma_{iq}^* P_{qt} + \sum_{t} \pi_t V_t + \varepsilon_t$$

where V_t= 1 for the tth period,

= 0 otherwise.

In this formulation each household is characterized by its own set of coefficients (except for the coefficients attached to the period dummy variables). This is probably unnecessarily general and in any case this number of parameters is impossible to estimate even with the large number of observations available to us. It seems reasonable to conjecture that the parametric differences between households are due to the differences in socioeconomic status. As an approximation we postulate that the socioeconomic status of each household is measured by its average total income ($\overline{Y}_i$) over the five periods for which we have observations. We assume that each of the coefficients of equation (7) (except ϕ_i^* and, of course, π_t), is a linear function of $\overline{Y}_i$, i.e.,

$$(8) \quad \alpha_{ik}^* = \alpha_{1k} + \alpha_{2K}\overline{Y}_i$$

$$\theta_{ik}^* = \theta_{1k} + \theta_{2k}\overline{Y}_i$$

$$\beta_{im}^* = \beta_{1m} + \beta_{2m}\overline{Y}_i$$

$$\delta_{im}^* = \delta_{1m} + \delta_{2m}\overline{Y}_i$$

and

$$\gamma_{iq}^* = \gamma_{1q} + \gamma_{2q}\overline{Y}_i$$

The coefficient of $C_{i,t-1}$, ϕ_i^*, is thought to depend not only $\overline{Y}_i$, but also on the direction of the adjustment, i.e.,

$$(9) \quad \phi_i^* = \phi_1 + \phi_2\overline{Y}_i + \phi_3 Z_{imt}$$

This implies that household A, whose socioeconomic status is, say, \$1,000 higher than that of household B, will have the intercept and each of the slopes (except perhaps for that of C_{t-1}) 1,000 times higher than household B. This will also be true of the slope of C_{t-1} unless the current incomes of the two households have moved in opposite directions, in which case the slope of C_{t-1} for household A would be $(1,000 \pm \theta_3)$ times that for household B.

Equation (7) - with the modifications spelled out in (8) and (9) - is derived entirely on the basis of _a priori_ considerations. To obtain further information about the model we utilize one-quarter of the sample observations for experimentation, the main purpose of which is to weed out some apparently irrelevant variables. This experimentation, however, is limited to the sets of variables specified in the model derived above. As a result of this initial data analysis, however, a number of the interaction terms suggested by equation (8) are deleted from the model. For example, the terms

$$\sum_{m}^{M} (\delta_{1m} + \delta_{2m}\bar{Y}_i) Y_{imt} Z_{imt}$$

which individually were found to make insignificant contribution to the explanation of the variation in C_{it} are replaced by

$$\delta Y_{it} Z_{it}$$

where Y_{it} = total income of the ith household in the t-period

and $\quad Z_{it}$ = 1 if $Y_{it} \geq Y_{i,t-1}$

$\quad\quad\quad\quad$ = 0 otherwise.

The resulting equation then becomes

$$(10) \quad C_{it} = \alpha_0 + \sum_{k=1}^{H} (\alpha_{1k} N_{ikt} + \theta_{1k} N_{ikt}^2)$$

$$+ (\phi_1 + \phi_2 \bar{Y}_i + \phi_3 Z_{it}) C_{i,t-1}$$

$$+ \sum_{m=1}^{M} \beta_{1m} Y_{imt} + \delta Y_{it} Z_{it}$$

$$+ \sum_{q=1}^{Q} \gamma_{1q} P_{qt} + \sum_{t=1}^{T} \pi_t V_t + \varepsilon_t$$

At this stage we have as yet not directly introduced any considerations regarding the appropriate functional form of the relationship. The linear-in-parameters form of equation (10) is certainly a candidate, but not one without serious competitors. In their pioneering study, Prais and Houthakker[1] considered the following functional forms as eligible on *a priori* grounds:

$$(11a) \quad v_i = \alpha + \beta/v_0$$

$$(11b) \quad v_i = \alpha + \beta v_0$$

---

[1] Prais and Houthakker (1955).

(11c) $\log v_i = \alpha + \beta \log v_0$

(11d) $\log v_i = \alpha + \beta / v_0$

(11e) $v_i = \alpha + \beta \log v_0$

where v_i is the expenditure on the ith commodity and v_0 is total expenditure (taken to be a surrogate for income). Prais and Houthakker made their final choice of functional form on the basis of more or less *ad hoc* tests and other considerations but some of the recent developments in the area of transformations make it possible to approach the problem in a much more rigorous and formal way.[1] In fact, it is now possible to represent all of the five different functional forms in the one equation:

$$(12) \qquad \frac{v_i^{\lambda}-1}{\lambda} = \alpha + \beta \, \frac{v_0^{\mu}-1}{\mu}$$

where the new parameters λ and μ determine the degree and type of nonlinearity in the variables. Each of the functional forms (11a) through (11e) can be represented as a special case of (12). Specifically,

if $\lambda = 1$ and $\mu = -1$, then (12) = (11a);

if $\lambda = 1$ and $\mu = 1$, then (12) = (11b);

if $\lambda \to 0$ and $\mu \to 0$, then (12) $\to$ (11c);

if $\lambda \to 0$ and $\mu = -1$, then (12) $\to$ (11d);

if $\lambda = 1$ and $\mu \to 0$, then (12) $\to$ (11e).

(ignoring signs and the composition of the constant term α)

---

[1] See Box and Cox (1964), pp 211-243; Zarembka (1974).

Thus instead of estimating five separate equations and using their R^2's and other *ad hoc* criteria to make a choice, we can estimate just one equation and the estimated values of λ and μ will tell us which special case (if any) is appropriate. This transformation is applied to the food expenditure, income and price variables of equation (10) to yield

$$(13) \quad \frac{c_{it}^{\lambda}-1}{\lambda} = \alpha_0 + \sum_{k=1}^{H} (\alpha_{1k} N_{ikt} + \theta_{1k} N_{ikt}^2)$$

$$+ (\phi_1 + \phi_2 \overline{Y}_i + \phi_3 Z_{it}) \left(\frac{c_{i,t-1}^{\lambda}-1}{\lambda} \right)$$

$$+ \sum_{m=1}^{M} \beta_{im} \left(\frac{Y_{imt}^{\mu}-1}{\mu} \right) + \delta Z_{it} \left(\frac{Y_{it}^{\mu}-1}{\mu} \right)$$

$$+ \sum_{q=1}^{Q} \gamma_{1q} \left(\frac{P_{qt}^{\mu}-1}{\mu} \right) + \sum_{t=1}^{T} \pi_t V_t + u_{it}$$

The above equation would be incomplete without the specification of the characteristics of the disturbance term u_{it}. To do this we have again used the initial quarter-sample to obtain information about the behavior of the disturbance. To start with, we consider the disturbance to follow a first-order autoregressive scheme, and to be heteroskedastic. That is, we specify

$$u_{it} = \rho u_{i,t-1} + v_{it}$$

where v_{it} is a normally and independently distributed random variable which is independent of $u_{i,t-1}$. Further, it is assumed that

$$E(v_{it}) = 0$$

and $\quad E(v_{it}^2) = w_{it} \sigma^2$

for all i, t. In order to test the hypothesis that $\rho=0$, and $w_{it}=1$, we proceeded as follows. First, the equation (13) is estimated from the data in the initial one-quarter sample by maximizing a likelihood function for normally and independently distributed random variables.[1] This maximization was accomplished by

---

[1] In the case where income was to enter in a reciprocal way we used the reciprocal of a linear combination of various types of income rather than treating the reciprocal of each type of income separately.

a two-dimensional search over various values of λ and μ. Second, using the estimated residuals from the resulting equation, we "test" for autoregression by using the method proposed recently by Durbin.[1] This involves regressing the residual $\hat{u}_{it}$ on all of the explanatory variables in the equation and $\hat{u}_{i,t-1}$. Lack of significance of the estimated coefficient attached to $\hat{u}_{i,t-1}$ indicates an absence of autocorrelation. This, indeed, turns out to be the case with our initial quarter-sample observations, so that we can then directly proceed to the "test" for homoskedasticity. For this purpose we use the same residuals as those used in the preceding test, but divided into several groups according to the magnitude of food expenditure. For each group we calculate the corresponding variance and used a chi-square test to see whether their differences are significant.[2] This test fails to reject the hypothesis of homoskedasticity, i.e., $w_{it}=1$.[3] Under these circumstances it appears reasonable to proceed further with the assumption that the disturbance u_{it} is non-autoregressive and homoskedastic. We further retain the assumption of normality and zero mean.

The likelihood function turns out to have a single peak at $\lambda = 0.4$ and $\mu = 0.8$. However, since the likelihood function is relatively flat in the neighborhood of the maximizing values of λ and μ, we have chosen $\lambda = 0.5$ and $\mu = 1$ as the preferred functional form, yielding a relationship to be tested with the remaining three-quarters of our sample. In addition, the data analysis performed on the initial sample of households suggests a model of household consumption expenditures incorporating the following particular sets of variables in addition to the interaction terms and dummy variables outlined above.[4]

---

[1] Durbin (1970).

[2] See Hoel (1954).

[3] A questionable aspect of this procedure is whether the transformation takes care of the nonlinearities in the regression equation or whether it actually serves to remove heteroskedasticity. Fortunately, Zarembka has shown that if the transformation leads to homoskedasticity of the error term, then the parameters of the relationship have been consistently estimated. This appears to be the case with our data.

[4] In the presence of various food subsidy programs, expenditures on food understate the value of food consumption. In order to have a more accurate measure of consumption, we have added the reported value of such items as "savings due to meals purchased at school," etc., to the basic food expenditure variable.

Household Composition

    Number of Adults (NAD)

    Number of Children 0-4 (NO4)

    "   "   "   5-9 (N59)

    "   "   "   10-12 (N1012)

    "   "   "   13-17 (N1317)

Prices[1]

    Food (P_F)

    Housing (P_H)

    Clothing (P_C)

    Transportation (P_T)

    Health and Recreation (P_{HR})

Income

    Transfer Income (Y_{TR})

    Imputed Income - Food Subsidy Program (Y_{FS})

    Other Income (Y_O) = Total Income - Y_{TR} - Y_{FS}

Table 13.1 contains the parameter estimates of the model based on equation (13) and selected from the data in our initial sample of households and yield the following suggestions regarding the nature of the budget process being studied.

a) *Economies of Scale and Food Expenditure*: The results presented clearly suggest the prevalence of economies of scale in family food budgets. All the quadratic terms relating to the age distribution of the household have the negative sign that reflects the realization of economies of scale in food expenditure. These effects, however, are not uniform over all age groups with such economies being apparently less important for the youngest age group.

b) *Price Effects*: All the price variables enter with the expected sign indicating a negative elasticity with respect to food prices and positive elasticities with respect to the prices of other items in the family budget. The parameter estimates in Table 1 yield the following measures of the impact and equilibrium price elasticities of household food consumption.

---

[1] The price variables are all components of the CPI and vary not only over time but across households at a point in time due to regional discrepancies in prices.

Price Elasticity	Impact	Long Run[*]
P_F	-1.89	-2.62
P_H	.65	1.18
P_C	.50	.91
P_T	.44	.80
P_{HR}	.44	.80

[*]Calculated with Z_{it}= 1.0 and $\overline{Y}_i$ set at its mean value.

c) *Speed of Adjustment*: The data of the initial one-quarter sample clearly reveal a mechanism of partial adjustment in the response of household food budgets to shifts in the determining variables incorporated in our model. The estimated speed-of-adjustment coefficient (ϕ) can be expressed as follows from the figures in Table 13.1

$$(1-\phi_i) = .360 + .00000648(\overline{Y}_i) + .03225(Z_{it}) .$$

Thus for households with rising income ϕ=0.549 while for other households the speed of adjustment is 0.581. As is evident from the above expression, however, ϕ is also a function of the household's average income ($\overline{Y}$). The higher the average income, the slower will be the adjustment in the food budget. Thus households with higher and rising incomes adjust their food expenditures relatively more slowly than others. The reader should also note that since the speed of adjustment varies with $\overline{Y}_i$ and Z_{it} so will the relationship between the impact and steady state price elasticities which were calculated above using the overall mean for $\overline{Y}_i$ and setting Z_{it}=1.0. The implication of the above estimate is that families with low average incomes not only respond more quickly but seem to exhibit lower steady state price elasticities.

d) *Income Elasticities and the Marginal Propensity to Consume*[1]: The parameter estimates presented in Table 13.1 suggest and support a number of interesting hypotheses regarding the relationship of household incomes to food expenditures.

---

[1]Given the functional form of the relationship being analyzed, this marginal propensity to consume ($\partial C/\partial Y$) is a transformation of the appropriate estimated parameter. The income parameter must be transformed as follows. If $\hat{\alpha}$ is the coefficient on income, the marginal propensity to consume is estimated by $\hat{\alpha}_C^{(1-\lambda)}$. The income elasticity would be estimated by $(\hat{\alpha})(Y/C^\lambda)$.

TABLE 13.1

Parameter Estimates of Household Consumption Expenditure (Equation 13)
Based on Initial Sample of Households

Independent Variables	Coefficient	Standard Error
CONSTANT	-28.69	19.00
NAD (Number of adults)	8.14	.79
$(NAD)^2$	-.95	.13
NO4 (Number of children aged 0-4)	2.40	.74
$(NO4)^2$	-.19	.32
N59 (Number of children aged 5-9)	4.96	.61
$(N59)^2$	-.93	.20
N1012 (Number of children aged 10-12)	4.08	.91
$(N1012)^2$	-.67	.42
N1317 (Number of children aged 13-17)	3.34	.59
$(N1317)^2$	-.33	.18
P_F (Local food prices)	-.33	.14
P_H (Local housing prices)	.23	.09
P_C (Local clothing prices)	.19	.12
P_T (Local transportation prices)	.16	.07
P_{HR} (Local health and recreation prices)	.16	.07
Y_{TR} (Transfer income)	$.84*10^{-3}$	$.17*10^{-2}$
Y_{FS} (Food subsidy income)	$.13*10^{-1}$	$.76*10^{-3}$
Y_0 (All other income)	$.11*10^{-2}$	$.01*10^{-2}$
Y*Z (Income x income increase)	$-.25*10^{-6}$	$.09*10^{-6}$
$Y*\overline{Y}$ (Income x average income over the years)	$-.21*10^{-4}$	$.22*10^{-5}$
V_2 (Year 1, shift function)	4.55	1.37
V_3 (Year 3)	1.94	.88
V_4 (Year 4)	5.44	2.33
C_{t-1} (Prior year's consumption)	.36	.02
$C_{t-1}*\overline{Y}$	$.65*10^{-5}$	$.11*10^{-5}$
$C_{t-1}*Z$	.04	.01

i) A steady state income elasticity of food expenditures is in the neighborhood of 0.25. This is substantially lower than in many previous studies, but is consistent with the results reported by Hymans and Shapiro (1973), Brandow (1961), Girshick and Haavelmo (1947), and Tobin (1950).

ii) The income elasticity of food expenditures is negatively related to the household's income--the higher the income the less responsive is the food budget to changes in income.

iii) Except for income generated through food subsidy programs, the marginal propensity to consume out of different income components is broadly similar. The corresponding income elasticities (evaluated at overall sample means) are, therefore, quite different. They are .02, .05, and .23 for transfer income (Y_{tr}), income generated from food subsidy programs (Y_{fs}) and "other" income (Y_o), respectively. The marginal propensity to consume also seems to be a function of the household's average income level--following an inverse relationship.

iv) Although the evidence is somewhat mixed, the parameter estimates presented above indicate that almost all of the income generated through food subsidy programs is actually spent on food. Our expectation had been that households would use some of this income subsidy for other purposes. The marginal propensity to consume out of this subsidy income is, as expected, considerably higher than out of other income components.

III.

The above results are both encouraging and illuminating. First, a good number of the initial hypotheses generated through our *a priori* model building have found some support in the evidence generated from the initial sample of households. Second, our extensive data analysis of this initial sample has served both to restrict some of the generality of our initial model and to suggest a number of issues requiring further investigation. Our research plans, therefore, involve two further steps:

i) The completion of the data analysis on the initial sample of households. This step will include a careful checking of the results and the investigation of a number of ideas generated by the work to date. When this work is completed, we will have a final model available for testing on an independent set of data.

ii) The model testing phase. Here we will bring to bear the standard tools of statistical inference to test the hypotheses developed on the basis of our *a priori* model building and the data analysis on the initial sample of households. We will complete the research by comparing our final results with those achieved by other researchers.

References

Brandow, P. E., Interrelations among Demands for Farm Products and Implications for Control of Market Supply, Pennsylvania State University College of Agriculture Extension Station, University Park, Pennsylvania, 1961.

Box, G.E.P. and Cox, D. R., "An Analysis of Transformations," Journal of the Royal Statistical Society, Series B, 26(1964), pp. 211-43.

Duesenberry, J., Income, Saving and Theory of Consumer Behavior, Cambridge, Harvard University Press, 1949.

Durbin, J., "Testing for Serial Correlation in Least Squares Regression When Some of the Regressors are Lagged Dependent Variables," Econometrica (May 1970).

Girshick, M. A. and Haavelmo, T., "Statistical Analysis of the Demand for Food: Examples of Simultaneous Estimation of Structural Equations, Econometrica, 15 (1947), pp. 79-110.

Hoel, P., Introduction to Mathematical Statistics, Third ed., New York: John Wiley, 1962.

Houthakker, H. S., "An International Comparison of Household Expenditure Patterns Commemorating the Centenary of Engel's Law," Econometrica 1957.

Hymans, S. H. and Shapiro, H. T., "The Allocation of Household Income to Food Consumption," Five Thousand American Families -- Patterns of Economic Progress, Volume II, Institute for Social Research, The University of Michigan, Ann Arbor, 1973.

Morgan, J., et al., Five Thousand American Families -- Patterns of Economic Progress, Volume I, Institute for Social Research, The University of Michigan, Ann Arbor, 1973.

Muellbauer, J., "Household Composition, Engel Curves and Welfare Comparisons Between Households," European Economic Review, 5 (August 1974), pp. 103-122.

Nerlove, M., "Distributed Lags and Demand Analysis for Agricultural and Other Commodities," Agricultural Handbook No. 141, U. S. Department of Agriculture, 1958.

Prais, S. J. and Houthakker, H. S., The Analysis of Family Budgets, Cambridge University Press, 1955.

Stigler, G., "The Early History of Empirical Studies of Consumer Behavior," Journal of Political Economy, April 1954.

Stone, R., The Measurement of Consumer's Expenditure and Behavior in the United Kingdom, 1920-1938, Volume I, Cambridge University Press, 1954.

Tobin, J., "A Statistical Demand Function for Food in the United States," Journal of the Royal Statistical Society, Series A113, 1950.

Zarembka, P., "Transformation of Variables in Econometrics," P. Zarembka (ed.) Frontiers in Econometrics, New York Academic Press, 1974.

LABOR MARKET DISCRIMINATION AGAINST WOMEN

Michael Conte
Research Assistant
University of Michigan

The persistent wage differential between men and women stands in defiance of basic economic theory. Theory would lead one to expect that the distribution of hourly compensation for work would differ between female and male workers only to the extent that their skill level or capacity is different. Neoclassical economists argue that the wage differential can be divided into two components: a "personal characteristics" differential, meaning a *deserved* difference in wages due to a different quality or productivity in the employee's work, and an unexplained portion resulting from *undeserved* discrimination arising from unequal returns to similar skills.

By controlling for 262 detailed occupations, Sanborn estimated the amount of discrimination in the market place to be approximately 13 percent[1] implying an average woman's wage is 87 percent of that of an equally qualified man's in the same job. I hope to show that a different method of estimation will yield a different (and higher) discrimination coefficient even after controlling for occupation and industry. Further, it is proposed that the existence of different (discriminatory) patterns of hiring and promotion for equally qualified women and men makes a fine division of occupational groupings nonsensical for the discrimination hunter.

Using the wage of white males as the norm, a discrimination coefficient is calculated for women. This is done by obtaining regression coefficients for men on the variables assumed to be important in predicting their hourly earnings and using these estimates to form an "expected" wage for women. Since women's lower wages are taken to result from a lower level of productive skills, the exercise of prejudice by firms, or both, any difference between the actual and predicted values of the wage is due to discrimination. The average percent difference

---

[1] Sanborn (1964) pp. 534-550.

between the predicted and actual wage for women yields the discrimination coefficient.

Since previous investigators have found that including industry and occupation variables in the male wage regression significantly reduces the estimate of the amount of discrimination, a second discrimination coefficient is derived by including ten categories of both occupation and industry to predict the male wage. While Oaxaca finds that controlling for differing distributions across occupational and industrial categories reduces the discrimination coefficient by 30 percentage points[1] (57 percent to 27 percent), I find the reduction to be only six percent (43 percent to 37 percent).

In order to ascertain whether there are subgroups in the sample which experience differing degrees of discrimination, the discrimination coefficient is then regressed on the variables used in predicting the male wage plus other factors which may differ in their impact on men and women. Examples of the latter are "household burden" variables--age of youngest child, number of children in family, and so on. These are included to indicate the importance in the wage determination process of variables which most analyses ignore.

Data on the seventh wave of the Panel Study of Income Dynamics will be used to identify any subgroups which experience differing degrees of discrimination. The inclusion of questions regarding the job experience of women will provide better estimates of the discrimination coefficient. Any discernible trends in discrimination will be investigated in so far as they bear on the main argument.

References

Sanborn, Henry, "Pay Differences between Men and Women," Industrial and Labor Relations Review, SVII (July 1964), pp. 534-550.

Oaxaca, Ronald, "Male-Female Wage Differential in Urban Labor Markets," International Economic Review, Volume 14, No. 3, (October 1973), pp. 693-709.

---

[1] Oaxaca (1973) pp. 693-709.

DETERMINANTS OF VOLUNTARY JOB CHANGE

Gregory F. Miner
Research Assistant
University of Michigan

INTRODUCTION

An individual's attitudes and behavior with respect to geographic and job mobility are important determinants of his ability to "climb out" of poverty. The purpose of this study is to isolate variables which motivate people to change jobs. We shall compare the importance of these variables in explaining job change over a one-year period to their importance in explaining job change over a five-year period. What we are really attempting to estimate is each individual's probability of changing jobs voluntarily. The only evidence that it is not zero is when the individual actually changes, but in any short period not changing does not necessarily indicate a zero probability. The longer the period, the more chance we have of distinguishing probabilities, but also the more the individual's circumstances and probabilities may change. Of course, those with multiple job changes have higher probabilities of change than those who changed only once.

Here we provide a relatively simple set of analyses using one-year job change and five-year job change as dependent variables, focusing our attention on examining a large number of variables that might affect these two dichotomies.

ANALYSIS

The method of analysis utilized here is the examination of one half of the available sample, using the information to formulate a more specific model. This model is then tested for explanatory power on the remaining one half of the sample. Two models are tested. One examines the variables from the 1972 survey and their effects on job changes between 1972 and 1973. The other examines the variables from the beginning of the study and their effects on job changes at any time in the following six years.

A number of caveats are in order prior to presentation of the analysis and the results. Job change is a relatively rare event and is strictly binary in character. This results in a spurious difficulty with least squares regression. Rare events have a small variance and consequently, the explanatory power appears to be quite small when in fact the model may predict quite well. There are other difficulties discussed in Volume I, Appendix E, but they are not serious for large samples and regressions using categorical predictors.

One difficulty arises from the fact that nearly all of the data utilized in this study are from interviews. Psychological variables present more difficulties than do economic or easily quantifiable variables. The respondent's interpretation of a particular question, the interviewer's interpretation of the response, and the researcher's interpretation of the response all present possible discrepancies and provide several sources of measurement error. Difficulties of this sort will be discussed as they arise.

A sequential inter-relationship of variable classes is illustrated in Figure 13.1. The analysis which is presented below is not a detailed discussion of all aspects of the illustrated flow but is instead concerned with a few parts of it. The main thrust of this presentation is to discover the variables which are relevent in determining which individuals will change jobs. This is accomplished for two overlapping samples.

The first set is composed of those families in the sample which did not change heads between 1972 and 1973, whose heads were employed at the time of the interview, and who worked more than 1,250 hours in 1972. This number of hours assures that all full-time workers are included in the sample, and that unemployed, retired, or student workers are for the most part excluded. In addition, this work-hours constraint permits inclusion of those full-time workers who missed some work due to sickness or strikes or other reasons. There are 1,542 cases in the sample. The second sample has the same constraints, except the families must have had the same head for the entire six years of the sample, and the constraints must have applied for each year in the period from 1968-1973. There are 893 cases in this sample.

A peripheral analysis of those variables which influence the formulation of plans is also included. This analysis uses the 1972-1973 sample and is included only as an indication of a possible thread which can be picked up for later analysis.[1]

The initial step in the analysis consists of examining a large number of variables which could affect a decision to change jobs and utilizing the Auto-

---

[1]Regression results for this are given in Appendix Table A13.1.

FIGURE 13.1

Determinants of Job Change

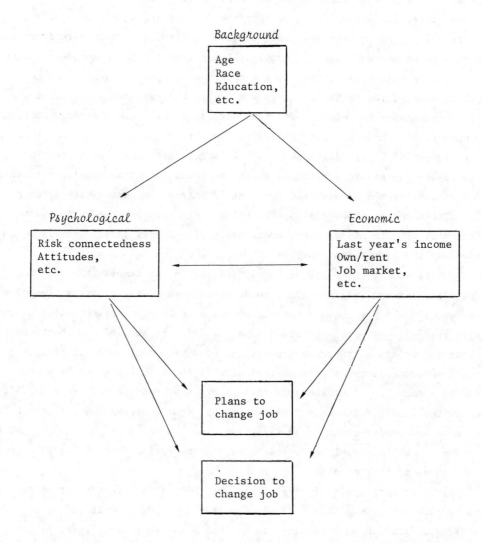

matic Interaction Detector (AID3) computer package. This package forms a series
of binary splits on the independent variable in accordance with the amount of
variance explained by each variable.

On the basis of results of AID3, a number of variables were rejected because
their effect on explaining voluntary job change was small overall and for all
subgroups. While this program is useful in describing the relative importance of
independent variables and rejecting some, it does not provide simultaneous estimates of the effects of each variable. After a number of variables were rejected,
the pared variable list was examined using Multiple Classification Analysis (MCA).

I.   The Dependent Variable

The dependent variable is a dichotomous variable designated 1 if the respondent in the sample voluntarily changed jobs and designated zero if he did
not change jobs or did so involuntarily. Table 13.2 describes the categories of
this variable and its distribution over the entire sample. Categories 4, 6, and
8 form values 1, and all others are zero. It should be noted that some respondents who reported voluntary job changes may not have changed jobs *voluntarily*
or may have done so only under duress. This would introduce error in the dependent variable; however, as there is no way to distinguish inaccurate responses,
it is hoped that their incidence is small enough so results are not affected. In
the 1972-1973 sample, 8.4 percent of the respondents voluntarily changed jobs; in
the 1968-1973 sample, 21.4 percent voluntarily changed jobs. Both samples restrict the individuals to those who have been working for the entire period under
consideration. Hence, they do not permit analysis of those who were unemployed
for a time and then found another job, those who were pregnant or ill, or those
who for whatever reason were temporarily not in the work force.

II.   Variables Not Included

It is frequently valuable to discuss those variables which are not relevant
to the explanation of the desired phenomenon and are consequently rejected from
further examination. Note that rejecting them from further analysis does not
imply that these variables are never and nowhere important, but merely that they
do not demonstrate significant explanatory power in this instance. Some of these
variables might be important at other times or places, or even if we could measure
them better.

Psychological variables or those which measure attitudes or behavior patterns
are the most difficult to measure. There are several of these in the panel, and
although an *a priori* argument can be established for each, the results indicate

TABLE 13.2

Reasons Given for Changing Jobs
1972-1973

Reasons Given	Percent of Sample
1) Company folded, changed hands, moved out of town, employer died, went out of business	.9
2) Strike, lockout	.0
3) Laid off, fired	2.0
4) Quit, resigned, retired, pregnant, needed more money, promotion, wanted a change, still has previous job (in addition to main occupation)	7.4
5) First full time or permanent job	1.0
6) Was previously self-employed	.3
7) Other (including drafted into armed service or any mention of armed service)	.7
8) Job was completed, seasonal work	.4
9) Not ascertained, don't know	1.0
10) Inappropriate; unemployed, retired, housewife, student, has had job for one year or more	86.4
	100.1

that they are not significant. One such variable is the "connectedness" index.
This composite variable is designed to indicate the opportunity for and extent
of social contact of the respondent. This aspect of behavior could be quite
important as many jobs are obtained through personal contact instead of adver-
tisement; thus one might expect those with more social contacts to make more
beneficial job changes.

Another behavior index is the "risk avoidance" index, which attempts to
measure the propensity of an individual to avoid unnecessary risks. There is an
inherent but calculated risk to changing jobs, as one is not assured of better
pay, better hours, improved working conditions, etc. Thus it might be expected
that those people who wish to avoid unnecessary risk would also be less likely
to change jobs and thus take on these associated risks.

"Achievement motivation" is another composite variable. A higher achievement score might indicate that the motivation for changing jobs would be higher.
This also is not significant in the analysis.

A test was conducted in the survey based on thirteen sentence completion
questions. It was expected that those with high scores would progress through
more jobs; this variable was rejected because it is not sufficiently exhaustive
and believed to be too closely related to education.

Marital status, whether the respondent owned his own home or rented, and
whether he said he was willing to move for a new job all demonstrate significant
differences within some subclasses (e.g., single persons are more likely to
change jobs than married); but the overall explanatory power of these variables
is too small to merit inclusion in the final model.

A "well-offness" variable has been constructed from the income and amount of
leisure time the respondent utilized. This could have been a powerful affirma-
tion (or negation) of the standard theoretical model, but there are difficulties
associated with the proper weighting of income and leisure. It has little explanatory power, but no argument against the standard theory is based on this
result.

The last of the psychological variables which was tried and rejected is
one in which the respondent was asked whether he planned his life or lived day
to day; the responses were on a five-point scale. Arguments can be developed
for increased job changes at either end of the scale, and the data indicate
equal probabilities at either extreme. Overall, however, there is very little
power of prediction in this variable--there is little difference in the probability of job change at either extreme.

Although these psychological and attitudinal variables have small explanatory power, this should not be used as a conclusive indictment against their use or importance. Better techniques of measurement could very easily show them to be quite important in understanding the behavior of man in the work environment.

The economic variables which were *not* used in the final model are predominantly proxies for financial burden. One might expect the respondents with increasing financial burdens to be actively searching for and changing to better paying jobs. Five such variables are: 1) the number of children; 2) the age of the youngest child; 3) whether the family is expecting more children; 4) the number of dependents which the family supports but are not part of the family unit; and 5) whether the family incurred any unusual or unexpected expenses during the past year. All save one need no further explanation; the age of the youngest child could determine whether or not the wife would be able to work or is required to care for a very young child.

In addition to these variables, four others related to extra work are rejected. One might expect an individual to search for and change to a better paying job if he needed to work extra hours or his wife had to work. The data did not show this to be the case, however, and the following variables are not used in the final model: whether the wife worked, whether the head of the household held more than one job simultaneously, whether overtime work was available to the head, or whether the head worked overtime if it was available. The industry in which the head was employed was also used initially, but not in the final model. It was believed that occupation and industry were so closely related that either one or the other should be used, but not both. Consequently, occupation is retained, and industry rejected.

The last of the rejected variables is the income change from 1969 to 1970 and from 1970 to 1971. The lack of explanatory power here is startling and quite contrary to expected results. The expectation is that if income were falling, the individual would change his job; if it were rising, he would either stay put or change to a job in which there was an income differential sufficient to overcome the seniority and security benefits of his present job. Income changes, however, prove to have very little power in explaining job change. Only 1970-1971 income change had sufficient explanatory power to be included in the model for planning to change jobs and even here, the explanatory power is quite low. This perhaps indicates that the past is easily forgotten, and could lead to the conclusion that the future is also out of mind, and consequently that planning horizons for changing jobs are extremely short. This would in turn lead one to conclude that, in a year to year study, job change appears to be spontaneous, not planned, which is in fact one of the conclusions of this study. This brings us to a discussion of the variables which *are* included in the model to explain voluntary job change.

A summary of the power of the eight predictors in the final model is given in Table 13.3. The most interesting comparisons are those between the one-year change and the five-year change, particularly the switch in importance of age and job tenure. The split-sample comparisons and the drop in power from the gross effects (Eta) to the net ones (Beta) are less interesting. For five-year change, how long the respondent had had his job at the beginning of the period was far more important than his age, but for one-year change, his age was more important. One possible reason is that only among some young age groups are the probabilities of changing jobs high enough to make substantial differences in the proportions who move in a single year, while how long the respondent has been in the same job at the beginning has a less dramatic but more persistent effect on future job changes. The longer on the job the less likely one is to change jobs.

Both occupation and education become more important and their relations more systematic with job change, when we allow five years to pass. This occurs in spite of the substantial reduction in sample size when we restrict ourselves to those in the labor force all the time.

Since only those respondents who changed jobs were asked why the current job is better, the differences shown reflect almost entirely whether there was a job change, not different reasons among those who changed. This variable is a second proxy for job tenure. Similarly, what the respondent is doing about a new job is largely a proxy for plans to change jobs.

Given the substantial shifts in importance when we go to five-year change, and the split-half evidence of the instability of some coefficients selected by ransacking and the proxy nature of two of the predictors, it seems necessary to to admit that we should reconsider the basic model and examine what matters for five-year voluntary job change. Hence this should be regarded as a progress report.

TABLE 13.3

Gross and Net Importance of Eight Predictors in Accounting for Voluntary Job Changes, One Year and Five Year

Variable	One-Year Job Change				Five-Year Job Change			
	First Half-Sample		Second Half-Sample		First Half-Sample		Second Half-Sample	
	Eta^2	$Beta^2$	Eta^2	$Beta^2$	Eta^2	$Beta^2$	Eta^2	$Beta^2$
Age of head	.047	.020	.062	.037	.060	.010	.772	.019
Job tenure	.049	.018	.035	.009	.062	.025	.103	.037
Why is job better	.042	.016	.052	.032	.242	.182	.202	.139
What are you doing about a new job	.038	.016	.043	.026	.064	.017	.064	.018
Real income/needs	.018	.014	.023	.014	.012	.004	.025	.014
Largest city	.012	.013	.002	.005	.008	.011	.002	.004
Occupation	.013	.010	.013	.009	.009	.012	.015	.027
Education	.009	.009	.016	.013	.024	.023	.013	.027
Multiple adjusted R^2	.114		.134		.287		.285	
Mean of dependent variable	.084		.092		.214		.235	
Number of cases	1542		1559		903		911	

APPENDIX 13.1

TABLE A13.1

Explanatory Variables for Plans to Change Jobs,
First Half-Sample

Variable	Eta^2	$Beta^2$
Age of head	.100	.046
Job enjoyability	.047	.042
Job tenure	.059	.030
Why is present job better	.035	.019
Education	.016	.016
Wanted overtime work	.016	.009
1971 Income higher than 1970	.006	.008
Income/needs	.019	.005

Multiple adjusted R^2 .189

Chapter 14

SUMMARY OF OTHER RESEARCH

In this chapter we summarize some recent analysis of the Panel data being conducted here at the University of Michigan and elsewhere. A similar summary appeared in Volume II, and here we attempt to bring that list of research completed and in progress up to date.

These analyses are in various stages of completion. Some have already been published in professional journals, some are currently at the "working paper" stage, and the remainder are just getting started.

Our list of analysis is certainly not complete. The task of contacting everyone working with the Panel data is impossible but our hope is that the following summaries will help to coordinate future research.

DETERMINANTS OF LABOUR FORCE PARTICIPATION AND
TIMING OF BIRTHS FOR MARRIED WOMEN, 1967-1971

E. R. Berndt and T. J. Wales
Department of Economics
University of British Columbia

In this paper we analyze empirically the determinants of labour force
participation and timing of births for married women in their family formation
years. We find that conception probabilities in a given year are significantly
affected by the birth gap, number of weeks head unemployed, and whether family
formation has already begun. For couples without children, the first birth interval is significantly related to the wife's potential wage rate in a U-shaped
fashion. However, neither transitory income nor wife's age significantly affect
the conception probability. We find that hours worked by the wife is affected
primarily by the age of the youngest child, and by the wife's potential wage,
results that are consistent with other findings in the literature.

Since our data are based on four panel waves, we have investigated the
temporal relationship among parameters and disturbances. We have derived and
tested the conditions required for pooling of the data. Although we cannot reject the hypothesis of parameter stability in the four years for the conception
and hours worked equations, we reject the disturbance covariance restrictions
that must be met in order to pool the data. Hence, our results are presented
for an eight equation model in which the parameters of the conception and hours
worked equations are the same in all four years.

A MULTIVARIATE LOGIT MODEL OF QUIT AND
RELOCATION AS A FAMILY LABOR SUPPLY

Martin David
Social Systems Research Institute
University of Wisconsin

The model presented indicates that past employment history is the most important determinant of job changes, both voluntary and involuntary. Although
the wage rate inhibits layoffs in a fashion predicted by the Holt-David model in
a linear version of the model presented in Volume II, it fails to attain significance in the logit version. Stated aspirations to move for higher paying work
do not have the relevance that is predicted by the Holt-David framework.

Attitudes toward job search and relocation appear to play a significant
part ultimately in decision making. Further investigation on attitude forma-

tion and the concrete implementation of search can be undertaken using the OEO panel data. Because of the importance of attitudinal information it appears that behavioral models based solely on establishment data will fail to capture an important aspect of job changes.

There appears to be validity to the structure that was imposed on the data. The partitioning of job changes into quits and layoffs appears to have sorted out different causal factors for the two decisions. The same is true of the distinction between employer-motivated moves in the transfer variable and the family-initiated search of a wide labor market that is captured in the job related move variable.

WELFARE PAYMENTS AND FERTILITY

Frances VanLoo Flanagan
Department of Economics
University of Illinois at Chicago Circle

The purpose of this study is to measure by multivariate methods the effect of welfare payments on fertility. More specifically, it attempts to assess 1) whether welfare families have more children than nonwelfare because of the availability of an additional stipend for each new baby born, 2) how any such effects vary with the education of the wife; the religion and race of the family; the degree of urbanization, and state welfare laws, and 3) the implications of these results for public policy.

DETERMINANTS OF WAGE RATES FOR MARRIED WOMEN: RESULTS FROM PANEL DATA

Ernst R. Berndt and Terence J. Wales
Department of Economics
University of British Columbia

A large number of empirical studies have investigated determinants of earnings for working males. The theoretical foundation for these studies is traditionally drawn from the theory of investment in human capital. With few exceptions, these empirical studies have been based on either a single cross-sectional body of data, or on a comparison of several cross sections. Although the latter permit some of the dynamic aspects of determinants of earnings to be investigated, such studies suffer from the problem of changes in sample composition over time.

In this paper we report results of an extensive cross-sectional and dynamic analysis of wage rate determination for married women in the United States over the five-year period 1967-71. To allow for possible differences in the structure of wage rate determination we split the sample into "career" and "occasional" workers. The 1967-71 period is of particular interest since the national unemployment rate for women age 20 and over varied considerably from 3.8% and 3.7% in 1968 and 1969 to 5.7% in 1971; further, toward the end of this period an increasing emphasis was placed on eliminating discrimination against working women.

Our principal findings include the following: 1) for both the career and occasional workers, wage rates increase with the level of educational attainment; urban, Jewish, and non-Southern women tend to receive higher wages than non-urban, non-Jewish, and Southern workers; and real wage rates are basically unaffected by variations in the rate of unemployment; 2) wages for career women tend to peak at about age 50, while for occasional workers wages peak at about age 40; 3) white career women tend to receive higher wages than non-white career women, but this difference declines considerably in 1970-71; for occasional workers the wage difference by race is negligible throughout the 1967-71 period; 4) structural changes in wage rate determination for career workers took place in the high unemployment years of 1970 and 1971; more highly educated career women obtained significantly larger real wages in 1970 and 1971 than during the 1967-69 period; and 5) although the evidence is not as strong, some structural changes in wage rate determination for occasional workers may have taken place in 1970-71; more highly educated women and urban occasional workers received larger real wages in this period than in the 1967-69 period.

EVOLUTIONARY CHANGES IN THE DISTRIBUTION OF INCOME, 1970-1971

Thad W. Mirer

Department of Economics
State University of New York at Albany

This study examines the impact of changing macroeconomic conditions on the distribution of income among families during 1970 and 1971. Cross section longitudinal data are used to develop an evolutionary characterization of the incidence of income changes on families as classified by income level, rather than by social, demographic, or other economic groupings.

SOME PROPOSED CHECKS OF THE DATA WITH THE CURRENT POPULATION SURVEY ESTIMATES AND WITH NATIONAL AGGREGATES

Joe Minarik
Economic Studies Program
The Brookings Institution

Given that the incidence and extent of poverty is a matter of grave national concern, the poverty counts of the Michigan Longitudinal Survey deserve some attention. This survey gives figures of poverty incidence which are uniformly lower than those drawn from the Census Bureau's Current Population Survey for all six currently available income years. It would be valuable for those concerned about poverty to know whether the Michigan Longitudinal Survey counts or the higher Current Population Survey figures are more accurate.

The purpose of this study is to compare the two surveys with each other and with income totals derived from other sources. Sampling variances are estimated to determine the significance of the differences in poverty proportions between the two data sources. Differences in completeness of income reporting are determined by comparisons with adjusted National Income Accounts totals and program totals for transfer payments. The vulnerability of the Michigan Longitudinal Survey to non-random sampling error and selective attrition are tested by cross-tabulations according to income-significant characteristics such as age, race, sex, and education of household heads. Finally, the possibility of improving or deteriorating reporting of income to the Michigan Longitudinal Survey with increasing contact with the panel over the years are tested by following the panel's results over time.

If the differences in poverty counts between the Michigan Longitudinal Survey and Current Population Survey are found to be irreconcilable, it would be worthwhile to see how those differences translate into the distribution of income as a whole. Of particular interest here are measures of the distribution of income including and excluding government transfer payments.

THE TIMING OF SPLITS BY YOUNG ADULTS

Martha S. Hill
Economics, University of Michigan

This study uses the Panel Study of Income Dynamics data to determine what factors affect the decision of young adults to separate or "split" from the parental unit. Previous analysis has shown that demographic changes resulting from marriage, birth, and departure of family members have substantial impacts on the economic well-being of family units. Researchers in the fields of demography, economics, and sociology have studied marriage and fertility decisions quite extensively, but have virtually ignored the decision of when to leave the parental family. The Panel Study provides a rich data set for examining this decision.

At this point in the analysis several preliminary results have been found. First, the factors important in determining age at split are quite different for females than for males. For males the most important factors are the financial ease of splitting and labor market conditions. Those males with non-labor income (i.e., transfer, or asset) leave the parental unit earlier than those without such income. For females, educational variables are the most important determinants of the age of departure. Females whose parents expect all their children to get a college education split later than those whose parents do not have such expectations.

Further work (which will be used in the author's doctoral dissertation) will include the following: 1) More detailed examination of the timing of splits, attempting to integrate the educational, labor force participation, marriage and split decisions facing young adults; 2) an examination of the impact of the split on the labor force participation behavior of both the splitoff and the parental unit; and 3) an examination of the relationship between the rate of splits and the business cycle.

SOCIAL CLASS AND THE SICK ROLE:
EXAMINING THE ISSUE OF MUTUAL INFLUENCE

David W. Britt
Department of Sociology and Social Psychology
Florida Atlantic University
(To appear in Journal of Health and Social Behavior)

Building on previous work which suggests that illness symptoms might stabilize into more permanent responses, it is argued that there should be a reciprocal relationship between self-reported illness and social class. Data from the Panel Study of Income Dynamics are used to test the hypothesis. Alternative explanations for the finding of a reciprocal relationship are discussed and additional data are presented to document more finely the effect of movement into the sick role on subsequent wage income.

THE PERSISTENCE OF THE DISCOURAGED WORKER EFFECT

Professor Stuart O. Schweitzer

Departments of Economics and of Community Medicine
and International Health, Georgetown University

and

Dr. Ralph E. Smith

Senior Research Staff of the Urban Institute

(Summary of an article which appeared in Industrial
and Labor Relations Review, January, 1974)

This study tests the hypothesis that the experience of unsuccessful job search increases the propensity to withdraw from the labor force, both immediately and in subsequent years. That is, the memory of past failure(s) in the labor market may influence subsequent labor force participation decisions, creating a persistent "scar effect." This dynamic modification of the discouraged worker effect postulates that one's perception of his present chance of success in securing employment is determined by past events as well as by present circumstances. Hence, past periods of unemployment are expected to have a significant additional effect on whether an unemployed worker will remain in the labor force.

As a preliminary test of the above hypothesis, the authors utilized data from a longitudinal survey being conducted by the Center for Human Resources Research at Ohio State University under the direction of Herbert Parnes. Data on the labor force status (E = employed; U = unemployed; and 0 = out of labor force) of male youths for the years 1966-1968 were extracted and subdivided by race. If unemployment reduces subsequent labor force participation, the following inequality of conditional probabilities is implied:

$$P \left[0_T \mid E_{T-J} \right] < P \left[0_T \mid U_{T-J} \right]$$

For example, the probability that an individual is out of the labor force in 1968 should be greater for an unemployed person in 1966 than for an employed. The results from these groupings were striking -- the probability that a youth would be out of the labor force in a given year was twice as high for those who had been unemployed previously than for those who had been employed.

Data to develop a more rigorous model were obtained from the Panel Study of Income Dymamics. The decision to participate in the labor market and the number of hours offered by an individual in a given year are assumed to be related to his demographic characteristics, educational attainment, other family income, assets, wage rate, and current employment opportunities. Since the data set is restricted to include only heads of households who had labor force activity in

420

1967, 1968 and 1969, it is important to note that this study only considers the quantitative decision of how many hours an individual chooses to be in the labor force once he decides to participate. Furthermore, on the assumption that all parameters interact with race and sex, separate regressions were run for each category.

The dependent variable is hours in the labor force in 1969. The regressor of primary interest, an individual's unemployment experience, is formed by the ratio of hours unemployed divided by hours in the labor force for the sample respondent in the observation year. Lagged unemployment terms are introduced in subsequent regressions to investigate whether past failures in job searches influence present labor force activity.

Multivariate regression techniques are utilized to control for the impact of other determinants of labor participation. The current year's (1969) unemployment experience enters the equations with the expected negative coefficient indicating the presence of a discouraged worker behavior pattern. The results imply that a difference in the unemployment experience by one percentage point between workers is associated with a difference in labor force participation of six hours per year for white males and by four hours for nonwhite males.

Investigation of various lag specifications reveal that when a two-year lagged unemployment term is coupled with the current year's unemployment experience, the former enters with a significant negative parameter for all groups -- indicating a remarkable persistence of the effect of unemployment on labor force participation. These latter estimates indicate that while the current year impact for white and nonwhite males are reduced to 4 and 2.5 hours per year respectively, a subsequent reduction of 7 hours for white males and 4.5 hours for nonwhite males is associated with the lagged unemployment term. Thus, the effect of including past unemployment rates is to reduce the immediate impact of current unemployment on labor force participation, but to raise its total effect. This strongly suggests that the discouraged worker effect has a significant dynamic component, implying that the costs of unemployment persist over time.

TWO STRUCTURAL MODELS FOR FAMILY INCOME, HOUSING CONSUMPTION,
HOME OWNERSHIP, AND THE LABOR FORCE PARTICIPATION
OF MARRIED WOMEN

Sherman David Hanna, Ph.D.

Cornell University, 1974

Two structural models for family choice behavior are derived in this study.
Both models have four endogenous variables: Family income, housing consumption,
dummy variables for home ownership, and the labor force participation of married
women. The exogenous variables used include: family size, age of husband, education of husband, race, the unemployment rate of the county of residence, the
occupation of the husband, city size, family public housing status, region, age
of the youngest child, an index for the relative price of housing in the area,
and the difference between the husband's age and the wife's age. Cross-section
interviews from the Panel Study of Income Dynamics for 1971 are used. A subsample consisting of families with both husband and wife present, with an income between $1,000 and $30,000, and with various other exclusions is used to estimate
the two structural models. The two models are identical except in home ownership
and wives' labor force participation, where housing consumption was used as a
proxy for normal income in one. Two-stage least-squares regressions are used to
estimate the parameters of the two models. The results suggest that the structural model approach may improve analysis of family choice behavior.

LOW WAGES AND LONG HOURS

Gerald E. Plato

Agricultural Economist in Economic Research Service, USDA

and

J. Patrick Madden

Department of Agricultural Economics
The Pennsylvania State University

The specific objectives of this study are to identify and measure the
effects of social and economic characteristics that are responsible for 1) low
levels of hourly earnings during a given year; 2) low levels of annual hours
worked; and 3) the slow improvement in hourly earnings over time of household
heads.

The theoretical framework for the determination of hourly earnings and of
annual hours worked is based upon the Neoclassical model of supply and demand

422

for labor. Reduced-form equations, suggested by the Neoclassical model, are
used in the analysis of these two variables instead of the Neoclassical model because of problems involved in specifying structural demand and supply equations
for labor. The independent variables in the two reduced-form equations are in-
tercept and slope shifter variables (i.e., predetermined or exogenous variables)
for the labor demand and supply curves in the Neoclassical model. It is postu-
lated that these independent variables 1) measure the quality of labor services
(i.e., human capital variables); 2) describe the structure of labor markets; or
3) measure the influence of the general social or economic environment. It is
also hypothesized that the disadvantaging characteristics that are found to be
responsible for low hourly earnings during a given year (i.e., the disadvantaging
determinants of hourly earnings) are also responsible for slow improvement of
hourly earnings over time.

Race and sex are found to have a large influence on both the determination
of hourly earnings and of annual hours worked. In general, the results for
hourly earnings reveal that the independent variables have a larger effect on
hourly earnings and that the level of hourly earnings is higher for each level of
a given independent variable for white males than for the other race-sex groups.
The most influential independent variables on the level of hourly earnings, other
than race-sex, are found to be age, education, occupation and labor union membership. In the analysis of annual hours worked it is found that white males in
general work considerably more hours per year than the other race-sex groups,
holding other characteristics constant. The other most influential variables on
annual hours worked are age, occupation, physical or nervous disability, annual
hours unemployed and family size (family size has a large effect for only the
female household heads).

The attempt to explain the change in hourly earnings between years as a
function of the independent variables used to explain the level of hourly earnings during a given year was not successful. The hypothesis that a disadvantaging determinant of hourly earnings has a negative effect on the change in hourly
earnings relative to advantaging determinant(s) "contained" in the same variable
is in general rejected.

EXPENDITURE PATTERNS OF WELFARE HOUSEHOLDS, AGED HOUSEHOLDS, AND DISABLED HOUSEHOLDS

Teh-wei Hu
Norman L. Knaub
Sharif Ghalib

Institute for Research on Human Resources
The Pennsylvania State University

Prepared for the Social Security Administration and The Social and Rehabilitation Service of the United States Department of Health, Education and Welfare, this study uses data from the Panel Study of Income Dynamics in conjunction with data from the Survey of Consumer Expenditures to answer four specific questions relating to welfare recipients and to the general expenditure behavior of the elderly and the disabled. The questions addressed for welfare recipients are:

1. What are the welfare families' expenditures on food, alcohol, cigarettes, housing, transportation, clothing, etc.?

2. Are there differences between welfare and nonwelfare families with respect to expenditure patterns?

3. What are the relevant marginal propensities to expend on these expenditure categories for changes in welfare payments?

4. Do food stamps, a welfare subsidy in kind designed to increase food consumption, alter the expenditure patterns of recipients as compared to nonrecipients?

The policy implications of the findings of this study appear in chapters 7, 11 and 14 of the report sent to the U. S. Department of Health, Education and Welfare in March of 1974.

THE EFFECTS OF WELFARE PAYMENTS ON FAMILY EXPENDITURES

Teh-wei Hu and Norman Knaub

Institute for Research on Human Resources
The Pennsylvania State University

This study first investigates the possible differences of expenditure patterns between welfare and nonwelfare families in terms of their level of expenditures and the marginal propensity to expend (MPE) on various items (food, housing, alcohol, cigarettes, and car). It is found that, although welfare families in general have lower levels of expenditures in these categories, the MPE's of welfare families for alcohol, food, and car are higher than those of nonwelfare families. However, the MPE's of housing and cigarettes are almost the same for both kinds of families. Among these five expenditure categories, both types of families show that food has the highest MPE followed by car, housing, alcohol, and cigarettes.

The second topic investigated in this study is the effect of welfare payments on family expenditures. The results indicate that there is no significant difference between cash welfare and nonwelfare income in terms of their MPE on various items. Among the cash welfare income and nonwelfare income, food has the highest MPE followed by car, housing, and cigarettes. There is no effect on alcohol expenditures. Among the in-kind welfare, food has the highest MPE followed by housing and car. There is no effect on cigarettes and alcohol.

SOCIAL SECURITY PAYMENTS AND THE AGED HOUSEHOLD EXPENDITURES IN THE U.S.

Teh-wei Hu and Sharif Ghalib

Institute for Research on Human Resources
The Pennsylvania State University

One of the objectives of this study is to estimate the impact of the proposed or enacted increases in incomes from Social Security benefits on expenditures of aged recipients. The increase will amount to about $200 for single persons and $400 for couples. The estimated marginal propensity to expend with respect to Social Security benefits, suggests that there will not be any significant effect on alcohol or cigarette expenditures but that there will be a significant increase in food and housing expenditures.

ESTIMATION OF THE ALLOCATION OF TIME FOR WORK, LEISURE AND HOUSEWORK

T. J. Wales and A. D. Woodland

Department of Economics
University of British Columbia

The utility maximization approach to estimation of labour supply response requires that leisure be defined as total time available minus time spent at a job and at any other endeavour that may not yield utility to the same extent as pure leisure. In this paper we show that for the simple case in which housework hours are excluded from the measure of leisure the estimates of labour supply response differ considerably from those in which leisure is defined as time not spent working at a job. Our results are consistent with cost minimizing behaviour of the household in the sense that the division of housework hours between husband and wife is responsive to the ratio of their wage rates, although the effect is not significant. In addition, for families without children, we find total housework hours to be significantly negatively related to income, while for families with children they are not.

ESTIMATION OF HOUSEHOLD UTILITY FUNCTIONS AND LABOUR SUPPLY RESPONSE

T. J. Wales and A. D. Woodland
Department of Economics
University of British Columbia

In this paper we estimate the labour response of both the husband and wife under the assumption that the household maximizes a utility function with after-tax income and leisure hours of both individuals as arguments. The results are based on a subsample of panel households that includes only those individuals who are not faced by binding institutional constraints on the number of hours worked.

In the aggregate an increase in husbands' wage rates leads to a reduction in hours worked by husbands, but virtually no change in hours worked by wives. On the other hand an increase in the wage rates of wives leads to no net change in their hours worked, but does increase hours worked by husbands substantially. In all cases these market responses are the result of positive and negative individual responses. Finally, both the education level and child status of the family have a statistically significant effect on the household's labour supply behaviour.

LABOR SUPPLY OF HUSBAND AND WIFE

Jonathan G. Dickinson
Research Associate
Institute for Research on Poverty
University of Wisconsin

A theoretical model has been developed which will permit the estimation of labor supply functions which are consistent with a generalized family utility function. The advantage of this approach is that it allows a consistent simulation of responses to large changes in tax rates or income supplement. This approach contrasts with previous studies which have been of two main types, those

426

which rely on a general model which is strictly applicable only to a very small
change in variables, and those which rely on specific forms of utility functions
and are thus subject to distortion if that function is inappropriate. Further
work has been devoted to adapting the model to account for complex ties of real
world employment opportunities. These include progressive marginal income tax
rates, premium pay for overtime work, time and money costs of travel to work, and
limits on available work time. Empirical implementation of the model is now in
process.

A STUDY OF PARTICIPATION IN THE FOOD STAMP PROGRAM
Maurice MacDonald, Research Associate
Institute for Research on Poverty
University of Wisconsin

From the 1972 wave of the Panel, Maurice MacDonald has selected a subsample
of households which were eligible for food stamps in 1971 and lived in counties
that had food stamp programs. The households which reported using food stamps in
1971, eligible participants, are being compared to eligible nonparticipants, to
isolate characteristics which best predict participation in the food stamp program. That comparison is based on multiple discriminant analyses of one split-
half of the eligible subsample. Resulting discriminant functions then allow
classification of the households from the other split-half into participant or
nonparticipant categories. As expected, preliminary results indicate participants are disproportionately drawn from the welfare population. However, variables representing relative need, access costs (e.g., transportation items),
and local employment conditions are also important. Attitudinal indices are only
marginally related to participation. Dr. MacDonald plans to repeat this study
for the 1974 wave of the survey.

FAMILY BACKGROUND AND LIFETIME EARNINGS
C. Russell Hill
Brookings Institution
and
Frank P. Stafford
University of Michigan

Extending the work presented in Chapter 11, Volume II, in this paper we try

to set forth a consistent explanation of the role of family background variables
in the earnings functions estimated by economists. We find that influences of
family background, particularly as measured by parental time inputs to the care
of children, fit well into the theory of investments of human capital (although
our preliminary efforts to integrate these and subsequent investments into a lifetime human capital model can certainly be improved upon). In particular, we show
that besides the well-known relation between investments in formal schooling and
family of origin variables, investments of time in preschool human capital are
also related to these variables (e.g., parental education, occupational status,
family size, religion.)

RESEARCH IN PROGRESS
Christopher Jencks
Lee Rainwater
Martin Rein
Harvard University

The Income Dynamics Panel data and several other data sets will be used for
analysis in four different areas: 1) estimation of path models of earnings,
2) extension of path models to explain *family* rather than individual income,
3) further work on social class and social position with more detail on occupation, and 4) "social consumption" of families with the effects of individual,
neighborhood and community factors in consumption.

THE DETERMINANTS OF SEPARATION AND REMARRIAGE
Isabel Sawhill
Income Maintenance
The Urban Institute

Families headed by women have grown very rapidly over the last decade, and
there is some evidence that changes in divorce and remarriage rates are the es-
sential demographic factors accounting for this growth. These developments provide the context for the Urban Institute's analysis of divorce and remarriage
using the Panel data.

Preliminary findings (from a linear probability model) show that those
marital separations or divorces which lead to the creation of a female-headed
family are more common among couples whose marriages are of relatively short
duration, who marry young, are renters rather than owners, do not attend church

regularly, and who live in the West and/or in the central city of a large metropolitan area. Separation is also more common where the wife's earnings are high
relative to the husband's and where the husband's income is not much higher than
what the wife and children would receive on welfare. The relationship between
separation and family income was weak and did not operate in the expected direction. Whites had higher expected rates of separation than nonwhites after controlling for all of the above variables.

The expected remarriage rate of female-headed families was found to vary
positively with family income and negatively with duration in female-headed
status and age of the woman. Women on AFDC remarry at much lower rates than
other women after controlling for income, number of children, and other factors.

Further work is under way to attempt to refine this analysis using a
specially-prepared tape (created by Beverly Harris at ISR). The final results
will be incorporated in a forthcoming book on female-headed families which is being written by Heather Ross, Isabel Sawhill, and others at the Urban Institute.

THE DISTRIBUTIONAL EFFECTS OF HIGHER UNEMPLOYMENT
Edward M. Gramlich
Senior Fellow, The Brookings Institution
(Summary of a paper published in the
Brookings Papers on Economic Activity, 1973:2)

The recent burst of inflation in the American economy has made the always
difficult problem in reconciling full employment with price stability that much
more so. In order to dampen inflation, it becomes increasingly likely that the
economy will undergo a prolonged period of unemployment, which may in turn imply
large losses in personal income for lower and middle income families.

This paper represents an attempt to measure these losses and how they are
distributed among families of various income classes. It first tries to measure
the earnings losses of family heads caused by direct unemployment, and then the
indirect responses of hours worked of family heads and the earnings of wives,
children, and others in the affected families. It also assesses the comprehen-
siveness of income protection provisions of various existing transfer payments.
It does not look into changes in wage rates or capital income which may also ac-
company periods of high unemployment, or any changes in income distribution due
to unanticipated inflation.

429

The paper tries to go beyond past work based largely on CPS aggregations by using micro-longitudinal data from the Panel Study of Income Dynamics. The panel observations are used to estimate relationships describing each of the sources of income loss, generally by pooling time series data for each family. Decomposing the aggregate losses in this way provides a way of making more precise tests of the impact of policy changes on the various reactions and checking the responses for consistency with other work at various stages.

Unemployment of Family Heads

The distributional incidence of family head unemployment is investigated through a two-step procedure. I first estimated very simple time series relationships on aggregate BLS data to determine how the major family head unemployment rates -- for adult white males, adult nonwhite males, and females -- are related to the overall unemployment rate. Then I used the panel survey data to determine how the unemployment of individual family heads is related to, or really allocated within the three groups, according to variables such as education, occupation, wage rates, and location. These equations also control for the influence of cyclical activity because they pool cross-section data for the six years of the panel survey -- three in which the unemployment rate was low and three in which it was high.

The results of this procedure are given in Table 1. The first table shows the average response in unemployment rates for family heads of the three types, and then uses the coefficients for education, occupation, and so forth to give the responses for families where six year average income was at the poverty level, at three times the poverty level, and at five times the poverty level.

TABLE 1

Response of Family Head Unemployment Rates
to One Percentage Point Change in Overall Rate

	Family Head		
	White Male	Black Male	Female
Average	.818	1.927	.814
If average family income at poverty line	1.311	2.140	.845
If average family income three times poverty line	.877	1.635	.776
If average family income five times poverty line	.652	1.307	.679

For all three groups sensitivity to movements in the unemployment rate declines with economic well-being, implying that high income people are not as susceptible to the business cycle, at least in terms of their unemployment. There is at least some impact on high income people, however. The unemployment rate for poor white male heads is estimated to rise by 1.31 percentage points for every one percentage point increase in the national rate, twice as much as for fairly affluent whites (income of five times the poverty line, or about $22,500 for a family of four in 1973). For black males the low income sensitivity is less than twice that of high income males, though more than for whites at every level. For poor females the sensitivity is less than for either type of male family head, and only slightly above that of high income female family head. The apparent reason that the disparities in income sensitivity are not sharper is the fact that generally medium wage rate occupations (craftsmen, operatives, etc.) suffer relatively large swings in unemployment, and these same occupations are heavily represented in upper income classes.

Other Earned Income

I then focus on two other types of losses in labor income which could result from swings in overall employment demand. The first involves hours worked by family heads the second involves the earnings of wives and children in families of various income classes.

Regarding the first source, I have used estimates by Stuart Schweitzer and Ralph Smith, also based on the panel survey data[1] which predict the additional reduction in hours worked undergone by family heads who suffered unemployment. Schweitzer and Smith indicate that white male family heads lose fifty percent more hours through this sort of worker discouragement factors than would be predicted by their unemployment alone, black males thirty-three percent, and females twenty-five percent.

Regarding the second source, I have again estimated pooled time series cross sections with the panel survey data, explaining the aggregate secondary (nonhead) earnings of families in the sample. The independent variables include semi-descriptive cross-section variables, the aggregate unemployment rate to measure any increases in secondary earnings when the head becomes unemployed. The latter term in the equations does show up statistically. When male family heads become unemployed, secondary earnings rise by about 11 percent. But for male headed families (not females) this increase is more than offset by the fact

---

[1] See Stuart O. Schweitzer and Ralph E. Smith, "The Persistence of the Discouraged Worker Effect," Industrial and Labor Relations Review, January 1974, p.249.

that aggregate secondary earnings for all families are decreased by reductions in labor demand, with a one percentage point rise in the unemployment rate lowering secondary earnings by from two to three percent.

These three sources of lost earned income are combined in Table 2, which shows the percentage loss in family income due to reductions in earnings from head's unemployment, lost hours worked, and losses in secondary earnings, all at various average income levels. The average loss in earned income for all groups combined is about 1.2 percent for every percentage point in the unemployment rate, roughly consistent with various macroeconomic estimates after account is

TABLE 2

Percentage Reduction in Family Personal Income
Caused by A One Percentage Point Increase in the Unemployment Rate,
No Accounting for Response of Transfer Payments

| | Family Head | | |
	White Male	Black Male	Female
Average	1.1	2.7	.9
If average family income at poverty line	2.9	3.9	1.0
If average family income three times poverty line	1.4	2.0	.8
If average family income five times poverty line	.9	1.3	.5

taken of certain biases and inconsistencies. The distributional implications are much the same as before when only the head's unemployment was measured: the impact of cyclical movements is relatively small for female headed families and only barely greater for poor than affluent families. Poor male headed families still fare much worse than affluent families for both races, with blacks faring somewhat worse than whites at every income level. On an overall basis, blacks fare much worse than whites, however, because their average income is much lower.

Transfer Payments

The final question regards transfer programs, which cushion the declines in earned income by various amounts for various family types and income groups. The degree of cushioning is again estimated with the panel survey data, though this time the equations are estimated only for 1971, a year after some important changes in these transfer programs took place. Separate equations are estimated for unemployment insurance, welfare, the nonaged portion of Social Security, food stamps, and private transfers.

The equations indicate that transfer payments cushion fully 56 percent of the decline in earned income for low income female headed families -- for every dollar reduction in earned income, transfer payments rise by 56 cents. The largest contributors to this response are welfare (20 cents), unemployment insurance (19 cents), with a surprisingly high (8 cents) impact of private transfers. High income female headed families do not receive any welfare but still have 25 percent of their loss cushioned. Low income male headed families have 37 percent of their loss cushioned, less than female headed families of comparable incomes, because welfare, private transfers and unemployment insurance are all less comprehensive, the latter because so much of the loss in labor income for male headed families is not attributable to direct unemployment. High income male headed families, on the other hand, have very little (9 percent) of their decline cushioned, with unemployment insurance being the only important cushioning transfer program.

These results for transfer payments are then combined with those in Table 2 to give the overall reduction in family personal income due to a percentage point increase in the unemployment rate. The high degree of cushioning for female headed families has made the cyclical impact even smaller and less regressive, in fact now low income female headed families are among the groups most

TABLE 3

Percentage Reduction in Family Personal Income
Caused by A One Percentage Point Increase
in Unemployment Rate

| | Family Head | | |
	White Male	Black Male	Female
Average	.9	2.1	.5
If average family income at poverty line	2.0	2.5	.4
If average family income three times poverty line	1.2	1.7	.5
If average family income five times poverty line	.8	1.1	.4

insulated for cyclical declines in employment demand. The regressivity has not been eliminated for male headed families of either race, however low income male headed families suffer declines in personal income between 2 and 2 1/2 times as great as fairly affluent families. Moreover, there is still a somewhat greater decline in black incomes at any level of well-being, and still a large difference

in the overall effect on whites and blacks in male headed families because blacks
fare worse at any level and because black incomes are lower.

A NOTE ON RANDOM EVENTS AND TURNOVER
AMONG THE POVERTY POPULATION

Terence F. Kelly

Senior Research Associate
The Urban Institute

In a previous study using data from the year-to-year matched component of
the current population survey, we find that nearly 36 percent of those families
which were poor in 1965 were not poor in 1966 and that in addition, about six
percent of the nonpoor families in 1965 became poor in 1966.[1] Similar magnitudes
of turnover are recorded in the Michigan Panel Study of Income Dynamics.[2]

Thad Mirer suggests that certain policymakers interpret the findings to mean
that the poor can work themselves out of poverty and, therefore, there is little
need for special anti-poverty programs.[3] Such a view of the world implies that
much of poverty is the result of transitory, often random, forces. If poverty
is generated by some set of purely random forces lying outside individual or
policy control, then programs designed to alter the structure of markets or the
characteristics of the poor are doomed to fail. Thus, the degree of influence
exerted by random, as opposed to controllable, events on the poverty process is
a matter of considerable policy concern.

As shown by Mirer, even if the distribution of permanent income is fixed
over time, a random pattern of distribution in temporary incomes could produce
considerable poverty flow. This calculation is useful in illustrating that the
observed flow of families crossing over any arbitrarily drawn income line need
not necessarily imply a real change in permanent family incomes. The most important policy implication is that we should not irrationally equate observed
turnover with real changes in permanent income capacity. To buttress this con-
tention, we may consider the fact that of those families "escaping" from poverty
between 1965 and 1966, one-quarter remained within $500 of the poverty line.
Many of those who do escape, then, do not escape very far. Of course, even if

---

[1] Kelly (1970).

[2] Morgan, et al. (1974), p.21.

[3] Mirer (1974), Vol. II, p.209.

434

it turned out that all income change was due to transitory forces, there would
still be considerable room for policy efforts designed to effect a more equitable
distribution of transitory incomes or to reduce the importance of the transitory
component of total family income.

By examining the distribution of poverty flows across demographic subgroups
of the population, it may be possible to estimate the degree of randomness in the
income distribution. If certain groups are known to lie behind their counter-
parts in terms of, say, escaping from poverty, then there is *prima facie* evidence
that other than random forces underlie the process. Evidence that can readily
be brought to bear on the question suggests that other than random forces operate
to produce poverty and turnover in the poverty population.

The quantitative importance of random events in the poverty process cannot
be stated with precision. Strictly speaking, the answer depends on one's point
of view about what constitutes a random event and about the tradeoff between
transitory and permanent poverty. There seems to remain ample room within the
limiting boundaries implied by the data for policy actions both to prevent sudden
income losses and to change the permanent earning capacities of poor families.

References

Kelly, Terence F., "Factors Affecting Poverty: A Gross Flow Analysis,"
President's Commission on Income Maintenance Programs, Technical Studies,
Washington, D.C., U.S. Government Printing Office, 1970.

Mirer, Thad, "Aspects of the Variability of Family Income," Five Thousand
American Families -- Patterns of Economic Progress, Vol. II, p.209.

Morgan, James N., et al., Five Thousand American Families -- Patterns of
Economic Progress, Ann Arbor: Institute for Social Research, 1974.

Appendix A

RESPONSE RATES AND DATA QUALITY

In the first five years of the Panel Study of Income Dynamics we attempted
to obtain a personal interview with each of our respondents. In some cases a
personal interview was not feasible and other arrangements had to be made in order to maintain contact with the respondents. In many of these cases we substituted a telephone interview for the personal interview. In the sixth wave, to
save costs, we interviewed our respondents by telephone whenever possible. For
those respondents without telephones, personal interviews were obtained. As seen
in Table A.1, over four-fifths of our sample were interviewed by telephone
in 1973. In previous years the proportion of telephone interviews did not exceed
2.5 percent.

TABLE A.1

Proportion of Interviews by Telephone

Year	Sample Size	Number of Phone Interviews	Percent of Sample
1968	4802	--	--
1969	4460	--	--
1970	4655	67	1.5
1971	4840	108	2.3
1972	5060	134	2.5
1973	5285	4047	81.8

In Table A.2 we present the response rates for each of the analysis years.
Response rates are calculated using as a base the previous year's sample size
augmented by splitoffs since that interview. In 1968 the response rate was a
relatively low 76 percent. In subsequent years the response rate was substantially higher, remaining at 97 percent since 1970. Thus, it does not appear that
switching to telephone interviews had an impact on the response rate.

TABLE A.2

Annual and Cumulative Panel Response Rates

| | Percent | |
Year	Annual	Cumulative
1968	76	76
1969	89	68
1970	97	66
1971	97	64
1972	97	62
1973	97	61

In order to get an indication of the impact of switching to telephone interviews on the quality of the data, we examine in Table A.3 the accuracy of reported 1972 money income by respondent (i.e., head or non-head) and by type of interview (i.e., personal or telephone). Rather than examine each component separately, we present in Table A.3 the sum of the accuracy codes on all the components of family money income. The accuracy code for each component is 0 if no estimates or assignments were made, 1 if estimates were made with a probable error under ten percent, and 2 if a major assignment was made. The results indicate very little difference between personal and telephone interviews. Some differences, however, exist between interviews with the family head and with someone other than the family head. For example, over 92 percent of interviews with family heads had no assignment in any of the income components; on the other hand, approximately 88 percent of the interviews with non-heads had no assignment in any of the income components. We may, therefore, conclude that switching to telephone interviews per se is not likely to have a serious effect on the quality of the data.

However, if switching to telephone interviews increases the likelihood of non-heads being the respondents, the impact on the data quality may be serious. In Table A.4 we examine the proportion of interviews with family heads over the years. The results indicate only a two percent reduction in the proportion of interviews with the family head between 1972 and 1973. It is unlikely that this slight reduction would have a significant impact on the overall quality of the data. The evidence, therefore, does not reveal any major impact of switching to telephone interviews.

To see whether the respondents interviewed by telephone seem to show different changes from those who were not, we controlled by regression for other differences between the two groups -- change in head's total work hours, and change in family money income. The results are shown in Table A.5. In both cases the

TABLE A.3

Accuracy of Money Income,
by Respondent and Type of Interview, 1973

| Sum of Assignment Codes on Income Components* | Respondent | | | |
| | Head | | Non-Head | |
	Personal	Telephone	Personal	Telephone
0	92.4%	92.5%	88.7%	88.0%
1	3.9	4.0	6.5	5.1
2	3.0	2.7	3.2	4.5
3	0.1	0.4	1.5	0.0
4 or more	0.6	0.4	0.1	2.1
TOTAL	100.0%	100.0%	100.0%	100.0%
Number of observations	1007	3702	159	345

*assignment code:

  0 = no assignment
  1 = minor assignment
  2 = major assignment

TABLE A.4

Proportion of Family Heads Interviewed

Year	Total Sample	Proportion of Interviews by Head
1968	4802	92.6
1969	4460	93.1
1970	4655	93.2
1971	4840	93.3
1972	5060	93.5
1973	5285	91.1

TABLE A.5

Effects of Nine Variables on Change
in Hours and Income Between 1971 and 1972
for Families with Same Head and Where the
Head Worked at Least 500 Hours Each Year

	Change in Hours Worked		Change in Family Income	
	Gross Effect*	Net Effect**	Gross Effect*	Net Effect**
Switched to phone***	.002	.001	.000	.000
Age	.005	.028	.010	.007
Education	.006	.003	.006	.019
Race	.000	.002	.001	.003
Region	.001	.001	.001	.002
Sex	.000	.001	.007	.003
Distance to center of city	.003	.003	.004	.008
Size of largest city in area	.003	.002	.004	.005
Level of Head's hours in 1971	.141	.194	--	--
Level of income in 1971	--	--	.023	.080

	Change in Hours Worked	Change in Family Income
Number of extreme cases removed	6	12
Number of cases used	n = 3512	n = 3506
Mean change	$\bar{y}$ = + 23 hrs.	$\bar{y}$ = $1025
Standard deviation of change	σ_y = 566	σ_y = $4060
Adjusted R^2	R^2_A = .174	R^2_A = .067

* Eta-squared = square of correlation ratio or fraction of variance of dependent variable accounted for.

** Beta-squared, analogue to partial beta of numerical regression, normalized regression coefficient.

*** Equals one if changed from personal interview to phone, and zero otherwise.

"dummy variable" distinguishing those who were changed to telephone interviews was not significant, indeed was the least powerful of the nine explanatory factors used. There did appear to be a smaller increase in work hours between 1971 and 1972 for those switched to phone, but by 40 hours, less than a tenth of a standard error. The phone respondents reported a slightly larger increase in family income, again completely insignificant. Rerunning the regressions unweighted to emphasize the lower income oversampled groups produced almost identical results.

The actual mean changes and adjusted mean changes are given in Table A.6 for those switched to phone and the others, for both weighted and unweighted regressions.

The correlations themselves are deceptively high because they largely reflect the regression to normalcy -- the effect of initial level on change, which is particularly powerful for hours. The young show the largest absolute increases in both hours and family income, but the middle-aged show the largest adjusted increases. The adjustment (for initial level and other things) slightly reduces the effect of education on increase in hours, but greatly increases the apparent tendency for the better-educated to have increases in income. Similarly, the advantages in income change of whites, and males, look greater *after* the adjustments.

There is, then, no evidence that changing to telephone interviews is associated with any systematic differences in reported changes in work hours or family income, absolutely or after adjustments for initial levels.

TABLE A.6

Changes in Head's Hours and Family Income
by Whether Switched to Telephone Interview

	Switched to Phone	All Others	Eta Squared	Beta Squared
Change in Head's work hours				
Weighted				
Unadjusted	14	74	.002	
Adjusted	17	57		.001
Unweighted				
Unadjusted	20	60	.001	
Adjusted	23	50		.000
Change in total family money income				
Weighted				
Unadjusted	$1018	$1060	.000	
Adjusted	1028	984		.000
Unweighted				
Unadjusted	971	867	.000	
Adjusted	1000	764		.001
Number of cases	2743	769		

Appendix B

CUMULATIVE NON-RESPONSE 1968-1973

Analysis of the effect of non-response in single cross-section surveys based on probability samples presents problems because of the lack of information about those who are not interviewed. The *subsequent* losses in a panel study, however, can be analyzed using any of the information collected in the first wave. We present here some data on differential non-response between the first wave and the sixth. We do the analysis using *individuals* rather than families because the splitting of families would make family data confusing. There were 18,272 individuals in the 4,802 families interviewed in early 1968, of whom 14,340 were in one of the 5,285 families interviewed in early 1973.[1] Most of the 21.5 percent were lost in the second wave, but it seems best to look at the total losses during the five-year period.

The overwhelming impression is that the losses are widely distributed and almost random (see Table B.1). Losses were higher among single persons (33.6 percent) and among Spanish-Americans (37.4 percent of 175 people), those 65 or older (39.3 percent) and "extra" family members (not head, wife or children) (41.2 percent).[2]

Figure B.1 shows the age pattern, with the young (mostly splitoffs) and the very old (these include senile and deceased) having higher rates of non-response.

Looking at factors which had no influence we find that among the indexes of attitudes and behavior patterns, none had a rank-correlation with response rate above .05 except "connectedness to sources of information and help" which had a

---

[1] There are actually an additional 49 people who are sample members and in the six-year individual-family file. They were not in the 1968 file because they were in institutions or were missed at the time and have been filled in later. Including them in this analysis would merely have raised the response rates slightly, since they are all still present and accounted for.

[2] Of course, we know from our individual-year non-response analysis that losses were also somewhat higher among the splitoffs, particularly young men and divorced men, but again the differences were not huge.

TABLE B.1

Relationships of Several Initial Variables
to Cumulative Response Rate 1968–1973

	Rank Correlation Tau-b	Rank-free Measure of Association Cramer's V
Individual income in 1967	-.01	.02
Which sample (SRC or Census)	.04	.04
Head's welfare income	.02	.02
Money income of family decile 1967	.01	.05
Income/needs decile 1967	-.01	.06
Family size	.07	.10
Race	-.02	.07
Unemployed or on strike 1967	.06	.08
Days unemployed in 1967	.02	.03
Background problems	.01	.03
Current handicaps	-.02	.05
Trust	.04	.05
Horizon expressed	.05	-.09
Horizon self-report	.01	.05
Connectedness	.07	.11
Efficacy	.01	.03
Ambition	-.00	.04
Real earnings acts	.05	.07
Economizing	.03	.05
Risk avoidance	.04	.06
Age	-.05	.12
Sex	.03	.03
Relationship to head	-.02	.15

MTR 1118

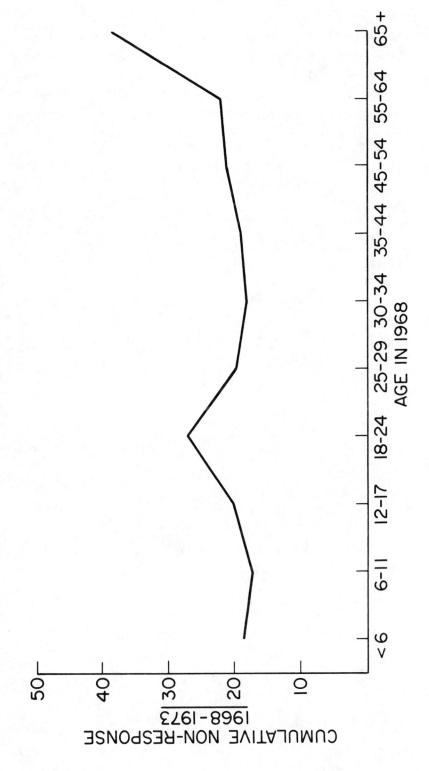

FIGURE B.1

Cumulative Non-response, 1968-1973, by Age of Individual
(For all 18,272 sample individuals)

443

MTR 1118

444

systematic negative effect (we lost the unconnected), Figure B.2. The non-response rates were identical for blacks and whites, varied less than two percent according to individual income (zero for the nonearners), were less than three percent higher in the Census (low-income) sample than the Survey Research Center sample, and actually two percent *lower* among those with any welfare income in 1967. There was no correlation with money income of the family in 1967 (rank correlation .01) or with the family income/needs decile in 1967 (rank correlation -.01).

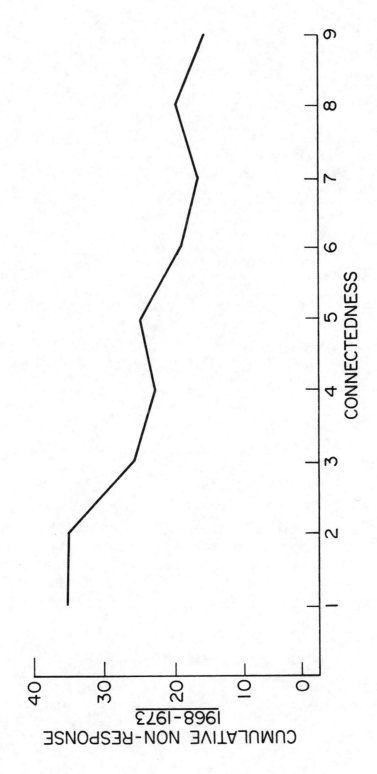

FIGURE B.2

Cumulative Non-response, 1968-1973, by Initial Connectedness of Family
(For all 18,272 sample individuals)

MTR 1118

445

Appendix C

SOME NATIONAL NORMS FOR A SENTENCE
COMPLETION TEST

Without answering the question of what tests really measure, we can be sure that they are often used to sort people, and that they at least measure one's capacity to handle the test. One trouble with most tests is that they have been developed and normalized on special groups -- students, draftees, applicants for special programs, and the like.

A very brief thirteen-item, sentence-completion test was developed for and used in our national panel study in the fifth year of that study. It was given to the head of the household, defined generally as the husband of the main couple or as the main earner.[1] It has proven to be a powerful explanatory variable in analysis of earnings, even in multivariate analysis jointly with education and many other variables.[2]

Hence, it seemed appropriate to provide other researchers with some national norms by which they could adjust the scores of individuals in special groups, eliminating the effects of years of school completed, age, race, sex, and farm background. We provide three ways of doing this. First, a nonadditive model using only education and race allows one to assign an individual to one of only six final groups (Figure C.1). Second, for those who may not have all the relevant information, a completely additive model allows one to start with the average of 9.51 and make any one of a number of additional adjustments using whichever of the five factors is available.

There is clearly an interaction between education and race, perhaps reflecting cultural differences or differential qualities of education received by whites and nonwhites (see Figures C.2 and C.3). Dropping out of high school seems to go with greater differences in scores for nonwhites than for whites.

---

[1] For documentation on the development of the test, see Veroff, et al. (1971).

[2] See Morgan, et al. (1974).

FIGURE C.1

Sentence Completion Test Score
by Education, Race, Age, Sex, Where Grew Up

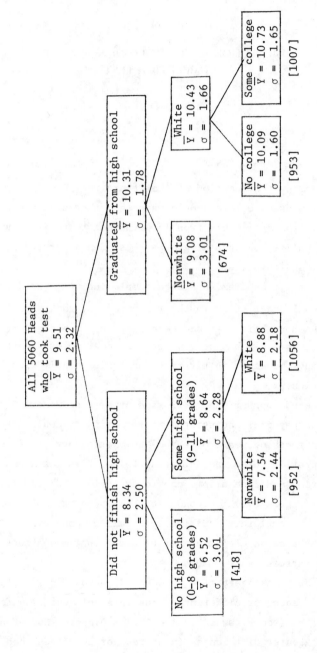

Six groups explain 25.8% of the variance.

[ ] = number of cases, but see sample design

MTR 1122

449

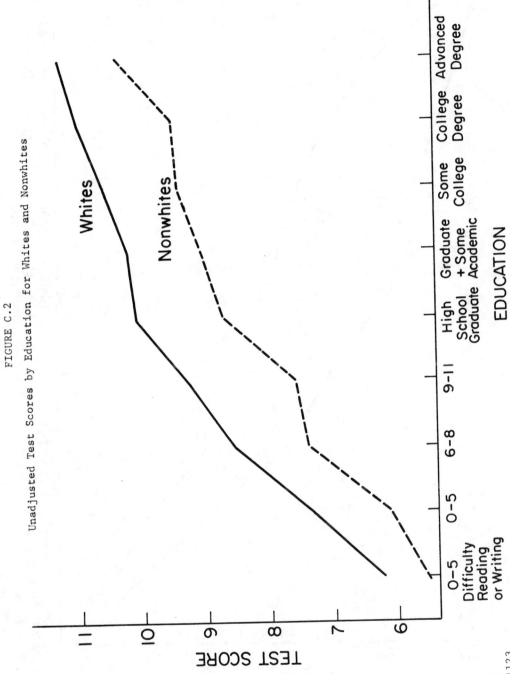

FIGURE C.2

Unadjusted Test Scores by Education for Whites and Nonwhites

MTR 1123

450

FIGURE C.3

Adjusted Test Scores by Education for Whites and Nonwhites

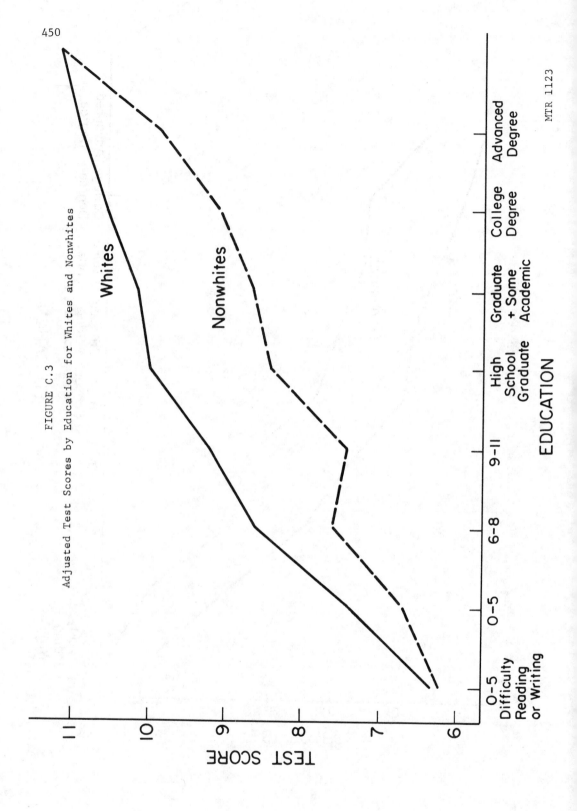

MTR 1123

There is also a differential effect of rural background on the scores of whites and nonwhites.[1]

Even age seems to matter more for nonwhites.[2] Hence, it seems appropriate to provide different adjustments for the other four factors (education, age, sex, and farm background) for whites and for nonwhites. Table C.1 shows the relative explanatory power of each of the predictors. Tables C.2, C.3, and C.4 provide such combined and separate norms. Tables C.3 and C.4 take the overall average (for that racial group) and then make adjustments for education, age, sex, and farm background or any subset of them for which information is available. Clearly the adjustment for formal education is the overwhelmingly powerful one.

TABLE C.1

Gross and Net Power of Predictors for All, Whites, and Nonwhites

	All		Whites		Nonwhites	
	Gross Effect Eta^2	Net Effect $Beta^2$	Gross Effect Eta^2	Net Effect $Beta^2$	Gross Effect Eta^2	Net Effect $Beta^2$
Education	.245	.175	.220	.194	.200	.119
Race	.084	.039			.005	.004
Age	.047	.006	.052	.005	.136	.048
Where Grew Up	.035	.003	.034	.002	.087	.026
Sex	.014	.002	.010	.003	.006	.003
	$R_A^2 = .289$		$R_A^2 = .226$		$R_A^2 = .267$	

Do such corrections remove too much? They imply that one does not want to attribute to test-passing ability differences clearly associated in a national sample with other factors that could account for differences in test scores. Given recent work on the distinction between perceptual and verbal skills and cultural differences in emphasis on them, it would seem sensible to avoid arguments

---

[1] Spanish-Americans and others were combined with blacks because their scores were similar and their numbers small.

[2] It is tempting to speculate that younger blacks got better schooling or that television is teaching standard English usage to younger people.

TABLE C.2

Sentence Completion Test Scores -- Raw and Adjusted
by Regression, for a National Sample of Household Heads, 1972

(All)

Education	Unadjusted Mean Score	Adjusted Score	Number of Cases	Standard Deviation of Unadjusted Data
0-5 grades, difficulty reading or writing	5.93	6.54	170	3.13
0-5 grades, no difficulty	6.90	7.37	748	2.87
6-8 grades	8.40	8.54	921	2.31
9-11 grades	8.88	8.96	1087	2.23
12 grades: high school graduate	9.88	9.82	1008	1.77
12 grades plus nonacademic training	10.09	9.97	407	1.69
College, but no degree	10.48	10.33	636	1.74
College degree	10.90	10.70	339	1.53
Advanced or professional degree	11.24	11.02	144	1.36
Not ascertained	9.31	9.46	100	2.64
Race				
White	9.78	9.69	3147	2.13
Black	7.76	8.36	1753	2.73
Spanish-American	8.28	8.83	124	2.60
Other	8.09	7.51	36	3.14
Age				
18-24	9.74	9.42	780	2.01
25-34	9.95	9.53	1101	1.95
35-44	9.89	9.67	957	2.11
45-54	9.70	9.75	928	2.25
55-64	9.05	9.34	707	2.57
65-74	8.89	9.37	384	2.51
75 +	8.25	9.09	202	2.82
Not ascertained	9.00	9.54	1	----
Where Grew Up				
Farm, rural area	8.90	9.34	1715	2.48
Small town, suburb	9.68	9.52	1673	2.27
Large city, city	9.51	9.44	109	2.00
Other, several places	9.65	9.63	83	2.61
Sex				
Male	9.66	9.57	3616	2.25
Female	9.03	9.31	1444	2.45

Overall average = 9.51, standard deviation = 2.32

R^2 (adjusted) = .29

MTR 1123

TABLE C.3

Sentence Completion Test Scores -- Raw and Adjusted
by Regression, for a National Sample of Household Heads, 1972

(Whites Only)

Education	Unadjusted Mean Score	Adjusted Score	Number of Cases	Standard Deviation of Unadjusted Data
0-5 grades, difficulty reading or writing	6.27	6.42	48	3.23
0-5 grades, no difficulty	7.35	7.49	83	2.94
6-8 grades	8.57	8.67	530	2.23
9-11 grades	9.21	9.21	526	2.07
12 grades: high school graduate	10.05	10.02	655	1.62
12 grades plus nonacademic training	10.18	10.15	298	1.58
College, but no degree	10.56	10.53	515	1.66
College degree	10.96	10.89	310	1.49
Advanced or professional degree	11.23	11.12	129	1.29
Not ascertained	9.64	9.67	53	2.65
Age				
18-24	10.03	9.67	447	1.85
25-34	10.16	9.74	692	1.84
35-44	10.18	9.90	524	1.88
45-54	10.03	10.01	523	1.96
55-64	9.32	9.64	456	2.40
65-74	9.18	9.74	328	2.35
75 +	8.65	9.52	177	2.48
Where Grew Up				
Farm, rural area	9.21	9.63	1053	2.27
Small town, suburb	9.99	9.83	1106	2.03
Large city, city	10.13	9.86	849	1.90
Other, several places	9.77	9.81	90	2.38
Not ascertained	9.95	9.96	49	2.46
Sex				
Male	9.89	9.84	2472	2.08
Female	9.39	9.57	675	2.25

Overall average = 9.78, standard deviation = 2.13

R^2 (adjusted) = .23

MTR 1123

TABLE C.4

Sentence Completion Test Scores -- Raw and Adjusted
by Regression, for a National Sample of Household Heads, 1972

(Nonwhites Only)

Education	Unadjusted Mean Score	Adjusted Score	Number of Cases	Standard Deviation of Unadjusted Data
0-5 grades, difficulty reading or writing	5.56	6.34	122	3.00
0-5 grades, no difficulty	6.15	6.75	165	2.62
6-8 grades	7.43	7.63	391	2.55
9-11 grades	7.62	7.46	561	2.36
12 grades: high school graduate	8.72	8.41	353	2.25
12 grades plus nonacademic training	9.07	8.64	109	2.38
College, but no degree	9.43	9.07	121	2.37
College degree	9.50	9.85	29	2.16
Advanced or professional degree	11.40	11.14	15	2.06
Not ascertained	8.35	8.10	47	2.40
Race				
Black	7.76		1753	2.73
Spanish-American	8.28		124	2.61
Other	8.09		36	3.14
Age				
18-24	8.43	7.88	333	2.18
25-34	8.70	8.28	409	2.10
35-44	8.48	8.32	433	2.56
45-54	7.80	8.04	405	2.86
55-64	6.93	7.40	251	2.91
65-74	6.32	6.92	56	2.41
75 +	4.79	5.92	25	3.28
Not ascertained	9.00	8.71	1	----
Where Grew Up				
Farm, rural area	7.05	7.56	662	
Small town, suburb	7.63	7.63	567	
Large city, city	8.99	8.48	631	
Other, several places	6.94	6.64	19	
Not ascertained	7.93	7.72	33	
Sex				
Male	8.01	7.97	1144	2.74
Female	7.57	7.65	769	2.70

Overall average = 7.86, standard deviation = 2.73

R^2 (adjusted) = .27

MTR 1123

455

about racial differences and their causes and look at differences in the test
scores only around norms that eliminate them. There should still be individuals
who score better or worse than those with the same cultural, geographic and eth-
nic backgrounds, and many researchers may want to see where such differences
lead.

Of course, even those differences may reflect many things, ranging from
fear of tests (or of failure) through parental inputs of time and other environmental influences to differences in motivation.

CORRELATIONS WITH ANOTHER MEASURE AND WITH EARNINGS

There are 234 cases in the sample where the same head of household is
given a variant of the Ammons Quik-Test in 1968 and the Sentence Completion Test
in 1972. If we select from them those where the head had some earnings in 1967
and in 1971, we can look at the correlations among the earnings at the two dates
and the test scores at the two dates. The correlations are reassuringly high,
except for a curious but insignificant negative correlation between the 1967
earnings and the 1972 test. The simple correlations are as follows:

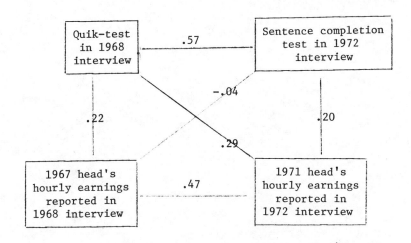

The correlations for whites and blacks using the same format were:

(70 Whites)　　　　　　(144 Blacks)

456

There is little in these findings that would help us select one test or the other and some comfort in the fact that their correlation is so high four years apart. The extent to which the Sentence Completion Test helps explain earnings in the full sample, even in a multivariate context controlling for education, age, race, sex, and other factors, makes it a clearly useful measure even though we do not know whether it is a proxy for acquired (verbal) skills, differential quality of education, lack of fear in taking tests, or some innate abilities. It may be that ability to do well on such tests is the passport to jobs even though it has little to do with performance on the job.

References

Morgan, James N., et al., _Five Thousand American Families -- Patterns of Economic Progress_, 2 volumes. Ann Arbor: Institute for Social Research, 1974.

Veroff, Joseph, McClelland, Lou and Marquis, Kent, _Measuring Intelligence and Achievement Motivation in Surveys_, 2 volumes. Ann Arbor: Institute for Social Research, 1971.

QUESTION SEQUENCE FOR SENTENCE COMPLETION TEST

Now here is something a little different. We would like you to take this word test.

There are some sentences written in this booklet I have for you--here they are. (HAND R THE BOOKLET.) In each one there's a word left out. I'll read each of the sentences to you and after I read it, you pick one of the words under the sentence to complete it. Say the word you think makes the best, truest, most sensible complete sentence. If you're not sure of the answer, take a guess.

1. For example, Lemons are sour but sugar is __"blank"__ ; which would you pick?
    (READ ALL ANSWERS AND NUMBERS, EVEN IF INTERRUPTED.)

    1. Bitter   2. White   3. Fattening   4. Sweet

    [ ] R PICKS SWEET (4)   [ ] R DOES NOT PICK SWEET (4)

O.K., let's try some more (GO TO 2)	I think the right answer here is number 4, sweet. Lemons are sour, sugar is sweet. (GO TO 2)

2. I don't have the answers for the other sentences here, so from now on I won't tell you if you're right or wrong. Just tell me which word you think is best.

INTERVIEWER:	a. USE TRANSITION STATEMENTS
	b. CIRCLE ANSWER GIVEN
	c. DO NOT ACCEPT "DON'T KNOW" ANSWERS
	d. DO NOT REINFORCE ANY ANSWERS

INTERVIEWER
TRANSITIONS

2a. We see _____ only at night.
    1)Children   2)Plants   3)Stars   4)Houses   5)Trees

Here's the   3. Not every cloud gives _____.
next one
    1)Weather   2)Shade   3)Sky   4)Climate   5)Rain

O.K.   4. In the spring the buds form on the branches of the _____.
    1)Trees   2)Rivers   3)Bugs   4)Leaves   5)Animals

Mm Hmm   5. There is an old _____, "An apple a day keeps the doctor away."
    1)Talk   2)Saying   3)Reader   4)Book   5)Man

The next   6. The ragged _____ may prove a good horse.
question
    1)Puppy   2)Child   3)Calf   4)Lamb   5)Colt

Let's try   7. The important thing is not so much that every child should be taught as
the next   that every child should be given the wish to _____.
one
    1)Learn   2)Play   3)Hope   4)Reject   5)Teach

458

O.K.   8.   The person who _____ another must make good the damages.

              1)Reforms   2)Improves   3)Instructs   4)Injures   5)Delights

All Right   9.   False facts are highly _____ to the progress of science.

              1)Injurious 2)Necessary 3)Devoted   4)Useful   5)Instrumental

Number 10   10.   It is better that ten guilty persons _____, than that one innocent
is   suffer.

              1)Suffer   2)Escape   3)Capture   4)Starve   5)Repent

Mm Hmm   11.   The winds and the waves are always on the side of the ablest _____.

              1)Soldiers   2)Statesmen   3)Navigators 4)Students   5)Weathers

O.K.   12.   The vanquished never yet spoke _____ of the conqueror.

              1)Ill   2)Well   3)Little   4)Nastily   5)Often

Here's   13.   Think long when you may _____ only once.
the next
one   1)Abstain   2)Live   3)Die   4)Decide   5)Eat

O.K.   14.   The coward threatens only when he is _____.

              1)Afraid   2)Surrounded 3)Safe   4)Conquered 5)Happy

Appendix D

REGRESSION WITH CATEGORICAL PREDICTORS

A major goal of the social scientist is the explanation of individual variations in socioeconomic conditions. Statistically, the explanation takes the form of estimating the portion of the original variation in a dependent variable which can be attributed to the variation of an explanatory or predictor variable. For example, if we are interested in the variation of wages, we might suppose that part of this variation is associated with variation in the job experience of the wage earner. If, for a particular sample, the original variance in wages was ten, and the variance remaining after taking account of the variation in experience (by least-squares regression) were eight, the percent of the variation explained by experience is 20 percent (10-8)/10 x 100.

The particular name applied to this fraction depends on the nature of the predictor variable and on the complexity of the analysis. In the example above, the 20 percent would be termed "R-squared" because the explanatory variable was continuous and the analysis was simple. If we had used race, a categorical variable, instead of job experience and found (via analysis of variance) that the variance of wage was reduced from ten to seven, the Eta-squared of race in explaining wage would be 30 percent. The major reason for distinguishing between R-squared and Eta-squared is not that their interpretations differ but rather that the statistical techniques used to estimate them differ.[1]

When more complex analysis is performed, the need for additional measures of explanatory power arises. Suppose in the above analysis that we wished to use not only race as an explanatory variable of wage but also the variable of whether

---

[1] By using the subgroup averages to predict, instead of the overall average, one reduces the error variance from the variance around the grand mean to the smaller sum of variances around subgroup means. The reduction can be calculated more simply as the weighted sum of the squares of the subgroup averages minus $N\bar{y}^2$.

or not the wage earner finished high school. If we computed the Eta-squared for each of these variables, we might find that the race variable accounted for 30 percent of the variation in wages, and high school completion accounted for 20 percent. The total portion of the variance explained by our multivariate analysis, however, would *not* be 50 percent but something less, perhaps only 40 percent. The reason for this is that race and the completion of high school are interrelated. Proportionately fewer blacks finish school than whites. Hence, the variance explained by race and high school education overlap, and the whole is less than the sum of the parts. The Eta-squared for race incorporates both the explanatory power of race and some of the power of education. In order to determine the unique power of race in explaining the variation in wages, we need a statistic which adjusts for the interrelation of race and education. Beta-squared is such a statistic. It measures the explanatory power of a predictor after the effects of all the other included predictors which are related with it are taken into account. If a predictor were not related to any other predictor included in the analysis, then its Beta-squared would equal its Eta-squared.

The analogue to Beta-squared when continuous variables are employed is the "normalized regression coefficient," or

$$\frac{b\sigma_x}{\sigma_y}$$

the number of standard units that y changes when x is changed by one standard deviation. Both beta measures are approximations of what is generally regarded as the true marginal effect of a predictor, namely its partial R-squared with the dependent variable. The two will be identical when the correlation of the dependent variable with the *other* predictors is as high as the correlation of the predictor in question with the other predictors. If the latter is large, beta will exaggerate the marginal power of the predictor.

For interpreting the results of categorical-predictor multiple regression (sometimes called dummy-variable regression), all the reader needs to remember is that Eta-squared measures the explanatory power of a single classification set of subclasses, while Beta-squared measures the net power of that set in a multivariate context.

For those concerned with the loss of explanatory power in using a few categories or classes instead of a numerical predictor, it should be pointed out that even if the relationship were truly linear, the fraction of explanatory power still available using k classes instead of an infinite set of numbers is only $(1-\frac{1}{k^2})$. With five subgroups of roughly equal size, one still has 96 percent as much potential explanatory power and with seven groups, 98 percent. In addition, if the relationship is nonlinear, one usually explains and learns *more* with categorical predictors.

GLOSSARY

The following is a description of some of the technical terms used in this volume. For more details on the measures used in these analyses see the documentation, A Panel Study of Income Dynamics, 2 volumes, Survey Research Center, Institute for Social Research, University of Michigan, Ann Arbor, Michigan, 1972, and A Panel Study of Income Dynamics: Procedures and Tape Codes 1973 Interviewing Year, Wave VI Supplement.

ACHIEVEMENT MOTIVATION - A personality measure from social psychology representing a propensity to derive satisfaction from overcoming obstacles by one's own efforts in situations where the outcome is ambiguous. It is believed to be developed by early independence training, to result in the taking of calculated but not extreme risks and in the raising of goals after success experiences. It was administered in the 1972 interview.

ASPIRATION-AMBITION - A seven-item index of attitudes and plans reflecting attempts to improve economic well-being; see Volume II of the documentation, p. 789. The items include the following:

> Might move on purpose
> Wanted more work, and/or worked more than 2500 hours last year
> Might quit a job if it was not challenging
> Prefers a job with chances for making more money to
>   one more pleasant
> Is dissatisfied with self
> Spends time figuring out how to get more money
> Plans to get a new job, knows what type of job and what
>   it might pay
> (Second and last items neutralized for those for whom
>   they are inappropriate.)

BETA - A measure of the explanatory power of an independent variable when considered in a multivariate context.

BETA WEIGHTS - When the independent and dependent variables in the regression equation $Y = a + b_1 X_1 + b_2 X_2 + u$ are measured in their "natural" units (e.g., in dollars, years, hours) then the parameters b_1 and b_2 reflect the effect on Y of a one unit change in X_1 and X_2, respectively. If all variables are standardized so that each has a mean of zero and a standard deviation equal to one, then the equation becomes $Y = \beta_1 X_1 + \beta_2 X_2 + v$ and the β's can be interpreted as the fraction of a standard deviation that Y changes as a result of a change of one standard deviation in the X's. The b's are regression coefficients (sometimes called "partial regression coefficients"), the β's are *beta weights* or standardized regression coefficients. The unstandardized and standardized coefficients are related in the following way:

$$\beta_1 = \frac{b_1 \sigma_{X_1}}{\sigma_Y}$$

COGNITIVE ABILITY - See TEST SCORE

CONNECTEDNESS (to sources of information and help) - The following eight-item set of reported behaviors measuring the extent to which the respondent has friends or habits likely to keep him informed or provide help; see Volume II of the documentation, p. 793.

> Attended PTA meeting within the year
> Attends church once a month or more
> Watches television more than one hour a day
> Knows several neighbors by name (2 points if 6 or more)
> Has relatives within walking distance
> Goes to organizations once a month or more
> Goes to a bar once a month or more
> Belongs to a labor union and pays dues
> (First item is neutralized for families without children)

COUNTY WAGE RATE for unskilled casual labor - An estimate of the wage rate for unskilled labor in the county where the respondent lives, secured by mail questionnaires sent each year to the state official in charge of unemployment compensation.

COUNTY UNEMPLOYMENT - An estimate of the unemployment rate in the county where the respondent lives, secured by mail questionnaires sent each year to the state official in charge of unemployment compensation.

CRAMER'S V - A measure of association between two nominal scale variables when they have no natural rank order. It is similar to the Chi-square measure except it is adjusted for the number of observations and is constrained to take on values between 0 and 1. The higher Cramer's V, the greater the association between the classification.

DECILE - If all units are arranged in ascending order on some criterion such as income and each tenth marked off and identified, the ten groups formed are called deciles. The actual dividing points of incomes are given in Volumes II and III of the documentation.

DESIGN EFFECT - The effect of departures from simple random sampling in probability samples, defined as the ratio of the actual sampling variance to the variance of a simple random sample of the same size.

ECONOMIES OF SCALE - As the size of a family increases, if the costs do not increase proportionately, then we say there are economies of scale in large families.

ECONOMIZING INDEX - An index of six reported behaviors taken to indicate parsimonious use of money; see Volume II of documentation, p. 790.

> Spent less than $150 a year on alcohol
> Spent less than $150 a year on cigarettes
> Received more than $100 worth of free help
> Do not own late model car
> Eat together most of the time
> Spent less than $260 a year eating out
> (The fourth item is neutralized for those not owning cars.)

EFFICACY INDEX - An index composed of six self-evaluations which reflect a sense of personal effectiveness, and a propensity to expect one's plans to work out; see Volume II of documentation, p. 787.

> Is sure life will work out
> Plans life ahead
> Gets to carry out plans
> Finishes things
> Would rather save for the future
> Thinks about things that might happen in future

ELASTICITY - Refers to the response of the quantity of a good consumed to a change in price or in income. If the percentage change in the quantity of food consumed, for example, is greater than the percentage change in the price, then the demand for food is said to be price-elastic; if it is less than the percentage change in price, it is price-inelastic.

ETA - A measure of the explanatory power of a set of subclass means based on a one-way analysis of variance. The square of eta for a single categorical variable is analogous to the unadjusted R^2 from regression with a single independent variable. Eta is sometimes called the correlation ratio.

EXOGENOUS VARIABLE - Variables whose levels and changes are determined by forces independent of those being studied, as contrasted with endogenous variables

466

which are interdependent with variables in the system.

EXPECTED VALUE - When a dependent variable is determined by a combination of systematic and random effects, the expected value is that part which can be predicted from the systematic relationship. In the case of regression, it is the value predicted by the regression equation.

F-TEST - A test of the significance of the proportion of the variance explained by a set of several predictors or several classifications of a single predictor; see *STATISTICAL SIGNIFICANCE*.

FAMILY - All persons living in a household who are related by blood, marriage, or adoption. In occasional cases an unrelated person has been included in the family unit if he or she shares expenses and is apparently a permanent member of the unit. The definition of family used in this study includes single person families. This contrasts with the Census Bureau convention of classifying single persons separately as "unrelated individuals."

FAMILY COMPOSITION - Contains several dimensions, most of them related to the family's position in the standard life cycle: marriage, birth of first child, youngest child reaches age six and starts school, children leave home, one spouse dies. The sex and marital status of the head, the number of children, and age of the youngest are the main components.

FAMILY MONEY INCOME - Family income, unless otherwise designated, is the total regular money income of the whole family, including income from labor, capital, and transfers such as pensions, welfare, unemployment compensation, workmen's compensation, and alimony. It includes neither capital gains (realized or unrealized) nor irregular receipts from insurance settlements.

FAMILY TAPE - A data file containing all the data on that family from all six interviews. There is one record for each sample family. The final six-year data tape includes only families interviewed in 1973, so that there are no partial records. Where there are several families derived from an original sample family, the early family information will appear on each of their records.

HEAD OF FAMILY - In nuclear families the husband is defined as the head. In families with a single adult, he or she is defined as the head. In ambiguous cases of more than one adult, the head is the major earner or the one who owns the home or pays the rent. Note that the head of the family may change due to marriage, divorce, or death. For splitoff families, the head is similarly defined.

HORIZON INDEX - A six-item index of reported behavior indicating a propensity to plan ahead; See Volume II of documentation, p. 792.

> Is sure whether will or will not move
> Has explicit plans for children's education
> Has plans for an explicit kind of new job
> Knows what kind of training new job requires
> Has substantial savings relative to income
> Expects to have a child more than a year hence, or
>   expects no more children and is doing something
>   to limit the number.

HOUSEHOLD - Probability samples usually sample occupied dwellings, which may contain more than one household, which in turn may contain more than one family. However, the term household is often used loosely to mean family, since the number of individuals living with unrelated adults is very small. A family is a group of individuals related by blood, marriage, adoption.

HUMAN CAPITAL - The economically valued skills which result from the investment in one's self through education or other training.

IMPUTED RENT - A form of nonmoney income for home owners who can be thought of as in the business of renting a house to themselves. It is calculated by taking six percent of the owner's net equity in his house (house value minus mortgage).

INCOME - Unless otherwise specified, this means total family money income including regular money transfers. (See *FAMILY MONEY INCOME*.) When a year is given, it is the year of the income, not the (later) year when the interview was taken.

INCOME/NEEDS RATIO - See *NEEDS STANDARD*

INDIVIDUAL TAPE - A data file with one record for each individual as of 1973, containing all the data for that individual over the whole period and all the data for the family that individual was in each of the six years. The file contains some individuals who are not in the sample and are thus excluded from the analysis but who are necessary in order to derive family information for those in the sample. Individuals and families have separate weights; see *WEIGHT* and the documentation, Volume I.

INELASTIC - See *ELASTICITY*

INTELLIGENCE - See *TEST SCORE*

KENDALL'S TAU - A measure of rank correlation between two classifications.

LEAST SQUARES ESTIMATOR - That method of estimation which minimizes the squared deviations of the actual value from the predicted value of the dependent variable. Such estimators are sensitive to extreme cases and nonnormal distributions.

LINEAR REGRESSION - See *REGRESSION*

MARGINAL PROPENSITY TO CONSUME - That fraction of an incremental increase in income which is spent on consumption.

MOTIVATION - See *ACHIEVEMENT MOTIVATION*

MULTICOLLINEARITY - A problem arising in estimation if two or more predictors are highly intercorrelated. It thus becomes difficult to estimate the separate effects of these variables.

MULTIPLE REGRESSION - See *REGRESSION*

MONEY EARNINGS ACTS INDEX - An index of behavioral reports that the family is doing things to increase its money income including working long hours, getting to work on time, changing jobs, looking for a better job; see documentation, Volume II, p. 794.

MTR - Tables and other computer output are indexed by a Machine Tabulation Request number for checking and filing purposes. The number appears at the bottom of each table.

NEEDS STANDARD - An estimate of the annual income necessary for a family. The standard is generated in the same way as the official Federal poverty line; food needs are determined according to age and sex, as estimated and priced by the USDA (in Family Economics Review), and food costs are adjusted for economies of scale; this figure is then multiplied by a factor to allow for other needs also differentially greater for smaller families.

The absolute level is to some extent arbitrary and is not adjusted for inflation in later years, but the standard adjusts for differences in family size and structure so the status of families that differ in composition can be compared.

The needs standard is corrected for changes in family composition during the prior year, so that it is legitimate to compare it with that year's income. See the documentation, Volume I, for further details.

NUMBER OF CASES - The actual number of families or individuals on which the estimate is based. The number does not reflect the proportion of the population represented by that group because of the differences in sampling and response rates. See *WEIGHTS*.

NULL HYPOTHESIS - See *STATISTICAL SIGNIFICANCE*

QUINTILE - If all cases are arranged in ascending order on some criterion such as income and each fifth is marked off and identified, these five groups are called quintiles.

PARTIAL CORRELATION COEFFICIENTS (partial R^2) - The partial correlation coefficient (squared) is a measure of the marginal or added explanatory power of one predictive variable or set of variables, over and above all the other predictors. It can be thought of as the correlation of two sets of residuals, after removing the effects of all other predictors from both the dependent variable and the predictor in question. It is also the fraction of the remaining distance to perfect explanation (1.00) the multiple correlation (squared) is moved by the added predictor. It is the best measure of the "importance" of a predictor or group of predictors.

PERCENT OF POPULATION - The fraction of the weight-sum represented by a subgroup is an estimate of the percent of the population (of families or of individuals) it represents. Aggregate estimates can be made by ratio-estimating procedures, i.e., multiplying the sample mean by the proportion of the population times an outside estimate of the aggregate number of families or individuals.

PLANNING INDEX - A subset of the efficacy index consisting of the following items:

> Plans ahead
> Prefers to save for future
> Thinks about the future

REAL EARNING ACTS INDEX - A five-item index, with neutralization of the inapplicable items, reflecting ways of earning nonmoney income or investing in self; see documentation, Volume II, p. 789-90.

> Saved more than $75 doing own additions or repairs
> Saved more than $75 growing own food
> Saved more than $75 repairing own car
> Head was taking courses or lessons with economic potential
> Head spent spare time productively

R^2 - The fraction of variance in the dependent variable which is explained by the set of explanatory variables.

REGRESSION - A statistical technique which estimates the separate, independent effect of each of several predictors on a dependent variable. It minimizes the sum of the squared deviations from predicted values (see *LEAST SQUARE ESTIMATOR*) and assumes that the dependent variable is a linear and additive function of the predictors and a random error term.

REGRESSION COEFFICIENT - The estimated effect of a predictor on the dependent variable obtained from a regression analysis. It shows the expected effect that a unit change in the predictor would have on the dependent variable if all other predictors were held constant.

RISK AVOIDANCE INDEX - An index of six reported behaviors indicating the avoidance of undue risks; see Volume II of the documentation, p. 791.

> Car (newest if several) in good condition
> All cars are insured
> Uses seat belts (2 points if all the time)
> Has medical insurance or a way to get free care
> Head smokes less than one pack of cigarettes a day
> Have liquid savings (2 points if more than two months
>   income in savings)

SIZE OF LARGEST CITY IN AREA - The primary sampling unit is a county or (rarely) cluster of counties and the size of the largest city in that area is intended to reflect the number and variety of jobs, as well as differences in costs and standards of living. When the city is 50,000 or more, the area is a Census Standard Metropolitan Statical Area.

SPLITOFF - A splitoff is someone who left a sample family and is living in a different household, Most splitoffs are children who left the parental home to set up their own households. When a couple is divorced, one of them is designated as the continuing family and the other is a splitoff.

SPLIT SAMPLE - In order to allow proper testing of the significance and explanatory power of the descriptive and explanatory models finally selected, we have divided the sample into independent subsamples. This requires attention to the original sample design and the allocation of whole primary sampling areas to one subsample or another, so that they are truly independent (households within a cluster in a clustered sample are more like each other than a purely random set). The sample is divided into four parts, so that some initial analysis can be done on half-sample and some on three-fourths depending on the amount of searching that may need to be done and the precision of the needed testing.

STANDARD DEVIATION - A measure of the dispersion of a distribution of observations around their average (or predicted) value. If random effects are normally distributed, roughly two-thirds of the observations fall in a range of the mean plus or minus one standard deviation. It is equal to the square root of the variance and is denoted by the symbol σ. The standard deviations presented in the tables should be considered in context of the design effect.

STATISTICAL SIGNIFICANCE - Traditional statistical inference tests the hypothesis that a finding (e.g., that some effect is greater than zero), is a chance result from the sample, not existing in the population. If the probability is suffiiently small, (e.g., less than 5 percent), this "null hypothesis" is rejected and it is believed that there is some effect which is "statistically significant." Tests of significance should consider the design effect.

In most initial searching of data for what matters, and in what form, the assumptions of statistical testing are violated because many alternative models are tried. In addition, there are problems of estimating sampling variance with complex samples. Hence, we have used only part of the sample for searching and have reserved an independent part of the sample for assessing significance and explanatory power.

T-TEST - Under certain assumptions, estimated regression coefficients have a frequency distribution known as the t-distribution. This fact can be used to form a test of significance for the coefficients, called the t-test. See also *STATISTICAL SIGNIFICANCE.*

TRUST IN OTHERS - An index composed of five self-evaluating items on trusting others, believing in the fairness of the system; see Volume II of the documentation, p. 788.

> Does not get angry easily
> It matters what others think
> Trusts most other people
> Believes the life of the average man is getting better
> Believes there are *not* a lot of people who have good
>   things they don't deserve.

WEIGHT - There are weights both for the file of individuals and families which make the weighted estimates representative of the national non-institutional population of the continental United States. They offset differences in sampling rates and response rates, and the extra probabilities of inclusion of those who married nonsample members. There will be more respondents in lower income and minority groups than the weighted proportions because of oversampling. The oversampling simply makes the estimates for those groups more reliable.

Weighted estimates essentially multiply each case by a number representing the number of households it represents. Each digit of the weight represents 500 households.

YEAR - Interviewing was done in the spring of 1968, 1969, 1970, 1971, 1972 and 1973, but the income questions refer to the year prior to each (1967-1972).

476